The Alchemical Harry Potter

The Alchemical Harry Potter

*Essays on Transfiguration in
J.K. Rowling's Novels*

Edited by Anne J. Mamary

McFarland & Company, Inc., Publishers
Jefferson, North Carolina

Another Brick In The Wall Part II, Mother, Hey You,
Waiting For The Worms, Stop, The Trial and *Outside The Wall*
Music and lyrics composed by Roger Waters, reproduced by kind permission
© 1979 Roger Waters Music Overseas Ltd
Administered by BMG Rights Management (UK) Ltd

ISBN (print) 978-1-4766-8134-4
ISBN (ebook) 978-1-4766-4083-9

LIBRARY OF CONGRESS AND BRITISH LIBRARY
CATALOGUING DATA ARE AVAILABLE

Library of Congress Control Number 2020047218

© 2021 Anne J. Mamary. All rights reserved

No part of this book may be reproduced or transmitted in any form or by any means, electronic or mechanical, including photocopying or recording, or by any information storage and retrieval system, without permission in writing from the publisher.

Front cover image of alchemist's study room
© 2020 Unholy Vault Designs/Shutterstock

Printed in the United States of America

McFarland & Company, Inc., Publishers
Box 611, Jefferson, North Carolina 28640
www.mcfarlandpub.com

For Minerva, Poppy, and Flitwick

Table of Contents

Acknowledgments ix

Abbreviations xi

Introduction 1

I—The Resurrection Stone and the Transfiguration of Desire

Why I Read Harry Potter Books Again and Again
 SOPHIA IMAFUJI, AGE 8   28

The Literary Alchemy of J.K. Rowling
 JOHN GRANGER   30

Harry Potter and the Transfiguration of Desire
 ANNE PARKER-PERKOLA   46

Re-Reading Harry Potter, Re-Creating Ourselves: Harry Potter as Resurrection Stone
 ISAAC WILLIS   63

Out from the Shadows into the Light: Persona and Shadow in Harry Potter
 ALICIA L. SKIPPER *and* KATE FULTON   79

An Anti-Oedipal Reading of Harry Potter and Alchemy
 ROBERT TINDOL   97

II—The Elder Wand and the Transfiguration of Power

My Harry Potter Journey
 ELLA VICTORIA GREER, AGE 13   116

The Missing Element: The Alchemy Experiment Inside the
Chamber of Secrets
    S.P. Şipal   118

On the Transmutation of Voldemort's Love of Power into
Harry Potter's Power of Love
    Lawrence W. Farris   140

Auror Magic: An Almost Alchemical Process
    Lorrie Kim   156

Tapping on Just Another Brick in the Wall
    Sean Paulsgrove   168

III—The Cloak of Invisibility and the Transfiguration of Self and Community

And All Was Well
    Tamyra Dixon-Rankin, Deputy Headmistress,
    Dumbledore's Academy   188

The Snitch, the Stone, and the Sword: Harry Potter the
Alchemical Seeker
    B.L. Purdom   190

Alchemy as a Metaphor for Learning
    Mary Pyle   209

Harry Potter and the Root of All Evil
    Charles M. Rupert   225

Soul Making and Soul Splitting: Alchemy of the Soul in
Harry Potter
    Julie Loveland Swanstrom   244

Ruddy Stargazers: Centaurs, Philosophers, and a Life
Worth Living
    Anne J. Mamary   265

Epilogue: Friendship Hallowed, Pure, and Ever-Present   287

About the Contributors   291

Index   295

Acknowledgments

I am grateful to all of the contributors to *The Alchemical Harry Potter*, some of whom have been waiting to see their essays in print longer than Nearly Headless Nick has been waiting to be admitted to the Headless Hunt. Gary Mitchem, Lisa Camp, and Layla Milholen at McFarland, are paragons of patience and support. Thanks to historian Dr. Christine Myers, who helped me hatch the plan for the collection (though fortunately not from a chicken's egg under a toad at the full moon!). For their friendship, encouragement, and assistance, I tip my hat to my colleagues at Monmouth College (and hope I do not shower them with spiders): Dan Ott, Ermine "Newt" Algaier, IV, C. Hannah Schell, B. Kathleen "Sirius" Fannin, Brianne "Hermione" Donaldson, Petra "the Honorary" Kuppinger, and David "Lert" Suda in Philosophy and Religious Studies; and Doug "Ollivander" Rankin, Barry "Rita Skeeter" McNamara, Nancy "Luna" Loch, Duane Bonifer, Jeff "Gred" Rankin, Brad "Fang" Rowe, Monie G. Hayes, Leisa Kauffmann, Kathy Wagoner and Mary Lou Pease, Carolyn Suda, Tim Pahel, Stacy, Simon, and Gareth Cordery, Mary Hanford and Mike "the Philosoraptor" Sostarecz, Amy Caldwell, Ken McBaaa, Ashwani Kumar, jak & cats, and Marlo!!!; Dr. V in the fullness of time, the Holschuh Simmons family, Amjad "the Wizard" Karkout, Kateryna Sylaska, and David Timmerman, Sir.

Thanks also to Mitchell Parks, Brenda Tooley, and Bill Young at Knox College; Michael Nieto Garcia, Arti Wulundari, Felicity Palmer, Jerry Gravander, and Annegret Staiger at Clarkson University; Jeffner Allen, Jeanne Constable, Tony Preus, and Eileen Boylan Rizo-Patrón at SUNY Binghamton; Charles Courtney at Monmouth College and Drew University; Todd McDorman at Wabash College; Dante "Crookshanks" Giarrusso at St. Lawrence University; Martha R. Merson and Myra P. Love at Hoggy Warty Hogwarts; "the gang" from your stray cat in Canton, New York; Dad and Mary, Joshie, Jonah, and Lea; Les Hyman, Margaret Ferranti, and Mike and Storm Tooley; Bird, Sara, and Stephanie "Rubea" Babcock; Michael Goldenberg, who traveled by Floo Powder to meet with my students in the fireplace in Poling Hall; Cera Finney at Easy Song Licensing and Kate Watkins of MFM Ltd. Music Management, London; the good souls at the 2019 meeting of the International Society for Neoplatonic Studies; and my Weasleys: Meredith, George, and Mark Manitzas, and Cary, Juliet, Jeremy, and Kristin "Hedwig" Manitzas Miles.

I am thankful to Janet Manbeck, April Backus, Malia, Ja'Tona Cody, Carole Grummons, Jacque Boneck, and Pam Pasquale for their forbearance; and to Celia and Jimbo, and my nieces, Hannah Rose and Lily Ruth, who always have something new to teach me about Hogwarts. Jernabi Coffeehouse in Potsdam, New York, and Innkeeper's Coffee in Galesburg, Illinois, are my Three Broomsticks.

My gratitude always to Peter Klosky for his help with the images and to Maria Hosmer-Briggs for her expert copyediting. To the B.F. Harridans, thank you for the dance—"a magic beyond all"—these many years. The young wizards and witches and Tamy "Celestina" Dixon-Rankin of Dumbledore's Academy at West Central Middle School in Stronghurst, Illinois, are an inspiration. To all of the students at Monmouth College who have shared your Harry Potter journeys with me: you are the Philosopher's Stone.

Abbreviations

Plato

Apology—Apol.
Republic—Rep.
Timaeus—Tim.

J.K. Rowling

Harry Potter and the Chamber of Secrets—Secrets
Harry Potter and the Cursed Child—Child
Harry Potter and the Deathly Hallows—Hallows
Harry Potter and the Goblet of Fire—Goblet
Harry Potter and the Half-Blood Prince—Prince
Harry Potter and the Order of the Phoenix—Phoenix
Harry Potter and the Philosopher's Stone—Stone
Harry Potter and the Prisoner of Azkaban—Azkaban
Harry Potter and the Sorcerer's Stone—Stone
The Tales of Beedle the Bard—Beedle

Introduction

In an interview with the Scottish newspaper *The Herald*, J.K. Rowling said, "I've never wanted to be a witch, but an alchemist, now that's a different matter. To invent this wizard world, I've learned a ridiculous amount about alchemy.... I [had] to know in detail what magic can and cannot do in order to set the parameters and establish the stories' internal logic" (Simpson). Although the novels do not focus overtly on alchemy, Rowling gives readers hints about the novels' alchemical internal logic, starting with the British title of the first book, *Harry Potter and the Philosopher's Stone*. On his first trip to school on the Hogwarts Express, Harry learns from Dumbledore's Chocolate Frog card that the Headmaster practices alchemy with his friend Nicolas Flamel and discovers later that Nicolas and Perenelle Flamel, two historical alchemists, are "the only known maker[s] of the Philosopher's Stone" (120, 220). If contemporary readers have one point of reference for the study and practice of alchemy, it is likely the Philosopher's Stone, known for its power to transform base metals into gold and to give immortality to its maker.

Despite the "fact" of the Stone in Rowling's novels and Dumbledore's alchemical practice, contemporary readers might think of alchemy as a misguided superstition at worst or as an early and undeveloped version of chemistry at best (Granger 49). But alchemy has a long and varied history. It has Chinese, Indian, and Egyptian roots, incarnations, and variations. The ancient Greeks studied alchemy with their Egyptian neighbors, and the practice journeyed northward as medieval northern Europe learned from their Arab neighbors in the Iberian Peninsula. It is much more about transformations or transfigurations, as the class at Hogwarts is called, than about unlimited money or life in an ordinary sense.

Perfectly Normal, Thank You Very Much

Harry Potter and the Sorcerer's Stone begins the series with an introduction to Harry's relatives' world: "Mr. and Mrs. Dursley, of number four,

2   Introduction

Privet Drive, were proud to say that they were perfectly normal, thank you very much. They were the last people you'd expect to be involved in anything strange or mysterious, because they just didn't hold with such nonsense" (1). By contrast, their nephew, Harry, is "as not normal as it was possible to be" (*Chamber* 9); he is "a highly unusual boy in many ways," not only because he actually wants to do his homework but because he "also happened to be a wizard" (*Azkaban* 1).

When Harry first meets Hagrid, he and his Aunt Petunia, Uncle Vernon, and cousin, Dudley, have been on the run from some "not normal" happenings at four, Privet Drive. Uncle Vernon dashes off with the family, trying to escape the letters on parchment addressed to Harry in green ink flooding from the living room fireplace or rolled up inside each of a dozen eggs left by the bewildered milkman on the front steps. The eve of Harry's eleventh birthday finds him and the Dursleys in a falling-down shack on a windswept rock out at sea when Hagrid knocks down the door in the middle of a fierce storm to deliver Harry's rather squashed birthday cake and, finally, the letter inviting him to attend Hogwarts School of Witchcraft and Wizardry.

It is one thing not to have any idea that another world or experience exists at all and so to be ignorant of it. But the Dursleys, knowing full well that a world of magic exists, consciously and persistently deny it on a metaphysical level, vowing to "stop … that rubbish, … [t]o stamp it out of him" when they took Harry into their home (*Stone* 53). The conflict readers encounter from the first pages of the novels is not mainly one of good vs. evil, of Harry vs. his family or Voldemort, or Magic vs. Muggle. It is instead, perhaps, a conflict of foundational metaphors for understanding human beings, human communities, the cosmos, and our relationships each to the other.

Hagrid's letter invites Harry to board a train to school on the first of September. The scarlet, steaming train will not only take Harry to Hogwarts but will also transport him to a new conceptual world in which he will undergo alchemical transformations in and through his relationships with other people and with a variety of magical items, from the Philosopher's Stone and the Mirror of Erised (the Mirror of Desire) in the first book to the Deathly Hallows (the Elder Wand, the Resurrection Stone, and the Invisibility Cloak) in the last. These magical objects and relationships reveal something of desire, power, and identity. The Mirror shows "the deepest, most desperate desire of our hearts" (*Stone* 213), while the Resurrection Stone brings back a pale shadow of the most desperately missed lost loved ones (*Hallows* 409). They show something of power. What would a person do with the Elder Wand's immense power or with the Philosopher's Stone's unlimited gold or life? These objects show something of who people are, singly and together. What would a person do with a Cloak of Invisibility, which would enable all sorts of behaviors one could not perform in plain sight, or with a Wand that could beat all others? Both items could be used to protect or harm the user or the user's community.

Dumbledore helps Harry and readers to see these transfigurations of desire, of power, and of people—from Harry's desire to find but not use the Philosopher's Stone in the first book, to his wish to end the destructive power of the Elder Wand in the last, and in his both remarkable and ordinary power to love throughout the series. Harry owes his life to his mother's love, to her sacrifice to save him from Voldemort. Voldemort has no understanding of this power. As Dumbledore explains, "If he could only have understood the precise and terrible power of that sacrifice, he would not, perhaps, have dared to touch your blood. ... But then, if he had been able to understand, he could not be Lord Voldemort, and might never have murdered at all" (*Hallows* 710).

Even as a young child, Harry understands. At the end of *Sorcerer's Stone*, Harry risks his life to save the Stone from Quirrell and Voldemort, wanting only to prevent Voldemort's return to power. Dumbledore reflects to Harry just how remarkable this desire is. Dumbledore had protected the Stone in the Mirror of Erised by making it possible for only the person "who wanted to *find* the Stone—find it, but not use it—[to] be able to get it" (*Stone* 300). As he peers into the Mirror, Harry sees reflected his deep desire to have the Stone simply to save his world from abuses of power. When Dumbledore and the Flamels agree that it is best to destroy the Stone, Harry's main concern is that Dumbledore will lose his two good friends, Nicolas and Perenelle. Dumbledore recovers alchemy from contemporary prejudices when he explains to Harry that death is not the worst thing in a mortal life. The Flamels have kept enough Elixir to set their affairs in order before embracing death, which Dumbledore says after nearly seven hundred years of living is both "but the next great adventure" and "like going to bed after a very, *very* long day" (*Stone* 297).

Harry's worry about the loss of friends, and Dumbledore and the Flamels' attitude about death, can help us to turn away from a petty conception of alchemy as an obsession with having "as much money and life as [we] could want," for as Dumbledore continues, "the trouble is, humans do have a knack of choosing precisely those things that are worst for them" (*Stone* 297). Dumbledore's caution invites Harry and readers to shift our modern preconceptions and to begin to understand the alchemists' work in its own context. When Rubeus Hagrid careens into the Dursleys' world on a flying motorbike, carrying Harry to Albus Dumbledore and Minerva McGonagall, readers see not only the brief meeting of two worlds with different social conventions but the touching of two worlds with different paradigms for understanding our lives. It is not only Dumbledore's appearance—his sweeping robes and purple cloak, with his high-heeled boots and a beard long enough to tuck into his belt—that makes him unwelcome on

Privet Drive. It isn't just that Hagrid stands nearly twice as tall as a normal person, quite apart from his arrival on a flying motorcycle (*Stone* 8–9). Professor McGonagall's transfiguration into a tabby cat might get more to the underlying differences. As an Animagus, she not only transfigures her own appearance but gives us a hint that we and the physical world are the closest of relatives, that we are all active agents, and that magic transforms minds, bodies, spirits—the three of which can be spoken of as if they were separate kinds of things, but which are thoroughly interwoven.

Rather than trying to control nature for the sole benefit of the practitioner, the alchemist worked with nature, understanding it as an active participant in the process. *Physis*, the Greek word for nature, sounds like the English "physics" and may carry modern European overtones of inert matter. But *physis* is "a biological metaphor." Its root is *phyein*, "to bring forth, produce, make to grow" (Reeve and Miller x). Nature, *physis*, itself is the source of its own growth. While the alchemist worked with metals, the metals also worked on the alchemist. As British Sufi teacher Nigel Hamilton puts it, alchemy transforms the practitioner, liberating him or her "from a 'dead, leaden state of mind'" (1). At its best, alchemy allows us to find the sacred in our mortal lives, to find the magic of the cosmos in ourselves. It is a practice of the very best of what it means to be human in conversation with our human communities, with magical creatures, and with the universe.

The modern foundational metaphor to which the Dursleys desperately cling posits humans in and above a vast, soulless, disenchanted universe—a world of "radical divisions between self and world" (Tarnas, *Cosmos* 47). In "Grandma's Story," literary critic and film-maker Trinh T. Minh-ha explains that there is a similar division in the modern mind between fiction and truth, which tends to think of fact and truth as identical. Stories, fairy tales, and imagination are devalued as a result, as fiction becomes a kind of lie or untruth. Trinh explains how imagination discovers, uncovers, and creates the truths in fiction. A culture that values storytelling values the storytellers' wisdom. Trinh writes, "The story depends upon every one of us to come into being. It needs us all, needs our remembering, understanding, and creating what we have heard together to come into being. The story of a people. Of us, peoples. Story, history, literature (or religion, philosophy, natural science, ethics)—all in one" (119).

Uncle Vernon embodies the modern Western view when he will do nearly anything to ignore or explain away things acting "abnormally." Upon hearing whispers of the Potters and being hugged by a complete stranger dressed in robes, Uncle Vernon rushed off for Privet Drive, "hoping he was imagining things, which he had never hoped before, because he didn't approve of imagination" (*Stone* 5). Voldemort, too, suffers from Uncle Vernon's failure of imagination. Dumbledore reminds Harry, "Of house-elves and children's tales, of love, loyalty, and innocence, Voldemort knows and understands nothing. *Nothing*. That they all have a power beyond his own, a power beyond the reach of any magic, is a truth he has never grasped" (*Hallows* 709–10).

Alchemical Foundations

Rowling's stories and the great long multicultural traditions of storytelling from which she drew share alchemy's powerful ability to inspire and free readers' imaginations, just as Harry is about to be freed from ten long years of a leaden existence with the Dursleys. In *Harry Potter and Imagination: The Way Between Two Worlds*, Travis Prinzi suggests that the Dursleys are not just Harry's miserable relatives but that they are "caricatures of Enlightenment rationalism" or the dominant modern western metaphysical paradigm, one that devalues the metaphoric, the poetic, and the imaginative (5). Rowling writes a way between the modern consciousness (a way of thinking about the world that began to develop during the Renaissance and became "perfectly normal, thank you very much" by the nineteenth century) and the world of alchemy. These world-shaping views are so deeply held that they are often believed without conscious awareness. In *Cosmos and Psyche: Intimations of a New World Order*, philosopher and historian of ideas Richard Tarnas writes that the development of the modern western metaphysical paradigm "brought about a deep schism between humankind and nature, and a desacralization of the world. This development coincided with an increasingly destructive exploitation of nature, the devastation of indigenous cultures, [and] a loss of faith in spiritual realities" (13).*

The Dursleys live in a desacralized world of individualism and capitalism, a world of literal truth, and disenchanted nature, with their lawn shorn into perfect submission and their midnight violations of hosepipe bans (*Phoenix* 1). They live in a world that has separated science from story and that substitutes accumulation as a mark of one's power—and, therefore, of one's value—for the power of imagination as a means to empowerment. Theirs is a world that made what we have come to know as different disciplines live in different neighborhoods. Although indebted to the work of the alchemists, the modern mind separated science from "superstition," sending alchemy to live with the "metaphysically batty great aunts," not to mention a rather medieval-looking headmaster and a Transfiguration teacher who, as a cat, reads signs and keeps watch from atop suburban walls (Moran 10).

---

*See also Cornel West's discussion of the "Age of Europe," from *Prophetic Thought in Postmodern Times*, which he says is at once grand and flawed, setting forth at once movements of liberation, the age of colonization, and environmental destruction.

Riding the train from the modern to the magical world, readers find that neither the metaphysics nor the great aunts are batty, whatever Ron says about Dumbledore being "[b]rilliant and everything, but cracked" (*Hallows* 133). At the start of *Distilling Knowledge: Alchemy and the Scientific Revolution*, historian of science Bruce Moran writes:

> There is something that does not quite make sense about including a subject like alchemy in a discussion of scientific revolution. Science, after all, is rational and ordered. Alchemy, we think, presumes disorder and irrationality. Common sense tells us that there are certain classes of objects, certain kinds of knowledge, and certain ways to go about discovering truths of nature that can be regarded as "scientific." Alchemy, because of its associations with magic and the occult, certainly does not belong here. To see things differently would be either crazy or intellectually counterfeit. Science, we know, is a particular form of knowledge made up of experimental facts, impartial observations, and specific theories. Anyone, no matter what his or her background, who would honestly seek objective truths in nature would ultimately have to reach the same conclusions about how the world works—right? (1)

In his *Quibbler*-like question, Moran challenges his readers to look at the internal logic of both science and alchemy. Moran writes that all manner of people practiced alchemy—men and women, Christians, Jews, and Muslims. As in all walks of life, "some were sincere, others frauds" (9). It was "never altogether something that people *believed* in; it was something that people *did*" (10).

Yet people's actions and practices grow from what they believe. For example, in *The Death of Nature: Women, Ecology, and the Scientific Revolution*, ecofeminist philosopher and historian of science Carolyn Merchant outlines the shift in the early modern European consciousness from an organic foundational metaphor for nature to a mechanistic one. Merchant shows how our current environmental crisis has roots in the shift in thinking about nature from the pre-modern period and that the status of women of all classes and of peasant women and men declined as the pre-modern metaphor for nature gave way to the modern one.*

In the first chapter of *Prisoner of Azkaban*, Harry—trying hard not to drip ink onto his sheets—works on his essay, "Witch Burning in the Fourteenth Century was Completely Pointless—discuss" (*Azkaban* 1). Although

---

*In *Unearthed: The Economic Roots of Our Environmental Crisis*, Kenneth Sayre shows how a shift in social values would result in a shift in behavior toward the planet. For another example from outside the European perspective, Paula Gunn Allen's "The Woman I Love Is a Planet, the Planet I Love Is a Tree" starts with the same premise as Descartes' at the start of European modernity: the human body and all physicality is the same sort of thing. For Descartes, all physicality is inert matter governed by mechanistic laws. For Allen, all physicality is also rational, spiritual, political—that is, there is no mind/body duality in her Laguna Pueblo perspective (118). For another study of how one's metaphors (or archetypes) shape one's attitudes and behaviors, see Richard Tarnas' *Passion of the Western Mind: Understanding the Ideas That Have Shaped Our World View* and *Cosmos and Psyche: Intimations of a New World Order*.

the point of Harry's assignment is well taken, the witch trials began in earnest with the publication of the *Malleus Maleficarum* (*The Hammer of Witches*) on the eve of modernity in 1480 and were at their most virulent between 1580 and 1660. The trials continued into the eighteenth century, when the modern consciousness was in full bloom.

One way Harry might have addressed the question, though, is precisely through applying the *Revelio* Charm to Europe's metaphysical shifts as it moved toward an early modern mechanistic model of the world from an ancient and medieval model. Merchant writes, "the world we have lost was organic," and that model was not only one of an enchanted nature but of a gendered enchanted nature (1). Merchant explains that the metaphor of earth as nurturing mother was replaced by the metaphor of earth as machine, while the metaphor of earth as unruly female led to modern attempts at human control of nature—and accusations of witchcraft against human women (132). From a model of human-nature interdependence, "two new ideas, those of mechanism and of domination and mastery of nature, became core concepts of the modern world" (1–2). The witch burnings might be understood as one among many struggles to wrest alchemical power from the "metaphysically batty great aunts," from the planet, and from story's imaginative powers, as Europe made the transition from a pre-modern to a modern consciousness.* One way Harry might earn top marks and extra house points on his essay, aside from describing Wendelin the Weird's use of a Flame-Freezing Charm to outwit the witch hunters and to enjoy "a

---

*See Barbara Ehrenreich and Deidre English's *Witches, Midwives, and Nurses: A History of Women Healers* for a discussion of the gendered nature of the shift from what might be called an alchemical way of thinking among the women healers accused of witchcraft, as men of the dominant classes began to practice "scientific" medicine at the start of the modern period in Europe.

Richard Tarnas also points out that technologies new on the European scene contributed to the development of the modern mind: gunpowder, the magnetic compass, the mechanical clock, and the printing press (*Passion* 225). The printing press made the transmission of ideas quicker and easier and increased literacy as books become more affordable. It also made the distribution of such books as the *Malleus Maleficarum* (*The Hammer of Witches*) quicker and easier. Soon a copy was on every judge's desk and probably contributed to the increased intensity and viciousness of the witchcraft trials (Ehrenreich and English 36–37).

William Cavanaugh's discussion of the religious wars of early modern Europe is also instructive here. Cavanaugh suggests that while it is certainly true that people do violence in the name of religion, he makes a case for those decades of wars as a struggle to shift from one foundational metaphor to another. Cavanaugh argues that, while it was true that Protestants and Catholics fought each other, a good part of the struggle was over the modern separation of the sacred from the so-called secular, both in the political and the conceptual spheres. He is describing one part of the shift from a pre-modern to a modern metaphysics, fought on a physical battlefield and on the bodies of those who might suffer most from the shift, since the peasantry also lost some measure of self-sufficiency in the move from pre-modern feudalism (an organic metaphor) to modern capitalism (a mechanistic one) (489–90).

gentle, tickling sensation," would be to explain that it was the metaphysics of the alchemical world—his world—under attack. Completely pointless (*Azkaban* 2).

Moran describes the alchemical work of Libavius, who worked in the late sixteenth and early seventeenth centuries, not as the work of trying to produce as much wealth and life in any (modern) conventional sense but as illustrative of the alchemists' organic model of the universe. Moran writes, "Libavius ... followed a long alchemical tradition in which the primary procedure was distillation and the principal purpose was to make the purest substance of all, something linked, it was thought, to the first stuff of creation" (11). This fifth essence, or Quintessence, according to alchemist John of Rupescissa, had healing properties; "extracting the fifth essence from things was really to extract the 'star stuff' and each metal, he reasoned, contained a heavenly essence that corresponded to a particular planet and acted on a particular part of the body" (Moran 18).

As the title of Rowling's Charms textbook, *Quintessence: A Quest*, reminds us, alchemy is aware both of the golden nature of the world and the person and that there is something eternal, something of the "star stuff," in metals and in alchemists. We are not just in the world; we are of it, a small reflection of it. The name of the author of *Advanced Potion Making* at Hogwarts, Libatius Borage, reflects this relationship. Borage, also called Starflower, is a food, an herb, and a medicinal plant. The ancient Greeks often poured a libation of wine for the gods; the name Libatius suggests pouring a libation of Potions to the flowering earth and to the star-strewn cosmos as a token of the relationship between potion maker and the planet.*

Transfigurations

We might wonder, then, why Alchemy is not a subject at Hogwarts. Alchemy includes the study and practice of many branches of knowledge, including reading patterns in the Heavens; understanding the magical and medicinal properties of plants and using them in brewing potions;

---

*Tara Nummedal's "Alchemy in Christian Europe" describes both a Catholic and Protestant embrace of alchemy, especially for its Christian symbolism. Each borrowed from the other regarding eternal life and the connection of the human, the divine, and the natural worlds. For example, Rupescissa "likens the third stage of the philosophers' stone, a distillation, to the crucifixion" (314). Yet precisely because of its "appeal to heterodox religious groups," alchemy sometimes became suspect. Nummedal writes, "Once confessional lines were sharpened, in other words, religious orthodoxy could impose intellectual orthodoxies as well" (320–21).

understanding how to use Charms in one's quest; understanding the power in numbers and in the symbols of ancient languages; learning to care for and work together with magical creatures; understanding the relationship of people to each other and to the enchanted cosmos; and understanding how people developed their magic and sometimes abused it. That is, Astronomy and Divination; Herbology, Potions, and Charms; Arithmancy, Ancient Runes, Care of Magical Creatures, and Muggle Studies; and History of Magic and Defense Against the Dark Arts, taken together, are an Alchemical education. They are Transfigurations, all.

The Greek philosopher Empedocles (like philosophers from many ancient traditions) held that everything was created from hot and dry fire, hot and moist air, cold and moist water, and cold and dry earth (Hamilton 1). In the *Timaeus*, Plato described a fifth element, the heavenly aether (58d), which became the alchemist's Quintessence, and which permeated the whole of the cosmos and the Earth. In particular, the most pure forms of mercury (water) and sulfur (fire) when combined would create gold. In other combinations, they created the other metals: silver, lead, tin, iron, and copper (1). In his laboratory at Johns Hopkins University, chemist and historian of science and technology Lawrence Principe has a ceramic model of an alchemical recipe depicted in a picture of a dragon in front of a hill on which "a rooster pecks at the back of a fox ... while the fox is devouring another rooster." Not only has Principe decoded and reproduced the alchemists' recipes, but he also explains how the image in his lab, the "Flying Red Dragon," is the key to creating the Philosophers' Stone. In his interview with Principe, Ben Guarino writes:

> "The rooster represents gold, which, believe it or not, makes sense because the rooster crows at sunrise," Principe said. "And the sun ... represents gold in traditional alchemical analogies." The fox is "a particular kind of highly acidic liquid," which Valentine described in a previous key. If you add gold to the acid, it dissolves: The fox eats the rooster. Distill the liquid, and the gold reappears. The rooster eats the fox.
>
> "As you keep doing this again, and again, and again, you're making a gold salt that, under just the right conditions, will actually sublime. It will rise in red crystals to the top of the distilling vessel," Principe said. "And that's the Red Dragon."

Professor Principe demonstrates alchemy's metallurgic and metaphoric transfigurations when he produces the red dragon, sublimated gold.

As Cerena Ceaser writes, the alchemists' transformations were not only brought about by physical transformations in the laboratory. "They must also incorporate symbolic relationships," which are revealed in the four alchemical stages: the *nigredo* (black) stage of decomposition; the *albedo* (white) stage of purification; the *citrinitas* (yellow) stage of the sun's light or the flame; and the *rubedo* (red) stage of the Philosopher's Stone. Ceaser further describes the process, explaining:

The basic alchemical sequence begins with a male and female sealing the *prima materia* (original substance) into a vessel. This process changes the substance from being red to black, *nigredo*, the dark side. *Calcinatio* is the application of fire to the substance, turning it from black to purple and then into ash. The ashes are dissolved in the *solutio*, or water. The sunlike substance, sulfur accomplishes the *coagulatio*, drying, of the solution. The pairing of opposites is possible in a gaseous state, *sublimatio*. Finally, an alchemical wedding of process and material leads to the reddish yellow/rosy pink philosopher's stone, *coniunctio*.*

In "Alchemy 101," John Granger explains that Ron, Harry, and Hermione's relationship is an alchemical one. Granger suggests that Hermione plays the role of Mercury, with her dentist parents and her initials Hg, the chemical symbol for the element (61–62). Fiery, red-headed Ron represents Sulfur, which Paracelsus described as the fire of burning wood. The alchemists also believed that the addition or removal of Sulfur could transform other metals. Ron and Hermione work to make Gold of Harry's Lead (63). The three of them together make the Philosopher's Stone, or the Stone of Wisdom, each transforming and purifying the others.

The Stone and the Hallows

The seventeenth-century "Chymist" Johann Rudolf Glauber illustrated the Philosopher's Stone with the *tria prima* (*tria principia*) of Sulphur, Mercury, and Salt (the central circle with the line through the diameter) symbols in the corners of the triangle surrounded by the four elements written in the corners of the square. In the outer circle of the left-hand illustration, the inscription reads, "The salt/wit/elegance of metals is the Philosopher's Stone." And around the square, there is a command: "Bring or continue through to maturity or perfection." In the right-hand illustration, the inscription around the circle reads: "The fifth essence of minerals/ores is the universal medicine." And the text inside the circle on the sides of the

---

*While contemporary readers might wonder about connecting "black" with decomposition, it might help to think of the fertile black soil, the Khem, of Egypt that gives alchemy its name (rsc.org). It is the product of decomposition and also the start of all growth. Contemporary readers might also rightly have second thoughts about what seems like the compulsory heterosexuality implied in the alchemical wedding imagery. On one hand, it seems important that the female was highly regarded among the alchemists while actual women and female metaphors for nature were devalued in the modern European mind. On the other hand, the contemporary imagination might think of other metaphors to tell the story of the prime material and its distillation and transformation. Ceaser explains the metaphor as showing the importance of joining material and process, so we also might see the metaphor as a refusal of modern European dualisms. There is a uniting of mind and body, human and cosmos; or rather, they are found, each in the other.

Introduction 11

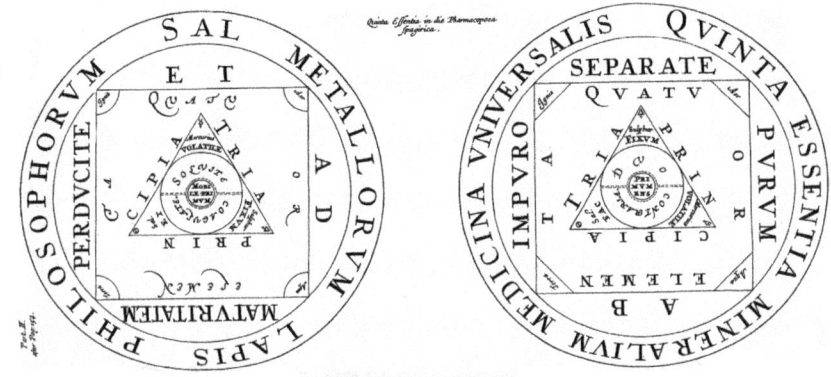

Johann Rudolf Glauber. "Quintessence."

square commands "Separate what is pure from what is impure or morally foul."*

Similarly, the alchemist Paracelsus (who also appears on a Chocolate Frog card) said:

> The beginnings of all material things ... were ... the "three primes," or *tria prima*, of Sulphur, Salt, and Mercury. These were as much symbolic categories as rudimentary components of matter. Salt represented an unburnable, nonvolatile ash or earth; Sulphur stood for combustible natures; and Mercury denoted the volatile and metallic constitutions of bodies.... From these ... came into being all the earthly, watery, airy, and fiery things of the world [Paracelsus, 1922–1922; rept. 1996: vol. 13, 393ff]. (Moran 72–73)

According to the Royal Society of Chemistry, the word alchemy (and chemistry, for that matter) "is derived from the Arabian phrase 'al-kimia,' which refers to the Egyptians' preparation of the Stone or Elixir. The Arabic root 'kimia' comes from the Coptic 'khem' that alluded to the fertile black soil of the Nile delta. Esoterically and hieroglyphically, the word refers to the dark mystery of the primordial or First Matter (the Khem)" (rsc.org).

The power of the sun to bring growth and life, the alchemists believed, was transmitted by Salt, part of the first matter and another way of saying earth. Along with the other two heavenly or prime substances, Salt and Sulfur, Mercury "transcended both the solid and liquid states, both earth and heaven, both life and death" (rsc.org). In addition to describing Harry as the "salt of the earth," Granger also portrays him as lead, the symbol for which, curiously, is lightning shaped. The four elements and the three primes (the powerful seven) of the Philosopher's Stone transform Harry

---

*Thanks to Robert Holschuh Simmons of the Monmouth College Classics Department for his help with the translation.

into Gold, and Ron and Hermione help Harry to heed the Stone's command: they help him to maturity and toward perfection.

If the Salt symbol in Glauber's illustration is rotated ninety degrees inside the triangle of the *Tria Principia*, we see something like Rowling's Deathly Hallows embedded in Glauber's square representing the four elements. In the illustration of the Deathly Hallows, the circle stands for the Resurrection Stone; the vertical line represents the Elder Wand; the triangle enclosing them is the image of the Invisibility Cloak. Like the Philosopher's Stone at the start of the series, the Deathly Hallows at its end are also real in the alchemical world of Harry Potter—"real, and dangerous," says Dumbledore (*Hallows* 713). Like the Stone, the Hallows might also teach us that there are better and worse ways to live our mortal lives.

The Deathly Hallows.

The Deathly Hallows

In Rowling's "Tale of the Three Brothers," the Peverell brothers meet with Death on a lonely road, and, after using some clever magic to avoid him, are each allowed to request a gift. The first brother requests the Elder wand that must always win, the second the Resurrection Stone that brings back a pale image of a deceased loved one, and the third the remarkable and infallible Invisibility Cloak (*Hallows* 411). The first brother, Antioch, drunk on the power of possessing the Wand and drunk on wine as well, is murdered while he sleeps. Overcome with a desperate longing, the second brother, Cadmus, uses the Stone to drag back the woman he loves and who had died. But she is so unhappy that he kills himself to join her. Using their choices against them, Death outwits and claims them; they were not empowered by their love of mundane and abusive power or by their desperate, self-absorbed desire. Only Ignotus, the third brother and Harry's direct ancestor, uses Death's gift, the Cloak of Invisibility, to enable his mortal life and joins Death as an equal when the time is right, handing on the Cloak to his heirs (*Hallows* 406–09).

The brothers who choose the Wand and the Stone understand the Hallows' alchemical properties not at all; they choose the most destructive form of power and indulge the most selfish desires, to their own and others' harm. Hermione suggests that the Philosopher's Stone might have been the inspiration for the Resurrection Stone (*Hallows* 416), and the two brothers' choices reaffirm Dumbledore's observation that people "have a knack of choosing precisely those things that are the worst for them" (*Stone* 297). The third brother, however, "the humblest and also the wisest," gives us a glimpse of the possibility of distilling the "starstuff," the stuff of the heavens—the Quintessence—from our earthly lives in his choice of the Cloak (*Hallows* 408).

It is possible, that is, to transfigure the Hallows and recover what is truly holy in them, while allowing them to transfigure us, to find or create what is truly hallowed in us. As the Philosopher's Stone is not mainly about riches and immortality in the most obvious sense of hoarding gold and defeating death, the Hallows are not mainly about becoming "master of death" in the sense of fearing or disdaining our own human fragility and mortality. It takes extraordinary care to retrieve them from Gellert Grindelwald's symbols of superiority and terror at Durmstrang. He would use the Hallows to achieve Wizarding Dominance over Muggles and manipulation of the Magical community. Those powerfully magical objects he would have used to dominate and torture, making them anything but sacred, sowing seeds of mistrust and fear as Voldemort did a generation later, when he used his grandfather's ring—his Peverell ancestor's unrecognized Resurrection Stone—to make a Horcrux.

In the liminal space between life and death at King's Cross Station, when Harry talks with his late headmaster about the Deathly Hallows, Dumbledore acknowledges that it would take a very special person indeed to unite the Hallows (*Hallows* 720). To understand those three objects and to join them is something like the alchemical process of creating and understanding the Philosopher's Stone. It requires a transformation of desire, of power, and of the possessor, which the Flamels and Dumbledore showed us in the *Harry Potter and the Philosopher's Stone* and which Harry and his friends live at the close of *Deathly Hallows*.

The Alchemical Harry Potter: Transfiguring Desire, Power, and the Person

The Alchemical Harry Potter: Essays on Transfiguration in J.K. Rowling's Novels reveals these alchemical transformations, whether considered literally or metaphorically.* The collection is divided into three sections: The Resurrection Stone and the Transfiguration of Desire; The Elder Wand and the Transfiguration of Power; and The Cloak of Invisibility and the Transfiguration of Self and Community. One of my colleagues told me she suggested that her then seven-year-old daughter, Sophia, should branch out from the Harry Potter novels. In response, Sophia gave her mother excellent reasons for why she planned to continue reading and re-reading the series. This young girl reminded me, of course, that children and young adults are the books' first audience and that Dumbledore encourages us very early in the series to take seriously house-elves and children's tales, love, loyalty, and innocence. The contributors range in age from eight to eighty, and young readers' voices begin each section.

The Resurrection Stone and the Transfiguration of Desire

Dumbledore tells Harry that most people would use the Resurrection Stone to drag back those who are at peace as he, Dumbledore, did when he put it on, forgetting it was a Horcrux hiding part of Voldemort's soul. Dumbledore hasn't moved so far from what Harry guessed his mentor might have seen in the Mirror of Erised—not "a pair of thick, woolen socks," but his family, hoping to assuage his own terrible guilt about the death of his sister, Ariana (*Stone* 214). Harry sees himself surrounded by his parents and other family members when he gazes longingly, nearly paralyzed, into that Mirror of Desire. Ron has a similar experience, seeing himself singled out and glorified, the Mirror reflecting his longing to stand apart from his many siblings.

Back on Privet Drive, Dudley's eleventh birthday confirms the Dursleys' view of "normal," in contrast to Harry's discovery of a new world the day he turned eleven. Dudley's father rewards his son for complaining he has only thirty-six presents, two fewer than the year before, saying "Little tyke wants his money's worth" (*Stone* 22). Yet, even on the first trip to school on the Hogwarts Express, Harry shows that he thinks differently, moves in the world differently from his uncle. It is not just the new wand

---

*Cerena Ceaser's "Alchemy and the Hermetic Tradition: Mircea Eliade and Carl Jung" explains the function of myths or foundational metaphors. She writes, "While both Eliade and Jung agree that myths are an integral part of human perspective, Eliade focuses on myths as reflecting the sacred in narrative synthesis, while Jung emphasizes mythology as a process similar to other natural phenomena." Granger, too, recognizes the importance of Jung's study of alchemy but also critiques its lack of a transcendent element (50). Jung's may be a modern adaptation of a pre-modern alchemy, and I wonder if modern or postmodern thinkers are in some ways always blinkered by the foundational shifts of those intervening modern centuries.

in his pocket or the wizard's robes in his trunk. When his new friend Ron is embarrassed by his dry corned-beef sandwiches, and Harry has, for the first time in his life, enough money to buy whatever he wants, we see the difference in his very character. Harry gets everything from the lunch trolley and thoroughly enjoys his afternoon with Ron, delighted both to have treats and a new friend with whom to share them (*Stone* 102).

Harry and Ron turn upside down the Dursleys' focus on material possessions and what it means to get one's money's worth. Even before looking into the Mirror, the two friends transfigure the fruitless desire each felt before it into something as pure and golden as Harry's first birthday cake. When Hagrid pulled back the curtain dividing the two worlds, he replaced Harry's "normal" marginalization and ostracization with love and affection and an appreciation for the singularity of one young boy's life. It is a rare moment during which Harry is treated neither as an abomination nor as a rising star but just as a child with a birthday which matters to someone else, just a kid covered in frosting as sweet as it is possible to be.

On their first day together and throughout the series, Harry and Ron become the Mirror for each other. Their friendship, however bumpy at times, becomes a life-affirming reflection and fulfillment of the other's desire: Ron and the Weasleys become the loving family for which Harry aches, and Harry shows Ron his own unique gifts. Under the influence of the locket Horcrux in *Deathly Hallows*, Ron storms out on Harry and Hermione but regrets his action immediately. After escaping the Snatchers and spending Christmas with his brother, Ron discovers that the Deluminator—the little silver instrument which when clicked sucks the light from any source only to return it with another click—Dumbledore has left him would guide him back to Harry and Hermione. After saving Harry from drowning, Ron says Dumbledore "must've known I'd run out on you," to which Harry replies, "No.... He must've known you'd always want to come back" (*Hallows* 391).

On the train, the two eleven-year-olds happily share candy and friendship. They begin a relationship that continues to the series' final book, in which Harry understands that Ron is part of him, that Ron would risk his own life to save Harry's. Harry *is* because Ron—fiery, impetuous, Sulfur-Ron—is part of him. Ron, too, understands that he is unique in Harry's world. They have learned to transfigure the burning desire reflected in the Mirror—a desire which might well have burned them out—when they reflect those desires to each other and burn brighter. As the Flamels decided it was best to destroy the Philosopher's Stone, Harry decides it is best to leave the Resurrection Stone in the forest where he had dropped it. The Stone, like the Mirror, teaches him its lessons: the dead he loves live in him (*Azkaban* 427); his mother's love lives "in [his] very skin" (*Stone*

299); that Prongs can ride again without Time Turners or Stones that bring back the dead (*Azkaban* 428); and that Hermione and Ron are part of his Transfigurations, even when he tries to push them away. He uses the Stone "to enable [his own] self-sacrifice" rather than to disturb those who are at peace (*Hallows* 720).

Sophia Imafuji, age 8, begins this section with "Why I Read Harry Potter Books Again and Again."

In "The Literary Alchemy of J.K. Rowling," John Granger introduces both Rowling's hermetic artistry and her probable sources and inspiration, Vladimir Nabokov and C.S. Lewis. Granger explains how the structure of Rowling's work follows the traditional pattern of chiasmus, what anthropologist Mary Douglas called "ring composition." The stylistic complement to this there-and-back-again structure is Rowling's use of hermetic colors, symbols, and sequences, a style Granger calls "literary alchemy." With his exploration of Rowling's use of chiasmus and her choices in names, plot points, and story parallels, Granger shows that Rowling's stories are alchemically driven, and that alchemy, as Rowling herself says, "set[s] the magical parameters" of her books.

Anne Parker-Perkola's "Harry Potter and the Transfiguration of Desire" sounds out some of the esoteric and alchemical resonances of *Harry Potter and the Philosopher's Stone*. Parker-Perkola reflects that books in general and the Potter books in particular are initiatory objects which, like the Mirror of Erised, are able to mediate an encounter for readers with their own unacknowledged desires and so become imaginative tools for transfiguring these desires into knowledge. Parker-Perkola argues that the Mirror facilitates an important moment of self-knowledge for Harry that later helps him achieve the object of the Great Work, the Philosopher's Stone, and, at the end of the novels, not only to face and conquer death but to return to life.

In "Re-Reading Harry Potter, Re-Creating Ourselves: Harry Potter as Resurrection Stone," Isaac Willis writes that he, like a lot of people who go on to major in English literature, was inspired by the books he read as a child. It so happens that Harry Potter was the first book he read for nobody but himself, and he fell in love with the series and with reading more broadly. In his junior year of college, he re-read all seven books for a class centered on the texts. But as the semester progressed, he realized something: The books he was reading were not the books he remembered. He had to mourn the idea of the books he had read as a child. As we grow up, and as we re-read, we are sometimes struck by grief—a different sort than that which attends us when we finish a good book for the first time. This is the grief that reminds us, at its loftiest, of our own transience and finitude and, at its most base, that all of our relationships—with books, people, pets—are subject to change, will someday come to a close. In the grief of re-reading, he at first thought he was after Harry Potter as a Resurrection Stone, but the resurrection he was after, like stoppering death, is probably impossible and, at the very least, is self-damaging in the end. He realized that what he needed instead was a re-creation, a recognition that, to paraphrase Albus Dumbledore, "the books we love never really leave us" (*Azkaban* 427).

Alicia L. Skipper and Kate Fulton's "Out from the Shadows into the Light: Persona and Shadow in Harry Potter" draws on Plato's "Allegory of the Cave" to show the distortion of reality as the prisoners emerge from the shadow of the cave to achieve enlightenment and confront reality, and Carl Jung's archetype of shadow and persona to explore the need to acknowledge and accept the different aspects of one's self in order to achieve balance. While Tom Riddle is Lord Voldemort's persona and Voldemort is Riddle's shadow, Severus Snape presents his shadow as his persona in order to work against the cruel and murderous Voldemort. Albus Dumbledore's persona, at first, seems to be one with his shadow; that is, he seems to be in all ways the good, wise, and kind mentor he plays to Harry. Yet, he himself tells us that he struggled with his shadow as a young man and by conscious choice keeps his fascination with power at bay. Harry, of the four, seems to come closest to a reconciliation of persona and shadow. He is able to plumb the hidden depths of his soul or personality to be the love he tries to bring to the world. He enacts the alchemical transformation from lead into gold helped by Dumbledore and, as readers learn, by Snape.

In "An Anti-Oedipal Reading of Harry Potter and Alchemy," Robert Tindol writes that Carl Jung saw alchemy as a means of unifying and reconciling the conscious and the unconscious. To Jung, a plot device such as a Philosopher's Stone would be best described as a metaphor but one that possesses true value in the real world. Gilles Deleuze and Felix Guattari's *Anti-Oedipus* effectively argues that Jung's theories can be updated to include the notion of alchemy as a "productive mechanism"—that is, as a means of bridging the gap between individuals' deepest desires and the countless ways that society impels us to conform. An Anti-Oedipal reading of Harry Potter focuses on alchemy as a dual pathway toward the balance of desire and interest. In particular, an Anti-Oedipal reading clarifies the reasons that Harry's self-effacing willingness to sacrifice himself for the greater good, coupled with his reluctance to claim greater power, is the key to defeating Voldemort.

The Elder Wand and the Transfiguration of Power

When discussing the Hallows with Harry at King's Cross Station, Dumbledore says that he, Dumbledore, "was fit only to possess the meanest of them," the Elder Wand (*Hallows* 720). Recognizing the dangerous appeal power held for him, Dumbledore resolved to tame the Wand and not to kill with it. Dumbledore transformed his remorse and, therefore, himself, in a way Voldemort remained unable to do. At the end of *Hallows*, as Voldemort and Harry face off, Rowling holds out the chance for redemption until the very last moment. Harry says to Voldemort: "Be a man ... try.... Try for some remorse..." (*Hallows* 741). Yet Voldemort is unable to rethink power or desire, unable to rethink what it means to be a human or a man.*

For Voldemort, the Wand is a Death Stick, enabling him to seek his Destiny (the Wand's third name) of self-aggrandizement (from his perspective) through the slaughter of any who stood in his way (and many who did not). He is only interested in the Wand, Dumbledore tells Harry, and neither knows nor cares about the other two Hallows, for whom would he wish to bring back from the dead, never having loved? He could make himself invisible well enough without need of the Cloak. By contrast, Dumbledore has allowed his lifelong, aching remorse to change him. He has resolved to transfigure not only the Wand's power but also what counts as power. He recognizes in Harry someone who has no desire for power over others, for the power of domination.

Handed leadership responsibilities without ever wanting them, Harry bears them well, learning that he needs his friends, needs the support of others along the way (*Hallows* 718).† He transforms power into mutual empowerment. The inadvertent master of the Elder Wand, Harry, to Ron's utter amazement, uses the Wand only once, not to kill but to heal—to repair the Phoenix Feather Wand that chose him in Ollivander's the first time he visited Diagon Alley (*Hallows* 748–49). Harry returns the Elder Wand to Dumbledore's grave, hoping to live a long life, to die a natural death, and to allow the Wand's power to die with him.

On being surrounded on their way to Voldemort in the Shrieking

---

*In "Love Potion No. 9¾," Gregory Bassham gives a moving discussion of Merope Gaunt and her use of the love potion to ensnare the elder Tom Riddle. Bassham argues that she saw the error of using magical means to have a relationship with Riddle and that she gave up any possibility for her own happiness to free him. Her remorse shows that her son, Tom Marvolo Riddle, is nothing like her. It seems to me remarkable that this abused and battered woman thought she could have and give love, despite experiencing only rejection and scorn her whole life. Anne Collins Smith's "Harry Potter, Radical Feminism, and the Power of Love" suggests that the series is radically feminist as it both unhooks sex from gender constructions and elevates those values and behaviors historically coded feminine. Harry suggests to Voldemort that he might reconstruct what it means to be a man when he urges Riddle to "try for some remorse" (*Hallows* 741).

†In "Harry Potter and the Young Man's Mistake: The Illusion of Innocence and the Temptation of Power," Daniel P. Moloney argues that Dumbledore's "old man's mistake" is not that he loved Harry too much, but rather not nearly enough. And Harry's "young man's mistake" is in his temptation to break away from his friends in his anger and pain.

Shack in *Deathly Hallows*, Harry, Ron, and Hermione nearly succumb to the dementors' soul-crushing hopelessness. That is until Luna Lovegood arrives. When Ginny stops people calling Luna "Loony," Ginny's good heart and Luna's brave and reliable friendship also transform power. We might imagine that Luna would have seen herself surrounded by friends, had we been able to watch her peer into the Mirror. Her hand-painted portraits of Ron and Neville, Harry, Ginny, and Hermione on her bedroom ceiling linked together with the word "friends" repeated over and over, like golden links in a chain, show that she transforms what might have been a desperate, draining longing into an empowered and actualized desire (*Hallows* 417). Luna is far braver than her father, far braver than Voldemort, who, faced with isolation, fails entirely at empathy, becoming less and less human as the years go by. Luna's strength is in her unwavering devotion to both her friends and to a sense of wonder, even over what many would consider to be entirely implausible. She keeps up morale when she, Dean Thomas, and Mr. Ollivander are prisoners in the basement of Malfoy Manor and gives everyone the strength to conjure Patronuses against the dementors in the Battle of Hogwarts. When Harry nearly mocks her for suggesting they think of something happy, she reminds them, "We're all still here, ... we're still fighting. Come on, now…" (*Hallows* 649).

"My Harry Potter Journey" by Ella Victoria Greer, age 13, launches this section.

In "The Missing Element: The Alchemy Experiment Inside the Chamber of Secrets," S.P. Şipal argues that as Harry Potter enters the Chamber of Secrets near the end of his second year at Hogwarts, he is unknowingly entering an alchemical experiment of J.K. Rowling's creation. In Tom Riddle's secret chamber, Harry must face his Shadow, rescue his hidden feminine side, and dissolve in basilisk poison to be reborn via phoenix tears into a higher, more-noble being. As Harry strives toward quintessence in this second phase of Rowling's Great Work, the hint of a magical missing element, one linked to the Eye of Horus—an important Egyptian life-restoring amulet—speaks to Rowling's greatest theme: the power of love.

Lawrence W. Farris' "On the Transmutation of Voldemort's Love of Power into Harry Potter's Power of Love," shows that a life journey is often shaped by one's relationship to money, sexuality, and power. Although Harry Potter and Voldemort share much in common—especially childhood deprivations—they choose very different paths regarding their relationships to those three shapers of life. Voldemort surrenders all else in the pursuit of power that he believes will give him immortality, while Harry comes to realize that the unique power that is love in its various forms—familial, friendship, erotic, and self-giving (as set forth by C.S. Lewis)—tempers the allure of raw power. Harry undergoes a true alchemical transformation that leads to the gold of personhood and relationship, while Voldemort chases what can only remain the basest of metals—isolation and defeat. J.K. Rowling's insight into both alchemy and love undergirds the setting forth of two lives so similarly begun which end so vastly differently.

In "Auror Magic: An Almost Alchemical Process," Lorrie Kim notes that Voldemort did not aspire to alchemy. He pursued a degraded version of immortality, making himself unkillable by splitting his soul through murder, rather than purifying his soul and producing gold. Yet on three occasions, without intending to, he produces golden light or flames when he casts a Killing Curse at Harry Potter and Harry's magic collides with his own. Harry did not set forth to learn alchemy either. With his momentous decision between "Horcruxes and Hallows," choosing to hunt the repositories of a Dark Wizard's destructive power rather than seeking greater magical power for himself, Harry pursues a different sort of soul magic (*Hallows* 484). As an aspiring Auror, his quest is not to transmute base metals into gold but to transmute an unnaturally debased soul, Voldemort's soul, back to its own humanity.

Sean Paulsgrove explores abuses of power that arise from dogmatic thinking and resistance to such abuses in both the Harry Potter series and in Pink Floyd's *The Wall* in "Tapping on Just Another Brick In the Wall." In "A Certain Blindness in Human Beings," American philosopher and physician William James suggests that each person sees the world through his or her own cultural and epistemic lenses. This is unavoidable. But, when a person is unable to see from another's perspective, he or she runs the risk of dogmatism. When Hagrid taps on the bricks in the wall behind The Leaky Cauldron, he opens a portal to the magical world. In *The Wall*, Pink Floyd's Pink decries the dogmatism in education that is designed to make children obedient and docile. Rowling's Professor Umbridge is just such a dogmatist in the magical world. This essay celebrates the power of imagination to resist dogmatism, whether it is in the form of Hermione studying Muggles "from the wizarding point of view," the antics of Fred and George, Dumbledore's Army, or Pink's determined resistance to the Schoolmaster's crushing control (*Azkaban* 57). When we tap on the correct bricks in a Wall, the doorway we make using imagination is not where we came in but is, instead, how we get out.

The Cloak of Invisibility and the Transfiguration of Self and Community

Harry with his friends makes the alchemical journey, transforming himself enough to be able to unite the Hallows and to become "the true master of death" by transfiguring desire, power, and the self in community

(*Hallows* 720). By contrast, Voldemort turns the Stone into a Horcrux, neither recognizing nor potentially appreciating the power embedded in a natural entity. He treats it like an inert thing, seeing it only as a servant to his project. He murders Snape hoping to bend the Elder Wand to his command, not recognizing the intention in wand wood. Even though Voldemort has commandeered Lucius Malfoy's wand, Harry's wand recognizes the person who shares a bit of his soul and whose own wand shares with Harry's the phoenix feather core. As Harry and Hagrid fly from the Dursleys' to the Tonkses' on the eve of Harry's seventeenth birthday, the wand so intimately bound with Harry acts of its own accord to shoot Golden flames at Voldemort. Perhaps reflecting the golden Transfigurations Hermione and Ron help Harry to achieve, the wand gives Harry enough protection to hurtle across the protective charms to safety in the Tonkses' garden (*Hallows* 61–62).

Not only does Harry understand the enchanted nature of the Hallows and the materials of which they are made, but he shows readers that the three of them together help us to reconsider ourselves and our communities. Harry uses the Resurrection Stone to enable his own self-sacrifice, calling forth his parents, Sirius, and Lupin, who are part of him, and later dropping the Stone in the forest. Dumbledore also reminds Harry that while the Invisibility Cloak can be used for selfish purposes, its real power is that it can "protect and shield others as well as its owner" (*Hallows* 720; 716). Harry embraces his own mortality, hoping to pass on the Cloak to his children at the moment that the power of the Wand dies with him.

The Sorting Hat is another woven item with a mind of its own that can give us a model for weaving community out of multiple talents and interests. As the version of the Hat's song in *Order of the Phoenix* reminds readers, the four houses recognize the variety of human strengths and talents, while recognizing that there is some of each house's virtue in each of us. The Hat reminds us that Hogwarts was founded by two pairs of best friends, Ravenclaw and Hufflepuff, Gryffindor and Slytherin (*Phoenix* 204). The Hat reminds readers that the ideal is for the four houses to work in harmony, sharing their strengths with each other, for the benefit of each and of the whole. The differences are not the problem; the problem is a failure of friendship (*Phoenix* 205).*

I teach a course at Monmouth College in Monmouth, Illinois, called "Harry Potter and the Philosopher's Soul," which of course plays on the

---

*See Steven W. Patterson's "Is Ambition a Virtue? Why Slytherin Belongs at Hogwarts" and Susan R. Matthews' "*Ich bin ein Hufflepuff*" for compelling discussions through an Aristotelean lens of how the four virtues or personalities (Patterson) or "human geniuses" (Matthews) are in each person and are in the collective.

title of the first book in the series and points in the direction of the series' alchemical transformations. The college juniors with whom I have had the pleasure of sharing the series grew up with Harry Potter. Many learned to read with the series, and some of the international students learned English, while Harry and his friends learned Potions, Care of Magical Creatures, and Transfiguration. Many of the students said that they escaped into the world of the novels when things were tough at home or when they were being bullied at school, that in those pages, they learned not only about friendship and acceptance but also about how to stand up to injustice. It is a privilege and an honor for me to have some part in their transformations and to see something new in the books each time I read them, in large part because of these young people's insights. The series empowers children, when too much in their young lives exists to make them docile and obedient.

Some of the students recalled being disappointed on their eleventh birthdays when no letter from Hogwarts arrived, either by Muggle Post or by owl, neither rolled up inside each of a dozen eggs on the front steps nor whizzing down the chimney. Yet, like the eleven-year-old wizards and witches who received their letters from Hogwarts, our students' college admission letters promised to take them to a new world. College is a time of transition, a time of self-exploration, and, we hope, a time of personal and social empowerment. By the end of the semester, we realize how the books have grown up with the students, giving them the courage to be playful and imaginative and to be brave when they "have to make a choice between what is right and what is easy," as Dumbledore urges when he remembers Cedric Diggory, that brave, smart, ambitious, and loyal Hufflepuff (*Goblet* 724). The four houses live in Cedric and, combined, show the Quintessence of friendship in him, when he, with Harry in the Triwizard maze, cares more for mutual survival and fair play than winning a cup for House or School. In the four houses with their four virtues, there is a reminder of the four elements—Earth (Hufflepuff), Air (Ravenclaw), Fire (Gryffindor), and Water (Slytherin)—and the fifth element in Cedric and Harry's journey of Transfiguration (Mugglenet).

As the Hat reminds the four houses to cooperate for mutual support and protection, the Cloak has the power to preserve its owner and others, to protect and give space for introspection in the face of danger. In one of the Harry Potter classes, we were talking about an article in the student newspaper that featured some of Monmouth's two dozen or so Syrian students. One spoke of his parents who had just fled Syria for Turkey and said the College had saved his education. One of the Harry Potter students wondered if we had saved his life, as if we had been able to draw the Cloak around him to give him a place to conjure his parents as sources of strength, even as he worried about them daily. Those students seemed to me to have transformed their thinking about themselves and about community, about their own unique strengths and about the importance of combining those strengths with the gifts of their friends and classmates. They, with Harry, their friends, communities, and countless readers, will have performed the transfiguration of the Hallows, uniting them in a way both golden and eternal, because the Hallows, like the Philosopher's Stone, will have made those transformations in them.

This section begins with "And All Was Well" by Tamyra Dixon-Rankin, science teacher at West Central Middle School and Deputy Headmistress of Dumbledore's Academy in Stronghurst, Illinois.

In "The Snitch, the Stone, and the Sword: Harry Potter and the Alchemical Seeker," B.L. Purdom writes that as a baby, Harry Potter becomes The Boy Who Lived and the Horcrux Voldemort never meant to make. Harry undergoes other significant transfigurations on his journey, chiefly that he becomes a symbolic Golden Snitch, a metaphorical Philosopher's Stone, and a human Sword of Gryffindor, which makes him, paradoxically, both a Horcrux and a consummate hunter/destroyer of Horcruxes. These transfigurations are indelibly linked to Harry's most transcendent and liminal role as a Seeker, a metaphysical title that marks him as an intercessor who has internalized the central philosophy of alchemy: all is one and death is an illusion, the same philosophy underlying the quest of the Deathly Hallows. This ultimately enables Harry, both the Master of Death and youngest Seeker in a hundred years, to destroy the most difficult Horcrux of all: himself.

Mary Pyle's "Alchemy as a Metaphor for Learning" analyses how alchemy can be a metaphor for learning and development in Rowling's Harry Potter series. Although alchemy is not taught as a discipline at Hogwarts, the core subjects at the school are closely linked to the topics studied by the alchemists. The alchemists did not confine themselves to scientific study; they were also concerned with base humans moving through enlightenment to a golden, more godly state. Pyle's essay addresses the emotional development of the protagonists as they grow through their seven school years.

Charles M. Rupert employs a Frommian lens through which to view the series as a psychological allegory in "Harry Potter and the Root of All Evil." Dumbledore and Voldemort represent two polarized moral identities that motivate their behavior: "being" in the case of Dumbledore and "having" in the case of Lord Voldemort. While "being" is understood as self-determination and actualization, "having" is more pathological, characterized by an internal inadequacy that pushes the "having" person to attempt to control and dominate the world around him or her in a doomed attempt at self-actualization. Rupert argues that the clash of these two psychologies drives the moral conflict in the series.

In "Soul Making and Soul Splitting: Alchemy of the Soul in Harry Potter," Julie Loveland Swanstrom explains that alchemy applies not only to external objects but also to one's entire being, including one's soul. Harry and Tom have a number of similar life experiences: rough childhoods rife with abusive situations; the feeling of belonging at school; a relationship to fame; a search for companions; and an exploration of eternal life. Their very different reactions to those experiences allow for an examination of how they do (in Harry's case) or do not (in Tom's) perform alchemy on their own souls. The evils Harry suffers feed his soul making; the more he refuses to replicate those evils, the more he drains them of their power and purifies his soul, making it more whole, more golden. By contrast, Voldemort *né* Tom returns evil for evil as he splits his soul in his quest to overcome what he sees as the weakness of human mortality. In the process, he amplifies and strengthens evils. Embracing opportunities to unify people, to become more moral, and to respect magic through appropriate secrecy, Harry discovers the divine cosmos in himself. Spurning those same opportunities, Voldemort remains lonely, selfish, and fractured.

Anne J. Mamary's "Ruddy Stargazers: Centaurs, Philosophers, and a Life Worth Living" observes that both Plato's *Republic* and Rowling's Harry Potter series draw readers into their texts with fantastic stories and compelling imagery, taking readers on journeys that challenge us to rethink what it means to be the best people we can be, both individually and together. Both texts assume an enchanted universe and play on the phrase "stargazers" (or "ruddy stargazers" in Hagrid's case) to contrast the all-too-human view of philosophers or centaurs as head-in-the-clouds dreamers with the ability of philosophers and centaurs to read patterns for our lives in the star-strewn skies. Rowling sorts her students into Houses, and Plato sorts his characters based on what is unique in each and also by the choices each has made. If the Hogwarts Houses and Plato's classes work together in harmony, bringing together the strengths each represents, they create together a just society and just people. In Rowling's "Tale of the Three Brothers" and in Plato's myth of Er, ordinary people choose gifts from death. If they choose well, they will live long lives in peaceful fellowship with their friends and neighbors, and "hand on a like life to their offspring," as Ignotus Peverell did in Rowling's tale and the citizens of the healthy city do in Plato's (*Rep.* 372c–d). Living lives as microcosms of the patterns woven into the heavens, the "stargazers" end Plato's *Republic* with hope: May we, all of us, "fare well" (621d). And Harry can conclude the series saying, "All was well" (*Hallows* 759).

Works Cited

Allen, Paula Gunn. "The Woman I Love Is a Planet, the Planet I Love Is a Tree." *Off the Reservation: Reflections on Boundary-Busting, Border-Crossing, Loose Canons*, Beacon, 1998, pp. 118–20.
Bassham, Gregory. "Love Potion Number 9¾." *The Ultimate Harry Potter and Philosophy: Hogwarts for Muggles*, edited by Gregory Bassham, Wiley, 2010, pp. 66–79. Blackwell Philosophy and Pop-Culture Series.
Cavanaugh, William T. "Religious Violence as Modern Myth." *Political Theology*, vol. 15, no. 6, Nov. 2014, pp. 486–502. W.S. Murray & Son Ltd., doi:10.1179/1462317X14Z 00000000094. Accessed 7 Jan. 2018.
Ceaser, Cerena. "Alchemy and the Hermetic Tradition: Mircea Eliade and Carl Jung." *Sutra Journal: Eternal Truths, Modern Voices*, Jan. 2016, www.sutrajournal.com/alchemy-and-the-hermetic-tradition-by-cerena-ceaser. Accessed 17 Aug. 2018.
Ehrenreich, Barbara, and Deidre English. *Witches, Midwives, and Nurses: A History of Women Healers*. 1973. Feminist Press, 2010.
Glauber, Johann Rudolf. *The Works of the Highly Experienced and Famous Chymist, John Rudolph Glauber* (Translated by Christopher Peck), 1689. "Unveiling the Secrets: The Evolution of Modern Chemistry." *Hay Exhibits*. Brown U Library. library.brown.edu/exhibit/exhibits/show/revolution-of-chemistry/alchemical-symbols-as-secret-c. Accessed 15 Aug. 2017. Used by permission of the Hays Library at Brown University.
Granger, John. "Alchemy 101." *Unlocking Harry Potter: Five Keys for the Serious Reader*, Zossima, 2007, pp. 47–76.
Guarino, Ben. "This Chemist Is Unlocking the Secrets of Alchemy." *Speaking of Science, The Washington Post*, 30 Jan. 2018, www.washingtonpost.com/news/speaking-of-science/wp/2018/01/30/this-chemist-is-unlocking-the-secrets-of-alchemy/?utm_term=.62af1bd9fe11. Accessed 5 Feb. 2018.
Hamilton, Nigel. "The Alchemical Process of Transformation." 1985, www.sufismus.ch/assets/files/omega_dream/alchemy_e.pdf. Accessed 1 Aug. 2018.
Matthews, Susan R. "*Ich Bin Ein Hufflepuff*: Strategies for Multiple Skill Management in J.K. Rowling's Novels." *Mapping the World of the Sorcerer's Apprentice: An Unauthorized Exploration of the Harry Potter Series*, edited by Mercedes Lackey, BenBella, 2005, pp. 133–44. Smart Pop Books.
Merchant, Carolyn. *The Death of Nature: Women, Ecology, and the Scientific Revolution*. 1980. HarperOne, 1990.
Moloney, Daniel P. "Harry Potter and the Young Man's Mistake: The Illusion of Innocence and the Temptation of Power." *Mapping the World of the Sorcerer's Apprentice: An Unauthorized Exploration of the Harry Potter Series*, edited by Mercedes Lackey, BenBella, 2005, pp. 7–26. Smart Pop Books.
Moran, Bruce T. *Distilling Knowledge: Alchemy, Chemistry, and the Scientific Revolution*. Harvard UP, 2005.
"New Interview with JK Rowling." *Mugglenet*, mugglenet.com/2008/03/new-interview-with-jk-rowling/. Accessed Apr. 2019.
Nummedal, Tara. "Alchemy and Religion in Christian Europe." *Ambix*, vol. 60, no. 4, 27 Nov. 2013, pp. 311–22, Taylor & Francis, doi: 10.1179/0002698013Z.00000000036.
Patterson, Steven W. "Is Ambition a Virtue? Why Slytherin Belongs at Hogwarts." *Harry Potter and Philosophy: If Aristotle Ran Hogwarts*, edited by David Baggett and Shawn E. Klein, Open Court, 2004, pp. 121–31. Popular Culture and Philosophy 9.
Reeve, C.D.C., and Patrick Lee Miller, editors. *Introductory Readings in Ancient Greek and Roman Philosophy*. 2nd ed., Hackett, 2015.
Rowling, J.K. *Harry Potter and the Chamber of Secrets*. Scholastic, 1998.
_____. *Harry Potter and the Deathly Hallows*. Scholastic, 2007.
_____. *Harry Potter and the Goblet of Fire*. Scholastic, 2000.
_____. *Harry Potter and the Half-Blood Prince*. Scholastic, 2005.
_____. *Harry Potter and the Order of the Phoenix*. Scholastic, 2002.
_____. *Harry Potter and the Prisoner of Azkaban*. Scholastic, 1999.
_____. *Harry Potter and the Sorcerer's Stone*. Scholastic, 1997.

Sayre, Kenneth. *Unearthed: The Economic Roots of Our Environmental Crisis*. U of Notre Dame P, 2010.
"Sign of the Deathly Hallows." *Harry Potter Wikia*. harrypotter.wikia.com/wiki/Sign_of_the_Deathly_Hallows. Accessed 29 Aug. 2017.
Simpson, Anne. "Casting a Spell Over Young Minds: Anne Simpson FACE TO FACE with J K Rowling: Casting a Spell Over Young Minds." *The Herald*, 6 Dec. 1998. www.heraldscotland.com/news/12021592.casting-a-spell-over-young-minds-anne-simpson-face-to-face-with-j-k-rowling/.
Smith, Anne Collins. "Harry Potter, Radical Feminism, and the Power of Love." *The Ultimate Harry Potter and Philosophy: Hogwarts for Muggles*, edited by Gregory Bassham, Wiley, 2010, pp. 80–95. Blackwell Philosophy and Pop-Culture Series.
Tarnas, Richard. *Cosmos and Psyche: Intimations of a New World Order*. Plume, 2006.
———. *The Passion of the Western Mind: Understanding the Ideas That Have Shaped Our World View*. Ballantine, 1991.
Trinh, T. Minh-ha. *Woman, Native, Other: Writing Postcoloniality and Feminism*. Indiana UP, 1989.
West, Cornel. "Prophetic Thought in Postmodern Times." *Philosophical Documents in Education*, edited by Ronald Reed and Tony Johnson, Longman, 2000, pp. 171–84.
"What Is Alchemy?" *Periodic Table*. Royal Society of Chemistry. 2017. www.rsc.org/periodic-table/alchemy/what-is-alchemy. Accessed 15 Aug. 2017.
"What Is the Deathly Hallows Symbol?" *Quora*, 2 Nov. 2016, www.quora.com/What-is-the-Deathly-Hallows-symbol. Accessed 10 July 2018.

I
The Resurrection Stone and the Transfiguration of Desire

Why I Read Harry Potter Books Again and Again

SOPHIA IMAFUJI, AGE 8

My friend Carter, who I bumped into in the public library, got me started reading the Harry Potter series. He said, "Sophia! Over here are the Harry Potter books," and said he thought I'd like them. And so I quietly followed behind him and checked out *The Sorcerer's Stone*. Since then Harry Potter books have changed me by showing me I can have a magical world in my head. Before reading Harry Potter books, I didn't know anything about Hermione, a clever witch at the top of every class, who shrank Professor Sprout's Devil's Snare. And there's Ron, someone who sticks up for his friends, like when he said, "If you want to kill Harry, you'll have to kill us too," and Harry Potter, the brave Gryffindor who conquered the Dark Lord Voldemort (*Azkaban* 339). These characters have shown friendship, courage, cleverness, and loyalty. I can think about this world and talk about it with my friends anytime.

I re-read Harry Potter books because they are great, great books. These books are funny, adventurous, and magical, and have fun-to-read-about characters. Draco might be the enemy to Harry Potter, but his actions are also exciting to read about. Hermione Granger's actions are fun too because of her smarts. I keep reading because I like to see what these characters and others will do next.

Another reason I re-read Harry Potter books is because I might get more details and notice something I didn't before, Latin words for example. I started realizing Latin words were in the books after a worksheet in school. The worksheet contained Latin roots and their meaning, such as *bene* means "well" or "good" and is in the word "benefit." Just as I approached the word "severe," a spelling word, and the Latin root in it, I giggled. "Severe" comes from the Latin word *severus*. As in Severus Snape! "Severe" means strict or harsh, and that's exactly how Professor Snape acts. Also, *malus* in

Latin means "bad," like the "mal" in "Malfoy." This root makes a lot of sense because Draco Malfoy and all the Malfoys are trouble. There's more Latin words in Harry Potter, so I should keep watching out for them. When my mom says, "Why don't you read something else?" I tell her, "Reading is educational, and Harry Potter books have Latin in them and other smart stuff." I will keep reading Harry Potter books.

The Literary Alchemy of J.K. Rowling

John Granger

No less an authority than the Russian American novelist, Vladimir Nabokov, told his students at Cornell University that literary artistry could safely be reduced to "structure and style" (*Lectures* xxiii). Close readers of J.K. Rowling's novels and screenplays have noted that the structure of all her work follows the same traditional pattern of chiasmus, what anthropologist Mary Douglas called "ring composition." The stylistic complement to this there-and-back-again structure is her use of hermetic colors, symbols, and sequences, a style I call "literary alchemy."*

This alchemical style is grafted from mysterious metallurgical texts of the Middle Ages which cryptically detail and describe the production of a Philosopher's Stone, the elixir from which will turn any object, even lead, to gold; this elixir, if drunk with any regularity, makes the drinker immortal (Linden, ch. 1). Though pervasive from Chaucer and Shakespeare to J.R.R. Tolkien and Angela Carter, literary alchemy as a stream running through English literature remains unknown to most readers. In order to set the stage for a survey of five signature elements or alchemical set pieces in Rowling's Potter series, I am obliged to introduce the subject's mechanism or "how it works on a reader or audience." I will do this by sharing the alchemical artistry of C.S. Lewis and Vladimir Nabokov, two writers who are obvious and admitted influences on Rowling's use of this alchemical tradition, both creatively and as, herself, an enthusiastic conformist.

Laden with Christian symbolism and meaning, Rowling's seven-book

---

*The first use of the term "literary alchemy" was in *Diacritics* magazine in 1971, but it is not about alchemical symbolism in literature. Stanton Linden's *Darke Hierogliphicks* is the standard text on the subject, though he does not use this phrase to describe it. Granger, *Hidden Key to Harry Potter* and subsequent books and weblog posts are the first contemporary use of the phrase "literary alchemy" in this sense.

series of Wizarding world schooldays novels invited comparisons with C.S. Lewis' septology of children's adventures stories in a magical fantasy realm, *The Chronicles of Narnia* (Groves, *Literary*; Granger, *Spell*). Much less obvious and consequently less explored is the influence of Vladimir Nabokov, whom Rowling has consistently listed as one of her three favorite authors.* Nabokov is infamous for the supposedly pornographic *Lolita* and famous as a writer of stratospheric sophistication and of difficult-to-penetrate literary novels. Unfortunately, those features have not invited comparisons between or the drawing of parallels linking his work and Rowling's, as has been the case with Lewis.

Lewis and Nabokov were contemporaries, and though a superficial look at their work and lives marks them as near absolute contraries, closer examination reveals remarkable points of congruence. Each, for example, lived in voluntary exile from the country of his birth and childhood. Both received Oxbridge educations between the two World Wars and were shaped by their life-altering experiences in the two greatest conflicts of the early twentieth century: the Bolshevik nightmare in Russia and the trenches of France in WWI. Lewis is justly famous for his Christian apologetics and allegories; Nabokov is too often misunderstood as only a great stylist, but his work also is suffused with spiritual content, moralizing, and otherworldliness.†

What makes these parallels between two of the most important influences on Rowling's *oeuvre* more than just interesting coincidences is that Lewis and Nabokov also shared a formalist understanding of literature and that each in his own work, different as their novels are in their audiences and accessibility, employed the signature elements of literary alchemy. A student in Nabokov's last class at Cornell, John Updike's wife, Martha Ruggles Updike née Bernhard, remembers that his "central dogma" was: "Style and structure are the essence of a book; great ideas are hogwash" (Nabokov, *Lectures* xxiii). Our principal pleasure in reading the best fiction, Nabokov declared, is the fruit of our ability in re-reading to "keenly enjoy—passionately enjoy, enjoy with tears and shivers—the inner weave of a given masterpiece" (4).

According to Michael Ward, author of *Planet Narnia*, "[C.S.] Lewis argues that it is the quality or tone of the whole story that is its main attraction.... Lovers of romances go 'back to the fruit tree for its taste; to an air

---

*Austen and Colette are the other two. See Michael Maar's "Why Nabokov Would Have Liked Harry Potter," in which Rowling says Nabokov is a writer she "really loves."
†On the morality of his work, Nabokov said, "I believe that one day a reappraiser will come and declare that, far from having been a frivolous firebird, I was a rigid moralist kicking sin, cuffing stupidity, ridiculing the vulgar and cruel—and assigning sovereign power to tenderness, talent, and pride" (*Strong Opinions* 74).

for ... what? For *itself*; to a region for its whole atmosphere—to Donegal for its Donegality and London for its Londonness'" (16).

Donegal was one of Lewis' favorite vacation spots as a child in Northern Ireland. Ward defines Lewis' stylistic atmosphere as his "Donegality," writing:

> By donegality we mean to denote the spiritual essence or quiddity of a work of art as intended by the artist and inhabited unconsciously by the reader. The donegality of the story is its peculiar and deliberated atmosphere or quality; its pervasive and purposed integral tone or flavor; its tutelary but tacit spirit, a spirit that the author consciously sought to conjure, but which was designed to remain implicit in the matter of the text, ... the more influentially to inform the work and so affect the reader. (75)

Ward's concern is especially with Lewis' character Aslan, in whom this donegality is "concentrated and consummated" as a "Christologically representative character," but the thesis of *Planet Narnia* is that the "kappa-element," Lewis' phrase for the informing, hidden "tutelary but tacit" style of a work, is astrological symbolism, each of the *Narnia* chronicles representing one of the seven traditional planets. Ward argues that Lewis' subliminal artistry, the "inner weave" or style of his work in Nabokovian language, is the embedded mythological and astral metaphors to be found beneath the surface of each story (75).

Nabokov, too, was a literary alchemist. In "Nabokov's Alchemical *Pale Fire*," Lyndy Abraham shows that the novelist's greatest work, *Lolita*, was suffused with hermetic images from the English tradition. Nabokov's 1930 short story "The Aurelian," too, is something of a transparency, revealing a man's transformation from darkness to light, lead to gold, as the title suggests. In short, both Lewis and Nabokov were expert in the alchemical tradition in English letters. Stanton Linden's *Darke Hierogliphicks* surveys this hermetic stream from Chaucer to the Restoration, but, though it has strong roots in Shakespearean drama, it is the subject of scholarship in authors as important and contemporary as Yeats, Joyce, Angela Carter, and J.R.R. Tolkien.* Add the important influence of Tolkien on Rowling to the alchemical Nabokov and Lewis, and any resistance to the idea that *Harry Potter* is written within this tradition is more like willful ignorance.

The first book is titled *Harry Potter and the Philosopher's Stone* and features real-world alchemist Nicolas Flamel as well as the fictional Albus Dumbledore. Rowling herself testifies to her use of alchemical symbolism. In an interview she gave in 1998 to a local newspaper in Scotland, Rowling said, "I've never wanted to be a witch, but an alchemist, now that's a

---

*See Gorski, *Yeats and Alchemy*; Dibenard, *Alchemy and Finnegan's Wake*; Cooke, "Alchemy of the Word: Alchemy, Allegory, and Individuation in Angela Carter's *The Passion of New Eve*"; and Brown, "From Abjection to Alchemy: Tolkien's Middle-earth Legendarium."

different matter. To invent this wizard world, I've learned a ridiculous amount about alchemy. Perhaps much of it I'll never use in the books, but I have to know in detail what magic can and cannot do in order to set the parameters and establish the stories' internal logic" (Simpson). Rowling has written more about this usage on her PotterMore website. She explains:

> Colours also played their part in the naming of Hagrid and Dumbledore, whose first names are Rubeus (red) and Albus (white) respectively. The choice was a nod to alchemy, which is so important in the first Harry Potter book, where "the red" and "the white" are essential mystical components of the process. The symbolism of the colours in this context has mystic meaning, representing different stages of the alchemic process (which many people associate with a spiritual transformation). Where my two characters were concerned, I named them for the alchemical colours to convey their opposing but complementary natures: red meaning passion (or emotion); white for asceticism; Hagrid being the earthy, warm and physical man, lord of the forest; Dumbledore the spiritual theoretician, brilliant, idealised and somewhat detached. Each is a necessary counterpoint to the other as Harry seeks father figures in his new world. (Granger, "PotterMore")

Rowling admitted recently at a London Museum exhibit on the history of Magic that even her dreaming life was consumed by alchemy when she began writing the series, recalling, "I had a really vivid dream about Nicolas Flamel, during the writing of *Philosopher's Stone*. I dreamt that I was in his alchemist's studio and this kind of symbolism was all over his walls. I didn't even ask questions, I was just watching. Typical writer, just observing. Didn't even ask!" (Rowling, "Flamel"). On her original website, JKR.com, Rowling shared that her original drafts of *Philosopher's Stone* were much more obviously alchemical. She wrote, "There were several discarded opening chapters for Book I, one of which had a Muggle betraying the Potters, one had a character called '[Argo] Pyrites,' whose name means 'fools' gold,' meeting Sirius in front of the Potters' house. Pyrites was a servant of Voldemort" and author of the textbook, *Alchemy, Ancient Art and Science*.

In a very short piece at her Pottermore.com website, fans were told that "[v]ery specialised subjects such as Alchemy are sometimes offered in the final two years, if there is sufficient demand." To which note Rowling added, "A slightly different list of school subjects appears in my earliest notes. Herbology is called 'Herbalism.' Divination is compulsory from the first year, as are Alchemy and a subject called simply 'Beasts,' whereas Transfiguration is called 'Transfiguration/Metamorphosis'" ("Subjects"). Readers learn near the end of the series finale, *Deathly Hallows*, that Snape was in Godric's Hollow the night Voldemort murdered Lily Evans Potter, Snape's true love. In *Half-Blood Prince*, Harry is given Snape's annotated Potions textbook, which is something of a link to the Pyrites book. As "Alchemy" became "Potions" and the "servant of Lord Voldemort" who had reason to be outside the Potters' home on the night of their murder was Severus Snape, it seems reasonable to conclude that the Potions Master who plays such a large part in Harry's adventures was originally conceived as the *Alchemy* instructor.

In addition to the hundreds of individual tokens listed in Abraham's *Dictionary of Alchemical Imagery*, there are five key markers of a work in the alchemical tradition:

1. The work is going to have three key stages marked by the use of specific colors and story events, namely, black, white, and red, which stages reflect, in sequence, the dissolution or break down of the subject character or main characters (*nigredo*) usually by heat, the purification or purgation of same (*albedo*) usually with water, and the revelation of the transformation undergone in the process in the story crisis (*rubedo*).

2. There will be story contraries that must be resolved by the principals' transformation, contraries like the Two Cities in Dickens' most popular novel or the Montagues and Capulets of Shakespeare's Verona, or just groups like the Quileute Wolfpack and Cullen Vampires of Meyer's *Twilight*.

3. Look for a "Quarreling Couple," a pair in opposition, one relatively feminine or lunar, the other masculine and solar, who engage the character being broken down to *prima materia* for illumination as "solid light" or gold. This duo are polar opposites and they either quarrel or draw the principal in contrary directions. This "Quarreling Couple" of alchemical Mercury and Sulfur, think Shakespeare's Tybalt and Mercutio in *Romeo and Juliet* or Meyer's Edward and Jacob in her *Twilight* books, are the catalysts of the reaction and character transformation.

4. Between the white and red stages noted above, there is an Alchemical Wedding of the Red King and White Queen that prefigures the conjunction of opposites signaling the golden moment of the Philosopher's Stone creation, i.e., *the* divinization of the main character and birth of the Philosophical Orphan or story savior joining contraries as a *Rebis* or hermaphrodite.

5. And there should be remarkable resurrection imagery—say, something as simple as light shining out of darkness or grander images of a hero rising from the dead, or even of a Phoenix, a Rose, or a Red Lion, symbols of the Stone and of Christ, the Light of the World. This is the story cipher for the illumination of lead to gold and the enlightenment of the alchemist.

All five signature markers are evident and obvious in the *Harry Potter* series. Rowling noted in a 2005 interview that the Hogwarts Houses represent the four elements of traditional cosmology: Hufflepuff being "Earth,"

Ravenclaw "Air," Gryffindor "Fire," and Slytherin "Water" (Anelli). Each House's defining qualities reflect these elements, as do the locations of their common rooms and dormitories. The principal conflict of the books, the defining polarity, is less between that of Muggle and Wizard than between fire and water, the Houses of Gryffindor and Slytherin, an archetypal set of contraries that Rowling represents as a rift that stretches back to a break between two of the Hogwarts Founders, Godric Gryffindor and Salazar Slytherin (Whited). At series end, the death of Lord Voldemort brings about a resolution of these contraries when all four Houses sit down together rather than at separate tables in the Great Hall after the Battle of Hogwarts.

The "Quarreling Couple" of *Harry Potter,* who represent the catalysts of Alchemical Mercury and Alchemical Sulfur in the transformative reaction taking place, are Harry's closest friends, Hermione Granger and Ron Weasley. The hermetic reagents represent the poles of existence with Mercury being feminine, cool, and intelligent, and Sulfur being masculine, volatile, and passionate. The story figures of these poles, brainiac Hermione and impulsive, raging Ron, are not only always bickering with one another, but their names point to Rowling's artistry. Mercurial Hermione's name is the feminine of Hermes, her initials are H.G. (Hg, the periodic table abbreviation for the element), and her parents are dentists, the only modern professionals who, until recently, used mercury on a day-to-day basis for fillings. Ron's hair is fiery red, and he is as brash and heated as Hermione is calm and collected; his middle name is Bilius, which highlights his sulfuric nature. The resolution of the Quarreling Couple in a kiss at the end of *Deathly Hallows* marks the beginning of the end of the Great Work itself and the beginning of the revelation of Harry's becoming the Philosopher's Stone.

We learn in the Epilogue that Ron and Hermione do get married, but the Alchemical Wedding of the series, the nuptials of the Red King and the White Queen between the *albedo* and *rubedo* stages of the Work, is the marriage of British Bill Weasley, red headed and lupine after his battle with a werewolf in *Half-Blood Prince,* and French Fleur Delacour, white-haired Veela. Their wedding in the opening chapters of *Deathly Hallows,* though the reception and celebration is interrupted by a Death Eater attack, is all in gold and yellow, Rowling's marking of the *citrinintas* or "yellow stage" of the metallurgical process, also before the red and after the white stages.

And the resurrection imagery? Every book and especially the finale ends with Harry's rising from seeming or near death in the presence of a traditional symbol of Christ. Book by book, the symbols are: the Philosopher's Stone, Fawkes the Phoenix, a White Stag, Phoenix Song and tears, Fawkes again in the Ministry duel between the Dark Lord and Dumbledore, a Hippogriff, and Harry himself in *Deathly Hallows* when he sacrifices himself to save his friends. Harry's return in *Hallows* from the King's Cross after-life conversation with Dumbledore, a destination to which he was dispatched by Voldemort's death curse, is bursting with Calvary and Easter references, most notably his victory over the Dark Lord and death as the sun rises and illumines the Great Hall (Groves ch. 4; Granger, *Spell* chs. 7 and 19).

These four markers of literary alchemy would be sufficient to convict Rowling of writing hermetically. The most convincing evidence, though, of her embedding alchemical "structure and style" elements is in the use of the black, white, and red color sequences and their attendant imagery in each book and in the series as a whole. Metallurgical alchemy and its corresponding equivalents in literary and spiritual alchemy are described in three stages, each of which has a signature color. Those colors are black, white, and red.

Alchemy as a spiritual work follows the revealed traditions in being a three-part task. The *nigredo* or "black" dissolution stage is the work of "renunciation" or "repentance." It is preparatory to the work of "purification" and "illumination" that in alchemy is done in the second, so-called "white stage," the *albedo*. Alchemy represents spiritual accomplishment or perfection in its *rubedo* or "red stage." "The *albedo* occurs after the blackened matter, the putrefied body of the Stone, has been washed to whiteness by the mercurial waters or fire" (Abraham, *Dictionary* 4). This is the stage of purification and the transformation of the subject, already broken down into *prima materia*, into the *rebis* or Philosopher's Stone. This work, though, is hidden; the accomplishments of the white stage are revealed in the drama of the red finale.

The three colors can be seen as metallurgical steps: dissolution or "blackening," distillation and purification or "bleaching," and recongealing or "reddening." The sun at day's end and human experience of it is analogous. As the sun sets, the sky darkens and the observer become less focused; the ego-self dissolves into sleep. In the night, there is reflected light, sun on the moon, which illumines the supraconscious self in secret. At dawn, in the light of day, the person is re-membered and different, even re-created, because of the purifying rest in the lunar light. The person is re-born every morning because of his or her rest in the darkness. This is not a bad summary of the alchemical work. The recongealing or perfection of the human person in the *rubedo* or red stage is really only a revelation of the renewing, purifying transformation that took place in the dark. Throw in a full moon and a long ablution or bath in that white stage at night, and the analogy of the predominant white stage imagery and meaning is complete.

This second step, the *albedo*, is represented in literature with the color white, the silver element or color, with light, especially the light at night (the moon or "Luna" frequently plays a part), and with water. These elements are used as backdrops and props to story events of purification, illumination, and reconciliation or healing. Again, think of a prophetic dream or insight while lying in bed under the moon after a long bath when recovering from a shattering day; that's an *albedo*. No one will know about it until it is revealed in the light and through the events of the coming day, but that change in the moonlight is the greater part of the Great Work.

The *rubedo* or third step is "the reddening of the white matter of the stone at the final stage of the opus alchymicum" (Abraham, *Dictionary* 174). In the *nigredo*, all form, color, and light are taken from the substance to reduce it to blackened "prime matter." In the *albedo*, a light like the moon's reflected colorless light is evident in the white stone produced. In the *rubedo*, the contraries are resolved, the white stage's accomplishments are revealed, and the Stone becomes red.

As important as the idea of light as a symbol is in understanding alchemical gold, perhaps it is best if the three stages of the work are understood in terms of light as well as color. As Burckhardt writes, "Black is the absence of color and light. White is purity; it is undivided light—light not broken down into colors. Red is the epitome of colors, its zenith and its point of greatest intensity" (182). Imagine the lunar light in the darkness of night shining through a prism to reveal all colors and especially their epitome, red.

That is evident first in the books being largely about the resolution of contraries, especially the battle between the hot and dry Gryffindors up in their tower and the cold and moist Slytherins in the dungeons beneath the lake. Harry's adventures are about his transcending this polarity, marrying the contraries, which purification happens in a black and a white and a red stage. Every book and the series as a whole come with a complete set.

In the individual books, the black stage or *nigredo* is almost always launched on Privet Drive, where Harry is treated horribly and, at least in *Philosopher's Stone*, lives in a cupboard under the stairs. The work breaking Harry down is continued each year when he gets to Hogwarts and Severus Snape takes over, a figure whose hair, eyes, and clothing are uniformly black. But Hogwarts is the home of Albus Dumbledore. The Latin root of "*albedo*" is "albus," meaning both "white" and "resplendent." There's a hint of "luminescent" or "brilliant"; "purification unto illumination" perhaps best describes the "albification" process. With Dumbledore as headmaster, Hogwarts is the "white house," where Harry is purified of some failing identified at the Dursleys' as he and the Quarreling Couple solve that year's mystery. The understanding he gets through these trials is revealed in the book's crisis, the confrontation with the villains, in which he always dies a figurative death and is re-born. From Privet Drive to his chat with Dumbledore at book's end, Harry is always purified and transformed.

The clearest illustration of this is in *Prisoner of Azkaban*. At the start, he is an angry teenage boy. He blows up Aunt Marge, quite literally, because she has a little too much to drink and, in a flood of Thatcherisms (Aunt Marge and her bulldogs can be read as metaphors for Margaret Thatcher and the patriotic John Bull Tories), says unkind things about Harry's parents. At the end of same book, though, he is so much changed that to prevent Sirius and Lupin from killing Pettigrew, Harry throws himself in front of Pettigrew, the man who had actually betrayed his parents and was almost solely responsible for their deaths. About his father's two best friends, Harry bellows, "I don't reckon my dad would've wanted [them] to become killers—just for you" (*Azkaban* 376).

The series taken all together has a black, white, and red stage, too: *Order of the Phoenix* is the series' Black stage, *Half-Blood Prince* is the White, and *Deathly Hallows* is the *rubedo* or Red stage.

The *nigredo*, again, is the stage in which the subject is broken down, stripped of all but the essential qualities for purification in the *albedo* or white work. *Order of the Phoenix*, darkest and most disturbing of all the Harry Potter novels, is this stage in the series, a fact to which Rowling cues us not only in the plot points, all of which are about Harry's loss of his identity, but in the "Black"-ness of the books. No small part of it takes place in the House of Black and it ends, of course, with the death of Sirius Black. More important, though, is that *Phoenix* details Harry's near complete dissolution. Every idea he has of himself is taken from him. Dolores Umbridge teaches him that Hogwarts can be hell. He learns his father was a jerk. No Quidditch! Ron and Hermione outrank him in the Hogwarts social hierarchy. The entire "Girl thing" eludes him except for the agonizing confusion and heartbreak. Everything, in brief, is a nightmare for him in his fifth year. His self-understanding and identity are shattered—except that, at the very end, after Sirius' death and with it any hope of a family life with his godfather, Harry learns about the Prophecy. That understanding replaces everything else. And that is the end and purpose of the black work.

When *Half-Blood Prince* begins, the reader seems to be in a different universe. Albus Dumbledore is not only back in Harry's life, he even comes to pick him up at Privet Drive. The Headmaster, largely absent in *Phoenix*, is everywhere in *Prince*. This is his book, which, given the meaning of his name and the work that is accomplished therein, might be called the "White book." Not to mention that, like Sirius at the end of the "Black book," Albus dies at the end of the "White." Through the tutorials with Dumbledore and the tasks he is given, Harry comes to a whole new understanding of himself in terms of the Prophecy and his relationship to Lord

Voldemort. Harry does not get the whole truth from the Headmaster, but at the end of *Prince* he has been transformed from a boy who does not believe Dumbledore will show up to one who defiantly tells the Minister of Magic, "[I'm] Dumbledore's man through and through" (649).

Deathly Hallows is the "Red book," the *rubedo*. As explained above, just as in *Romeo and Juliet* and *Tale of Two Cities*, a wedding has to be revealed, contraries have to be resolved, and a death to self must lead to greater life. The reader attuned to alchemical tropes would expect to see a Philosopher's Stone and a philosophical orphan as well. The *rubedo* of *Deathly Hallows* is the crisis of the whole series.

Deathly Hallows bears a much closer look because it is not only a *rubedo* and finish to the series' alchemical artistry but an encapsuled and near-perfect black-white-red story-telling piece in and of itself. Before looking at it in this way, though, two points need to be made about the series' artistry over the course of seven books, to answer an obvious question. If the last three novels are *nigredo, albedo,* and *rubedo* of the series, what function do the first four books serve?

First, William Sprague and Joe Packer independently have noted that the first three books are as alchemical as the last three books, but, in keeping with Rowling's ring composition structural artistry, they are in reverse order, i.e., red-to-white-to-black, in parallel with each of the closing books. To make the reverse parallelism complete, the end of each book is an upside-down version of the three stages: *Philosopher's Stone* closes with Dumbledore destroying rather than creating a Stone; *Chamber of Secrets* ends with Harry filthy with Basilisk blood, Horcrux ink, and Chamber dirt rather than having been through an ablutionary *albedo*; and *Prisoner of Azkaban*, instead of breaking Harry down and stripping him of his identity, reveals his godfather, Sirius Black, to him with the promise that he might once again have a family and home. The literary alchemy of Rowling's artistry is in itself the "structure and style" of the series as well as being fully integrated with and complementary to her over-arching structural design.

Second, *Goblet of Fire*, the fourth and "crucial" book of the series, according to Rowling, is not any one of the three specific colored stages at the series' pivot but all three at once, a transition from the reverse alchemy of the opening books to the straightforward hermetic coloring of the closers ("Book Four"). The three Triwizard Tournament tasks in *Goblet of Fire*, most notably, are snapshots of the three stages:

- The *nigredo* is Harry's agonizing lead-up to his confrontation with the Hungarian Horntail in the first task. Everyone at Hogwarts, it seems, and his best friend Ron most importantly, think he has entered the Tournament himself and decided he is a conceited anti-

hero whom they can openly despise. This breakdown in his identity is complemented by the very real danger of his being burned alive by the fire-breathing Horntail.
- The *albedo* or ablutionary stage is Harry's reconciliation with Ron and the school as a whole before the second task. He figures out what the task is under water in the prefect's bathroom; and the challenge itself is about being able to breathe underwater in the Great Lake.
- The *rubedo* finale in the Labyrinth Hagrid creates on the school's Quidditch pitch is a collection of obstacles that reveal all that Harry has learned and has become through the other stages and tasks.

Each of the events of the Triwizard Tournament and Harry's preparation for each trial by fire, water, or labyrinth in *Goblet of Fire*, then, is from the alchemical work. Not only do the nature of the tasks themselves reflect the three stages, but the specific tokens or story elements Rowling uses in *Goblet* are also traditional symbols of the stages in their appropriate sequence in the tale. Dragons, the egg, the prefects' bath and the water trial, the labyrinth, and the graveyard resurrection and fight are each alchemical tokens.

Dragons: The first task in the tournament involves dragons, which are used in alchemy to represent "matter at the *beginning* of the work being resolved into philosophical sulphur and mercury" (Abraham, *Dictionary* 59).

The egg: Harry and the other champions then have to solve the mystery of the egg, which appropriately is the name given to "the alchemist's vessel of transmutation in which the birth of the Philosopher's Stone takes place … also known as the griffin's egg" (i.e., from beginning to the place of the work) (66).

The bath: Harry solves his egg puzzle in the prefects' bath, a word used by alchemists to describe "the secret, inner, invisible fire which dissolves and kills, cleanses and resurrects the matter of the Stone in the vessel" (that is, the element that makes the work proceed in the alchemist's alembic, or distilling flask) (17–18).

Water immersion/flood: The second task in the tournament is the trial underwater in the lake. Interestingly, one of the alchemist's maxims was "Perform no operation until all be made water." Water immersion, it turns out, is "a symbol of the dissolution and putrefaction of the matter of the Stone during the black or *nigredo* stage" (78–79) and, more importantly, the ablutionary agent of the *second stage*, "the circulation of the matter of the Philosopher's Stone in the alembic when the blackness of the *nigredo* is washed and purified into the whiteness of the *albedo*" (1; 4–5).

Labyrinth: The third task, which is supposed to be the end of the tournament, is a maze and is a metaphor for life in the world, or "the dangerous journey of the alchemist through the *opus alchymicum*.... While Harry is in the labyrinth of the opus, illusion and confusion reign and the alchemist is in danger of losing all connection and clarity" (113).

Grave: Harry and Cedric are transported to the graveyard, where they witness Voldemort's rebirthing party. The graveyard is also what alchemists and poets refer to as "the alchemist's vessel during the *nigredo*" (90–91), when everything is broken down into formless elements—a metaphor for what happens to Harry there.

The graveyard scene includes a Black Mass of sorts in which the Dark Lord creates a new body for his fragmented soul, whose potion elements are an inversion of Christian sacramental liturgy. Harry's survival there is a Great Work in miniature as he endures a *nigredo* torture while tied to a grave marker, an ablutionary trial in his forced duel with the Dark Lord, and a *rubedo* revelation and triumph in the sphere of Phoenix Song that allows his escape back to Hogwarts with Cedric Diggory's corpse.

The seven-book series, then, is a mirrored alchemical work, first in reverse with a story turn featuring all three stages and a Great Work in miniature at its close, and finally the work in order, *nigredo, albedo,* and *rubedo*. The last book, as noted, is not only a *rubedo* to the series but a black-white-red story sequence in itself. *Deathly Hallows* begins, as mentioned, with Bill and Fleur's alchemical wedding, in which France and England are married in a sort of sitzkrieg before the shooting war with Voldemort's Nazis begins. The first eight chapters of *Deathly Hallows* are a lead-up to this union of opposites, of choler and phlegm. The wedding itself is a meeting of contraries, of solar and lunar. That is why in addition to the Gallic/Briton jokes, the lunar Lovegoods show up in sunlight bright yellow. Luna, the moon in solar outfit, explains that it is good luck to wear gold at a wedding (141). This is not just Luna being "loony" (the nickname unkind characters give her); everything at the Weasley–De la Couer wedding is golden: the floor, the poles, the band jackets, the bridesmaids' dresses, even Nymphadora Tonks' hair (139–46).

The wedding, though, is only the entrance ramp to the long story journey to the conjunction of the Slytherin and Gryffindor opposites. The wedding breaks up with the arrival of Kingsley's lynx Patronus with the message that Rufus Scrimgeour is dead and the Death Eater blitzkrieg has begun. With that, the death of the first character whose name means "red," the real action of *Deathly Hallows*' alchemical work begins.

The rest of the book is best understood as black, white, and red stages. In summary, the *nigredo* stretches painfully from chapter nine, "A Place to Hide," to chapter eighteen, "The Life and Lies of Albus Dumbledore."

Harry's purification and illumination stage begins in chapter nineteen, "The Silver Doe," and ends with the trio's return to Hogsmead in chapter twenty-eight, "The Missing Mirror." The crisis of the book and the series is in Harry's return to Hogwarts, destruction of the remaining Horcruxes, and victory over Lord Voldemort, as told in the last eight chapters of *Deathly Hallows*.

The ten *nigredo* chapters are as dark and gothic as anything ever offered as "children's literature." We get a trip to the House of Black, we visit the Orwellian "Magic is Might" black statue in the new Ministry (accessible only by flush toilet…), and we go camping, where, for some reason, it is always night, or overcast, or the three friends cannot get along. Ron finally just up and leaves. "The camping trip" of *Deathly Hallows* is only nine chapters in length, fourteen through twenty-two, but they are unpleasant reading, and the three after Ron departs are agony to the young reader.

These are the Christmas chapters about Harry's holiday trip with Hermione to Godric's Hollow, which are the climax of the book's *nigredo* and end with Harry's crisis of faith. At the end of *Half-Blood Prince*, Harry proclaims that he is "Dumbledore's man." In *Hallows*, he reads one article by Rita Skeeter, and his faith is shaken. He talks to Aunt Muriel and Elphias "Dogbreath" Doge at the wedding, and he is struggling to believe. At the end of the *nigredo*, when Harry reads *The Life and Lies of Albus Dumbledore*, Harry denies Dumbledore as mentor, denies that he loves Albus, denies that Dumbledore loved him. Harry's holly and phoenix wand has been broken in battle with Nagini, and he is left with a broken wand, a broken piece of glass, and shattered faith. He keeps these fragments, though, in a bag around his neck. He denies Dumbledore, denies his mission, and, in something like despair, he keeps these remnants or relics of the person he once was close to his heart.

The *nigredo*, however, mercifully ends here with the brilliance reflecting off the Silver Doe in the snow-covered Forest of Dean. "The Silver Doe" chapter, with its meeting of Christian, alchemical, and Arthurian images in one spot, is probably the height of Rowling's achievement as a writer. "Ron the Baptist" saves Harry from his watery grave; Ron's ablutionary exorcism destroys the Locket Horcrux; Harry's death to self and his discovery of remorse, repentance, faith, and love in Dobby's grave; and the pale dragon in Gringotts are all images of purification, with water on hand or nearby (Granger, *Lectures*).

The white stone on the red earth of Dobby's grave and the dragon's pink eyes are chromatic signs of the story's movement from white to red. The *rubedo* of *Deathly Hallows* begins, I think, when Harry refuses to listen to Aberforth's complaints and criticism of his brother Albus. When Harry shows his faith and his choice to believe, Neville appears to take him into the castle and the Battle of Hogwarts has its beginning. You could say the red stage really begins when Rubeus, the half-giant whose name means "red," flies through the window of Hogwarts Castle. It is in this battle, of course, to include Harry's sacrifice in the Forbidden Forest and his ultimate victory over Voldemort, that the contraries are resolved and all the Houses sit down at one table. The battle also causes the creation of the "philosophical orphan" when Nymphadora and Remus Lupin are killed. And we get a Philosopher's Stone, too; Hermione and Ron's daughter, we learn in the Epilogue, is named Rose, which is another name for the Stone.

The turning-into-its-opposite transformation in the last novel of the series is how the world has been changed by Harry's internal victory and destruction of the scar-Horcrux. Lord Voldemort tortures and murders the Hogwarts Muggle Studies teacher in the first chapter of the book. Her name is Charity Burbage, and her corpse is dinner for Nagini. Charity or Love is destroyed by Death. Via Harry's death to self in the white stage's Dobby burial, revealed in his willing self-sacrifice before Voldemort, death's power is broken. Lily's and Harry's sacrificial and selfless love sustains life and has its victory over death.

We see a complete transformation in Harry, too. He is Dumbledore's man by confession as the story begins, but his disbelief and lack of trust come to the fore after his fight with Nagini in Godric's Hollow. After choosing to believe, however, when he is in Dobby's grave, and choosing to pursue the Horcruxes, as instructed, rather than Hallows, he becomes almost Christ-like in dying and rising from the dead to vanquish death. Even the near-omnipotent Dumbledore begs Harry's forgiveness and tells him that he has known for a long time that Harry was "the better man" (*Hallows* 713).

Harry becomes the conjunction of contraries by acquiring the seemingly contradictory views and qualities of both Albus, champion Gryffindor, and Severus Snape, Slytherin House Master and icon, by the end of *Deathly Hallows*. He becomes the better man, because he embodies the Gryffindor/Slytherin union himself—something like "Albus Severus Potter," as Harry and Ginevra name their younger son. The *Deathly Hallows* Epilogue is the return to the gold of the Alchemical Wedding and to a peaceful, post-*rubedo* version of the opening chapters' challenge, much as *Deathly Hallows* is a return to and re-telling of *Philosopher's Stone*'s story and events. In the Epilogue's seven pages, we meet the Rebis, the Orphan, and the Stone in the children of the next generation. The work is simultaneously complete and ready for its next beginning, like a serpent eating its own tail, an *uroboros* loop or ring.

The relative absence of critical discussion of Rowling's alchemical artistry, then, may seem a great curiosity. Mark Twain, however, is supposed to have said, "If you would have your fiction live forever, you must neither overtly preach nor overtly teach, but you must *covertly* preach and *covertly* teach." Lewis, believing as he did that "an influence which cannot evade our consciousness will not go very deep," wrote in astrological glyphs to reach covertly his reader's unconscious depths. I offer as a conclusion the possibility that the neglect of the subject in interviews and criticism, especially when taken in tandem with the unprecedented success of Rowling's work, speaks to her success in writing, as Twain admonished, "covertly," and as Lewis recommended, "evading consciousness." Occult artistry—the word, itself, means "hidden"—is at its best when unnoticed and still penetrating.

Works Cited

Abraham, Lyndy. "Nabokov's Alchemical *Pale Fire.*" *Dutch Quarterly Review of Anglo-American Letters*, 20 (2), pp. 102–19.
_____. *A Dictionary of Alchemical Imagery*. Cambridge UP, 2001.
Alexandrov, Vladimir E. *Nabokov's Otherworld*. Princeton UP, 1991.
Anelli, Melissa, and Emerson Spartz. "The Leaky Cauldron and Mugglenet Interview Joanne Kathleen Rowling: Part Three," *The Leaky Cauldron*, 16 July 2005, www.accio-quote.org/articles/2005/0705-tlc_mugglenet-anelli-3.htm.
Brown, Sara. "From Abjection to Alchemy: Tolkien's Middle-earth Legendarium." PhD Dissertation, U of Salford, 2013.
Burckhardt, Titus. *Alchemy: Science of the Cosmos, Science of the Soul*. Fons Vitae, 1997.
Carter, Angela. *The Passion of New Eve*. Virago, 2005.
Cooke, Alana Bolton. "'Alchemy of the Word': Alchemy, Allegory, and Individuation in Angela Carter's *Passion of New Eve*." Masters Thesis, U of Canterbury, 2005.
Dibenard, Barbara. *Alchemy and Finnegan's Wake*. SUNY, 1980.
Douglas, Mary. *Thinking in Circles*. Yale UP, 2007.
Gorski, William T. *Yeats and Alchemy*. SUNY, 1996.
Granger, John. *The Deathly Hallows Lectures*. Zossima, 2008.
_____. "Guest Post: The Connection of Ring Composition and Literary Alchemy in the Layout of the Seven Book Harry Potter Series." *Hogwarts Professor*, 20 Aug. 2011, www.hogwartsprofessor.com/guest-post-the-connection-of-ring-composition-and-literary-alchemy-in-the-layout-of-the-seven-book-harry-potter-series/.
_____. *Harry Potter as Ring Composition and Ring Cycle*. Unlocking Press, 2010.
_____. "Hogwarts Professor Mailbag: The Super, the Silly, the Sublime." *Hogwarts Professor*, www.hogwartsprofessor.com/hogwarts-professor-mailbag-the-super-the-silly-the-sublime/.
_____. *How Harry Cast His Spell*. Tyndale, 2008.
_____. "PDay Minus Three—Prediction #5: The Rubedo." *Hogwarts Professor*, 18 July, 2007, www.hogwartsprofessor.com/pday-minus-three-%E2%80%94-prediction-5-the-rubedo/.
_____. "PotterMore: J.K. Rowling Discusses Alchemical Colors." *Hogwarts Professor*, 1 Oct. 2013, www.hogwartsprofessor.com/pottermore-j-k-rowling-discusses-alchemical-colors/.
Groves, Beatrice. *Literary Allusion in Harry Potter*. Routledge, 2017.
Lewis, C.S. "The Literary Impact of the Authorized Version." The Ethel M. Wood Lecture, University of London, 20 March 1950, biblicalstudies.org.uk/pdf/kjv_lewis.pdf.
Linden, Stanton J. *Darke Hierogliphicks: Alchemy in English Literature from Chaucer to the Restoration*. UP of Kentucky, 1996.
Maar, Michael. "Why Nabokov Would Have Liked Harry Potter." *Hogwarts Professor*, 16 Feb. 2017, www.hogwartsprofessor.com/guest-post-why-nabokov-would-have-liked-harry-potter-michael-maar/.

Nabokov, Vladimir Vladimirovich. *Lectures on Literature*, edited by Fredson Powers, Harcourt/Bruccoli Clark, 2002.
_____. *Strong Opinions*. Vintage International, 1990.
Parker, Joe. "The Chiastic Structure of Harry Potter." *St. Mark Reformed Church Pastor's Page*, 16 July 2017, stmarkreformed.com/pastors-page/the-chiastic-structure-of-harry-potter/.
Rowling, J.K. *Harry Potter and the Deathly Hallows*. Scholastic, 2007.
_____. *Harry Potter and the Half-Blood Prince*. Scholastic, 2005.
_____. *Harry Potter and the Prisoner of Azkaban*. Scholastic, 1999.
_____. "Hogwarts School Subjects." *Pottermore*, www.pottermore.com/writing-by-jk-rowling/hogwarts-school-subjects. Accessed 24 May 2019.
_____. "J.K. Rowling Discusses Nicolas Flamel, Avada Kadavra Origins in Harry Potter BBC 2." *Snitchseeker*, 28 Oct. 2017, www.snitchseeker.com/harry-potter-news/j-k-rowling-discusses-nicolas-flamel-avada-kadavra-origins-in-harry-potter-bbc2-doc-108554/.
_____. "JK Rowling Talks About Book Four," *cBBC Newsround*, 8 July 2000, www.accio-quote.org/articles/2000/0700-cbbc-mzimba.htm.
_____. "JKR.com: Very Early Page of Philosopher's Stone." www.hp-lexicon.org/source/other-canon/jkr/jkr-com-scrapbook/earlyps/. Accessed 24 May 2019.
Simpson, Anne. "Casting a Spell Over Young Minds; Anne Simpson FACE TO FACE with J K Rowling." *The Herald*, 6 Dec. 1998, www.heraldscotland.com/news/12021592.casting-a-spell-over-young-minds-anne-simpson-face-to-face-with-j-k-rowling/.
Sprague, William. "Ring Alchemy." *Hogwarts Professor*, 20 Aug. 2011, www.hogwartsprofessor.com/guest-post-the-connection-of-ring-composition-and-literary-alchemy-in-the-layout-of-the-seven-book-harry-potter-series/.
Twain, Mark. en.wikiquote.org/wiki/Mark_Twain. Accessed 24 May 2019.
Ward, Michael. *Planet Narnia*. Oxford UP, 2008.
Whited, Lana. "Here Be Dragons (and Phoenixes)." *Hogwarts Professor*, 14 Feb. 2019, www.hogwartsprofessor.com/the-beasts-within-of-fantastic-beasts-here-be-dragons-and-phoenixes/.

Harry Potter and the Transfiguration of Desire

Anne Parker-Perkola

> Look how the potter forms his vessels on the swift wheel,
> Whilst with his foot he mixes the clay with the water;
> He relies always on two things,
> So that by his dexterity the liquid quenches the thirst of the dry substances.
> Act in the same way, now wiser by this example,
> That the water may not dominate over the earth, but neither be dominated by it.
> —Michael Maier (*Atalanta Fugiens*)

Accompanying emblem XV in Michael Maier's book of Alchemical Emblems, the *Atalanta Fugiens*, this epigram describes something as ordinary as a potter at the wheel (135). Several other emblems in this series depict skills exercised in ordinary work, like washing or cooking, that, when properly applied, can become part of the larger, alchemical work of creating the Philosopher's Stone. These tasks, in esoteric context, become part of a story of balance, transformation, elimination, purification, and sublimation—of the reconciliation of opposites, of death and of birth. The story told by the epigrams and the emblems of the *Atalanta Fugiens*, as many spiritually rich and emblematically layered stories do, also undermines other dualities that might be taken for granted, like inner and outer, creator and created work, or, indeed, quotidian tasks and transfiguration of the soul. As Maier's translator, Helena Maria Elisabeth De Jong, notes, in seeking to create the Philosopher's Stone, the elements participate in a mutually transformative relationship, whereby outer processes are tied directly to the inner "process of transmutation and purification in the alchemist or in the human soul itself" (141).

Harry Potter and the Philosopher's Stone* stands on its own as an enjoyable adventure story, yet the novel also benefits from readings which allow for the dense magical, psychological, and mythic resonances and references with which it teems. Like the esoteric texts and traditions this novel so often invokes, Harry Potter and the Philosopher's Stone speaks a slanted, symbolically dense language right alongside, or within, its fantastical and fairy-tale elements. At once ordinary and extraordinary, Rowling's Harry Potter—a connection to Maier's potter too enticing to miss—must learn to balance the opposing parts of himself as he undergoes an initiation into a hidden, though always-present, magical world. In this essay I trace the way Harry Potter and the Philosopher's Stone addresses the key esoteric themes of the proper place of desire, how to discriminate between different kinds of knowledge, and the delights and dangers of initiation.

Harry Potter and the Philosopher's Stone begins with strange happenings on an ordinary doorstep, a boy-who-saved-the-world, and a snake. In my focus on the trifecta of Harry's transformations—desire, knowledge, initiation—I begin with the snake. Harry is with his Aunt Petunia, Uncle Vernon, and cousin, Dudley, in the reptile house at the Zoo, standing in front of the snake that Dudley has failed to rouse and feeling sorry for it. "He wouldn't have been surprised," Harry thinks to himself, "if it had died of boredom itself," drawing sympathy from his own experience locked in the cupboard under the stairs (27). But then, something peculiar happens, and the snake, as if drawn by some aspect of Harry that he himself does not yet understand, "opened its beady eyes. Slowly, very slowly, it raised its head" to look directly into Harry's eyes, and then, "*It winked*" (*Stone* 27).

It is a moment heavy with esoteric and biblical symbolism. It was, after all, a trickster snake in the Garden of Eden who tempted Adam and Eve with the opportunity to become "like gods, knowing good and evil" (Genesis 3:5). It is also two snakes who twine around Hermes' rod, the caduceus, when he acts in his role as a messenger, bringing word from the realms of the gods on his winged feet. A wink, too, is weighted toward the secret, indicating silent collusion and alliance. Harry's conversation with the Brazilian Boa Constrictor becomes a symbol not only of his immanent initiation into the magical world but also into the realm of moral choice—indeed, his ability to speak Parseltongue itself eventually becomes the way he is able to find and to enter the hidden Chamber of Secrets. Harry's encounter with the Brazilian boa is also a revelation of the capacity for empathy and sympathy, which, as the reader gradually learns, are as much a part of Harry as his

---

*Though as an American reader I first read *Harry Potter and the Philosopher's Stone* as *Harry Potter and the Sorcerer's Stone* and all references are to the American version of the book, I use the *Philosopher's Stone* throughout this essay because of its more precise connection with the esoteric lineage of these books.

magic. In contrast to Dudley's pounding on the glass, Harry approaches the captive boa constrictor quietly and sympathetically, and from this very first strange happening the reader already begins to suspect that Harry's capacity for magic, and what he does with it, will be closely tied to what might be his moral qualities, his faults and virtues.

Isolated behind the reflective surface, the Brazilian boa and Harry, isolated even among his family members, are both being kept in environments too small for them, far from their natural homes. In one of the first pivotal moments of psychological mirroring in the text, these two captives recognize each other, and Harry feels sympathy for the snake, who then responds to Harry's sympathy. When the snake winks at Harry, and Harry, as secretly as he can, winks back, the circle of communication is complete. Harry and the snake move from shared, ordinary eye-rolling to shared knowledge and an alliance predicated not only upon Harry's hidden magical power but also upon emotional resonance. The snake in his cage makes a friend, and Harry is initiated, by a wink, into the certainty that he is not so alone as he thinks.

Dudley and Uncle Vernon, seemingly unwilling to let Harry enjoy anything, come up and push him violently away. In response to this physical violence—and being called, as he is repeatedly, a "freak"—Harry's magic acts to protect him and the Brazilian boa without Harry's conscious intent. The glass dividing Harry from the snake, symbol of and impetus to magic, vanishes not only for the Brazilian boa but for all the other reptiles, and magic is loose and out in broad daylight, though still quite unexplained. As in the Garden of Eden, it is through conversation with a snake—a quasi-forbidden, or at least problematic, action even in Rowling's wizarding world, let alone the Muggle one—that Harry is initiated into a new kind of knowledge about himself and his ability to communicate with others through sympathy, shared desires, and reflection.

However, this knowledge does not come without cost. As soon as the Dursleys learn from Dudley's friend Piers that Harry was talking with the snake, they punish him, shutting him away in the cupboard with no dinner and, again, with nothing to do but wait; there is a hint, though, that Harry might soon follow the path of the once-discontented snake he freed. Just as the snake begins its journey "home" to Brazil where it has never been, the events in the reptile house foreshadow Harry's own return to a magical world he scarcely remembers (*Stone* 28–29). The power as well as knowledge that Harry unconsciously carries with him—in this case, of the reality and potency of the magical world—are quite literally pushed back into hiding, away from the conscious awareness of the Dursleys, who live in a state of almost constant anxiety concerning its revelation.

Following the escapade with the snake, magical activity builds around

Harry and comes to a peak on his eleventh birthday. Letters addressed to Harry in his cupboard under the stairs pour, first one at a time, and then in a fluttering river, through the Dursleys' mail slot (*Stone* 31–45). The removal of the barrier that separated Harry from the mass of quivering snakes is only the first of many initiations for him, and the letters are a second connection with the world and the powers that the Dursleys attempt so forcefully, but unsuccessfully, to repress and eradicate. In the wake of his conversation with the Brazilian boa, Harry, like Eve after she first listens to the snake and tastes the apple, is led to many other kinds of knowledge and eventually to new, non-Edenic dangers. Magic, once expressed, gains momentum, and Harry receives increasing access to an entire series of revelations about others, himself, and the world, each of greater intensity. Life with the Dursleys may have been boring and, much worse, abusive, but the dangers the Dursleys have to offer pale in comparison to that of a Dark Lord who sought to kill Harry at birth.

In the first chapters of *Philosopher's Stone,* through a snake, through letters calling him to education in an entirely new world, through Hagrid, through Ron, Hermione, and many others, Harry is initiated into new kinds of power and responsibility. He discovers that magic, like his own identity slashed on his forehead, has been hidden in plain sight and that even among the peculiar and the magical he holds a special place. In the aptly named *The Serpent's Gift: Gnostic Reflections on the Study of Religion,* Jeffery Kripal reads comic books, particularly the X-Men comic books, as coded (and even not-so-coded) stories of spiritual awakening to the burgeoning powers of the adult self. Mutants becomes college students studying the history and origins of religions, and Professor X becomes Every Professor, engaged in the difficult process of initiating these students into esoteric and dangerous knowledge of the world and of themselves, of their desires and of their own abilities (Kripal 126–37).

In *Harry Potter and the Philosopher's Stone*, Harry, like the young mutants at Xavier's School for Gifted Youngsters, discovers that there is something very special as well as peculiar about himself. Like them, he is also called to a school where he is trained in the mysteries of the right use of his own and others' powers, and this occurs precisely at the moment of his transition from childhood to adulthood. Also like many of the young X-men and X-women, Harry's powers are judged and repressed by his family, and family itself becomes a location of trauma both outside the magical world and within it, where he is confronted once more by his loss of his parents. Harry's fraught awakening to the world of magic is at the same time an invitation into a deeper relationship with himself. It is also, as it is for the young mutants, an initiation into a moral and magical community in which much larger conflicts are taking place, and he will be given the opportunity to discover both who he really is and to decide how he wishes to be.

Each of Harry's subsequent transitions from year to year, from Muggle to Magical, and from childhood to adulthood, can be seen as further grades of initiation into magical and psychological selfhood. In *The Mystical Qabalah*, twentieth-century occultist Dion Fortune writes, "The ceremony of initiation, and the teachings that should be given in the various grades, are simply designed to make conscious what was previously subconscious, and to bring under the control of the will, directed by the higher intelligence, those developed reaction-capacities which have hitherto only responded blindly to their appropriate stimuli" (246).* Over the course of his first year at Hogwarts, Harry slowly gains the ability to channel and direct his unconscious magical outbursts with the help of his friends, his professors, and his wand. Each level of control Harry gains is also associated with a deepening knowledge, not always pleasant, of himself. In his time at Hogwarts the magical powers that were previously subconscious become conscious, and Harry learns to channel these powers to achieve desired results.

Harry's encounters with the Mirror of Erised, the Mirror that shows "*Erised stra ehru oyt ube cafru oyt on* … (not your face but your heart's desire)," are key moments of initiation in which Harry discovers something new and hitherto latent in himself, just as when he speaks with the snake in the reptile house or finally reads his letter from Hogwarts (*Stone* 207–08). First alone, and then with Professor Dumbledore, Harry is brought face to face with the depth of his own desire for his parents' love. He is also instructed in the deceptive delights of the Mirror, an object that could hold him forever in its thrall, but which, if properly understood, is a portal into himself just as the brick wall beyond the Leaky Cauldron is a portal into the Magical World. The key, in both cases, is not to be taken in by appearances and to know how the object—or the portal—works.

Harry's first encounter with the Mirror of Erised occurs alone, in secret, and in an out-of-the-way room. It is midnight, and Harry has just been given his father's Invisibility Cloak for Christmas with the instructions "*Use it Well*" (*Stone* 205). Harry, in his exploration out of bounds, is already beginning to answer this mysterious note-writer's unwritten, invisible invitation to seek secret knowledge, to use the power granted by the cloak "well" (205). Under the cloak and out of bed late at night, Harry seeks knowledge about the mysterious Nicolas Flamel in the Restricted Section of the library until a screaming book gives away his position. Running from

---

*This is from Fortune's explanation of the process of initiation for Hod, the Sephirah on the Tree of Life particularly associated with magic.

Filch and Mrs. Norris, Harry stumbles into a deserted classroom and onto the Mirror of Erised (*Stone* 205–07). In good gnostic style, because Harry uses his father's Invisibility Cloak to search for the answer to a mystery outside him, Harry encounters the depths of the mysteries contained within him. The anonymous gift of his father's cloak grants Harry the opportunity to access his own heart and the secrets hidden within it as well as giving him he first glimpse of his parents he can remember.

"'Mum?' he whisper[s]. 'Dad?'" when Harry sees the man and woman in the Mirror (*Stone* 209). Though at first Harry is not able to recognize his parents, through his knowledge of himself, his own eyes, his own hair, his own knobbly knees, he is slowly able to know and remember them. At last, after careful scrutiny, Harry becomes certain that "Mum" and "Dad" are who the pretty, red-haired woman and the man with messy hair smiling at him really are. The Mirror mediates a reconnection with his absent parents for Harry, even though he does not yet know what it is or what it does. Harry gains conscious awareness of what had before been unconscious: not only his parents' looks but their idealized images.

It is no surprise that during this first encounter the Mirror is an object to which Harry grows close, to which he even clings. Harry transfers his desire for what the Mirror shows—his parents' loving faces—onto the mirror itself. In psychological terms, the Mirror becomes a powerful, albeit not entirely innocent, transitional or comfort object, mediating to Harry his own memory of the love of his parents in their absence, like a child's blanket or an object that belongs to a deceased loved one. As psychoanalyst and pediatrician D.W. Winnicott is careful to acknowledge, the fact that this process of transference between a child and an object which comes to represent the security of a parent's power to soothe is unconscious for Harry or any other child does not make it any less effective (211–19).

In Harry's case, however, this unconscious transference has additional dangers, because the Mirror engenders dependency rather than autonomous functioning, unless the observer is guided to proper knowledge of the sort of truth it shows. Drawing on Winnicott's theories of psychological development, the organizational psychologist Manfred Kets de Vries uses the term "charismatic attribution" to denote those transferences which take place in leader-follower relationships when "the past is transferred to the present in the interaction between a dynamic leader and his or her followers…, reactivating former developmental interaction patterns and bringing a hunger for idealization to the fore once again" (169). Charismatic attribution also plays a role in the power that the Mirror exerts over Harry by showing him his own most intense, unconscious desires. Though Harry does not find a dynamic leader in the mirror, he is certainly faced with an idealized past he can no longer access in the present, and the desire he feels for the image the Mirror shows him in representing his parents' love is transferred to the Mirror itself. In the Mirror of Erised, Harry's present fantasy is tied up, like almost all fantasies, in longing for the resurrection of past goods as much as hope for their future extension.

But, in spite of the dangers offered by the Mirror, it is also through its mediation that Harry is for the first time able to perceive himself as a recipient of nurturing and responsive attention. In a moment of literal mirroring that functions much as the mother's facial and emotional mirroring does for the developing child, and with a similar amount of consecutive fantasy on Harry's part, the magical object is able to do what the Dursleys never did: provide Harry with visual evidence of his belonging and belovedness through his parents' loving glances and in particular through his mother's affectionate smile. In front of the Mirror, for the first time Harry's deepest need is not repressed—as both Harry and his magic have been silenced, called names, and stuffed in a cupboard under the stairs—but instead is reflected back to him, is met. Petunia Dursley, with her horse-like face, her jealousy, and her cruelty to Harry, is an inverse, a distorted mirror of the idealized, smiling mother Lily becomes in the Mirror through its reflection of Harry's desire.

Rowling's slow, careful catalogue of the shared features between Harry and his mother, then Harry and his father, in this passage, and then their answering smiles, is itself a textual mirroring of Harry's glance and the Mirror's reflective action. In the medium of the text itself, the reader's own inner gaze turns first from one imagined face to another, then back. Cradled in this exchange of glances, Harry becomes part of an extended familial and visual context he lacked before. This contextualization builds for the reader as it builds for Harry himself, and Harry, remarkable for his very lack of resemblance to his aunt, uncle, and cousin, suddenly belongs. Harry is entranced by the Mirror, which, in Winnicottian terms, shows him precisely the facilitating environment he has most longed for and, though he did experience it, cannot remember. Though Harry later receives a photo album from Hagrid full of pictures of his parents, the reflection in the Mirror is the first moment in which Harry's parents appear to him where he can consciously see them and know that he belongs.

Just as the episode with the Brazilian boa that begins Harry's series of initiations into the wizarding world is thick with psychological, mythic, and esoteric resonances, so are Harry's first and subsequent encounters with the Mirror of Erised. Sounding just one of these resonances, the myth of Narcissus also centers around a boy entranced by his reflection. Narcissus, older than Harry, though not by much, is also caught before a reflective surface, unable to look away from what he desires, and misunderstands the kind of knowledge this reflection gives him. In his ninth-century

Metamorphoses, Ovid's narrator describes Narcissus' first encounter with his reflection:

> He [Narcissus] knows not what he sees, but what he sees
> invites him. Even as the pool deceives
> his eyes, it tempts them with delights. But why,
> o foolish boy, do you persist? Why try
> to grip an image? He does not exist—
> the one you love and long for. If you turn
> away, he'll fade; the face you discern
> is but a shadow, your reflected form. (Naso 94)

Narcissus does not understand the kind of knowledge the pool gives him. Rather than realizing that it shows him himself, Narcissus mistakenly attributes his own appearance to a fabricated other as if the reflection were real, unaware that the one he desires only illusorily appears to return his affection. Like Harry, Narcissus, fascinated and attracted by what he sees, does not perceive the true nature of the empty image and so is caught, unable to separate himself from his love-object, the object of charismatic attribution and of transference. Narcissus cannot perceive that, in a very real way, he already is what he most wants, and of course in his self-absorption misses the frantic attentions of Echo.

But, as much as Narcissus' and Harry's experiences have in common, they also differ. The Mirror of Erised colludes in the deception of its observer in a way that Narcissus' pool does not. Narcissus is engaged in a great deal more foolishness and self-deception than Harry is—and what he most desires, in the end, is someone who looks and acts, even sounds, just like himself. Harry, while entranced by the Mirror, does not see himself alone, but instead, held in loving relationship. Harry is able not only to recognize himself—showing an initial baseline self-awareness greater than Narcissus'—but is also able to see and recognize others and to desire a relationship with then more than his own isolated, idealized self. Age is also a factor to consider; where Narcissus is an adolescent fascinated by his own physical beauty, his relationship to his reflection charged with auto-erotic longing, Harry is still a child in need of his parents. The need reflected back to Harry—though it is of course especially developmentally keen in childhood—even for many adults never really goes entirely away, though it may indeed, as it does for Harry, transform into something else.

In acknowledging the different kinds of longing, of eros, that both Harry and Narcissus experience, it is also essential to recognize that their desires seem equally intense. As different as Harry's and Narcissus' love-objects are, their experience of longing seems analogously consuming and potentially dangerous. Harry's reaction to the reflection of his desires in the Mirror is highly reminiscent of Ovid's description of Narcissus' reaction to the refection of his in the pool. Harry stands, "hands pressed flat against the glass as though he were hoping to fall right through it and reach them" and leans toward his parents with "a powerful kind of ache inside him, half joy, half terrible sadness" (*Stone* 209). And both boys ultimately find themselves reluctant, and almost—in the case of Narcissus, utterly—unable to leave.

Likewise, in both cases, the impulse to reach out physically toward an immaterial reflection is too strong for either Harry or Narcissus to resist. "Why try/to grip an image?" Ovid's narrator asks—but we know all too well why (94). While an image makes a poor substitute for a loved one, it is no easy thing to resist the draw of an idealized image that we love and that loves us. Desire, emotional and physical, pulls Harry away from his senses towards his internalized, idealized images of parents (his imagos), reflected in the Mirror. Desire attracts Narcissus toward the beautiful boy in the water, reaching futilely for the hand, for the lips, the mouth of his reflection. As Maier remarks in his epigram, "the liquid quenches the thirst of the dry substances" only enough to lend the clay pliancy and must not overwhelm it in the hands of the skillful potter. Likewise, in Narcissus' and Harry's cases, desire itself, liquid and luminous, the fuel for shaping and for work, is only helpful so long as it does not wash away the stability of the more ordinary, physical self, the earth. Out of balance, Narcissus quite literally dissolves into mud, flowers, and pool, and if it were not for Dumbledore, one suspects Harry might also have vanished, washed away by the intensity of his own longing. Harry's and Narcissus' lack of awareness that these images are realities they themselves create is a source of real danger. It is only Dumbledore's interference that averts this dangerous dissolution for Harry.

On the night Harry meets Dumbledore in front of the Mirror of Erised, Harry has returned to the Mirror against Ron's advice, his obsession too strong for even his best friend to prevent him from going back (*Stone* 210–12). The power of Harry's own unconscious, now semi-conscious, desire to see himself encompassed by his parents' love, fed by images, prevents Harry from exercising other core qualities, including his curiosity and loyalty. It also causes Harry to disengage with his surroundings to the extent that, upon his arrival in front of the Mirror, he does not even realize Dumbledore is in the same room with him.* Like Narcissus, Harry is immediately absorbed in his reflection, dangerously unaware of himself,

---

*Read analogically and alchemically, Harry's character must be purified before he can progress, and so it seems quite appropriate that Dumbledore's first name is Albus, a possible reference to the white lead which Maier notes in the *Atalanta Fugiens* is an essential catalyst in the processes involved in the creation of the Philosopher's Stone. For a description of the process, see pp. 71–72.

unable to look away from the Mirror which seems to promise the fulfillment of Harry's deepest desire.

But Dumbledore does not stay silent for long, and just as the letters from Hogwarts helped Harry to decipher the "strange things [that] often happened around [him]"—like removing the glass at the zoo, speaking to the snake, or turning his teacher's wig blue—Dumbledore provides Harry with a key to understanding the Mirror and himself when he carefully explains to Harry that the "happiest man on earth would look into it and see himself exactly as he is" (*Stone* 24; 212–13). Through this and other hints Dumbledore leads Harry to understand that what he actually wants, that is, his parents and their love, is not something that the Mirror can actually give to him, and that, furthermore, it is dangerous to think it could. Dumbledore's description of those who "wast[e] away before it, entranced by what they have seen" is almost straight out of Ovid, increasing the mythic overtones of the scene (*Stone* 213). In Harry's conversation with Dumbledore, it becomes clear that conversation itself may be a kind of transfiguration, of magic.

Breaking the charm that the Mirror exerted for Harry, Dumbledore points Harry in the direction of wisdom, noting that circumstance and history as well as family often play a role in what we want and what is most tempting to us. Ron, Dumbledore is swift to point out, wants something different from Harry, because his life circumstances have made this the case; Ron sees himself alone, the best of his brothers, precisely because he has been overshadowed by them and wishes to prove himself. Harry, on the other hand, having lost his parents, is shown an ideal image of their love and his place with them. Dumbledore enables Harry to understand that desires, even—or perhaps especially—unconscious ones, have histories. They also have futures; read across the *Harry Potter* books, this scene foreshadows Ron's potential for jealousy and his profound motivational differences from Harry, as well as Harry's own tendency toward over-identification with and unrealistic idealization of his parents. It also lays the foundation for many future conversations in which Dumbledore initiates Harry into a deeper understanding of the hidden forces which drive him and others to act. As Dumbledore demonstrates to Harry repeatedly in his sixth year, even Voldemort's horrific actions originated in childhood need and the actions of Voldmort's own mother and father—and Voldemort himself was inclined by his circumstances to make choices that turned him into something ghostly, inhuman, out of balance, and hungering always for more life, no matter the cost to himself or others.

Harry's conversation with Dumbledore in front of the Mirror of Erised is the first of many moments in which Rowling invites the reader to consider the complexity of human motivation and its causes while at the same time suggesting that individuals are still responsible for how they act. In this particular scene, Harry's desire to love and be loved in return is not dismissed, but the actions he took and might take based upon that desire are also not condoned uncritically. Through the symbol of the Mirror of Erised and Dumbledore's and Harry's conversation about it, Rowling also suggests that people do what they do for understandable reasons even if they do not themselves always understand them.

But the dangers of such mirrors and mirroring are also clearly not to be underestimated. Even as Dumbledore verbally mirrors Harry's and Ron's desires back to Harry, he also suggests that mirrors—and any other objects that might purport to hold their satisfaction—are potentially deceptive and dangerous. He encourages Harry to reflect rather than to remain entranced by his reflection. In this, Dumbledore speaks from experience. Though unknown to the first-time reader of *Philosopher's Stone*, read retrospectively, Dumbledore's explanation of the workings of the Mirror to Harry seems closely tied to Albus' own experience of the lures of power and their close ties to grief. As Harry learns when he meets with Dumbledore in the space between life and death at King's Cross Station in *Deathly Hallows*, Albus has also known what a powerful pull grief and the fantasy of its eradication may exert when reflected back by another person or an object like the Mirror. Gellert Grindelwald and Albus had also been mirrors for each other in the summer Albus spent with Gellert after his mother's death. Albus and Gellert's desires to bring Witches and Wizards out of hiding are shown to be understandable, especially as readers learn of the Muggle boys who tormented Ariana Dumbledore and the imprisonment of her father for his vengeance (*Hallows* 564).

But these desires, just like Harry's desire for his parents' love, or Ron's desire for specialness and recognition, are also shown to be opportunities for exploitation, manipulation, and violence. In Albus and Gellert's case, such desires become part of the mix of motivations which result in the fight during which Ariana is killed, and the potent forces of grief, desire, and revenge only lead to more death (*Hallows* 574). Read with these events in mind, it is clear that Albus understands the power of the temptations presented by the Mirror precisely because, just like Harry, he has lost so much. Dumbledore and Harry's midnight conversation before the Mirror of Erised foreshadows the continuation of the work initiated by a serpent's hiss and is merely the first of many moments in which Harry is given the opportunity to understand and transform unconscious aspects of himself through supportive relationships.

Dumbledore's advice for Harry also has much in common with advice given by another figure poised at the intersection of esoteric, psychological, and spiritual currents. In his letters to his friends, confidants, patrons, and students, the fifteenth-century scholar, priest, and philosopher Marsilio Ficino gives philosophical and personal counsel on issues of love, loss, grief, creativity, diet, astrology, and innumerable other topics with bright humor and earnest sympathy. In particular, the advice he gives to his friend Gismondo della Stufa, lost in grief after the death of his beloved Albeira, in his letter, "Consolatio in Alcuis Obitu," bears a striking resemblance to Dumbledore's advice to Harry. Ficino writes:

> If each of us, essentially, is that which is greatest within us, which always remains the same and by which we understand ourselves, then certainly the soul is the man himself and the body but his shadow. Whatever wretch is so deluded as to think that the shadow of a man is man, like Narcissus is dissolved into tears. You will only cease to weep, Gismondo, when you cease looking for your Albiera delgli Albizzia in her dark shadow and begin to follow her by her own clear light. For the further she is from her misshapen shadow the more beautiful you will find her past all you have ever known. (54–55)

Ficino maps "shadow" onto the temporal and bodily and "clear light" onto the eternal and soulful in a way that Dumbledore does not. Unlike Ficino, Dumbledore does not separate the luminous soul from the shadowy body. Harry's desire for his parents' love and presence is only dangerous because they are gone, not because desire for loved ones, complete in their bodily forms, is itself a mistake or dangerous. Ficino makes an extreme divide between the merits of the body and the soul, even as their relation is mediated by the spirit. Instead of counseling a deeper engagement with other people and with life, Ficino counsels Gismondo to withdraw himself further, into God, where "[he] will contemplate the beautiful idea that through which the Divine Creator fashioned [his] Albiera; and as she is far more lovely in her Creator's form than in her own, so [he] will embrace her there with far more joy" (55). This is almost the opposite of the reminder Dumbledore gives Harry: "It does not do to dwell on dreams and forget to live" (*Stone* 214), and it also seems to be opposed to the life-affirming ethic which undergirds *Harry Potter and the Philosopher's Stone* and the rest of Rowling's series.

If we transpose Ficino's articulation of the dynamics of grief and desire into Harry's encounter with this vision of his parents, however, Ficino's warnings still hold true. As long as Harry seeks to find his parents through the Mirror—through their mere shadows, projected in response to his own fantasy and profound need—Harry will never escape the Mirror's power. Entranced by "shadows" like Ficino's friend, Gismondo, like Narcissus, he would never "cease to weep" and would be "dissolved into tears." As long as he mistakes the ideal parent imagos in the Mirror for his actual parents, Harry will not shake his desire to return and stand in front of it, regardless of the consequences to himself and others.

Later, in *Deathly Hallows*, Harry's heroic acceptance of death meets the courage to appreciate life. Instead of vanishing away into a communion with the radiant forms of his dead loved ones, Harry chooses to come back to those he loves who are still in their physical forms and are not in any way lessened by them. Seven years after his first look at the Mirror of Erised, as if the books were themselves mirrors, gazing at each other, Harry makes much the same choice he made as an eleven-year-old: friendship with the living and embodied over fulfilling his spectral fantasy of ideal parental love with all those he has lost. In both choosing to die and choosing to live, Harry truly becomes Death's Master. In the end, he also discovers that he does not have to choose one or the other, as becomes apparent after he drops the Resurrection Stone in the Forest. He walks on and returns knowing "the dead we have loved [never truly] leave us"—and that death itself is something a great deal more mysterious than any simple end (*Azkaban* 427).

In this emphasis upon the value of corporeal life and relationship across the *Harry Potter* books, Rowling offers a corrective to Ficino and others like him who denigrate the physical body to heroize the spirit and soul. Harry is clearly not wrong to desire his parents and their love, but he also comes to understand the importance of the love that is given to him by others, in particular, his friends. Harry's mistake in front of the Mirror of Erised is not in desiring love, but, like Narcissus, in thinking that love is something that he can find in a reflection, in a fantasy, rather than in his relationships with other people, and finally in his own body and blood. It is this last location of Harry's connection with his parents, especially his mother, that is pivotally important in his confrontation with Voldemort at the end of the *Philosopher's Stone*, when Harry challenges Quirrell as he tries to steal the Stone for Voldemort.

Quirrell, utterly confused by the Mirror, stands in front of it angry and unable to recognize what it reflects. Unlike Harry, he does not ever have the opportunity or the help he needs to move beyond his confusion, and because Quirrell's deepest desire is to use the Stone, he is not able to find it (*Stone* 290). Dumbledore explains this to Harry later, remarking to him as they sit in the hospital wing that the magic of the Mirror and the Stone depended upon the necessity of wishing for a desired object as an end in itself rather than as a means to an end (300). The kind of singleness of purpose, wherein desire for an object is separate from fantasies of its use, is a transfiguration of ordinary desire to extraordinary, magical will. In his influential *Liber Al vel Legis*, polymath and practitioner of Magick Aleister Crowley writes, "For pure will, unassuaged of purpose, delivered from the lust of result, is every way perfect." Quirrell is caught in limbo by his own fantasies of what he will do once he gets the stone—in Crowleyan terms, by his "lust for result" (I: 44). This man with two faces, quite literally a divided self, is unable to achieve what either he or his master wants. Harry, by contrast, initiated into the mechanisms of the Mirror and his own desire, is able to think and to wish his way through the puzzle set by this final task. Harry reasons to himself that if he wants nothing more than to find the Stone, he should be able to see where it is hidden. Harry chooses to use the tricks of the Mirror and his own capacity for wish and wanting to enable himself to discover something he does not yet know. In doing so, he receives not only something pure and perfect outside himself—the Stone—but discovers something more knowing and loving wrapped around him, contained within his blood itself.

The exchange Harry has with his reflection is brief and does not go as he expects. The reflection "put its hand into its pocket and pulled out a blood-red stone. It winked and put the Stone back in its pocket—and as it did so, Harry felt something heavy drop into his real pocket. Somehow—incredibly—*he'd gotten the Stone*" (*Stone* 292). Instead of seeing the Stone hidden somewhere else, as he expects, Harry discovers the Stone hidden within his own pocket. With a wink, just as in his conversation with the snake, Harry, through the quality of his attention and the direction of his will, receives access to the object of the alchemical Great Work. With Dumbledore's help, Harry has come far from being the one, like Voldemort, reaching out in frustrated longing, "star[ing] hungrily" at his own fantasy (290).

To return once more to Maier's evocative emblem, in this moment Harry becomes not only the skillful potter shaping clay at the wheel, but the clay itself that he molds and smooths, the liquidity of desire tempered by experience. When Harry's reflection winks at him, the relationship between a subject and object, between a young boy and his fantasies of familial love and belonging, between potter and clay, active and passive, becomes ambiguous. Harry, gazed at by his reflection, himself becomes a kind of object and a kind of subject, and the Mirror, instead of being a transitional object, is a transmissional one—an object that directly links Harry to the physical manifestation and fulfillment of his desires. Harry looks into the Mirror, and the Mirror, unexpectedly, winks back.

In the moment when the Stone slips into Harry's pocket, the image that reflects Harry doing as he most wants becomes Harry as he actually is. As the glass that divided Harry from the Brazilian boa literally vanishes from the reptile house, so, too, does the still-present Mirror of Erised symbolically vanish. There is no longer a division but a communion between Harry and his reflection. It is as if Narcissus' reflection not only spoke with Echo's voice, but took on form, and actually kissed him back—a languid, tangible spirit of the water all along. It is a compelling moment, dream-like and wry. At the heart of its power the fantasy that if we only understood desire well enough and wanted what we want desperately enough, it can slip into our pockets. It is as if Orpheus did not look back, or as if Gismondo's ideal loved one could return to him, summoned back to being by his grief. Harry may get a Stone rather than his parents, but in this entrancing moment of intersubjective exchange, the world of reflective, divine images winks at the material realm, and reveals itself, when approached rightly, to be not quite as remote as it at first appeared.

But, even though Harry's parents' images are no longer the reflections shown by the Mirror, Harry's love for his parents and their love for him are not absent from this confrontation. In fact, after he retrieves the Stone, the love and belonging that Harry so desperately wishes to experience in his late-night visits to the Mirror becomes manifest and embodied, as if this love passed with the Stone from the Mirror to Harry. When Voldemort attacks Harry physically through Professor Quirrell to take the Stone, it is his mother's love, living "in [Harry's] very skin," that protects him. It is this love which burns Quirrell beyond endurance when he touches Harry (*Stone* 299). Mirroring across the series, in the *Deathly Hallows*, it is Snape's love for Lily that is revealed to be a primary instigator of all sorts of action, from acceptance of death, to betrayal, to redemption. It is sense of his heroic duty as well the depth of an idealized, spectral mother's love that enables Harry to walk alone to his final confrontation with Voldemort, knowing he goes to his own death (*Hallows* 659–90). The love that was instrumental in the infant Harry's defeat of Voldemort and in his first subsequent confrontation with him is also essential to Harry's defeating him at the last.

In her emphasis upon maternal love in particular, Rowling also touches upon what D.W. Winnicott sees as an essential aspect of human development: the holding environment provided by a good-enough-mother or good-enough-caretaker that permits children to learn to manage their own overwhelming affect through soothing and mirroring. In providing a fantasy of motherly love in Harry and Lily's relationship, and a humanization of that love in Snape and Lily's relationship, Rowling imagines a compelling narrative testament to the power of such loves to transfigure overwhelming fear, bitterness, or despair into heroic action. It is also a spectral, haunted kind of love, manifest at gateways to both life and death, whether in the sacrifice that lives on in Harry's skin, or in the color of Harry's eyes, into which Snape asks to look as he dies (*Hallows* 658).

Much of what Suzanne Juhasz writes in the Epilogue to her book, *Reading from the Heart: Women, Literature, and the Search for True Love*, is illuminating for readings of the *Harry Potter* series. Juhasz concludes:

> What this book about reading and loving relationships has revealed, I think, is the importance both of our need for true love and the fantasies we create about getting it…. The stories revolve around fantasies not because they are the opposites of life but

because they are integral to life. There is no perfect mother-infant relationship, and the mother-infant relationship can never be experienced again. Yet our needs persist. For intimacy. Connection. Recognition. Those essential conditions for a real self to come into being and to be maintained. One way, if not the only way, to address the need is to imagine how it might be fulfilled.... Fiction can make these dreams of love and identity come true—for the characters; for the reader who is participating wholeheartedly in their story; for the author. (249)

In *Harry Potter and the Philosopher's Stone*, it is precisely these needs—for a relationship with his mother, "[F]or intimacy. Connection. Recognition."—which the Mirror of Erised enables Harry to see inside himself, even as it also fails to meet these needs. It is, indeed, a looking glass, a lens that reveals to him something that was already present but not yet known, secret within himself.

Rowling's imagined world provides a service not unlike the Mirror of Erised or the wink of the snake. If readers do not take trouble to engage with asking what kind of truth, what kind of knowledge, and what kind of solace these and other fantasies of magic and idealized maternal love, of good and evil, provide, then they do enthrall us as surely as Harry was first enthralled by the Mirror, Narcissus by the pool, or Gismondo by his grief. If we see the source of love as always originating outside us, without seeing where it begins within us, its goods will always remain alienated from us, just out of reach. If, however, we read these books with the awareness that they themselves dramatize of desire and fantasy, they may also inspire us to reflect upon our desires and understand their origins. Read in this light, *Harry Potter and the Philosopher's Stone* itself becomes not only a text about magic but a magical text if we let its themes—which are as old as initiation, heroic journeys, and the difficulties of relationship itself—transfigure us as we consider them.

Works Cited

Crowley, Aleister. *The Book of the Law. Liber Al vel Legis. Internet Sacred Text Archive*, www.sacred-texts.com/oto/engccxx.htm. Accessed 30 Nov. 2016.
Ficino, Marsilio. *The Letters of Marsilio Ficino*, vol. 1, Shepheard-Walwyn, 1975. 12 vols.
Fortune, Dion. *The Mystical Qabalah*. Ernest Benn Limited, 1979.
Freud, Sigmund, and Ritchie Robertson. *The Interpretation of Dreams*. Oxford UP, 1999.
Juhasz, Suzanne. *Reading from the Heart: Women, Literature, and the Search for True Love*. Viking, 1994.
Kets de Vries, Manfred F.R. *The Leader on the Couch: A Clinical Approach to Changing People and Organizations*. Jossey-Bass, 2006.
Kripal, Jeffrey J. *The Serpent's Gift: Gnostic Reflections on the Study of Religion*. U of Chicago P, 2006.
Maier, Michael. *Atalanta Fugiens: Sources of an Alchemical Book of Emblems*. Translated by Helena Maria Elisabeth De Jong, Nicolas-Hays, 2002.
Naso, Quintus Ovidius. *The Metamorphoses of Ovid*. Translated by Allen Mandelbaum, Harcourt, 1993.

Rowling, J.K. *Harry Potter and the Deathly Hallows*. Scholastic, 2007.
_____. *Harry Potter and the Prisoner of Azkaban*. Scholastic, 1999.
_____. *Harry Potter and the Sorcerer's Stone*. Scholastic, 1997.
Winnicott, D.W. "Transitional Objects." *Freud and Freudians on Religion: A Reader*, edited by Donald Capps, Yale UP, 2001, pp. 211–19.

Re-Reading Harry Potter, Re-Creating Ourselves
Harry Potter as Resurrection Stone

ISAAC WILLIS

Grief is itself a med'cine.—William Cowper

Had we but world enough and time.—Andrew Marvell

Memory / has a fly's dumb enthusiasm, rubbing its antennae / in blessing or ablution, dropping its sticky edges / circling back fiercely, fiercely / trying to forget the touch of so many small deaths.
—Janice N. Harrington

It is a cold February morning. Twenty-something twenty-somethings rearrange linoleum tables and plastic chairs in order to transform a hundred-year-old classroom into a seminar space. Nylon bags plop haphazardly on the ground, and the metal legs scraping along the glued-down carpet sound like an organized stampede on the second floor of the oldest building of our very old campus.

Once the tables more or less resemble a rectangle, we settle in. Paper coffee cups are arranged among collages of scanned and printed articles, spiral notebooks with illegible scribbles, and smartphones all being switched to silent. Like characters in a play, we all drop—as if on cue—our copies of *Harry Potter and the Prisoner of Azkaban* on our tables in a chorus of paperbound thuds.

It is a perfect day to discuss dementors, I think, as the stuck-open sliver of open window admits enough wind to chill me into a heightened awareness of all things dreary. This, seemingly in spite of our old building's unremitting steam radiators that usually keep us in summer year-round. Waves of steaming heat are marked by bone-chilling gusts that seem to punctuate our discussion about dementors-as-symbols-of-depression. But these feelings, of hot and cold and lukewarm coffee and heavy, heady conversation, are not symbolic; they merely are. I grow irritated, restless, not a little hopeless, and even a little bit angry, which is odd. Our stop isn't King's Cross; the steam ebbs. The space is colder than I expected.

As of late, a shadow has settled over my reading self. A specter that feels at once familiar and foreign falls down around me, which I attribute to the caffeine and cold. Someone across the rectangle chimes in, "If dementors are depression, then what is Azkaban? Like, our minds? And the Patronus?"

"Good memories we can use to block out the bad?" another student ventures.

And with that, I am transported to my own good memory. It is exactly eight years and one semester earlier. I am standing in a very different, temperate sort of room: the Morton Junior High School library. I have snuck in to lengthen my study hall bathroom break, but to keep up the pretense I scan the stacks around me, picking up some volumes and turning them over to read the blurbs on the back. While I am acting the part, a white-haired woman in a blue denim dress watches me from behind a massive oak desk with a small nameplate that reads, in white block letters, **Mrs. Andrews**. I can't tell which is older—Mrs. Andrews or the library itself—but I do know she guards a world I know very little about: the world of books.

As if she can see right through me, she gestures to a display shelf with six hardcover tomes arranged in a semicircle. From left to right, the dust jackets depict the same black-haired boy smiling, sometimes riding a broom or brandishing a wand. In the middle is a short stack of identical, orange-yellow volumes, much newer than the rest. But I think I recognize the same boy, although he's older now. I am drawn to these covers in a way I cannot put into words. I feel, without even consulting a blurb, that I must read them. I respond to the silent pull and grab the worn copy of *Harry Potter and the Sorcerer's Stone*, approach Mrs. Andrews' imposing desk, and—having no clue how this transaction works—stammer, "Can I use this book?"

By the time I'm back in study hall, I have been transported to Privet Drive, to a world as magical to me as Hogwarts, to cats that transfigure into humans and back again, to motorcycles and the half-giants they bear, and an old man with half-moon spectacles who reminds me simultaneously of Mickey from *Fantasia* and a magician my mom hired for my sixth birthday party.

I become, in a word, a reader. I begin thinking differently. In my spare moments, I daydream about Hogwarts, am enchanted by the castle grounds, the inimitable groundskeeper, the castle's many hidden rooms, enchanted objects, and mercurial ghosts.

But the farther I follow this memory of reading, the blurrier it becomes. It is as if the day in the library is a centrifuge, and every day after is spinning and spinning out into something beyond memory—if we can think of memory as events that definitely transpired in our past—into something like sensuous impressions. What I remember more than anything, looking back, is not the plot of Harry Potter or its characters' arcs, the *what* of the story, but rather how I *felt* reading. The images circle around and around. I see myself sneaking the books to bed, reading them after lights out with a small book light I keep clipped to the nightstand. Then, in earth science, I am daydreaming about Quidditch, tracing the beveled dust jackets with my fingers while the teacher prattles on none the wiser.

One of these images stands out among the others, especially on this frigid day. I am alone in my childhood bedroom; I have just finished the Epilogue of *Deathly Hallows*. For the first time in my life, I am in mourning. These texts, these objects on which I relied so much, to which I devoted so much time, were irrevocably torn from me in a way I was not expecting. I was still holding the book, but it had lost something essential and vital.

Interviewing J.K. Rowling shortly after the US release of *Deathly Hallows*, Oprah Winfrey addressed this sense of grieving:

> **OPRAH:** "When I came to the end of *Hallows* ... I mourned not only for the end of the series but for you…"
>
> **ROWLING:** "It was a bereavement ... although I knew it was coming. We all know that the people we love are mortal. We know it's gonna end. You cannot prepare yourself for it."

So, I guess I couldn't direct my anger, my sense of betrayal and bereavement at Rowling, the author and creator of all my splendor that fall semester of my junior high years. She was grieving too. But she does articulate and give shape to the twinge of grief I was feeling in that moment. In that same interview, Rowling continues, "It was not just the world [I mourned]. It was the discipline of working, and it was the structure it gave to my life."

When we read, especially as children, we are clay to be molded. I fell in love with the world of Harry Potter—its castles, its sports, its language of spells and lore of wand-making and house-sorting. "Fairy tales matter," insists Potter scholar Travis Prinzi. "Fantastic literature often imagines a more accurate and more edifying vision of reality than what the so-called 'realists' give us" (1). I was transported to a different and, if not "more accurate," then certainly more "edifying," reality, richly textured and alive. It was only when the series was over that I realized what it all meant to me, could grasp that sense of structure to which Rowling alludes. I wasn't aware how much the world of Harry Potter changed my own world, and it would take some time before I could begin to make sense of that change.

That "making sense of" is at the heart of the grieving process. Of mourning, literary critic Philip Fisher writes:

> It is not a question of one person's mere subtraction but of this event's changing everything, striking at the heart of life ... there is a near-death of the world itself, that is, of "my world." In the aftermath of such a death a new life has to be built; some other life has to be started. (213)

So it is, on a smaller scale, with the grief of reading. One of the many advantages of reading fairy tales, of course, is that we are allowed witness to the characters who mourn. When Harry loses Sirius, his godfather, he experiences the stages of grief, those that Elisabeth Kübler-Ross first described in 1969 as denial, anger, bargaining, depression, and acceptance.* His belief that, after Bellatrix Lestrange had sent him beyond the veil, Sirius "would reappear from the other side any second" is undoubtedly denial. The outburst that follows—"HE—IS—NOT—DEAD!"—is a broken, felt expression of anger commingled with that denial (*Phoenix* 807). The denouement of *Order of the Phoenix* through the opening chapters of *Half-Blood Prince*, when read with an eye for signs of grief,† are rife with bargaining, depression. All this is accompanied by occasional pangs of anger and denial.

Rowling writes of Harry, not long after the death of Sirius, "There was a terrible hollow inside him he did not want to feel or examine, a dark hole where Sirius had been, where Sirius had vanished. He did not want to have to be alone with that great, silent space, he could not stand it" (*Phoenix* 821). While the grief that attends us after we finish a good book, or series of books, might pale in comparison to the feelings of losing a loved companion, it is still grief. There is still a process that sometimes feels like being alone with an imposing silence, of avoiding any examination of what was

---

*The online APA *Dictionary of Psychology* says of Kübler-Ross' stages of grief, "The model is nonlinear ... moreover, [the stages] can recur and overlap before some degree of psychological and emotional resolution occurs" ("Stages of Grief"). I draw my framework of grief, mostly, from Philip Fisher's *Vehement Passions*. Fisher does discuss some of the stages of grief, but primarily as lenses for reading and analyzing characters.

†This is a different sort of reading than Mercedes Lackey's in her "Harry Potter and the Post-Traumatic Stress Disorder Counselor." Lackey analyzes Harry's never-ending trauma as from the standpoint of a psychologist. The article is still helpful as Lackey rightly insists that Harry undergoes several severe traumas. However, her observation, "Harry is repressing all this," downplays Harry's active transfiguration catalyzed by grief (162).

lost and how we, as the bereaved, must get on.* How do we begin to rebuild our world? Part of the answer lies, I think, in validating and attending to the complicated and soul-constituting ache of grief.

When I finished Harry Potter for the first time, I felt a sudden and terrible rend in my own world—the numbing understanding that I could never experience the novelty of reading Harry Potter again. If Rowling had set me on a quest for reading, then almost as soon as it had begun it was over. I took to the Internet for support and consolation. I came to learn, as a novice of both reading and grief, that I was experiencing PPD, or "Post-Potter Depression," which, according to *Urban Dictionary*, is "the feeling that a chunk of your heart was just ripped out after having finished *Harry Potter and the Deathly Hallows*, knowing that you will never again feel the anticipation, the excitement, the pre-release hype that ... accompanies a Harry Potter book release" ("Post-Potter Depression"). The Pottermore site, probably in response to so many cases of PPD, features a poignantly humorous and helpfully pragmatic article about dealing with life after Harry Potter. Its step-by-step guide offers such practical tips as "Assess your surroundings" and "Re-establish contact with family and friends." The first step, though, is quite direct: "Mourn" ("How to Deal..."). We have been given permission to wallow.

After one has spent a relative time mourning, though, she must begin the process of tending to her broken world. Fisher says, "Grief or mourning draws a horizon line between those who do and those who do not make up our world. Grief discovers or reveals a bright line between those who are not really part of the inner fabric of my world" (215). Tracing and redrawing those horizon lines is part of distilling the medicine of grief and underscores the alchemical nature of mourning.

Fisher describes grief as that feeling or passion that "[articulates] the boundary conditions of existence" (205). One of those conditions is our own mortality, our finite existence, or, simply, time. Another is the will, which paradoxically and unhelpfully "strives to go on existing without limit of time" (206). To say it another way, grief lies at the complicated intersection of, on the one hand, our limited time, and on the other, the will to keep plotting, making more plans. Grief, then, is being confronted with the things time has rent from us—the things we were renting from time.

---

*I want to be clear that I am not conflating getting on with life with getting over grief. Any insistence that one should simply "get over" his or her pain is rarely helpful and probably, on the other hand, harmful to the psyche. Megan Devine ("'Stay Strong,' and Other Useless Drivel We Tell the Grieving") articulates that even though the people who offer suggestions such as "Get over it" or "Stay strong" usually mean well, they end up minimizing the weight of grief.

I—The Resurrection Stone and the Transfiguration of Desire

The grief of reading is multifaceted. Seen in one light, it is the dreadful realization that, given an average lifespan, one cannot ever hope to read every book ever published, despite one's intentions otherwise. In another, it is more delicate and nuanced, like the desire to go backwards in time. It is this feeling, this baggage, that I carried with me, after reading Harry Potter, into every subsequent book checked out of the library. I wasn't being a generous reader. My horizon, marred as it was after finishing *Hallows*, closed my mind in a sense. After Harry Potter, I tried to fill the hole in my life with more books, different stories. I hadn't yet reconciled my will as a reader to the time I was taking to read. I didn't yet realize I was chasing a ghost, a specter of a story I'd already read.

But so much of grieving is chasing ghosts. As I write this now, I can look to the shelf near my desk and see a 5 × 7 picture of my childhood dog, Buster. He is long-dead, but something in me wants to keep him close at hand. Ghosts such as these are touchstones, those images we can reach out and touch in order to remember something lost. For Harry, an obvious touchstone is one he carries with him at all times: his scar. One of Dumbledore's first lines of the series calls to it: "He'll have that scar forever" (*Stone* 15). It is the ever-present signal of his parents' tragic death, and later in the series will cause Harry a great deal of physical pain and prove to be a dangerous link between him and Voldemort. C.S. Lewis writes, "Images, whether on paper or in the mind, are not important for themselves. Merely links" (65). My framed picture, Harry's scar. Both are links, reminders of pasts lost, ghosts of our own mind.

One integral touchstone for Harry is the Mirror of Erised, which we know, thanks to Dumbledore, is not a representation of reality but rather an image borne of desire—Erised is literally a backwards or scrambled kind of desire. Still, it is undeniably powerful. Rowling describes Harry's first encounter with the Mirror, articulates the heart-wrenching feeling of coming face to face with his mother as if for the first time. Harry sees the smiling reflection of a woman in the mirror, though he can neither see nor touch her in the room where he stands (*Stone* 208). After I read Harry Potter that first time, my mom encouraged and rewarded the endeavor by purchasing me a hardbound set of the novels. But I, like Harry, was chasing a phantom of a feeling that was retreating farther and farther from reality with every half-hearted conjuration.

The books were my own, and they were beautiful, but as companions they may as well have been dead. When C.S. Lewis' own wife died, he reflected: "I have no photograph of [Joy] that's any good" (15). By Lewis' logic, images are links to, but no substitute for, the real things they call to mind. Even before Dumbledore explains to Harry the manufactured nature of the images in Erised, Harry understands the sad fact about the Mirror.

As Rowling puts it, "He had a powerful kind of ache inside him, half joy, half terrible sadness" (*Stone* 208–09). The books, the picture of Buster, they are on the shelf, in the frame; a more accurate way to phrase it is, *I have shelved them, I have framed him*.

One of the cruel ironies of grief is that we can't rush it. There are no shortcuts—merely stop-gaps. Framing, shelving, these activities are vital and helpful. While Erised, like all ill-conceived desire, is destructive, the moving pictures of Harry's world serve the same function as our Muggle ones. One of Harry's most important touchstones, which exists mostly in the background of the text, is the photo album Hagrid gives to Harry at the end of his first year at Hogwarts. It is full of pictures of his family. When Hagrid asks Harry if he likes it, Harry is so moved he can't respond. Rowling writes, "Harry couldn't speak, but Hagrid understood" (*Stone* 304).

The stop-gaps, the chasing of ghosts, can be distracting if not necessary respites along the complicated, non-linear path of mourning. But at some point, the long, winding path opens up to a clearing. This is grief as medicine—not a cure-all but a remedy that invites self-reflection, the kind needed to begin redrawing our horizon. Months after the death of Sirius Black, after Harry's anger and denial has subsided, Dumbledore offers his own consolation: "It was cruel ... that you and Sirius had such a short time together. A brutal ending to what should have been a long and happy relationship" (*Prince* 76). This consolation is, in fact, an articulation of the boundary conditions of our existence, that the will and time are an ill-suited match. And Harry's response reveals a learned understanding, one that sounds like acceptance: "It's just hard ... to realize he won't write to me again" (77). There is no way around it; grief is *just hard*. "I realized I can't shut myself away or—crack up," Harry continues (77). Harry's world, his horizon, has been irrevocably altered, but he also finds a certain peace between his own will and his limited time.

This talk of medicine, grief, and touchstones is reminiscent of the work of the early alchemists, one of whose primary aims, historian of science Bruce Moran posits, "was to find a means to prolong life" (24). To achieve this, most alchemists sought to create a Philosopher's Stone, that object which would transfigure base metals to gold and even "produce the elixir of life," granting its distiller immortality (Granger 8). While the science, in its earliest settings, was practiced to achieve different aims, alchemists like John of Rupescissa, Roger Bacon, and Hieronymus Brunschwig were after that which would stay death: "What they were all looking for was a super-medicine, an elixir or *aqua vitae* that could purify physical bodies of their impurities, rid the human body of disease, and prolong life" (Moran 9, 11).

The work of these early alchemists was that of ascensional

transmutation—always of turning the baser thing, metal, or body to that which is less corruptible. They aimed to make the terrestrial heavenly, to distill the heavenly from the terrestrial.* Though they would not have used the language, their project was one of lengthening their lives and therefore expanding the potential of the will, pushing back against the boundary conditions of life.

This is the very reason the Stone is so attractive to Voldemort. But we know it is this very desire (again, a scrambled or backwards desire) that prevents Voldemort from obtaining and using it. Dumbledore explains that the Stone offers "as much money and life as you could want! The two things human beings would choose above all—the trouble is, humans do have a knack of choosing precisely those things that are worst for them" (*Stone* 297). Further, he reveals that "only one who wanted to *find* the Stone—find it, but not use it—would be able to get it, otherwise they'd just see themselves making gold or drinking Elixir of Life'" (300). Voldemort sees the Stone as a means to an end.

But John Granger explains that even the earliest alchemists did not pursue the Stone solely in order to transform lead to gold, to become immortal: "As important, … it creates a transformed person who is the conjunction of opposites, the resolution of contraries" (53). In this way, alchemy was not merely ascensional. Its transmutations could be thought of as descensional; that is to say, the vitality in alchemy lies not in what it affords the practitioner but in the process or the practice itself. Granger says that the relationship between alchemist and work was one of "correspondence" (51). Through the very process of distilling the Stone and transfiguring baser materials to make them more "perfect," the alchemist would undergo correspondent changes. The work is ascensional as much as the opposite. Grief is always tied to the correspondent process of alchemy, so long as we are open to its stages. Granger writes, "Death is the necessary part of the alchemical work; only in the death of one thing, from the alchemical perspective, is the greater thing born" (74).

So it is with the grief that attends us after a great book series, perhaps more so when we are children. When I finished *Hallows*, I was angry and bitter. Angry that the story was over. Bitter that no one had prepared me for it. But that is the thing about grief: like alchemy, it reveals a deep, profound relationship between subjects—a correspondence. Take the wedding guest in Coleridge's "Rime of the Ancient Mariner," who

---

*We might say the early alchemists actually distilled the heavenly already present in the terrestrial. That is, they recognized the sacred in the mortal rather than rejecting the mortal outright. I will show later that Voldemort confuses these aims, not that these alchemists were in any way like Voldemort. You might say that Voldemort's reading of alchemy is a cursory or poor one.

> Went like one that hath been stunned,
> And is of sense forlorn:
> A sadder and wiser man,
> He rose the morrow morn. (152)

Grief, at the outset, stuns us. Rowling expresses this another way in her novel for adults, *The Casual Vacancy*, where she writes, "Was it love when somebody filled a space in your life that yawned inside you, once they had gone?" (436). We can only hope that grief will allow us, at some future date, a wiser if not sadder vantage or horizon. To use Fisher's language, I didn't know it till it was over, but *Deathly Hallows* did fill a space in my life, and after I finished it there was a yawning that lasted for some time.

Another blistering gust bites the back of my neck and I am in the classroom again, out of the world of images and memory. Yet I still can't place my finger on this anger or dis-ease I'm feeling.

We're still on dementors, and someone else in the rectangle is describing his experience of watching the film adaptation of *Prisoner of Azkaban* for the first time: "I was just so disappointed the dementors in the movie didn't look like the ones in my head. They were scary, but not what I had pictured."

I look down at my blank notepad and empty cup of coffee and pause when I scan the cover of *Prisoner of Azkaban*. My friend's comment stuns me in a way I wasn't expecting—like an answer to a question I was just barely forming in my head. This copy of the book is new to me. My hardbound set of the novels is long-lost, maybe still sitting on a shelf at my childhood home. This cheap paperback is like a burning light in the dark, chilly room, signaling to me that I'm about to enter another season of grief.

Just as I was stunned twelve years ago, so I am now. I am betrayed. I am once again caught off guard by mourning. I know now that I am angry because these books I am reading for class are not the books I remember reading eight years earlier.

Eventually, the cold or the conversation leaves me weary. We are out of time. And, as if to block the stage for the next scene, in which we have no parts, we turn the seminar room back to a lecture hall. Tables are arranged once again into neat rows, chairs all facing front, and we shuffle out of the room, tossing empty paper cups into the wastebasket on the way out.

The fault, I begin to realize in the subsequent weeks and months, lies with me. Whereas when I finished the books as a child I sought to blame Rowling or the books themselves, now the grief is more a product or piece of my own tangled memories.

As readers, we grow and understand over time that a deep sadness attends the ending of any good book—which is, again, a sadness at the loss of connection to the book's world as well as the way the book structured our own world, for a time. What I didn't realize was that there was another grief in reading, one particular to the act of re-reading. And this grief has a lot less to do with written texts and everything to do with our expectations and preconceived notions. This was the key my friend had given me in articulating his own sadness that the film adaptation didn't live up to his expectations. And in unlocking that door I realized that what was grieving me was that I was betrayed by my own memory—my memory of what the books were, not of the books themselves. I had attached so much weight to these books that had caused me both great joy and profound sadness that I was blind to what they could mean to me now.

Part of this new grief was a result of the class I was taking, I have to think. Turning a critical eye to these fairy tales I had loved as a child was an interrogation of an idea with which I had mostly positive associations. Another, larger part was that I was dredging up that old grief, one which I clearly hadn't come to terms with completely. Horizons, it turns out, are never done being drawn and redrawn; the grief of re-reading has once again forced me to take up my pen and hew what belonged and what still needed remembering, that delicate business of recalling memories to restore something temporarily lost or forgotten.

And the part of my horizon that needed the most remembering was precisely this jumbled memory of images I carried: images of me reading. I thought that taking this Harry Potter class would put me in touch with those feelings of falling in love with reading once more. And what I wasn't expecting was that it really would and moreover that the feeling would be more complicated than I remembered, that my act of loving the books and letting them transform my life had, in fact, set me up for loss, for mourning.

C.S. Lewis said that he wanted his wife "back as an ingredient in the restoration of *my* past" (41). When we re-read, we are treading ground that's simultaneously old and new. The text, objectively speaking, is the text of our past, but we bring with us everything between the past and now and, in that way, the experience is alien and shocking. The grief of reading Harry Potter was long behind me, became its own sort of ghost. But when we come face to face with the ghosts of our past, we are often ill-prepared for what follows.

There are more than a few characters in the series who carry grief about their past lives with them everywhere they go. Hagrid's expulsion hangs over him like a cloud. Dumbledore is haunted by his youthful quest for power that ultimately led to the death of his sister. Filch prowls Hogwarts' halls with Mrs. Norris with the intent to make the students' lives difficult, and it is only later we learn that his bitterness is a result of his status as a non-magical Squib. Aunt Petunia, too, harbors a deep resentment of Harry and all things magical because her sister became a witch and she, to her great disappointment, was destined to live as a Muggle.

Writing about Severus Snape's complicated past in "Choosing Love: The Redemption of Severus Snape," Catherine Jack Deavel and David Paul Deavel claim that Snape, whom Harry once blamed for Sirius' death (*Phoenix* 833), is both haunted and ultimately redeemed by his love of Harry's own mother, Lily Evans Potter. Although Snape ruins any chance of a reciprocal relationship with Lily by calling her a Mudblood, Deavel and Deavel argue that over time "Snape's love for Lily pushes him beyond selfish desire and changes him fundamentally" (60). Eventually, as Snape's love evolves and in turn changes him, he sacrifices himself on behalf of Harry (62). Snape, unlike Petunia and Filch, looks back to the ghosts of his past and chooses not to be paralyzed by them; in fact, he learns from his past how best to live in the present. Snape's transformation is nothing short of alchemical.

If the ghost of Snape's love and grief are a kind of Resurrection Stone for Harry, then Harry is also that Stone for Snape. Subjected to Snape's incessant torture all throughout his education, Harry, through Lily, allows for his redemption. It is Lily's eyes, after all, and not Harry's, that Snape sees in his last moments (*Hallows* 658).

Filch and Petunia, like Snape, are haunted by what they could have been. In blind, misplaced pursuits of magic and fitting in, of power and gold, of a perceived or manufactured desire, we fail to achieve the correspondent aim of alchemy and instead become trapped, paralyzed by grief. This is Voldemort's downfall. In all his attempts to find the Philosopher's Stone, master the Deathly Hallows, and split his soul into eight fragmented pieces, he fails to love truly, even at Harry's insistence that he "Try for some remorse" (*Hallows* 741).

Voldemort's mission, in seeking immortality, prevents him from forming any meaningful or lasting relationship. Voldemort is immune, in a sense, to loss, and I think he in turn believes that this makes him immune to the many griefs of his own past. To the contrary, his fractured state is a direct result of his refusal to mourn, to come to terms with the boundary conditions of life.

To a certain extent, I empathize with Voldemort. To be human is to grieve, so why be that way at all? Why not at least try to master death? Even Dumbledore recounts, "I too sought a way to conquer death, Harry" (*Hallows* 713). The Philosopher's Stone, if he would let it, might actually transform Voldemort. The Resurrection Stone might teach him about living a golden, mortal life, but he turns it into a Horcrux. To love is to lose. To read, in the most basic sense, is to *finish*, to come to an end. To frame, to shelve, to love again, to re-read—all these aims recall old grief, resurrect forgotten feelings.

But the point of resurrection, I learned from reading Harry Potter, is not to cheat death. Voldemort, like Dumbledore before him, would seek the Resurrection Stone to reawaken the dead, to stay the inevitability of death. He cares little about the Hallows beyond their means to grant him power and immortality. Harry, on the other hand, aligns himself with Snape and uses it to allow for his own self-sacrifice. Dumbledore explains that Harry's awareness that death can sometimes be embraced and not only feared or resisted makes Harry "the [true] master of death" (*Hallows* 720–21).

What I was searching for in my Harry Potter course was the resurrection of those parts of my past I remembered fondly. Instead, re-reading awakened old and new griefs. I did not yet understand that while resurrection was the thing I wanted it was not what I needed. Resurrection implies a going backwards, which is impossible. If it's true that we can't step in the same river twice, it is equally true that we can't read the same book over again. I should have opened myself up to the transfiguration inherent in grief, allowed myself to change with my memories of the texts and the texts themselves.

One of Harry's last companions to die at the hands of the Death Eaters is Dobby the house-elf. But Harry's understanding of grief has matured since the death of his godfather. Voldemort tries to penetrate Harry's mind at the same time Harry realizes that Dobby is gone. In the intensity of Harry's anguish, Voldemort's fury "became a distant storm that reached Harry from across a vast, silent ocean.... Grief, it seemed, drove Voldemort out ... though Dumbledore, of course, would have said that it was love" (*Hallows* 478). When Rowling writes that grief drove Voldemort out, she means it drove everything he stood for out, as well. Harry and Voldemort both know, more than I, that to live is to grieve. But Voldemort fails to realize what Harry discovers: that to grieve is to love, which is that one magic that transcends Harry's world and crosses over into our own.

I realize that what I am after now is not resurrection but re-creation. When I re-read a beloved book, I was crushed to realize it wasn't the book I remembered it being. This is because the resurrection I was after, like stoppering death, is probably impossible and, at the very least, self-damaging in the end. As a young adult, I could not make the books mean everything they had meant to me as a child. I can merely re-member them as best I am able. Next to and behind my photo of Buster, if I look to my left, I can see seven tattered paperback books on the shelf. They can never be the books I want them to be again. But, as Dumbledore asks, "You think the dead we loved ever truly leave us? You think we don't recall them more clearly than ever in times of great trouble?" (*Azkaban* 427).

I am still, and think I will always be, on the path to re-creation when it comes to working through my grief. One's horizon is never static; it is always in flux, can change in an instant. I wanted Harry Potter to restore my horizon. In fact, I should have been re-reading in order to draw a new one.

Perhaps Dumbledore, sadder and wiser than most, knew about this alchemical nature of grief. It was he, after all, who refused to remove Harry's scar, even at McGonagall's insistence: "Even if I could, I wouldn't. Scars can come in handy. I have one myself above my left knee that is a perfect map of the London Underground" (*Stone* 15). Scars, like ghosting stones, are not unlike maps. They allow us to consider where we've been and where we have yet to go.

The grief of re-reading is a winding journey. It forces us to confront our past in order to make sense of the present, that we might be made more whole sometime in the future—or at least less fractured. But we do not draw and re-draw our horizons alone. As a final thought, I offer four strategies or insights to keep in mind as you re-read your own treasured favorites and come face to face with the specters of the past.

   1. Feel the grief of re-reading; don't try to rationalize it. Because the grief of reading and re-reading is inherent to the world of books and ideas, it is tempting to analyze your feelings, to abstract from them to the broader reality of reading and being. Understand that the grief of re-reading, like all grief, is natural and particular to you. My wife didn't read Harry Potter until adulthood, and therefore it doesn't mean the same thing to her as it did to me. Whereas when I re-read the series, I was shocked and saddened that the books weren't what I was wanting them to be, that same feeling might be awakened for Andi if she were to re-read Madeleine L'Engle's *Wrinkle in Time*—a book she treasured as a child. Another of my friends once told me about his disappointment when, in graduate school, he re-read *The Chronicles of Narnia* and wished he hadn't.

   2. The grief of re-reading allowed me to better appreciate Wallace Stevens' line, "Death is the mother of beauty" (55). Fisher says the boundary conditions that make up grief are the time we are given and our will. The grief of re-reading could be better defined as the intersection of transience and memory. All death, all loss, is change. But that is what allows for transformation. To say death is the mother of beauty is another way of saying that change is pregnant with possibility—the possibility for transformation and re-creation.

   3. Cherish first readings now. You can only read a book the first time once. I didn't know that, which is why after I finished Harry Potter for the first time, I was in a state of denial and depression. Grief has a

way of shocking us out of our expectations. Since I had never read a novel—or series of novels—cover-to-cover before, I had no idea Harry Potter would end in such a final sense. The novelty of reading is what I was chasing in re-reading. So, while you can, allow yourself to wonder at the seams of a good plot, to be surprised at a certain character's arc, be stunned by a description of a setting. At the very least, take stock of the way a book makes up your life or structures your world, if only for a moment.

4. Grieving books helps us process present mourning. It was only looking back to the grief I felt as an eleven-year-old that helped me make sense of the grief of re-reading as a twenty-year-old. While each grief is unique to what is lost and where you are at a given time, you are not starting from scratch. You can fall back, to an extent, on prior horizon lines in order to draw new ones. With reading, this is doubly true. Not only did I learn much about grief from my experience of reading, but I also found strategies for grieving in the text itself. I have done my best to highlight the characters who successfully—and sometimes unsuccessfully—grieve in the very pages that caused me so much joy and so much pain, that I love and grieve myself. It was Victor Frankenstein who told Walton, after all, "Learn from my miseries, and do not seek to increase your own" (Shelley 213). Draw from your own experience and learn from good books how best to get through, and not over, grief.

It is a hot summer day. It's been more than three years since the day in the classroom. Time, as it tends to do, has revealed even more about reading that I should clarify.

This whole project, of reaching back into my memories in order to construct a narrative of reading and reading again, has been one of selective remembering. And that has resulted in its own kind of misreading.

The Harry Potter course I took as an undergraduate was one of the most rewarding I attended. Most days it was anything but dementors and cold. Most days it was a treat to come to a steaming classroom, as if we were all boarding the Hogwarts Express. My fellow students and I could go down many rabbit holes together, were given space to reminisce about our favorite books. We were also challenged, on a daily basis, to see the books in a new light. We discovered with hard work and happily tired eyes some secrets the books, like Hogwarts, had withheld from us as children. What I remember most of all was being transported, for one warm hour every winter day, to the world of books I fell in love with nearly a decade earlier.

The grief, however, is real and was a byproduct of my taking the class.

But that, too, has mellowed with time. I have yet to pick the books back up, but I know I will again farther down the road—perhaps when the memories are even more distant, when I feel a twinge from an old scar that reminds me not of pain but of healing.

Grief is, more than anything, the process of remembering more rightly. It reminds us of our boundary conditions, lifts our heads to the horizon. The grief of reading, then, is taking a look at the bookshelf (which is not unlike a horizon) and recalling what each text means—not in the objective sense but as an answer to the question, *What does the text mean to me?*

John Steinbeck recalled certain books he read as "realer than experience—*Crime and Punishment* was like that and *Madame Bovary* ... I remember them not at all as books but as things that happened to me" (qtd. in Lisca 4). Remembering the books we've read, acknowledging the pain we feel when we must put them down or resurrect them, involves the most important alchemical step in grief: The object, person, animal, idea we have lost carried its own autonomy, had its own life. This very fact awakened in me feelings of betrayal; in my friend, it underscored the feeling of the film's failure to live up to his expectations. We are caught, in these moments, at the crossroads of memory and reality, of the will and its other enemy: the wills of others. Grieving for books is grieving for our memories, for the objects we expect them to be rather than the complicated, unexpected, beautiful subjects they are. Steinbeck recalls books not as texts to be mined or objects to be admired but dialogic agents of his past; they left lasting impressions on him.

It is our responsibility, as readers, to grieve and to remember rightly. If we don't, we are likely to confuse loving and living a good life with mastery and immortality. We will confuse the opportunity of re-reading with the disappointment of foiled expectations. After all, to adapt Dumbledore's phrase, the books we love never truly leave us.

Works Cited

Coleridge, Samuel Taylor. "Rime of the Ancient Mariner." *The Portable Romantic Poets*, edited by W.H. Auden and Norman Holmes Pearson. Penguin, 1978, pp. 130–52.
Deavel, Catherine Jack, and David Paul Deavel. "Choosing Love: The Redemption of Severus Snape." *The Ultimate Harry Potter and Philosophy*, edited by Gregory Bassham. John Wiley & Sons, 2010, pp. 66–79. Blackwell Philosophy and Pop-Culture Series.
Devine, Megan. "'Stay Strong,' and Other Useless Drivel We Tell the Grieving." *WBUR*, 7 Mar. 2018, wbur.org/cognoscenti/2018/03/07/how-we-manage-grief-megan-devine. Accessed 27 Dec. 2018.
Fisher, Philip. *The Vehement Passions*. Princeton UP, 2002.
Granger, John. *Unlocking Harry Potter: Five Keys for the Serious Reader*. Zossima, 2007.
Harrington, Janice N. "Before a Screen Door." *The Southern Review*, Winter 2004. thesouthernreview.org/issues/detail/Winter-2004/137/, p. 28. Accessed 19 July 2019.

"How to Deal with Life When You've Finished Reading Harry Potter." *Pottermore*, 2019, pottermore.com/features/how-to-deal-with-life-when-youve-just-finished-reading-Harry-Potter. Accessed 28 Dec. 2018.
Lackey, Mercedes. "Harry Potter and the Post-Traumatic Stress Disorder Counselor." *Mapping the World of the Sorcerer's Apprentice: Science Fiction and Fantasy Writers Explore the Bestselling Fantasy Series of All Time*, edited by Mercedes Lackey. BenBella, 2005, pp. 157–62.
Lewis, C.S. *A Grief Observed*. Harper One, 1996.
Lisca, Peter. "John Steinbeck: A Literary Biography." *Steinbeck and His Critics: A Record of Twenty-Five Years*, edited by Ernest Warnock Tedlock and Cecil Vivian Wicker. U of New Mexico P, 1957.
Moran, Bruce. *Distilling Knowledge: Alchemy, Chemistry, and the Scientific Revolution*. Harvard UP, 2006.
Prinzi, Travis. *Harry Potter & Imagination: The Way Between Two Worlds*. Zossima, 2009.
Rowling, J.K. *The Casual Vacancy*. Little, Brown and Company, 2012.
_____. *Harry Potter and the Deathly Hallows*. Scholastic, 2007.
_____. *Harry Potter and the Half-Blood Prince*. Scholastic, 2005.
_____. *Harry Potter and the Order of the Phoenix*. Scholastic, 2003.
_____. *Harry Potter and the Prisoner of Azkaban*. Scholastic, 1999.
_____. *Harry Potter and the Sorcerer's Stone*. Scholastic, 1998.
_____. Interview with Oprah Winfrey. *The Oprah Winfrey Show*. ABC, Chicago, 1 Oct. 2010.
Shelley, Mary. *Frankenstein*. Penguin, 2003.
"Stages of Grief." American Psychological Association *Dictionary of Psychology*, 2019. dictionary.apa.org/stages-of-grief. Accessed 1 Apr. 2019.
Stevens, Wallace. "Sunday Morning." *Collected Poetry & Prose*. Edited by Frank Kermode and Joan Richardson. Library of America, 1997, pp. 53–56.
Urban Dictionary: Post-Potter Depression. urbandictionary.com/define.php?term=post-Potter%20depression. Accessed 20 Dec. 2017.

Out from the Shadows into the Light

Persona and Shadow in Harry Potter

ALICIA L. SKIPPER *and* KATE FULTON

J.K. Rowling's Harry Potter series is filled with mythological, classical, and alchemical influences. Her characters have choices to make about who they will be as individuals, but those choices are shaped by their cultural contexts, which characters sometimes critique, sometimes embrace, and sometimes do not notice at all. Their true personalities often exist in the shadows, which have long been a literary and cultural trope representing darkness, mystery, and the unknown. The symbol of the shadow was readily developed into a psychological theory through Swiss psychiatrist and psychoanalyst Carl Jung's theory of persona (one's public face) and shadow (the often-private depths of one's personality). Jung believed that the personality contained both conscious and unconscious elements. He called the conscious element of personality "ego." The unconscious element, Jung said, is divided into the personal unconscious, where our own experiences and memories reside, and a deeper layer called the collective unconscious that contains thoughts and behaviors, or archetypes, which are "universal images that have existed since the remotest times" (*Basic Writings* 288).

Jung's theory grew from his fascination with alchemy. Although the common belief is that alchemy was the desire simply to turn common materials into gold, there is a long spiritual history associated with the process, essentially the process of transformation. Inspired by dreams, Jung wrote in his autobiography, *Memories, Dream, Reflections*: "Only by discovering alchemy have I clearly understood that the Unconscious is a process and that ego's rapport with the Unconscious and [its] contents initiate an evolution, more precisely a real metamorphosis of the psyche" (22). Inspired by ancient processes and scientists, Jung's analytical theory and alchemy became important influences in both psychological and cultural realms. Jung's alchemically influenced theory of the relationship of persona and shadow against the backdrop of the collective unconscious can be readily applied to many of Rowling's characters.

While Tom Riddle is Lord Voldemort's persona and Voldemort is Riddle's shadow, Severus Snape presents his shadow as his persona in order to work against the cruel and murderous Voldemort. Albus Dumbledore's persona at first seems to be one with his shadow; that is, he seems to be in all ways the good, wise, and kind mentor he plays to Harry. Yet, he himself tells us that he struggled with his shadow as a young man and by conscious choice keeps his fascination with power at bay. Harry, of the four, seems to come closest to a reconciliation of persona and shadow. He is able to plumb the hidden depths of his soul or personality to be the love he tries to bring to the world. He enacts the alchemical transformation from lead into gold, helped by Dumbledore and, as readers learn, Snape.

Lord Voldemort/Tom Riddle

An important part of bringing the conscious and unconscious into balance is acknowledging conflicting aspects of ourselves, our persona and shadow, and the anima (the unconscious feminine side of a man, according to Jung) and animus (the unconscious masculine side of a woman). This is similar to the alchemical wedding in which the masculine and feminine are united to make a whole (Sweeney 178). The shadow, anima, and animus are part of our personal unconscious, the part that contains the thoughts, memories, and experiences that are accessible to us. They can also be archetypes of the collective unconscious (Cloninger 258). The persona is defined as the public face we show to the world. It is who we say we are and who we become through education, experience, and social interaction (Stein 158). The persona is the mask we show to the world. Jung said, "The persona is nothing real; it is a compromise between individual and society" (*Basic Writings* 159). The shadow is the result of what is rejected by our ego consciousness. That which the ego accepts and identifies with becomes the persona; what the ego rejects becomes shadow (Stein 159).

The character of Tom Riddle/Lord Voldemort is a direct example of persona and shadow and, further, of the shadow becoming the persona. When Dumbledore describes Tom Riddle as a student at Hogwarts, he reveals that Riddle's persona as a child, the "I" he showed to the world, was of an intelligent, likeable young man who gathered followers and showed the talent and leadership to become a prefect (*Prince* 360–61). He even used his persona to his advantage when framing Hagrid for opening the

Chamber of Secrets, bragging: "On the one hand, Tom Riddle, poor but brilliant, parentless, but *so brave*, school prefect, model student ... on the other hand, big, blundering Hagrid" (311). The mask Tom Riddle showed to the world was certainly that of a charming, charismatic hero. Many believed this was the "real" Tom Riddle.

The persona not only provides an impression of us to others, it can also serve to disguise who we truly are (Jung 162). As Dumbledore tells Harry upon learning it was Tom Riddle's diary that enchanted Ginny Weasley in *Chamber of Secrets*, "Very few people know that Lord Voldemort was once called Tom Riddle.... Hardly anyone connected Lord Voldemort with the clever, handsome boy who was once Head Boy here" (329). Even while the title "Lord Voldemort" was in its shadowy, nascent state, Tom Riddle worked to present his shiny schoolboy persona to the world. Most people do not accept the negative aspects of their personality, since the shadow "contains features contrary to the customs and moral conventions of society" (Stein 106). However, Lord Voldemort was an exception to the rule that the shadow is the repressed negative aspect of one's self and was what Jung called a "rare exception"; someone who had consciously embraced evil as their identity and repressed their positive qualities into a "positive shadow" (Cloninger 50).

Jung believed in a balance of opposites in order to achieve optimum health. He believed in a balance between conscious and unconscious awareness—too much of either leads to disequilibrium and mental instability. Through the process of individuation, a person develops his or her true Self, with neither the unconscious nor the conscious dominating, but having a balance among all aspects of the personality (Feist, et al. 349). The Self contains opposites, but the goal of the Self is unity (Stein 107). Voldemort does not obtain a balance between his two selves, and as a result, neither his soul nor his psyche is united. In reality, Tom Riddle embraced his shadow as his identity, as well. While in the orphanage prior to Dumbledore's visit, which changed not only Tom Riddle's life, but eventually the entire wizarding world, Tom Riddle stole items from other children, hung a child's pet rabbit from the rafters, and lured two children into a cave to an unmentioned experience, although Mrs. Cole, the head of the orphanage, said they "were never quite right afterwards" (*Prince* 268).

The wizarding world, in its early ignorance of Tom Riddle's shadow, might have been illuminated through the story of the prisoners in Plato's "Allegory of the Cave." Plato's Socrates tells Glaucon and his other interlocutors a parable of prisoners chained underground facing a wall and perceiving the world through shadows. Not realizing there are powerful image makers projecting shadows onto the wall of the cave, the prisoners mistake the images of such things as animals, people, and trees for the real things.

The shadows are interpreted by the prisoners in a manner which they can understand so that they can make sense of the world and perhaps find comfort and meaning (*Rep.* 514a–515b).

When Cornelius Fudge, in large part to maintain his own position of power, launches a campaign to convince the magical community that Voldemort has not returned, he acts as image maker or puppet master. Yet, Fudge acts from fear and political expediency to deny the evidence of Voldemort's return until the evidence becomes so strong that he cannot deny it. Most witches and wizards do not choose to remain ignorant. They are like the prisoners who simply do not understand the world beyond the cave. When the Order of the Phoenix and Dumbledore's Army try to turn others toward the light, they convince some. But many others respond like the prisoners in Plato's allegory when an escaped prisoner returns to tell them about the world beyond the shadows. Socrates asks Glaucon, "'And if it were possible to lay hands on and to kill the man who tried to release them and lead them up, would they not kill him?' 'They certainly would,' he said" (517a).

While Harry is not killed for his campaign to warn the Wizarding World of Voldemort's return, he certainly suffers in the form of societal ostracism and even torture at the hands of Dolores Umbridge. *The Daily Prophet* and the Ministry of Magic launch a media campaign to discredit him, and he is shunned by classmates like Seamus Finnegan. At the end of *Order of the Phoenix* the truth of Voldemort's return is finally revealed and the entire wizarding world is freed, in spite of itself, from its ignorance. For Plato, education was a means by which one could attain freedom and enlightenment. Education, Plato writes, is not putting "true knowledge into a soul that does not possess it, as if ... inserting vision into blind eyes." Instead, education is awakening the "indwelling power in the soul" as an eye is "converted to the light from the darkness ... by turning the whole body" (518b–c). Education, then, sets one on a path to what Jung described as "unity."

Tom Riddle's early actions of tormenting children at the orphanage when they are on a field trip occurs in a literal cave, the same cave where he would later hide a piece of his soul. For Voldemort, the cave becomes a place where he attempts at the same time to hide and protect his transgressions, for he does not see them as transgressions at all. The scenes of the cave early in his life underscore Voldemort's development, a reality that is not yet evident to many. The persona of Tom Riddle and the shadow of Lord Voldemort reveal Voldemort as the ultimate puppet master. When Dumbledore and Harry unlock the secrets of the cave in their search for the locket Horcrux, they begin to understand the depths to which Voldemort will go to achieve immortality. When Harry, Ron, and Hermione take up Dumbledore's challenge to discover and destroy Horcruxes, they are on the path to enlightenment, the long and difficult path to defeat Voldemort.

Socrates notes that a prisoner emerging from the cave would "be able to look upon the sun itself and see its true nature, not by reflections in the water or phantasms of it in an alien setting, but in and by itself in its own place" (516b). He also explains that this process of education or enlightenment is often very difficult, reminding his friends "that there are two distinct disturbances of the eyes arising from two causes, according as the shift is from light to darkness or from darkness to light, and, believing that the same thing happens to the soul too" (518a). Like the prisoners breaking out of their chains in Plato's allegory, Harry, Ron, and Hermione come to their understanding of just what is required of them—three teenagers on their own without direct help from their professors, family, or Dumbledore—slowly and painfully. With every ounce of courage, intellect, cunning, love, and loyalty they possess, they work to perceive the world around them, to understand the Horcruxes and the Hallows, and to inform as many others as they can about the Ministry's misuse of power.

Readers repeatedly learn that love is the most powerful magic and that it was Harry's heart that saved him (it didn't matter that he could not close his mind in Occlumency). Harry, Ron, and Hermione use their free will, and their growing knowledge, to pursue their quest for the light: Voldemort's defeat. Along the way, they learn of and are inspired by others who were and are willing to turn toward the light, such as Regulus Black who gives his life to recover and attempt to destroy the Horcrux from Voldemort's cave to help the whole magical world break free from the shadows, accept that Lord Voldemort has returned to power, and, more importantly, understand that he must be destroyed (*Hallows* 196).

Lord Voldemort hides in the shadow and also emerges to allow his shadow to consume him fully. The shadow is like the id. It does what it wants to attain power, success, and pleasure. It dominates and controls without feeling or conscience (Stein 199). Sharp says, "The shadow is composed for the most part of repressed desires and uncivilized impulses, morally inferior motives, childish fantasies and resentments" (173). This is evident in Voldemort's actions from his childhood as Tom Riddle in the orphanage, through his adolescence at Hogwarts, and most prominently in his adulthood as Lord Voldemort.

Tom Riddle was embarrassed by his mother. He did not believe she could possibly possess magic, because she died. He was convinced that his father must have been a great wizard, and was thrilled to learn that indeed he was "special" and that he would take his rightful place in a special world (*Prince* 271). He developed the "persona" of charming Tom Riddle, the "poor but brilliant" orphan, in order to bide his time and learn what he needed in order to rule the wizarding world and beyond (*Chamber* 311). However, he never accepted any part of that persona as his true nature, although it is possible that some of those positive qualities could have grown and developed had he not rejected those parts of himself. Jung said, "Coming to terms with the Other in us is well worth while, because this way we get to know aspects of our nature which we would not allow anybody else to show us and which we ourselves would never have admitted" (Sharp 123). The more one aspect of a person is denied, either persona or shadow, the more difficulty one will have with that unacknowledged side (Sharp 127). Because Voldemort is determined to be special, to transform himself from common Tom Riddle, son of a Muggle, his identity as Lord Voldemort supersedes his identity as Tom Riddle.

Tom Riddle/Voldemort wants power and control and is not concerned about whom he harms or destroys in the process. The only emotion he seems to possess is anger. He has no sensitivity or compassion. He does not understand love, which proves to be his undoing. Love saved Harry as a baby, and love saves the surviving wizards at the Battle of Hogwarts when Harry willingly sacrifices himself (or tries to) in order to save them. If Voldemort had ever known the love of parents or allowed the love of friends as Harry has, he might not have denied and rejected the positive qualities he acted out in his persona, denied love and true friendship, and only fully embraced his shadow. His shadow became his persona. As Stein explains, "The shadow is the inferior personality, the lowest levels.... A person identified with and primarily living out of the Shadow quaternity ... is more or less limited to ... a state of moral and spiritual underdevelopment" (164).

Considering the image of the snake as a deceiver in the Garden of Eden and as an archetype associated with moral corruption, it is fitting to note that the only "being" to whom Voldemort has ever shown any attachment is Nagini, the snake, an animal with whom he communicates and whom he controls. Of course, Nagini also houses a piece of Voldemort's soul, so his fondness for something that contains a part of him is really not so surprising. In *Half-Blood Prince*, Harry and Dumbledore are discussing the Horcruxes when Dumbledore explains why he thinks Nagini may be the sixth Horcrux. He says, "She underlines the Slytherin connection, which enhances Lord Voldemort's mystique; I think he is perhaps as fond of her as he can be of anything" (506). The fact that Lord Voldemort can only express fondness for a snake reveals to Dumbledore that Nagini may in fact, be a Horcrux. After all, the only affection Voldemort has is for himself.

Voldemort's decision to create Horcruxes, to tear apart his soul, also defies the unity and balance Jung describes as necessary for the Self to be whole. Jung used the word psyche, which means spirit or "soul" in Latin (qtd. in Cloninger 48). Jung, however, delineated between psyche and soul, saying the psyche was the "totality of all psychic processes, both conscious as well as unconscious" and soul "is best characterized as a 'personality'" (*Collected Works* 6: 48). Therefore, Voldemort tears apart the pieces of himself that could have become a unified whole and instead creates Horcruxes in order to "protect" his soul in his quest for immortality. Most people journey through the process of individuation described by Jung in order to understand and accept the opposite parts of themselves. Voldemort does the opposite. He ignores, rejects, or denies any aspect of himself that did not help him reach his goals of power and success and domination: his shadow. This rejection tears apart the soul, the very essence of his being. As Dumbledore tells Harry, "Lord Voldemort has seemed to grow less human with the passing years, and the transformation he has undergone seemed to me to be only explicable if his soul was mutilated beyond the realms of what we might call 'usual evil'" (*Prince* 502). Jung said that transformation was "the modification of psychic energy to higher purposes" (Cloninger 53). Voldemort certainly achieves transformation, but, as he never thinks of his actions in the cave as "transgressions," he does not see the evil in his so-called "higher purpose." Finally, he is who he seems to be, dropping the pretense of the young Tom Riddle. The Voldemort persona and shadow are one.

One cannot complete the discussion of persona and shadow in Lord Voldemort, exploring the unconscious and coming to terms with the opposites within us, without exploring the persona and shadow in the character of Harry Potter. In some ways, it seems as if Harry and Voldemort are connected in more than just dreams and thoughts or through the mind connection forged when a part of Voldemort's soul attached to Harry when he tried killing Harry as a baby. Harry and Voldemort are both orphans, raised outside the wizarding world, who find their home and their place in the world when they learn their magical identity and enter Hogwarts. Both become the most famous wizards of their time but for very different, though connected, reasons. Severus Snape is one such connection, one man who helps decide both of their fates.

Severus Snape

Snape is arguably the most complicated characters in the series. From the outset he is established in the minds of readers and characters alike as untrustworthy and evil. From Snape's first appearance in *Harry Potter and The Sorcerer's Stone*, Harry and later Ron and Hermione suspect that Snape is out to get Harry. During Harry's Quidditch match against

Slytherin in the first book, Ron and Hermione believe that Snape is jinxing Harry, and Hermione sets fire to his robes to create a diversion (191). Every book in the series establishes reasons to believe that Snape is reprehensible, and Harry continually questions Snape's motivations and loyalties, even as he learns that Snape is trusted by Dumbledore and so implicitly by The Order of the Phoenix. In the denouement of the series, readers learn that Snape is actually projecting his shadow and hiding his persona in his actions that seemingly make him loyal to Voldermort. Yet, because Harry, Ron, and Hermione have been suspicious of Snape from the beginning, it is easy for him to maintain the façade. They project their own fears and suspicions and find it easy to accept Snape's shadow as his persona.

In his *Collected Works,* Jung examines the tendency to believe the perceptions of others. He writes:

> Just as we tend to assume that the world is as we see it, we naively suppose that people are as we imagine them to be. In this latter case, unfortunately, there is no scientific test that would prove the discrepancy between perception and reality. Although the possibility of gross deception is infinitely greater here than in our perception of the physical world, we still go on naively projecting our own psychology into our fellow human beings. In this way everyone creates for himself a series of more or less imaginary relationships based essentially on projection. (6: 307)

Harry, Ron, and Hermione are easily deceived into believing that the face Snape shows to the world is his persona. Yet, Snape reveals the opposite of Jungian theory of persona and shadow. Snape hides his persona from the world and shows his shadow, his former self, the darkness that he has mastered in his former allegiance to Lord Voldemort. As a result, he distorts the reality of the characters around him, and because they are quick to project their own fear and concerns, he succeeds. In their ignorance of Snape's shadow, Harry, Ron, Hermione, and many of the Hogwarts faculty and members of the Order of the Phoenix, not to mention Rowling's readers, have to work their way out of the cave. The example of Snape shows just how difficult that journey can be. All of the evidence points … to a false reality. The prisoners, who Socrates says are "like to us" (515a), are ordinary people who do not often make the extraordinary effort to look into evidence deeply and to challenge their own preconceptions. Those who do ascend into the light, though, come to understand that the shadows only represent a false reality and that reality can only be experienced by looking past the shadow. This experience can easily be likened to the revelation that not only was Snape not a villain, he was in fact a hero, playing the role of a double agent to help save Harry and thwart Lord Voldemort's rise to power.

From the outset, Harry's perceptions of Snape cloud his judgment and act as shadows, much like the prisoners experience on the wall of the cave. He cannot move past his perception that is born first from his physical impressions of Snape, with "greasy black hair, a hooked nose, and sallow skin" (*Stone* 126), and later develops into a more emotional response to Snape as he learns of the enmity between Snape and his father. Like the prisoners in the cave, Harry makes sense of Snape using the emotion of inherited prejudice and only partial facts as a guide. Snape looks the part of a villain and, in fairness, acts the part very convincingly as well. As a result, Harry rejects Dumbledore's proclamations of trust, and because he does not see any evidence for that trust, pursues Snape as an enemy. Of course, the killing of Albus Dumbledore by Severus Snape in *Order of the Phoenix* convinces the remaining characters and readers alike that Harry, Ron, and Hermione had been right all along.

Harry is not able to emerge from the cave and truly see Snape until the end of *Deathly Hallows*, when Harry obtains Snape's memories, falling like tears into a vial as he lies dying. When they are placed into Dumbledore's Pensieve, they reveal Snape's true self, the light that existed beneath his persona of darkness. Through viewing Snape's memories in *Deathly Hallows*, Harry is able to bear witness to a conversation between Snape and Dumbledore and learn that his destiny is to kill or be killed by Voldemort. When Dumbledore asks if Snape has grown fond of Harry, Severus produces his silver doe Patronus who takes wing through the office window. His eyes on the Patronus Snape had in common with Lily, Dumbledore asks "'After all this time?' 'Always,' said Snape" (687). This scene reveals that Snape's prime motivation was love not for Harry but for Harry's mother, Lily. To find redemption for his past loyalty to Lord Voldemort, Snape pledges his life to keep Harry safe. This means that he serves as a double agent, even killing the mortally injured Dumbledore at his request to protect his identity while also keeping Dumbledore from the pain and humiliation Bellatrix Lestrange or Fenrir Greyback would have inflicted on him (683).

Snape was forced to confront his shadow when Lily died because he had relied upon Lord Voldemort to save her. It is after her death that Snape originally makes the promise to Dumbledore that he will protect Harry. Snape understands the facts of Voldemort's persona and shadow precisely because he loves and loses Lily. He presents his own unlikable shadow to the world, purposefully and deliberately. He does not love Harry, but he uses supreme force of will to save him for Lily—for love. Harry, too, finally understands the truth, when he grants Snape's dying wish: "Look ... at ... me..." (*Hallows* 658). It is Lily's eyes Snape sees, looking out of her son's face. Harry, to his credit, changes, too, when he is confronted with the complexity of Snape's motivation: that he devoted his existence and sacrificed himself to save the son of his beloved. To honor his sacrifice, Snape lives on in Harry's youngest child, Albus Severus Potter, the middle name, like

Snape's position in the middle, is the name of "the bravest man [Harry] ever knew" (758).

Jung examines what happens when the shadow is revealed. He explains, "To confront a person with his shadow is to show him his own light. Once one has experienced a few times what it is like to stand judgingly between the opposites, one begins to understand what is meant by the self. Anyone who perceives his shadow and his light simultaneously sees himself from two sides and thus gets in the middle" (*Memories, Dreams, Reflections* 872). When Snape comes to Dumbledore, the headmaster confronts him about placing his trust in Voldemort and how Lily was not spared. Dumbledore's confrontation about Snape's persona inspires him to embrace his shadow: his love for Lily, which is so strong that he devotes and risks his life to save her child. Snape's revelation of his shadow literally places him in the middle—between good and evil, between Dumbledore and Lord Voldemort. Snape's ability to adapt his shadow thoroughly as his persona enables him to hide his true self and straddle the realms of darkness and light.

Through the process of individuation, a person develops his or her true Self, with neither the unconscious nor the conscious dominating, but having balance among all aspects of the personality (Feist, et al. 265). Snape does not fully embrace his shadow or his persona. Instead, he embraces both. His jealousy of James prevents him from truly being a benevolent force in Harry's life. He torments Harry at every turn and mocks Hermione for her knowledge. He favors Slytherin as head of the house and his affection for Draco Malfoy seems real, as the act of killing Dumbledore saves Draco from failing at Lord Voldemort's task. He shows the world the persona of a loyal and heartless Deatheater. Nevertheless, his shadow is one of love and loss. Snape is forced to reconcile both parts of himself, presumably achieving the unity that Jung believes is possible when both aspects of the personality are embraced. Snape is ultimately forced to embrace both in order to achieve his mission fully. Snape's love for Lily is his redeeming quality. Nonetheless, readers can suppose that his subterfuge is not without its difficulties. Readers are left to wonder if Snape's loyalties would have shifted from Voldemort and the Deatheaters had he not felt betrayed when Voldemort killed Lily. As a result, his ability to navigate the darkness and the light may have come to him gradually, spurred on by his loss. In essence, love saves Snape in much the same way it saved Harry.

Albus Dumbledore

Albus Dumbledore is another of the main characters who finds balance between his shadow and his persona. Although Dumbledore's persona is one of goodness, his past, or his shadow, certainly reveals darkness. Harry does not learn of this until after Dumbledore's death when Rita Skeeter publishes *The Life and Lies of Albus Dumbledore*. The biography reveals that Dumbledore was once associated with the evil wizard Grindelwald. Prior to reading the book, Harry had only been aware that Dumbledore had defeated Grindelwald, making him known in the magical community as a great wizard and a champion for both magical and non-magical people. As he had counted on Ron's friendship, Harry counted on Dumbledore's insight, support, and sagacity. Yet, the Albus Dumbledore who is revealed in the book is the opposite of everything that Harry has known, and it makes him question his beliefs, just as he questioned his judgment the night Ron walked out on him and Hermione. (*Hallows* 360).

Throughout the *Harry Potter* series, Dumbledore serves as a father-figure to Harry, and naturally, the thought that his mentor, his hero, his surrogate father, would be less than what he had previously believed is a devastating revelation, as hard to believe as the revelation that Snape was on his side all along. In her article, "Colours," on *Pottermore*, Rowling outlines Dumbledore's role in Harry's life and explains how it is connected to alchemical process. She writes:

> Colours also played their part in the naming of Hagrid and Dumbledore, whose first names are Rubeus (red) and Albus (white) respectively. The choice was a nod to alchemy, which is so important in the first Harry Potter book, where "the red" and "the white" are essential mystical components of the process. The symbolism of the colours in this context has mystic meaning, representing different stages of the alchemic process (which many people associate with a spiritual transformation). Where my two characters were concerned, I named them for the alchemical colours to convey their opposing but complementary natures: red meaning passion (or emotion); white for asceticism—Hagrid being the earthy, warm and physical man, lord of the forest and Dumbledore the spiritual theoretician, brilliant, idealized, and somewhat detached. Each is a necessary counterpoint to the other as Harry seeks father figures in his new world.

Because of his connection to Dumbledore, Harry struggles with the revelations of Dumbledore's past, and it is Hermione who reminds him that just because Dumbledore once believed that Muggles should be controlled and ruled by those in the magical world does not mean that his persona of "goodness and wisdom" did not fully represent the true Dumbledore. Hermione attributes Dumbledore's previous ethnocentric leanings to the folly of youth and reminds Harry how Dumbledore stood up to Grindelwald, pressed for Muggle-protection legislation, and gave his life to protect the world from Voldemort (*Hallows* 361).

Yet, as Harry learns in the "King's Cross" chapter, Dumbledore came to his senses over the body of his sister, Ariana, never knowing if he had killed her (*Hallows* 717). His relationship with Grindelwald and his early beliefs that championed the rights of the magical world over the non-magical were clearly not quite as "simple as that." It is likely, as Jung suggests, that Dumbledore learned to recognize and master his shadow. Certainly it is even very likely that Dumbledore's past and the recognition of his shadow would have motivated him to become a champion for those whom he would have once sought to control. Jung discusses the impact of coping with the shadows of the past and the struggle to control it: "If it comes to a neurosis, we invariably have to deal with a considerably intensified shadow. And if such a person wants to be cured it is necessary to find a way in which his conscious personality and his shadow can live together" (*Collected Writings* 11: 12).

Based on the way that Dumbledore lived the remainder of his life and his devotion to good, it seems that he found a way to live with his shadow. Dumbledore wanted to be, as Jung states, "cured" of the control of the shadow. As a result, Dumbledore rejected Grindelwald and the past to embrace his persona. This is very similar to Harry's own choice to reject the part of him that is connected to Voldemort. This transformation can also be connected to alchemy and Rowling's choice to associate Dumbledore with whiteness. Albedo is one of the four alchemical stages in the process of Magnum Opus, the alchemical term for the creation of the Philosopher's Stone. In this stage impurities are washed away (van den Broek and Hanegraaff 158–59). This can be likened to Dumbledore severing his connection to Grindelwald and seeking a life in pursuit of goodness and justice as opposed to one of fame and power.

In spite of Dumbledore's ability to manage his shadow, it appears that he does still struggle at times with his shadow. This is best exemplified in Dumbledore's attainment of Marvolo's ring in *Harry Potter and the Half-Blood Prince*. Dumbledore is unable to resist the allure of the ring precisely because it represents a way to atone, as Snape atoned, for the one misguided summer of his youth that cost him his sister. When he found the Resurrection Stone ring, Dumbledore did not give a thought to Horcruxes or curses. His only thought was to see his sister and parents again to give them his deepest apology (*Hallows* 720). In his grief, he forgot to master his attraction to power completely, which leads to his eventual demise.

The ring did indeed carry a curse, which blackened his hand and would have spread more quickly but for Severus Snape's quick intervention. Dumbledore is still tempted by power, the power to master death. Dumbledore recognizes his hubris, explaining how his near-fatal encounter with the ring proved him still unable to bring together the Hallows and their power (720). On the warlike nature of the shadow and the persona, Jung writes, "Nothing is so apt to challenge our self-awareness and alertness as being at war with oneself. One can hardly think of any other or more effective means of waking humanity out of the irresponsible and innocent half-sleep ... bringing it to a state of conscious responsibility" (*Collected Writings* 6: 964).

Jung's comparison of the conflict between the shadow and the persona is apt. For Dumbledore it is ongoing war in spite of an ability to recognize and control his shadow self. His lapse, which causes him to try on the ring, to feel the power to master death, results in a mortal mistake. Yet Dumbledore seizes the opportunity and transforms his moment of weakness into one of triumph as he acts upon the chance to save Draco Malfoy from committing murder, his murder. Because Dumbledore is dying as a result of the curse, it is easier for him to convince Snape to be the one to take his life, thus preventing Draco from destroying a piece of his soul through such an immoral act and seeming to secure Snape's identity as a double-agent (*Prince* 595–96). In agreeing "to help an old man avoid pain and humiliation," Snape once again redeems himself for his past transgressions (*Hallows* 683). He and Dumbledore collude one last time ultimately to aid Harry in the quest to defeat Voldemort, thus ensuring that Dumbledore is indeed master of his shadow.

In spite of Dumbledore's heroic actions, his brother, Aberforth, cannot let go of the past and holds on to Dumbledore's shadow as the whole reality of the man. When Aberforth recounts the events of the past and the tragic death of their sister Ariana, it is clear that he has remained bitter and blames Dumbledore for their sister's death. Aberforth's reaction is based upon his own knowledge of Albus' shadow. Aberforth witnessed Albus colluding with Grindelwald for "the greater good" and never accepted the change that he underwent in an attempt to master the shadow. Aberforth declares that after Ariana's death Dumbledore was "free," but the war with the past of which Jung speaks was one that never ended for Albus. Harry corrects Aberforth by recounting how Dumbledore had relived the agony of witnessing Grindelwald hurting his brother and sister on the night that he drank the potion as he and Harry attempted to recover a Horcrux. Harry says to Aberforth, "It was torture to him, if you'd seen him then, you wouldn't say he was free" (*Hallows* 568).

Dumbledore is never free of the past, which highlights the inability to exist without both parts the self. Even if one rejects the desires, the longings of the shadow, any acts committed as a result of the shadow self are never fully diminished. It is undoubtedly the actions and results of the past that serve as a constant reminder to Dumbledore of the need to recognize and control his shadow. In his defeat of Grindelwald and the rejection of his early thoughts regarding magical rule, Dumbledore rejects the shadow that had sought to control him. Persona and shadow are often opposites of each other, but Jung says that both must be realized in order to integrate our personalities (*Basic Writings* 233). Dumbledore recognizes both within himself and is therefore aware of his propensity to be tempted. Daryl Sharp writes, "The ideal is to have an ego strong enough to acknowledge both persona and shadow without identifying with either one" (96). Because Dumbledore struggled with his shadow when he was younger, he understands fully that he has both aspects to his personality. At times the shadow emerges in the form of his tendency to keep secrets when others need information or when he puts on the Resurrection Stone-turned-Horcrux ring, but ultimately, he is in control. The type of balance Jung describes is the type of balance Dumbledore achieves.

Harry Potter

When readers meet Harry as an unremarkable, skinny ten-year-old boy, he is forced to live in a cupboard under the stairs and barely tolerated by the Dursleys—his aunt, uncle, and cousin. He has nothing apart from the hand-me-downs from his quite over-indulged cousin, and a lightning-shaped scar on his forehead. When mysterious letters start arriving for him from an equally mysterious writer, and Hagrid blasts his way into the "Hut-on-the-rock, The-Sea" (*Stone* 51), Harry learns he is different. He is not an afterthought, a burden to an unloving "family." He is a wizard, and he is the son of a famous witch and wizard killed by the most evil and powerful wizard of their time. Harry is famous in this other world as well. He is known as "the boy who lived." This is the first evidence of a difference between Harry and Tom Riddle. Where Tom Riddle demands proof from Dumbledore of his ability to perform magic and refuses any assistance in preparing for his trip to Hogwarts, Harry eagerly accepts Hagrid's help and asks questions about his parents and this world of which he has no knowledge. He realizes he always knew something was different about him, but now he understands why. He feels "normal" for perhaps the first time in his life. There is a place where he belongs.

When Hagrid takes Harry to the Leaky Cauldron and Diagon Alley for the first time, Harry is fascinated. He drinks in the surroundings and is quite stunned at the reception he receives, wizards and witches bowing and shaking his hand, some in tears. The kind of reception Tom Riddle would have loved is all a mystery and a bit overwhelming to Harry. His brief interactions with Draco Malfoy leave him disgusted and fearful of being placed in Slytherin, the house Malfoy hopes to be in at Hogwarts. As Hagrid tells him, "There's not a single witch or wizard who went bad who wasn't in Slytherin" (*Stone* 80). Harry is also well aware that Voldemort was a Slytherin. These early interactions before his arrival at Hogwarts inform Harry's perceptions about Slytherin and make him resistant to the possibility that anyone in Slytherin could be anything but evil, even though he later realizes that his perceptions are false.

Readers see more glimpses into who Harry Potter is in *Sorcerer's Stone*. He is excited to have money, since he has been poor and underfed all of his life, but he does not use it to feel better about himself (even though he is tempted to buy a gold cauldron and a Nimbus 2000 during his first foray into Diagon Alley). Instead, he recognizes the poverty in Ron's family when they ride together on the Hogwarts Express. He buys out the food cart and shares it with Ron, trading for one of Ron's sandwiches so Ron will not feel he is a charity case. "'Go on, have a pasty,' said Harry, who had never had anything to share before, or indeed, anyone to share it with" (*Stone* 102). This scene with Ron underscores Harry's years of loneliness and his joy at having a friend for the first time in his life, and presents a stark contrast to young Tom Riddle, who does not share with any of his fellow orphans but instead chooses to steal from and torment them. Both Harry and Riddle have endured traumatic childhoods, but Harry is still able to be kind and empathetic. In befriending Ron from the outset, Harry breaks his cycle of loneliness and builds a support system that will enable him to weather the trials to come. In addition, Harry also refuses Draco's invitation to know the "right" people and lets him know that he can make those choices for himself (*Stone* 108–09). Harry is the poor orphan that Tom Riddle presented himself to be, but Harry has the empathy, courage, and humility not to play games and manipulate his way to power. If there were ever anyone who could have cashed in on his reputation, it would have been "the boy who lived." Instead, Harry fears he would arrive at Hogwarts not knowing anything and would be sent back to the Dursleys.

His fear also extends to where he will be placed at Hogwarts. His encounters with Draco Malfoy and information received from Hagrid color his perception that only evil wizards are placed in Slytherin, and he is afraid what will be revealed in the sorting ceremony. The process of sorting at Hogwarts separates the students based on the Sorting Hat's ability to discern their underlying nature. At the first sorting, the Hat recognizes that Harry possesses characteristics of all of the houses—Gryffindor bravery, Ravenclaw intelligence, and a dose of Slytherin ambition. The Hat argues that residence in Slytherin will help Harry to develop his talents most fully, even as Harry silently pleads not to be placed into that house (121). The Sorting Hat could see the fear of the shadow in Harry. If Harry had so chosen, he could have been placed in Slytherin, where his shadow might have developed and led him to "greatness." The shadow is not all bad, and the Sorting Hat recognizes this. The shadow is not just the "dark underbelly of the personality," but also "consists of instincts, abilities and positive moral qualities that have long been buried or never been conscious" (Sharp 125).

However, Harry insists he not go to Slytherin. At age eleven, it is because he does not want to be associated with the likes of Malfoy or the murderer of his parents. He has not journeyed to meet his shadow yet. He identifies more with his persona, a boy who behaves with Hufflepuff friendliness, kindness, and empathy. Add brave, loyal, curious, and a bit reckless and impulsive, and you have the Harry we grow to know throughout the series, one whom most Hogwarts teachers enjoy and whom Dumbledore admires. Dumbledore's perceptions of Harry in the memory in the Pensieve vary from Snape's, because they are not clouded by jealousy and because Dumbledore has spent time getting to know young Potter (*Hallows* 679).

The desire to do the right thing and the willingness to acknowledge both the positive and negative qualities in oneself separates Harry from Voldemort. While Voldemort never questions his superiority, cruelty, or methods, Harry wonders if he is really a good person and questions whether he too perhaps has a "dark side." The answer to his question, according to Jung, would be, "of course you do!" Although Harry does not have Carl Jung to consult, he does have Albus Dumbledore, who calms his fears in *Chamber of Secrets* when Harry reveals his fears that he is like Tom Riddle. Dumbledore points out the qualities—the often positive qualities—Harry shares with Salazar Slytherin, including "Parseltongue—resourcefulness—determination—a certain disregard for rules.... Yet the Sorting Hat put you in Gryffindor.... [Y]ou [are] *very different* from Tom Riddle. It is our choices, Harry, that show what we truly are, far more than our abilities" (333). Confrontation with the shadow is a moral issue, as the ego is responsible for the shadow. This confrontation can cause doubt and confusion about ourselves and our decisions (Sharp 258). Harry experiences this doubt and confusion throughout the series. He has internal conflict as he wonders if he is more like Voldemort than others recognize, even though he has an overwhelming desire to do the heroic and noble thing.

There are many more times that Harry is confronted with the negative qualities he possesses. His anger and jealousy erupt in *Order of the Phoenix* when he feels left out of the loop during his summer at Privet Drive, when Dumbledore will not look at him or speak to him, and when Hermione and Ron are made prefects. Each time, he has to examine his feelings and he feels ashamed of his behavior towards his friends. Murray Stein said, "The persona protects one from shame, and the avoidance of shame is probably the strongest motive for developing and holding on to a persona" (121). Stein also explains that "where the persona ends and the shadow begins makes us ashamed" (122). Harry is capable of exploring his shadow and feeling ashamed; Tom Riddle is not.

Perhaps the most frightening encounter Harry has with his shadow comes when he enters Voldemort's mind in *Order of the Phoenix* when

Nagini attacks Mr. Weasley at the Department of Mysteries. Harry is the snake at that moment and feels the viciousness of the attack. Shortly after, when leaving Dumbledore's office to travel by portkey to the Burrow, Harry and Dumbledore lock glances and Harry feels an overwhelming hatred toward and need to attack Dumbledore. He learns later that Voldemort and he are able to enter each other's minds and that these were Voldemort's thoughts and feelings, not his own. The experience shakes him, though, and he continues to wonder if something is wrong with him. Again, the difference between Harry and Voldemort is clear—when sharing Voldemort's thoughts, Harry is frightened and repulsed because of the violence and cruelty of Voldemort. He also knows he is capable of anger and perhaps cruelty as well and fears that part of himself. Jung says: "If we are able to see our own shadow and can bear knowing about it, then a small part of the problem has already been solved.... The shadow is a living part of the personality and therefore wants to live with it in some form. It cannot be argued out of existence or rationalized into harmlessness" (*Basic Writings* 304).

Harry sees his shadow in himself and portrayed in its most reprehensible form in Voldemort. Jung says this journey to meet the shadow is necessary and takes courage. We must meet our shadow if we ever want to truly know ourselves (*Basic Writings* 305). In meeting his shadow, Harry is able to make a conscious choice to control the unsavory characteristics of his shadow parts and embrace the positive qualities of his persona. Harry accepts all of what makes him Harry. He accepts the opposites, thereby journeying toward individuation and the unity of the Self. As Harry realizes how choices make us who we are, he even tries to give Voldemort one last chance to save himself, to make a different choice. Harry says: "Think, and try for some remorse, Riddle.... It's your one last chance, ... it's all you've got left.... I've seen what you'll be otherwise.... Be a man ... try ... Try for some remorse..." (*Hallows* 741). Of course, Voldemort cannot and does not try for some remorse and ends up defeated, killed by his own rebounding Killing Curse. Harry is able to meet his shadow, acknowledge and accept it. He is closer to the unity of the Self, the goal for which Jung said we all strive.

The characters of Tom Riddle/Lord Voldemort, Severus Snape, Albus Dumbledore, and Harry Potter, all struggle with finding a balance between their personas and their shadows. Tom Riddle embraces his shadow and fully becomes Lord Voldemort. Severus Snape's shadow emerges as his persona while his goodness is masked within himself. Albus Dumbledore struggles with the shadow self that emerged briefly in his youth to gain control over the shadow and embrace the goodness that came to define the whole of the rest of his life. Harry Potter struggles with his persona and shadow, eventually recognizing and accepting that he contains both. All of these characters and the dilemmas they encounter represent the struggle that exists within each of us.

Just as alchemy was the pursuit of transforming base metals into gold, Jung believed that the psyche, too, could be transformed to reject the impurities that exist within us, the evil of the shadow, and could lead us to embrace the goodness of the persona and the creating of the shadow. In the same way that Jung's theory of persona and shadow helps people to understand the various aspects of their psyches, Rowling's works are a testament to the power of transformation, the transformation of the characters who come alive and develop in the progression of each novel, and most importantly, the transformation of the readers undertaking the journey with Rowling. These transformations emerge throughout the Harry Potter series. Rowling's characters and the moral dilemmas they encounter inspire readers to confront the darkness that lurks within us all and to move out from the shadows and into the light.

Works Cited

Cloninger, Susan C. *Theories of Personality: Understanding Persons*. 6th ed., Pearson, 2013.
Feist, Jess, et al. *Theories of Personality*. 8th ed., McGraw-Hill, 2013.
Jung, C.G. *The Basic Writings of C.G. Jung*. Translated by Violet S. De Laszlo, Modern Library, 1959.
_____. *Collected Works of C.G. Jung, Psychological Types*, vol. 6. Edited and Translated by Gerhard Adler and R.F.C. Hull. Princeton UP, 1971. 20 vols.
_____. *Collected Works of C.G. Jung, Psychology and Religion; East and West*, vol. 11. Edited and Translated by Gerhard Adler and R.F.C. Hull. Princeton UP, 1970. 20 vols.
_____. *Collected Works of C.G. Jung, Structure and Dynamics of the Psyche*, vol. 8. Edited and Translated by Gerhard Adler and R.F.C. Hull. Princeton UP, 2014. 20 vols.
_____. *Memories, Dreams, Reflections*. Edited by Aniela Jaffé, Random House, 1963.
Plato. *Republic*. Translated by Paul Shorey. *Perseus*. Tufts University, www.perseus.tufts.edu/hopper/text?doc=Perseus%3Atext%3A1999.01.0168%Abook%3. Accessed 2 July 2019.
Rowling, J.K. "Colours." *Pottermore*, www.pottermore.com/writing-by-jk-rowling/colours. Accessed 11 July 2019.
_____. *Harry Potter and the Chamber of Secrets*. Scholastic, 1998.
_____. *Harry Potter and the Deathly Hallows*. Scholastic, 2007.
_____. *Harry Potter and the Goblet of Fire*. Scholastic, 2000.
_____. *Harry Potter and the Half-Blood Prince*. Scholastic, 2005.
_____. *Harry Potter and the Order of the Phoenix*. Scholastic, 2003.
_____. *Harry Potter and the Prisoner of Azkaban*. Scholastic, 1999.
_____. *Harry Potter and the Sorcerer's Stone*. Scholastic, 1997.
Sharp, Daryl. *Personality Types: Jung's Model of Typology*. Inner City Books, 1987.
Stein, Murray. *Jung's Map of the Soul: An Introduction*. Open Court, 2008.
Sweeney, Erin. "Cracking the Planetary Code: Harry Potter, Alchemy, and the Seven Book Series as a Whole." *Harry Potter for Nerds*, edited by Travis Prinzi, Unlocking Press, 2011, pp. 171–97.
van den Broek, Roelof, and Wouter J. Hanegraaff. *Gnosis and Hermeticism from Antiquity to Modern Times*. SUNY, 1998.

An Anti-Oedipal Reading of Harry Potter and Alchemy

ROBERT TINDOL

In any project that involves both alchemy and literature, surely Carl Jung's name comes to mind. The venerable Swiss psychoanalyst, far more than any other individual, made the case for a connection between the early scientific discipline of elemental transformations and their symbolic manifestations in the arts. If Hermione Granger were to have broached the topic of alchemy and psychoanalysis during her formative years at Hogwarts, we might have seen her curled up in the library with her dog-eared copy of *Mysterium Coniunctionis*. What she would have found in investigating the Muggles' ancient art of alchemy via Jung was not primarily about the oft-stated goals of turning base materials into actual gold, or of discovering the Philosopher's Stone and its Elixir of Life that leads to immortality, but rather a symbolic explanation. As Jung said, "The physical goal of alchemy was gold, the panacea, the elixir of life; the spiritual one was the rebirth of the (spiritual) light from the darkness of Physis: healing self-knowledge and the deliverance of the pneumatic body from the corruption of the flesh" (*Mysterium* 90). While Jung recognized the alchemists' practice as both physical and metaphysical, he saw alchemy as a metaphor.

However, we can't end our analysis of *Harry Potter* and alchemy with the insight that alchemy is a metaphor, because doing so would be no better than summing up J.K. Rowling's celebrated series with the severely reductionist insight that "it's all a fantasy." With such a facile definition of alchemy as a representation rather than a deeply involved plot development, surely our work in explicating alchemy in *Harry Potter* is done if we rely solely on Carl Jung. On the other hand, if alchemy were nothing more than a metaphor and not really a dynamic element in the plot, then why is the ancient science involved in the convoluted pathway that finally leads to ridding the magical world of the archenemy Voldemort? Why is Voldemort so hard to kill, and why does killing him require such indirect and counter-intuitive means? Also, why are the fruits of the alchemist's labors so casually brushed aside and occasionally not even fully employed throughout the entire series? What's more, if alchemy is to be thought of as a mere metaphor in the story-line, then why are certain physical products of alchemy nonetheless required in order to bring about the needed transformations to fight Voldemort? And finally, in understanding *Harry Potter* and alchemy, is it better to trade in our decades-old copies of *Alchemical Studies* and *Mysterium Coniunctionis* for a more contemporary understanding of alchemy's place in the history of science, such as Bruce Moran's 2005 book *Distilling Knowledge: Alchemy, Chemistry, and the Scientific Revolution*? Moran's subtitle alone suggests that the classification of alchemy as a "pre-science" is an inadequate and historically naïve grasp of the way in which alchemy is related to modern chemistry. If we are going to argue that alchemy is a structurally important plot mechanism in *Harry Potter*, then why not trade metaphor for early scientific tradition?

My answer to these questions is that we do not have to choose. A postmodernist reading of *Harry Potter* via Gilles Deleuze and Felix Guattari's *Anti-Oedipus* effectively argues that Jung's theories can be updated to include the notion of alchemy as a "productive mechanism"—that is, a means of bridging the gap between an individual's deepest desires and the countless ways that society impels us to conform. In other words, the plot devices involving the age-old concept of the Philosopher's Stone (renamed Sorcerer's Stone in the US version of the novels) in the first book of the series, *Harry Potter and the Sorcerer's Stone*, and the two duels between Harry and Voldemort in the final book, *Harry Potter and the Deathly Hallows*, all invoke traditional alchemy as Jung saw it in its capacity to unify and reconcile the conscious and the unconscious. However, alchemy in *Harry Potter* can also be thought of in more contemporary terms as a commodity that manifests its value in the real world, and moreover, as an entirely new commodity that may or may not conform with social conventions.

Anti-Oedipus is the first volume of a two-volume series by the French theorists that seeks to explain the functioning of the human psyche through a sort of amalgamation between the traditional Freudian concept of the id, ego, and superego, and the dominant capitalist economy of the West. To simplify, we have our basic desires (the Freudian id) that are tempered by social constraints (the superego), the latter of which can be summed up as the "Oedipus Complex," which imposes socially-normed limitations on our behavior. The details are far too complex for this essay, but the basic idea is that Anti-Oedipus can explain everything from youthful rebellion (where the social constraints are ignored) to the situation in which we move in exactly the opposite direction by continuing our support for a political system that clearly works to our personal detriment.

The economy of this unification is best described by Deleuze and Guattari as a process in which a bright line is to be drawn between desire and interest, and this is what brings us back to *Harry Potter*. Desire is that which Harry manifests in his unconscious without regard to utility, the needs of his friends, or even the "greater good" (a concept shown to have its paradoxes when we finally are privileged to see a few of Dumbledore's shortcomings in *Deathly Hallows*). Interest, by contrast, is any activity for which there is a perceived social need. This is not to say that desire and interest do not influence each other—in fact, Deleuze and Guattari argue precisely the reverse. If alchemy is a dual pathway toward balancing desire and interest, then it is imbricated in Harry's self-effacing willingness to sacrifice himself for the greater good. Such a transformation, moreover, can be understood as a pursuit that can only achieve its goal through a "non-pursuit" of sorts. Actually striving toward the transformation is precisely what paradoxically makes the goal unachievable, and perhaps this is the very counterintuitive touch that brings Jungian alchemy into conformity with the modern temper. Just as a physicist cannot measure the position and momentum of a particle simultaneously, as the Heisenberg Uncertainty Principle explains, perhaps the modern-day alchemist cannot truly put the Philosopher's Stone to its direct use without paradoxically rendering the Stone useless.

However, to explain the relevance of alchemy to Harry's balance of desire and interest, we must first stipulate that Harry has been primed during his early years, as have all adolescents in the nonfictional world, to behave and perform in a certain way in his social milieu. Thus, the lessons he learns are often irrespective of whether magic really exists in the world or not. Deleuze and Guattari argue that the socialization of desire can have both its oppressions and its pathways to a certain type of liberation. My argument is that this is precisely the way that alchemy functions in the *Harry Potter* series. That is, alchemy is restrictive in certain ways but allows these restrictions to be circumvented. This is a complicated idea that will require additional explanation, but the basic assumption is that we have to work through the complexities of our desires because we have been socialized to suppress them. This is reflective of the way that alchemy works throughout the series: alchemical transformations are never achieved in a straightforward manner.

If the distinction between desire and production is a bit murky, then a few additional words of explanation about Gilles Deleuze, Felix Guattari, and their strangely-named "Anti-Oedipus" theory will perhaps help. I'll begin with "Anti-Oedipus," which refers not so much to the great play by Sophocles, *Oedipus Tyrannus* as to Sigmund Freud's appropriation of the mythical Greek hero in psychoanalysis. To sum up the plot of the play very briefly, Oedipus is the monarch who is quite worthy in many respects, but unfortunately kills his own father by accident and, not recognizing him, proceeds inadvertently to marry his own mother. Freud takes the name of Oedipus and applies it to psychiatric patients whose problems stem from a fixation on their own mothers and overall familial dysfunction.

Deleuze and Guattari introduce their own innovation by arguing that society itself is vested in this enterprise of stipulating certain individuals to be suffering from the Oedipus Complex as a means of socialization. In other words, we are all socialized to assume a certain family dynamic, and this dynamic in turn prevents us from straying too far from social norms. But this creates a conflict, given that modern capitalist society also strongly motivates us to achieve original and innovative things. Thus, we are conflicted with a desire to become, say, the next Steve Jobs, even though we have at the same time been primed since infancy not to depart too far from the "straight and narrow." We have our desires, but how we act on them is highly complicated and will almost certainly require passage through the "Oedipus filter," so to speak. In fact, we may even be obliged to depart so far from the norms that we even seem a bit "crazy" in certain ways. Hence, the subtitle of Deleuze and Guattari's book is "Capitalism and Schizophrenia."

This is not to say that Harry Potter is schizophrenic or mentally diseased in any sense. Nor is it precisely accurate to simplify the *Anti-Oedipus* argument to proffer the notion that a little craziness can be a good thing in certain ways. Rather, the relevance of Deleuze and Guattari can be seen as an interpretation of the commodity via desiring-production, which refers to the hybrid objects that result from putting our most basic desires to good use. Just as the Anti-Oedipal program is a potent method of explaining why members of the working class continue to engage in economic activities that do not lead to their liberation, we can also understand the analogue of a Philosopher's Stone that does not physically and literally lead to the production of actual gold.*

---

*To provide an example, we may consider any typical contemporary ad for an expensive luxury product, such as a $200,000 watch or a $1 million sports car. Are these ads directed only toward the few privileged individuals who can afford the products? Is any viewer of the ad who struggles along on minimum wage merely sinking into neurotic fantasies by contemplating an item that he or she will never afford? If the answer to both questions is yes, then perhaps Karl Marx was correct in predicting that the "have-nots" would eventually try to rid themselves of their self-destructive fantasies and struggle for a world in which the "haves" would no longer work them for less than the value of their productivity in order to purchase those very luxury items. After all, why would anyone tolerate an economic system in which only a few are able to purchase luxury items solely because they have exploited the labor of others? But Marx's prognostication has clearly not happened, and one explanation may be that the contemporary consumer has much more in mind than the mere acquisition of commodities.

Why is desiring-production relevant at all to the *Harry Potter* series? My argument is that various plot details reinforce this view, and further, that the most striking instances often involve alchemical transmutations. It is almost always the case that Harry performs best against Voldemort when liberated from the social restraints that call for a traditional devotion to family and responsibility. If a budding Wizard or Witch possesses a Resurrection Stone that has proven effective in certain transactions, then he or she does not normally discard it, and yet Harry does so. Even if the budding Wizard or Witch is inclined to hold onto his or her trusty Invisibility Cloak, he or she would normally act on prior socialization by mouthing some platitude about devotion to family and friends in order to deprecate the act of possessiveness, and yet Harry announces that he will retain his cloak without further explanation. If standard socialization of the young Wizard to utilize alchemy for the greater good is the norm, then Harry breaks this norm consistently in the most crucial moments.

Therefore, "a little craziness can be a good thing" is an oversimplification, because we are not talking merely about spontaneous acts that come out of nowhere, but instead about ways in which nonconformity can amalgamate with standard practice to lead to a good result. Thinking about alchemy—as metaphor, metallurgical practice, and social and political transformation—sets the stage for my assertion that Harry breaks this norm especially in his encounters with Voldemort in the first and last books. Rowling indeed employs alchemy within the *Harry Potter* story-line, but invoking Deleuze and Guattari provides added detail about these precise transformations. Moreover, parsing the transformations along the lines of desire and production points to the uniqueness of the *Harry Potter* series in children's literature. That is, *Harry Potter* is an exemplary postmodernist children's story, and I believe that the way in which desire and production are handled in the plot are the very elements that make it so.

While it may seem counterintuitive at first glance to discuss pre-modern alchemical practices and postmodern interpretations in the same breath, the pre- and post-modern are actually compatible. Drew Chappell views the distinction between the modernist children's tale (as exemplified by Dorothy Gale and a host of others) as ultimately dependent on positive associations with adults, while the postmodernist children's story features the children themselves in the struggle for agency and legitimacy. Chappell writes, "Harry and his friends encounter considerable ambiguity in their adventures and learn as they age that the dualities seem more like continua and that the easy answers they receive from wizarding society are in fact influenced by those in power" (282). Ambiguity, of course, is a hallmark of postmodernism, but one may also forge an additional link between this ambiguity and the pre-modern tolerance for ambiguity in the cultural alchemy throughout the series.

The point is that we can shy away from standard Freudian interpretations with good textual cause. And because *Anti-Oedipus* calls for a viewing of the human psyche outside the Oedipal orbit, Rowling's parade of failed or flawed surrogates gives us grist for a Deleuzian/Guattarian interpretation. Furthermore, the general association of alchemy as a means of achieving an indirect and counterintuitive balance underscores the manner in which transformation throughout the series is served not by merely strong-arming adversity, but rather by achieving consensus and cooperation. Magic may be a powerful gift for those lucky enough to inherit it, but real transformation and realization of human potential requires much more.

The most productive angle in performing a Deleuzian/Guattarian reading of *Harry Potter* regards the question of whether Harry pursues his desires entirely for his own self-centered gains, or is attempting to meet social demands. Now as we all know, the "correct" answer for any work of children's literature is the latter. Of course Harry must think of his friends first, or else he is a bad kid. But the point that Deleuze and Guattari argue in *Anti-Oedipus* is that human society is structured just so that we will arrive at this kind of socialization. This is not to say that failing to look out for others is a good thing, but it is also not to say that self-centered activity is automatically to be regarded as a *bad* thing. Instead, the territory of unconscious desire uncoupled from social bonds is an interesting region to explore because of the raw creativity that so often erupts from its wild ramblings. Here, I will return to "desiring-production," an aforementioned term of Deleuze and Guattari, which, according to Ian Buchanan, is differentiated from Freud's notion of the id in that the former interfaces more directly with the world (28).

Those who have seen the classic 1950s film *Forbidden Planet* may recall that the rampaging invisible monster which is threatening the space travelers is actually the id of their host on the planet, a congenial man who at first doesn't even realize that his subconscious is running amok. This is pretty much the opposite of the Deleuze/Guattari conception, because they see desire as something that can interact in a much more integrated manner, and not merely as a separate entity that is like a second being totally separated from the conscious being. In other words, we may think of desiring-production as a potentially good thing. In fact, if it were not for desiring-production, and moreover, for the occasional breaches of public decorum in individual pursuits of this desiring-production, then the world would be artistically a much poorer place. And if alchemy is ultimately the human art of Transfigurations (which is the class where Hogwarts students would come closest to studying Muggle alchemy), then it is especially important to investigate the areas in which the rules have been breached.

The most obvious alchemical manifestation in *Sorcerer's Stone* on desire uncoupled from social context is the Stone itself, but the first example is the Mirror of Erised. According to Dumbledore, the mirror has the magical property of allowing the viewer to look at the visual embodiment of his or her fondest desire. Harry looks at it and sees living images of his long-dead parents, for his fondest desire is to unify his family. His friend Ron's desire is to be Head Boy, because becoming so would allow him to compete head-to-head with his older and more accomplished brothers. As Dumbledore explains, the mirror reflects the "most desperate desire of our hearts." As a consequence, "[t]he happiest man on earth ... would look into it and see himself exactly as he is" (*Stone* 213).

These and other statements by Dumbledore call for a bit of unpacking. First, he states that the mirror shows us exactly our deepest yearnings. This, though, is the beginning of a journey of self-discovery, not an ending place. And lest Harry has missed the point, Dumbledore further adds that "it does not do to dwell on dreams and forget to live" (*Stone* 214). Finally, Dumbledore reveals that his own reflection in the mirror shows him wearing a pair of nice wool socks. We learn in *Deathly Hallows* that Dumbledore lives with lifelong grief over the death of his sister Ariana, for which he considers himself at least partly to blame. While Harry suspects that Dumbledore might not have been entirely honest with him about the woolen socks, if we rely on Deleuze and Guattari we can conclude that the physical significance of the object itself (both socks and mirror) can be dismissed as things of lasting value, and that something in the process itself is worthy of further consideration.

The Sorcerer's Stone is the central alchemical feature of the first book, both because of its reference in the title and because of its central importance in the history of alchemy. Here, it is probably useful to review the precise differences between Rowling's magical rendering of alchemical history and a more nuanced approach such as that of Moran, which is grounded more thoroughly in the history of science. As one may infer, my assumption is that Rowling is essentially Jungian in her utilization of alchemy throughout the series, although she adds her own postmodernist twists. In fact, readers of Moran's book may well conclude that the Jungian conjoining of the physical and spiritual sides of alchemy is only a small and limited corner in the long history of alchemy as an early science. Instead, Moran writes, "Rather than cutting away the scientific lean from the presumed pseudoscientific fat when carving up knowledge in the 'early modern' world, we should try to understand how both fat and lean worked together to support intellectual life and to promote the process of discovery" (2).

In other words, we should step away from the "grand narrative" of the history of science as a "triumph of human reason over mysticism, magic and the occult" in order to reach a more nuanced understanding of alchemy in its broad historical context (4). Jung fits into this history because of the relatively late development during the eighteenth and nineteenth centuries of a belief "that personal transformation is somehow connected with doing alchemy" that "has lingered into the modern era" (67). Moran closes this particular discussion with the following observation: "As many readers may know, it became a prominent feature of psychology when the psychoanalyst Carl Jung argued that alchemical imagery was a product of a universal or 'collective' unconscious and could be read as revealing stages of individual psychic development" (67).

What is the reward for doing so? Moran's answer sounds almost as if it could serve as a mission statement for Hogwarts:

> Human divinity was, so to speak, smothered in material obsessions. If, however, a person could ever get free from such excessive affection for physical things and purify the soul in the process, that person might not only obtain a knowledge of God but regain his or her true, unblemished divine nature, and further, such a transformation would allow the person to become a *magus*, or magician. A magician possessed an intimate understanding of the operations of nature and knew how to manipulate natural processes so as to direct the powers and virtues of earthly things for good purposes. (69)

Granted, Moran is no longer talking about Jungian psychoanalysis in this section, but it becomes apparent that the fruits of the alchemist's endeavors can be individually transformative. One way of reading Rowling's series, then, is to consider alchemy as a metaphor for personal transformation. The alchemists sought personal transformations as they attempted to produce the Stone, and likewise, the magical doings of the *Harry Potter* world provide a productive mechanism through which human potential can be realized.

Obliquely introduced to the reader, as is so common in Rowling's plot developments, the Stone is the only point in which Rowling directly broaches the actual history of alchemy. Thus, it is worth quoting directly from the words in the text as Harry, Hermione, and Ron discover them in an old book on the history of magic:

> *The ancient study of alchemy is concerned with making the Sorcerer's Stone,* [which] *will transform any metal into pure gold. It also produces the Elixir of Life, which will make the drinker immortal.* (*Stone* 220)

Flamel, as the three discover, has not only been the only person known to have produced a Stone, but also celebrated his 665th birthday, having partaken of the Elixir of Life with his wife Perenelle, who is 658. "A stone that makes gold and stops you from ever dying!" exclaims Harry to his friends. "*Anyone* would want it!" (*Stone* 220).

Ron, for one, says that he could find a good use for such a stone in purchasing his own Quidditch team, which means that his interest as a utilization of newly acquired capital is a bit different than his ideal self-image. One is merely to gain social respectability and influence, while the other is to gain a new familial positioning. Neither may be what he *really* wants, which is a moot point, because the Stone will soon be sacrificed. An additional enjoinder from Dumbledore that Harry should avoid "brooding about that mirror" by "keeping busy" is presumably a foreshadowing that the same message will soon be made implicit about the Stone as well (*Stone* 224).

Sure enough, the Stone holds the potential for restoring Voldemort, who for the last decade has existed in severely weakened form due to the consequences of his *Avada Kedavra* death spell when he directed it toward the infant Harry. At this point the Mirror of Erised proves that it has not quite lived out its narrative usefulness, because Harry's wishing to keep the Sorcerer's Stone out of evil hands is reflected back to him, somehow causing the stone to materialize in his pocket. A brief struggle later, Harry wakes up in the Hogwarts hospital with Dumbledore at his side. The headmaster explains to him that the Sorcerer's Stone has been destroyed because of its danger. "You know, the Stone was really not such a wonderful thing," Dumbledore says. Although acknowledging that it indeed could create gold and eternal life, he continues: "[H]umans do have a knack of choosing precisely those things that are worst for them" (*Stone* 297).

The key is easy to miss on first reading, but the very thing that keeps Voldemort at bay and ultimately will defeat him is that either Harry or a like-minded person "who is prepared to fight what seems a losing battle" will willingly confront him (*Stone* 298). Moreover, Dumbledore reveals that the reason the Stone materialized in Harry's pocket was because he most earnestly wished to find it rather than to employ it in making gold or the Elixir of Life. Desire liberated from mundane concerns of family, society, or wealth is thus as much a key as the willingness to fight a losing battle. The end result must be insubstantial, or else it will be no end result at all. As for the actual object—in this case the Sorcerer's Stone—it is also insubstantial and easily sacrificed as other exigencies become apparent.

All of the alchemical elements of *The Sorcerer's Stone* are reprised in the final volume of the series, *The Deathly Hallows,* in which Voldemort achieves his most deadly manifestation in the series. Not only do the elements reappear, but we discover that both the devices and the pathways of transformation are deeply woven into the denouement of Harry Potter's story. Desire and production once again enter into the equation, and once again the manner in which the characters interact with the elements of alchemy demonstrate that the pathway to transformation is by no means a simple one sanctioned by existing social norms. Interestingly, Voldemort himself is an integral part of these transformations, and even more interestingly, his very malevolence in no way removes him from the alchemical matrix. Each of the final encounters between Harry and Lord Voldemort involves a life-and-death struggle that further defines the very nature of the desire for transformation and transcendence.

Those readers who stood in long bookstore lines in 2007 in order to grab a first-edition copy of *Deathly Hallows* must have been convinced near the book's end that rumors of Harry's demise at the close of the series might perhaps turn out to be true. Chapter 34, "The Forest Again," begins with the emphatic assertion that "Harry understood at last that he was not supposed to survive" (*Hallows* 691). While he has already learned that the "will to live" is stronger than the "fear of death" (*Hallows* 692), this time it looks as if his number is finally up. He is even visited by the shades of his parents and the departed Sirius and Lupin, who assure him that the death which will come to him in the next few moments will not be such a bad thing. Soon readers discover that Harry has a choice even about his own life or death when he meets with his departed headmaster in King's Cross Station. Harry himself wonders, "Is this real? Or has this been happening inside my head?" to which Dumbledore responds, "Of course it is happening inside your head, Harry, but why on earth should that mean it is not real?" (*Hallows* 723). Both pre-modern and postmodern in its outlook, *Harry Potter* empowers the imagination, as the Mirror empowers a searching of one's very soul, as the Stone empowers a questioning and transfiguration of one's most deeply held values.

The *Harry Potter* series is simply not a traditional story that beats children and adolescents over the head with its conventional morals. There is a great deal of indeterminacy in the books, and their young characters often intervene in the social structures into which they have been born. The example most relevant to Deleuze and Guattari's *Anti-Oedipus* is the very historical event that at least in part motivated their work, according to Buchanan. In May of 1968, protests broke out in Paris that essentially paralyzed regular business and also launched the country into an extended period of soul-searching. As Buchanan explains, anti-establishment types such as the older generation of leftists tacitly assumed that they were the natural allies of younger people who were inclined to protest the establishment, but this turned out not to be entirely true (7–10). Instead, the protesters were quite independent of both the establishment figures who thought that they should conform, and also of those who considered themselves to be the natural allies of protesters. Rowling's characters thus echo the May 1968 student protests in Paris in that they act in a spontaneous manner with apparent disregard not only to those who wish them to conform, but also to those who think that they should rebel in a sanctioned and acceptable manner.*

At any rate, Harry once again survives a potentially deadly encounter with Voldemort, partly because there is something about his selfless sacrifice that can at times undermine the bonds of family and the economy of social relations. After all, death takes one out of the family just as surely as it terminates economic productiveness. But an Anti-Oedipal interpretation does not reduce the rules to a Pauline contradictoriness of the "he who loses his life shall find it" variety. After all, the traditional interpretation of St. Paul's statement is that willingly sacrificing one's life is a means of having a life of a more everlasting sort, but I think that there is an ineffable hard core of stubbornness in the series that resists this very interpretation. A stable rule in which one redeems oneself and achieves some sort of everlasting reward, after all, is a metanarrative of the sort that postmodernism tends to avoid. But the point is not that *Harry Potter* strives to preserve its postmodernist credentials, but rather that the manner in which rules are broken throughout the series tends to be highly counterintuitive and resistant to generalization. The alchemical transformations of the *Harry Potter* series undermine rule-making in an Anti-Oedipal manner in that the series does not even attempt to state an overarching rule, or even imply one, about how the rules may be broken.

Harry survives this second-to-last encounter with Voldemort. We have been fully prepared to assume that the *Avada Kedavra* will kill Harry, although it may succeed in protecting those for whom he has sacrificed from harm. After all, that is the way it worked out for Lily Potter. But when Harry wakens in limbo after the Voldemort death-curse, he is informed by Dumbledore that Voldemort's prior actions have provided Harry with a new form of protection. For one thing, Voldemort harvested some of Harry's blood in *The Goblet of Fire* in order to regain human form, and for another, Voldemort's first attack left a bit of his soul in the infant Harry. In some complicated manner, the protection afforded by selfless sacrifice has been passed on to Voldemort. Therefore, his death-curse neither kills Harry nor backfires on himself this time—the blood harvesting apparently accounting for the survival of both. It does, however, take Voldemort one step closer to his death in the final battle. In his attempt to kill Harry, Voldemort has destroyed the fragment of his soul that once lived in his accidental Horcrux. Of the flayed and raw-looking creature whimpering nearby, Dumbledore says, it "is beyond either of our help" (*Hallows* 708).

During this final encounter with Dumbledore, Harry learns quite a

---

*For further contextualization of *Anti-Oedipus* in light of the May 1968 events, see Ian Buchanan's guidebook *Deleuze and Guattari's 'Anti-Oedipus.'*

few other interesting things that solve earlier mysteries, and he also learns the full significance of the Deathly Hallows, which turn out to be his Invisibility Cloak, the Elder Wand, and the Resurrection Stone which he discarded with little regard just prior to his encounter with Voldemort. Taken together, the three objects will afford the bearer certain unheard-of powers. But with the Invisibility Cloak long having been in Harry's possession and the stone lying on the forest floor somewhere, only the Elder Wand is still unaccounted for.

Although Voldemort is unaware of the significance of the Deathly Hallows as a triad, he is fully knowledgeable of the Elder Wand, and in fact has robbed Dumbledore's tomb to recover it from its last owner. The wand is an especially powerful one, which is precisely why Voldemort desires to possess it. He knows a great deal of the prophecy about his and Harry's destiny, and sees the wand as a means of gaining the upper hand. However, he doesn't fully understand its significance, for it turns out that he is not the rightful owner of the wand, and the result of his and Harry's last encounter is a death-curse that has backfired, finally killing the curser himself.

But the exact dynamics of how all these machinations work out is not my focus. Rather, I once again draw attention to the casual way the objects of the alchemist's art are discarded. Harry and the others decide among themselves that the Resurrection Stone will be left wherever it has been dropped in the forest. The Elder Wand will presumably be reburied in Dumbledore's tomb, with the hope that its power will die with Harry, should he die a natural death. As for the Invisibility Cloak, Harry announces that he will keep it because of its proven usefulness, both to himself and others. As Ron points out, the cloak has never failed even once, and it is also a gift, a token of affection from Harry's father, James. Perhaps the notion of what qualifies as "useful" has been as transformed as Harry himself.

In case the precise connection with Anti-Oedipal desiring-production and economics is still murky, the final encounters with Voldemort can be restated in more specifically Deleuzian/Guattarian terms. This is also helpful in understanding why certain seemingly irrational things often spontaneously occur—whether involving Harry's kicking a Resurrection Stone aside in fiction, or French students stupefying the Marxists who until 1968 thought they had the liberal youth of the day completely figured out. Voldemort's linking to and decoupling from Harry can be likened to the MCM' formula from the works of Karl Marx. In *Anti-Oedipus*, Buchanan writes, the formula "describes the basic working of the unconscious as Deleuze and Guattari see it" (54).

As Buchanan explains, the M stands for liquid capital initially available for investments, but its equivalent in Anti-Oedipus is the connective synthesis, which is a sort of gathering of psychic energy. A modern analogy involving smartphones might be the inventor who has gotten rich with his brilliant application and now has the capital available to try a new avenue of technological endeavor. Naturally, the inventor will not proceed in a vacuum, but instead will wisely cast about for ways in which his capital can be put to good use.* The C stands for commodity capital in Marx (in other words, money invested in factories or products with the goal of making more money), which Buchanan links to the disjunctive synthesis in *Anti-Oedipus*, or a critical period when one must decide whether to continue investing or "cash out." In other words, it is "disjunctive" because we tend to be cautious and conservative in such instances. Is our investment showing anemic returns? Then perhaps it is better to return to liquid assets. Finally, the M' is capital that is withdrawn from the commodity endeavor and is free for reinvestment in new ventures, or the conjunctive synthesis, which joins together the fruits of an earlier capital-driven investment with a fresh new venture (54).

These are closely related, for as Deleuze and Guattari explain:

> [T]he real truth of the matter—the glaring, sober truth that resides in delirium—is that there is no such thing as relatively independent spheres or circuits: production is immediately consumption and a recording process … without any sort of mediation, and the recording process and consumption directly determine production, though they do so within the production process itself. (4)

As a consequence, the interactions between Voldemort and Harry are dynamic, and furthermore, are always involved in continuous production. Just as business ventures are born, flourish, and die, Voldemort's bondage with Harry has its ups and downs, but ultimately only the latter. He could have perhaps done things differently (and the text supports this possibility), or he could have been smarter (also supported), and he could definitely have had more human compassion (a point that is overdetermined).

---

*If the investor is merely taking the next logical step, and that step is in conformity with the regular operations of society, then there is likely to be very little controversy. However, some of the most noteworthy innovations have run counter to the conventions of society, and I will suggest an analogy by way of the Beatles that may illuminate the point. When the Beatles first came along, rock and roll was already an established genre, and certain expectations of Western society for its youth were also well established. In regard to the latter, one may consider the hackneyed moral message that the "good" child or teenager was one who willingly and selflessly looked out for others. However, the title of the early Beatles song "Please Please Me" essentially says that hedonism is good. Or does it say so? Many adults were discomfited by the upstart Beatles and their influence on the youth, but in fact, the song merely says that interaction is a two-way street: "Please please me oh yeah like I please you" is not at all a selfish disregard for others. Therefore, the capital accumulated by the Beatles—in effect, the eagerness of the youth culture to have an anthem to articulate their feelings—led to a connective synthesis which was not especially pleasing to the adults, but not aggressively confrontational, either. Instead, it was an amalgamation of desire and interest. For an in-depth discussion of the spiritual component of alchemy, see Hauck's *The Sorcerer's Stone*.

To explain how this works, we can take Voldemort's gaining a piece of Harry's soul inadvertently in their first encounter as an extremely poor investment, but, nonetheless, one with a miserly yield. It is a poor investment, because Voldemort has lost his body and been rendered impotent for more than a decade, but not a fatally bad investment, because the piece of soul from Harry is apparently the very thing that allowed him to survive the backfiring of his own *Avada Kedavra*. Nonetheless, Voldemort lies in wait for an additional investment of "capital" (Harry's blood), which this time turns out to be a capital investment of much greater yield. He regains his body, and steadily consolidates his power through the last four volumes of the series.

However, as Buchanan explains, the "C" stage is closely linked with bivalent choices, which in economic terms is most clearly stated as the solution to the question of whether to stay invested or to take the money and run while the running is good. Here, Voldemort makes the sort of mistake that might cost others a high-paying job with a Wall Street investment firm but in fact costs him his life: he chooses to interact further with Harry in a fight-to-the-finish. And although he survives the second-to-last encounter, the final one finishes him off when it turns out that he has gambled away the entire bulk of his available capital (his inadvertent protection from his complicated blood/sacrificial bond with Harry). The Elder Wand proves to be a tool that does him no good at all, and he becomes an economic loser in Marxist terms and a life-loser as well. He has simply failed to know when to quit.

Now that the Elder Wand and the Resurrection Stone can create no additional surplus value (or at least none in immediate sight), they are discarded. Harry hangs onto his Invisibility Cloak for several reasons, however: one, it is far superior to any other cloak and perhaps to any other magical pathway to invisibility, as Ron has informed us; two, the cloak being flawlessly useful, it clearly possess residual value far beyond that of the wand and stone; and three, its residual value is multifaceted, in performing well against the enemy and in solidifying friendships, alike.

Taken in this manner, the *Anti-Oedipus* linkage explains how certain actions regarding the discarding of alchemical artifacts do not amount to a rejection of capital, but rather reflect a new way of seeing the residual value of those artifacts. To quote Deleuze and Guattari once again:

> Capital is indeed the body without organs of the capitalist, or rather of the capitalist being. But as such, it is not only the fluid and petrified substance of money, for it will give to the sterility of money the form whereby money produces money. It produces surplus value, just as the body without organs reproduces itself, puts forth shoots, and branches out to the farthest corners of the universe. (10)

But do the authors truly intend the application to literature as I have utilized it? The answer is yes, in part because they quote a plethora of writers of imaginative literature themselves throughout the book. In terms of general principles, they offer the following:

> [W]e hold ... that art and science have a revolutionary potential, and nothing more, and that this potential appears all the more as one is less and less concerned with what art and science mean, from the standpoint of a signifier or signifieds that are necessarily reserved for specialists; but that art and science cause increasingly decoded and deterritorialized flows to circulate in the socius, flows that are perceptible to everyone, which force the social axiomatic to grow even more complicated, to become more saturated, to the point where the scientist and the artist may be determined to rejoin an objective revolutionary situation in reaction against authoritarian designs of a State that is incompetent and above all castrating by nature. (379)

Cast in these terms, it is hard to imagine how Deleuze and Guattari would fail to value a close look at how Voldemort has squandered the family jewels, so to speak.

The seven-volume series ends with a very brief postscript which finds Harry and his friends married nineteen years after the final confrontation with Voldemort and standing at the train station to see their own children off to Hogwarts. The postscript is low-keyed and restrained, and except for a brief mention that children and perhaps parents alike are staring at Harry, there is little to tie their present circumstances to the earlier adventures of their student days. And even though Harry is presumably still famous, he was just as famous and recognizable the very first time he boarded the Hogwarts Express twenty-six years earlier. It is not even clear whether he eventually achieved his rather pedestrian goal of becoming an Auror after leaving school, although we do find out that Neville Longbottom is now the Herbology professor at Hogwarts, while Draco Malfoy has married, reproduced, and seemingly continues to have a relationship, though strained, with Harry, Ron, Hermione, and Ginny.

Therefore, the series closes with the economy of social relationships, and this brings us back once again to *Anti-Oedipus*. If Deleuze and Guatarri are correct about desiring-production, then the very vagaries encountered throughout the *Harry Potter* series can be understood as a form of potentiality that sidesteps the normal requirements of decorum and investment of interest (behaving well in the family, marrying a worthy spouse, having a meaningful career, and so on), although it does not cancel them. The best way to conclude with this point is to draw attention to both the rules and the continuous rule-breaking that occurs in all seven of the *Harry Potter* books. The formal rules and punishments are literally too numerous to mention, but a brief list should include the constant threats of expulsion, proscriptions of underage magic, tribunals for the trying of derelict witches, prisons like Azkaban for the incarceration of the worst offenders, and on and on. One of Hermione's primary plot functions, in fact, is to provide a source of fretting about the breaking of the rules, even though she often breaks them herself, though always with a high goal in mind, and never to be merely recalcitrant. In sum, there are scads of rules, and umpteen that are broken in the course of events.

Granted, the *Harry Potter* series is by no means a clarion-call for young readers to rebel against their elders and all sources of authority. In fact, there are many instances of rule-breaking and the repercussions that parents and teachers undoubtedly point out as beneficial for moral instruction. But the point is that the *Harry Potter* books embody no blanket statement on the nature of rules, which in fact is another argument that their outlook is postmodernist. This is not to say that the series takes no position on individual instances of rule-adherence or rule-breaking, but that there is *probably* no "meta-rule" on rules—and note that the word "probably" is important in this instance, for a blanket negation would itself be a meta-rule. Again, because the theme concerns alchemy, the question is whether all this rule-breaking somehow ties into the nuanced alchemical transformations that occur in the course of the series.

In fact, a fairly frequent instance in the entire series is the begrudging exception of normal punishment for rule-breaking—or sometimes even the perception of rule-breaking, as when Harry narrowly escapes expulsion from Hogwarts by barely prevailing in a vote of judges at the Ministry of Magic. In various other instances throughout the series, Harry and his chums sometimes are found out when they bend the rules, and sometimes not. Even when they are caught, the punishment is by no means consistent—in fact, it is occasionally rewarded, as in the case of Harry being made the Seeker of the Gryffindor Quidditch team after a fight with Draco Malfoy. Moreover, the argument that there is simply no "rule for rules" is in keeping with the notion that alchemy is best interpreted in the *Harry Potter* world as a free mechanism for social production rather than an inviolable law of nature, as would befit a more naturalistic application of the science of alchemy.

Finally, we may conclude that even attempting to create a rule for rules would be disruptive. In short, the way that the *Harry Potter* universe handles the topic of morality is consistent with the manner in which the physical manifestations of alchemy are handled: as manifestations that may become self-contradictory if they are held as eternal and inviolable concepts. This is not an undermining of alchemy so much as a qualification, but one that fits well with a postmodern outlook.

Harry Potter fits into the postmodern world of the arts at least in part because of how the series portrays alchemy. I do not claim it to be a postmodern novel that tests or questions all statements of principle, because an analysis of the recurring theme of diversity and tolerance might reveal a fairly traditional and unoriginal moral argument, as might a consideration of the themes of bravery and loyalty. The same is true of certain instances of rule-manifestation. But recalling Dumbledore's advice in the first book that one should not get caught up in desperate dreams of mingled joy and sadness shown by the Mirror of Erised but instead should get on with the business of living (*Stone* 209; 214), it seems that the series in many ways confirms Chappell's aforementioned definition of the postmodernist children's book.

In other words, the purpose of life is not necessarily to fill the shoes of the father, mother, or beloved teacher, but rather to get on with life—a tautology if there ever was one. Therefore, we may advantageously read the alchemy of Harry Potter in Jungian terms because of the insubstantiality of the alchemist's works, but we should not stop with Jung. A Philosopher's Stone may have vast applications for achieving power and wealth, but ultimately it is no more and no less than a pathway that leads to the securing of one's most natural desires. One indeed may use an available magic stone to achieve a good result. But after doing so, one is at liberty simply to kick the stone aside in the forest.

Works Cited

Buchanan, Ian. *Deleuze and Guattari's 'Anti-Oedipus.'* Continuum, 2008.
Chappell, Drew. "Sneaking Out After Dark: Resistance, Agency, and the Postmodern Child in JK Rowling's Harry Potter Series." *Children's Literature in Education*, vol. 39, issue 4, 2008, pp. 281–293. doi:10.1007/s10583-007-9060-6. Accessed 25 Feb. 2015.
Deleuze, Gilles, and Felix Guattari. *Anti-Oedipus: Capitalism and Schizophrenia*. Translated by Robert Hurley, et al., Penguin, 1977.
Hauck, Dennis William. *Sorcerer's Stone: A Beginner's Guide to Alchemy*. Citadel, 2004.
Jung, Carl G. *Alchemical Studies*. Translated by R.F.C. Hull, Princeton UP, 1967.
———. *Mysterium Coniunctionis: An Inquiry Into the Separation and Synthesis of Psychic Opposites in Alchemy*. Translated by R.F.C. Hull, 2nd ed., Princeton UP, 1970.
Marx, Karl. *Capital: A Critique of Political Economy*. Translated by Ben Fowkes, vol. 1, Penguin, 1990.
Moran, Bruce T. *Distilling Knowledge: Alchemy, Chemistry, and the Scientific Revolution*. Harvard UP, 2005.
Rowling, J.K. *Harry Potter and the Deathly Hallows*. Scholastic, 2007.
———. *Harry Potter and the Goblet of Fire*. Scholastic, 2000.
———. *Harry Potter and the Sorcerer's Stone*. Scholastic, 1997.

II

The Elder Wand and the Transfiguration of Power

My Harry Potter Journey

Ella Victoria Greer, age 13

I first read the Harry Potter series in sixth grade. I was eleven years old, just old enough to be enrolled in Hogwarts. My friend Claire had been pestering me for years to read this series of books that I thought was for old people just because my grandmother read it. I confess, Claire may have told me it had magic and wizardry in it (which I love), but in my stubbornness I refused to listen to anything she had to say on the matter. Eventually I ran out of "Excuse Books," books that I used to explain why I wasn't reading Harry Potter. I'm pretty sure that I borrowed the first book from the local library. I fell instantly in love. To this day Claire will never let me live it down. That year, for Christmas, I opened a big gift bag to find the whole Harry Potter series, just for me. I almost forgot the rest of the presents entirely.

Have you ever had a book trigger? I read Harry Potter mostly in the wintertime. I remember that Christmas I also had been given a rice-bag dog with a lavender scent. Every night I would heat up that dog, climb into bed, and read Harry Potter until the wee hours when my parents would see the light seeping underneath the crack of my door and order me to go to sleep at last. Now, every time I heat up my rice-bag dog, I get hit by a wave of nostalgia, and get the strongest urge to get lost in the land of witchcraft, wizardry, and beyond.

In *Harry Potter and the Philosopher's Stone* in the first Potions class, "'Potter,' Snape said suddenly. 'What would I get if I added powdered root of asphodel to an infusion of wormwood?'" (137). I was curious enough about this phrase to look it up on the website, www.bustle.com, "The Heartbreaking Truth Behind Snape's First Words." It turns out, asphodel, in the Victorian flower language, means "lily," or "my regrets follow you to the grave." Wormwood, also, means "absence," or symbolizes bitter sorrow. If you put it together, Snape's first few words to Harry were actually reaching out to him by saying, "I bitterly regret Lily's death." Harry just didn't know enough to understand it. Sadly, Harry will never know, truly, what his stingy Potions teacher (or suspected ex-Death Eater) was trying to imply to him.

Harry Potter has absolutely transformed my life with the charming characters (even the not-so-charming ones), the mystery, and the magic. I went from sort-of liking books to absolutely loving books and everything to do with them beyond all measure. I prefer fantasy, fiction, and sci-fi. Occasionally I also like realistic fiction because I can truly relate it to my life. Ever since *Harry Potter*, I have been going on a constant adventure in reading *and* in real life. I've been finding newer, better books, optically tasting new things, smelling new smells, seeing things that had never been dreamed of (except by the author of course— ;^]). That's why I have decided to be the world's next great author! Of course I'm never going to be as good as the legends, J.K. Rowling, E.B. White, Lewis Carroll, J.R.R. Tolkien, but I do aspire to write thick novels wrapped in whimsy and mystery, and it all started from my maiden voyage into *Harry Potter and the Sorcerer's Stone*.

These, I sincerely think, are some of the greatest things that have happened to me. If my life were a book, I would have no idea what it would be titled, but it would be along the lines of: *A Little of This, and a Bit of That … Plus Some More Books*. Many things have happened in my short thirteen years of life, but nothing so wonderful and *adventurous* as those in the wizarding world of *Harry Potter*.

P.S. If you're looking for new books to read, don't snoop around in the restricted area of the Hogwarts library, just ask your own personal Claire.

The Missing Element
The Alchemy Experiment Inside the Chamber of Secrets

S.P. ŞIPAL

For the contemporary reader, images of alchemy often involve a mad scientist conducting arcane experiments in a medieval laboratory to transform lead into gold, often for greedy purposes. However, for the alchemists of yore, the practice held an inner secret that was essentially spiritual. The idea underpinning the Great Work (the experimental process of creating the Philosopher's Stone) was that the sacred, whether conceptualized as the power of God or as the sanctified in nature, could be found outside of a consecrated holy building and inside a person, indeed in all of creation. As alchemists worked their experiments to transmute metals, the Great Work transfigured each of them in turn. Truly, the adept alchemist cared not so much for the materialistic pursuit of turning lead into gold but rather for the ennobling quest to transmute their own base nature into something divine. By seeking their own quintessence, the fifth, or sacred, element which represented the purest essence of the metal or person, they believed they would produce the Philosopher's Stone in their own lives and become spiritually immortal.

Azoth of the Philosophers, a seventeenth-century alchemical manuscript attributed to German alchemist Basil Valentine, shows a plate depicting the seven stages of the Great Work: calcination, dissolution, separation, conjunction, fermentation, distillation, and coagulation. According to Dennis William Hauck, author of *The Emerald Tablet*, this meditative medallion was used to guide the alchemist through each succeeding experiment as he or she sought to reveal this inner spirit (182–83). Each experiment sought the same goal, the refinement of the base material, *prima materia*, into something higher, a more pure metal, a nobler spirit, which was part of the whole all along. Thus from lead, if one would keep applying similar process of heat, distillation, and refinement, one could achieve the final most noble element of all: Gold. Gold of the physical metal. And Gold of the alchemist's own spiritual illumination.*

In J.K. Rowling's alchemical experiment of seven stages performed over the seven books of the Harry Potter series, this transformation from lead into gold takes place within Harry himself. Following the seven steps of alchemy, each book of the series represents an experiment to refine Harry and reveal the inner divinity that has resided within him all along. Harry must undergo this often painful transformation to prepare him to face and defeat the man, the shadow, who represents the epitome of evil. Yet Voldemort does not have a corner on evil any more than Harry is a solitary hero. Harry's battle with the Tom Riddle hidden in the diary in *Chamber of Secrets* also reveals a shadow in himself, not only as the seventh and unintentional Horcrux, but as a fallible human being, like Rowling's readers, like all people. Harry's confrontation with Tom's diary is as much an inward journey of transformation as it is an outward one.

Rowling wrapped this alchemical journey of transformation within the trappings of a genre mystery ... one with many threads. Some questions were solved by the end of a particular book. Was Sirius out to kill Harry in *Prisoner of Azkaban*? Why was Dumbledore avoiding Harry throughout *Order of the Phoenix*? Other questions lingered from one book to the next. What exactly happened that Halloween night so long ago in Godric's Hollow? Whose side was Snape truly on? Among this strung-out trail-of-clues, the longest and most important is: how would Harry, a young, inexperienced boy, defeat the most feared and skilled dark wizard of the century? And the key to unlocking this mystery was presented for the first time in *Chamber of Secrets*. In the form of a book.

Riddle's seemingly blank diary gives Harry his first glimpse of young Tom Riddle, an important process for understanding the man. When Harry destroys the diary, neither he nor the reader yet knows that the diary once held "a fragment of Voldemort's soul" (*Hallows* 686). Nor do the reader or Harry fully comprehend how Voldemort has sacrificed his humanity for a baser cause: immortality through terror, violence, and murder. Yet this private diary unlocks secrets of Lord Voldemort which will be the key for Harry's later understanding of the man and for his quest to destroy the Horcruxes.

---

*The pillars are well documented throughout history. Known as the Pillars of Hermes, they were later brought together and moved to a third temple. According to Hauck, Herodotus said: "One pillar was of pure gold, ... and the other was as of emerald, which glowed at night with great brilliancy" (Hauck, *Emerald* 344). On his website, Hauck adds, "In *Iamblichus: On the Mysteries*, Thomas Taylor quotes an ancient author who says the Pillars of Hermes dated to before the Great Flood and were found in caverns not far from Thebes. The mysterious pillars are also described by Achilles Tatius, Dio Chrysostom, Laërtius, and other Roman and Greek historians" ("AZoth Ritual").

This quest Harry embarks on is quite alchemical. Harry enters the Chamber of Secrets to sacrifice himself to a noble cause: saving the life of Ginny Weasley. Without conscious awareness, he enters a metaphorical sealed alembic—an alchemical vessel used for distillation. Inside this alembic, Harry experiences a transformation which allows him to defeat Voldemort for the third time ... and to dissolve the first Horcrux. The as-yet-unnamed Horcrux is the key not only to defeating Voldemort but also to understanding one of the most important underlying themes of the whole series: transformation of self.

Seeking Inspiration from the Ancient Home of Alchemy

To understand how Rowling contrasts this theme of transformation from Harry's growth to Voldemort's decline, it might be helpful first to explore her development of the Horcrux. Rowling hid a sly clue of its origins in the name itself, Horcrux. The first Horcrux is fully revealed, and destroyed, in the Chamber of Secrets. Earlier in the story, Ron says that the Chamber "rings a sort of bell," and it "might've been Bill" who mentioned it. Might've been Bill (145)? Bill ... his brother who was a curse breaker in Egypt (*Azkaban* 8)? This subtle nod in the direction of Egypt, the reputed home of alchemy, tells the reader where to search to unwrap Rowling's cunning linguistics in naming the receptacle for fragments of Voldemort's soul. A wizard skilled in breaking Egyptian curses would come in quite handy, for it is in ancient Egypt where we find hints of the Horcrux' namesake in the falcon-headed god, Horus.

Like many deities who existed over millennia, Horus is a god of many and often seemingly contradictory identities. In early development, he is known as Horus the elder, a brother of Osiris, god of the afterlife and rebirth, who fought as an adult god against Seth, god of chaos, disorder, and violence. In later myths, Horus becomes Horus the younger, the son of Isis and Osiris. When Seth murders Osiris and cuts his body into pieces, scattering them across Egypt, it is Isis, the goddess of magic and wisdom, and later her son Horus, who seek vengeance on Seth and to regain Horus' rightful rule.

During this fight, Horus loses an eye (sometimes both), which is then restored to him by Thoth, the god of magic and wisdom. Horus' restored eye became one of the most powerful, protective amulets, prized through the centuries and even transported across countries (and it bears a strong resemblance to Mad-Eye Moody's mad eye!). Both Osiris and Horus were considered the spiritual embodiments of the Pharaohs—Osiris of the deceased Pharaoh and Horus of the living. Horus was thus the resurrected soul of Osiris.

This association with resurrection was even codified in the hieroglyphs. While many Egyptian deities were depicted carrying the Ankh—the hieroglyph for eternal life—it was commonly associated with Isis, Osiris, and their son, Horus. Shaped like a cross with a loop on top, the Ankh resembles a key and was often referred to as the key of life. Some early Egyptologists, such as Flinders Petrie, called it the Horus cross (*Ancient Egypt* 98). It seems likely, then, that this Ankh, this Cross of Horus, is the etymological source for the Horcrux—Hor from Horus and crux from cross in the Latin.

Horus played an important role in the embalming process, during which the organs that were removed from the mummy were stored in four canopic jars depicted with gods who were referred to as the "sons of Horus" (Gahlin 32–33). It was the job of these four minor deities to protect the internal organs of the deceased Pharaoh during the journey through the underworld, and the most important ritual of the weighing of the heart against the feather of Maat, until they could be gathered back into his living body in the afterlife. Thus the sons of Horus guarded parts of the Pharaoh's body that ensured eternal life—much as Voldemort is depending on his Horcruxes to do for him. However, while the sons of Horus protected parts of the deceased Pharaoh on his righteous journey to resurrection, Voldemort's Horcruxes are meant to keep him forever from tasting death. And his heart has been so weighed down with evil that it is shown in Harry's King's Cross vision as a pitiful, maimed creature who will never know rebirth (*Hallows* 708).

Legends of Thoth

The Horcrux is not the only symbol of the power of alchemical transformation within Rowling's Chamber of Secrets. There is a nod to the legendary founder, Thoth, himself. The most learned of all the gods, Thoth provided Horus with the key knowledge and magic to defeat Seth and restore Horus' rightful rule. Often portrayed with an ibis head (a heron-like bird with a crescent beak) or as a baboon, Thoth was associated with wisdom, learning, and magic. The ancient alchemists considered him their founder. While Thoth is credited with inventing astronomy, geometry, medicine, and music, he is best known for inventing writing, and was called "the scribe of the gods" and "the lord of books" (Doty 4).

According to legend, he authored *The Emerald Tablet*, the most sacred text of alchemy, and the famous *Book of the Dead*, which was a guidebook of spells to help the deceased pass through the dangers of the underworld and attain eternal life (Budge 3). Thoth "succeeded in understanding the mysteries of the heavens [and] revealed them by inscribing them in sacred books which he then hid here on earth, intending that they should be searched for by future generations but found only by the fully worthy"—a task reminiscent of the alchemists' quest to share their knowledge with other adepts while also hiding their secrets from those not worthy (Fowden 33). All of Thoth's books were later hidden. According to varying legends, the hiding places included a golden box that was buried in a tomb, or a secret chamber, an inner sanctuary of a temple, or, according to another version, in the twin pillars at Heliopolis and Thebes.*

In one of the legends of the book of Thoth, Setna, a son of Ramses, goes searching in an ancient tomb for the sacred book, already a thing of legend in his time. In the tomb of a long-dead prince, Setna discovers not only the book but the prince and his deceased royal family guarding their treasure. During his lifetime, Prince Naneferkaptah, who was also a scribe and magician, found the book buried at the bottom of the Nile, hidden within a series of seven nested, locked boxes, each one increasing in alchemical value from iron to gold (perhaps inspiring Mad-Eye Moody's trunk), and guarded by all types of dangerous creatures. The last and most deadly of these magical beasts was a deathless, invincible serpent who changed form, growing deadlier with each strike against it ... very Voldemort-like. Naneferkaptah defeated the serpent and claimed the book as his own by dissolving the rewritten text in beer and drinking it down, an action which brought about Thoth's wrath and resulted in the death of his family and their separated burials in far-apart tombs.

Now, to steal the book from the dead, Setna must battle against both the deceased prince in a board game of chance (as in *Sorcerer's Stone*) as well as the kas (the souls in human form) of Naneferkaptah's wife and son, who serve as living memories. Setna triumphs and steals the book but suffers the calamities Naneferkaptah and his wife had foretold. In understanding of, and remorse at, what he has done, he returns his prize and restores the deceased prince's loved ones into the same tomb, thus redeeming himself with Thoth and perhaps mirroring Dumbledore's words to Harry at the end of *Sorcerer's Stone*. The one worthy to claim the Stone is the one who seeks to find but not use the treasure (300).

---

*Translated from an ancient scroll of papyrus (housed in the Cairo Museum), by the eminent Egyptologist W.M. Flinders Petrie in *Egyptian Tales*, pp. 87–141.

The Missing Element (Şipal)

Truly the secret knowledge of the hidden Thothian texts is very old magic. Of the various translations of *The Emerald Tablet* that have come down through the centuries, two are notable to Harry Potter fans: one by Dr. John Everard in 1650 and one by H.P. Blavatsky, author of the late nineteenth-century *Isis Unveiled*. Maybe not coincidentally, there are an Everard and a Vablatsky in Rowling's series. Everard is one of the old headmaster portraits who goes to check on Mr. Weasley when he is bitten by the snake (*Phoenix* 414). Cassandra Vablatsky is the author of Harry's third-year Divination book, *Unfogging the Future* (*Azkaban* 53). With such references, Rowling demonstrates that her research into alchemy likely also included intense study of its origins in ancient Egypt and its legendary founder, the wise god Thoth.

The Greeks knew Thoth as Hermes, then in an amalgamation of Hermes and Thoth as Hermes Trismegistus (Hermes the Thrice-Greatest). Hermes Trismegistus is the legendary author of the *Hermetica*, Egyptian-Greek wisdom texts that included teachings on alchemy, of which *The Emerald Tablet* is a part. Much later, Medieval and Renaissance alchemists revered *The Emerald Tablet* as the guide to create the Philosopher's Stone. Its message is presented in seven rubrics, each of which advances the practitioner's spiritual transformation. For some alchemists, like Basil Valentine, these seven rubrics are interpreted as seven steps in alchemical experimentation. For Rowling, each of those steps corresponds to a year of Harry's growth at Hogwarts.

> Level 1: Calcination is the heating of a substance over flame until it turns to ash. Harry passes through flames to face Quirrell-Voldemort, and it is his touch that burns Quirrell to death, and visually to ash in the film.
> Level 2: Dissolution dissolves the ash from level 1 in a liquid solution. In *Chamber*, Harry enters the watery, cavernous room deep underground, where the acidic poison of the basilisk dissolves him.
> Level 3: Separation takes the dissolved solution and separates out the impurities. In *Azkaban*, Harry is separated from friends and family as the escape of Sirius Black threatens his safety and haunts his thoughts of the parents he can't remember.
> Level 4: Conjunction brings the purified forms of the desired elements together into a new union. It is in *Goblet* that Harry's heart first feels the call of the opposite sex, and the union of opposites is celebrated with the Yule Ball. Voldemort has a body reborn of the union of his father's bone with Harry's blood.

Level 5: Fermentation brings new life into the conjoined union. However, death is always a part of fermentation; the alchemists refer to this as putrefaction. Harry not only loses his newfound substitute father, Sirius, but his old relationship with Dumbledore dies in *Phoenix*, to be reborn at the end into something more mature.

Level 6: Distillation boils down and condenses the solution to purify it even further while releasing and then collecting its essential vapors. The silvery memories through which Harry and Dumbledore peer in the Pensieve to understand Tom Riddle "swirled and shimmered, neither liquid nor gas" and are the beginning of condensation (*Prince* 199). Together, Harry and Dumbledore must sort through these condensed memories to understand the essence of the Dark Lord.

Level 7: Coagulation unites the fermented new life of the fifth stage with the spiritual essence of the sixth to give birth to the noble substance, the Stone. Hallows and Horcruxes come together and Harry must choose his path, which he does nobly. He sacrifices himself and is reborn. Along with his resurrection, Harry saves his community. He is a true Philosopher's Stone.

Step One: Calcination

In the first step of Rowling's Great Work, in the underground chamber at the end of *Sorcerer's Stone*, Harry and Hermione (the feminine name for Hermes) face fire as they attempt to rescue the Stone. Hermione solves Snape's puzzle, revealing which potion she must drink to allow her to return to revive Ron and seek Dumbledore. She hands Harry the potion that will enable him to pass through the flames, where he finds Voldemort and his host, Professor Quirrell, attempting to steal the Stone. Quirrell tries to kill Harry but cannot touch him without suffering fatal burns, precisely because Harry's mother's love lives in his "very skin" (*Stone* 299). When Quirrell tries to hold Harry down, the flesh of his hands is burned beyond endurance. To protect himself from Quirrell's impending curse, Harry simply "grabbed Quirrell's face—" (*Stone* 295). The embers of his mother's love that burn within Harry tortuously blister the professor who harbors Voldemort.

Quirrell is burned away through the power of alchemical calcination. Though the blistering fire of Quirrell's touch nearly kills Harry, he survives, transformed and strengthened, because he sought to "find ... but not use" the Stone (300). He descended into the underground chamber and found something of the quintessence in himself, like seeking wisdom from Thoth's books in their subterranean hiding places.

Throughout Harry's first year and book, he and the reader are merely introduced to Lord Voldemort. We find out that He-Who-Must-Not-Be-Named killed Harry's parents and was thus "killed" himself. However, why or how this happened remained a mystery. Those clues start in the Chamber of Secrets with the second alchemical step.

Step Two: Dissolution

In dissolution, the ash resulting from the first experiment must be dissolved in a solution for its internal essence to be released. The material is put into a retort or an alembic and an acidic solution added. Heat and pressure are used to refine it further. Exactly how this was done, and which solution added, varied from alchemist to alchemist. They all, however, involved heating the substance in liquid.

Water flows freely throughout *Chamber of Secrets*, from the water Moaning Myrtle splashes continuously inside her bathroom to the water pipes which the basilisk uses to move about the castle. In their coded texts, alchemists frequently illustrated their dissolution ingredients and processes with images associated with water and dissolving, including people in baths (as Myrtle highlights), but also poisonous toads, basilisks, and tears (Hauck "AZoth Ritual"). Thus Neville's toad, Trevor, continually hops away, drawing the reader's attention, Hagrid's rooster is killed as a hint about Slytherin's basilisk, as the crow of a rooster is fatal to the beast, and, finally, the water of Fawkes' tears heals Harry's dissolution.

In the spiritual understanding of alchemy, dissolution is where the alchemist's world is broken down and the transformation gets more internal (Hauck, *Stone* 189). Throughout his second year, Harry's world is torn apart, and everything he gained from the first seems lost. The support and respect he has earned from many of the students and staff in his first year falters when it is revealed in the duel with Draco that Harry is a Parselmouth. Some look at him with doubt or distrust, and a few assume he is the Heir of Slytherin.

Not only is Harry's social world collapsing, but the structures and mentors that surround him are as well. Fudge, in the first shown corrupt act of the Ministry, arrests Hagrid and sends him to Azkaban, with no supporting evidence. At the same time, Lucius Malfoy, through apparent blackmail and bribes of the school governors, has Dumbledore removed from Hogwarts. And the teacher who is supposed to prepare them to face danger through Defense Against the Dark Arts is revealed as a complete fraud.

After Hermione's Petrification deprives them of her direct guidance, Harry and Ron follow her last clue in the note she clutches and seek the Chamber to rescue Ginny from the Heir of Slytherin—with the somewhat dubious help of Lockhart. As they slip down the passage from Moaning Myrtle's bathroom, they describe the wet, underground chamber. "'We must be miles under the school,' said Harry, his voice echoing in the black tunnel. 'Under the lake, probably,' said Ron, squinting around at the dark, slimy walls" (*Chamber* 302).

At the sight of the basilisk's giant shed skin, Lockhart's attempt to hex Harry and Ron backfires and a rock fall separates the two boys. Harry must go it completely alone. Entering the chamber in its forbidding half light, Harry saw "towering stone pillars entwined with more carved serpents [rise] to support a ceiling lost in darkness.... [He] had to crane his neck to look up into the giant face above: It was ancient and monkeyish" (306–07).

The parallels between Thoth's secret chamber and Rowling's are quite striking: a secret hideaway underground (even under a large body of water) that strongly resembles a temple with towering pillars, housing a god-like statue, protecting a book of secret knowledge with a memory come to life, and guarded by a fearsome, invincible snake (and a snake-like villain who changes form with each "death"). Ancient Egypt is well known for its worship of the serpent, especially in the cult of Thoth. According to Claudius Aelian, a second–third century Roman naturalist, basilisks were kept in Egyptian temples, and whoever they happened to bite were divinely favored (*Ophiolatreia*). As we are about to explore, Harry was thus blessed.

That "ancient and monkeyish" statue, whom Tom Riddle later addresses as Salazar Slytherin, could be inspired by Thoth, who was often associated with monkeys. At the temple of Thoth in Hermopolis, several colossal statues of baboons stood guard. Perhaps Rowling designed Slytherin's statute as a tribute to the father of alchemy. It is fitting, then, that the alchemical experiment for this second book be performed in his secret chamber under his very nose. Young Tom calls to the statue in Parseltongue: "Speak to me, Slytherin, greatest of the Hogwarts Four" (317).

The serpent spilling out of Slytherin's mouth is compelled by dark magic, unlike what we would expect from Thoth. Except Rowling plays a long game. In ancient Egypt, Thoth equipped Isis with words of power to resurrect her dead husband, Osiris, and later her son, Horus. In *Harry Potter and the Deathly Hallows*, Slytherin's long-dead basilisk provides the necessary magic to save Harry's life. When Ron and Hermione return to the Chamber of Secrets during the Battle of Hogwarts, they retrieve fangs from the dead basilisk to kill one of Voldemort's Horcruxes. As Hagrid has so painstakingly shown throughout the course of the series, deadly beasts are not evil in their nature, but rather reflect the witch or wizard who manipulates their powers. Channeling the powers of the basilisk, Hermione and Ron use Voldemort's own magic to bring about his defeat and ensure that Harry, in his final and most powerful resurrected form, survives their final battle.

Even within the Chamber, the serpent offers the promise of resurrection. Each serpent-entwined pillar lining the chamber is actually a gigantic caduceus, the staff of Thoth and Hermes. According to legend, upon encountering two serpents trying to devour each other, Hermes threw his wand between them. The serpents entwined about it reach toward the top, toward a winged solar orb (sometimes a bird, symbolic of the bennu or phoenix). As they seek to devour the bird, the serpents strive toward a higher awareness, represented by the winged orb as the flight of the spirit, the eternal life of the phoenix (Hauck, *Stone* 456). In Hermeticism, the philosophical and spiritual practice based on the writing of the Hermes Trismegistus discussed earlier, the entwining snakes of the caduceus are understood to balance basic opposing forces, good and evil—and in alchemy, solar and lunar, or male and female. The alchemical union of the two snakes results in the birth of the Philosopher's Stone "represented as a golden ball with wings at the top of the caduceus" (Hauck, *Stone* 247).

In Harry's first Quidditch practice, Oliver Wood shows Harry the Golden Snitch: a "tiny [ball], about the size of a large walnut. It was bright gold and had little fluttering silver wings" (*Stone* 169). The solar orb at the top of the caduceus is golden in color. And those silver wings on Rowling's Snitch could be an homage to Mercury who also carries the caduceus and whose element, mercury, is also silver. In other words, the Snitch is the head of the caduceus brought to life, which makes it very fitting that Harry is the Seeker, the player whose job it is to chase and catch the little, winged ball. At the end of *Hallows*, after Harry casts the final disarming charm at Voldemort, his ultimate Seeker role is fulfilled: "And Harry, with the unerring skill of the Seeker, caught the wand in his free hand as Voldemort fell backward, arms splayed, the slit pupils of the scarlet eyes rolling upward" (744). Seeker Harry has caught the final Snitch that returns peace to the Wizarding World.

Into the Alembic: Unsealing the Chamber

In addition to transforming them into powerful magicians, the original Thoth book of secrets enabled readers to know the language of animals, gain knowledge of the universe, and be granted immortality. In Rowling's Chamber of Secrets, the knowledge in the second experiment, in the dissolution, also comes by way of a secret book, Tom Riddle's diary literally come to life. Riddle emerges from his diary, a shadowy figure, drawing life from the one who poured her heart out to him: Ginny Weasley. Sucking out and corrupting the hopes and desires of others is a skill the parasitic Dark Lord will perfect in his later years. Young Tom Riddle may have started his quest in the Dark Arts here in Rowling's secret chamber, studying and practicing the forbidden knowledge of the Horcrux to make himself immortal.

The revelations from the diary are not about the sum of universal wisdom, as they are in the books of Thoth. Instead, Riddle's diary exposes the more personal secrets of how Tom Riddle became Lord Voldemort. It shows how Riddle possessed the skill to charm the people he needed, like little Ginny Weasley, and as we later learn, Hepzibah Smith and Helena Ravenclaw. And most importantly, it shows how even the shadow of young Tom Riddle is quite obsessed with how Harry Potter, a seeming nobody, might defeat the most powerful dark wizard since Grindelwald.

Entering the Chamber of Secrets, Harry first deliberately uses his ability to speak and understand Parseltongue, gains knowledge of Riddle's life through the diary, and suffers a death and resurrection experience through the Basilisk-and-Phoenix caduceus. Although Harry had intuitively spoken in Parseltongue to the snake in the zoo in *Sorcerer's Stone* and called the snake off Justin during the duel earlier in *Chamber of Secrets*, it is breaking into the tunnel and unsealing the Chamber itself where he deliberately uses this "dark magic" to save Ginny. Opening the dark magic chamber requires him to unseal a hidden, dark corner within himself as well. One that will introduce him to his Shadow. As the last in a long line of Slytherin descendants, Riddle has rested secure in the belief that no one but himself would be able to access the Chamber. But by marking Harry as an infant, he had unwittingly given to another the power to open the Chamber of Secrets, find the secrets within, and, thus, ultimately vanquish him by use of his own magic, profoundly transfigured.

In the final moments of Voldemort's life, Harry tries to give Riddle back his magic, transformed, when he says he knows things Riddle does not, including that love is the most powerful magic and that he, Harry, understands how the Elder Wand has, for the moment, given him its allegiance. In the final fight with the Basilisk in the Chamber, Harry demonstrates the skills and instinct of the Seeker to thrust the fang through the diary. His skill and instinct come to fruition in *Hallows*, finally to claim the wand "spinning through the air toward the master it would not kill, who had come to take full possession of it at last" (*Hallows* 743–44). It is worth noting that young Tom's eyes gleam red, not gold, when he and Harry face off in the Chamber (*Chamber* 313). In the final moments of his life in the Great Hall, Riddle's "red eyes stared" tauntingly at Harry (*Hallows* 737).

Red is the last stage of development before the final gold of the

Philosopher's Stone (Hauck, *Stone* 106). At the moment before Voldemort hurls his Killing Curse and Harry his Disarming Charm, "[a] red-gold blur burst suddenly across the enchanted sky above them." And when the spells collide, "golden flames ... erupted between them" (*Hallows* 743). Voldemort is not yet fully immortal. Because he refuses to undergo the dissolution and reconstitution begun in the Chamber, refuses to learn the alchemical lessons that might move him from red to gold, he dies diminished, less than human. The opposite of Harry, Tom sought immortality to live forever. As we learn in the first book, he wants the Philosopher's Stone in order to use it. Harry, however, seeks what the Philosopher's Stone represents, knowledge and transformation of the self, in order to save others.

Inspiration from *Splendor Solis*

Rowling's Chamber-alembic is filled with symbols of alchemy that tell the story of the Great Work within. Ancient alchemists guarded their secrets well, hiding their ingredients and steps behind coded words and fanciful imagery. Like the adepts who came before her, Rowling camouflages her secrets with subtext and metaphors for the discovery of readers "if you've got your wits about you" (*Accio Quote*). To decode some of the symbolism inside Rowling's creation, it might be useful first to consider a beautiful depiction from an ancient alchemist. One of the best known texts illustrating the Great Work is the *Splendor Solis*, a sixteenth-century illuminated manuscript. The image in *Splendor Solis* for the dissolution stage plays out symbolically across Rowling's pages.

In the illustrated alembic are three birds—white, red, and black—possibly representing alchemy's three primary elements: salt, sulfur, and mercury. The red and white birds are pecking away at the black, the salt, representing the corporal body of the *prima materia*. Overhead, peacocks pull the carriage of Jupiter. And surrounding the alembic are scenes of a coronation, of a scribe with a manuscript, and a couple of men working a still. Perhaps Rowling's biggest nod to the *Splendor Solis* involves the peacock pulling Jupiter's coach. When Fawkes enters the Chamber, Harry likens his tail to a peacock's. "A crimson bird the size of a swan had appeared, piping its weird music to the vaulted ceiling. It had a glittering golden tail as long as a peacock's..." (*Chamber* 315). Alchemists speak of the appearance of the peacock's tail as a moment of great significance. What they mean is that an iridescent, oily color surfaces on the solution within their flask (Hauck, "AZoth Ritual"). Its appearance is a sign of a significant accomplishment and transition, as Fawkes' appearance is for Harry.

130 II—The Elder Wand and the Transfiguration of Power

Harry first meets Fawkes earlier in the book, when Dumbledore says to Harry, "It's a shame you had to see him on a burning day" (*Chamber* 207). Not only is Harry young in his alchemical journey, but the newborn Fawkes is too, just as the peacock stage in alchemy comes before the phoenix stage at the end. As Fawkes is representative of the peacock, so too is Dumbledore linked to Jupiter, the king of the gods. Although Dumbledore is absent from the castle, his aide is sent ahead of his return.

Finding His Feminine

In addition to writing Fawkes, Rowling uses her superb skills with metaphor and subtext to bring in other important elements for the dissolution. In studying the *Splendor Solis* or any other alchemical text, the iconography of the masculine and the feminine is striking. Sometimes this union is represented as sexual. At other times, it is shown in the person of a hermaphrodite. But underlying it all is the alchemist's belief that the union of the masculine and feminine represents the joining of opposing natures, the harmonizing with one's repressed nature, thus achieving the state of balance and enlightenment that the twining snakes of the caduceus represent.

It is no coincidence that Rowling chooses Ginny Weasley to be taken into the chamber for Harry to rescue. Ginny has been teasing at his consciousness all year, with her obvious crush. But it is here, in the Chamber of Secrets, where her fate is first linked to his and commands his full attention. Ginny is the Lunar Queen to Harry's Sun King, she is the female to his male who will one day be both romantically and alchemically united. And it is in this second step of the Great Work that their alchemical dance begins.

Confronting His Shadow

However, before Harry will be free to fully join with his feminine nature, he must first face his shadow. The shadowy young Tom Riddle points out the striking resemblance between him and Harry: "Both half-bloods, orphans, raised by Muggles. Probably the only two Parselmouths to come to Hogwarts since the great Slytherin himself. We even look something alike..." (*Chamber* 317). Only through confronting and harmonizing with their shadow, the negative and repressed side, are alchemists able to find peace within themselves. How fitting it is, then, that in his internal

Opposite: Plate 13 from *Splendor Solis*, a 16th-century illuminated alchemical text representing dissolution and showing the three birds.

Chamber of Secrets, as part of his alchemical dissolution, Harry comes face to face with the person he is most afraid of becoming. He pleads with the Sorting Hat, "Not Slytherin, not Slytherin" (*Stone* 121). He meets Tom Riddle at an age close to his own, when the evidence for their disparate choices is first starting to transform their lives.

Later, Harry will internalize more and more of his Shadow's anger and even hatred, directed toward those who have harmed the people he loves. However, through fighting to transform these emotions to effect positive change, Harry's choices propel him on a transformative course that Riddle will never know, despite his thirst for immortality.

Absorbing the Poison

To begin the dissolution's transformative alchemical process, however, a corrosive must be applied to dissolve the substance and release its spirit. On his way to the Chamber, Harry steps "over a gigantic snake skin, of a vivid, poisonous green, lying curled and empty across the tunnel floor. The creature that had shed it must have been twenty feet long at least" (*Chamber* 303). Green is the color of the Green Lion of alchemy, the color of acidic vitriol. Alchemists believed that vitriol could break down any metal, including gold.

Upon entering the Chamber, Harry feels as if followed by the numerous gazes of the stone snakes entwining the pillars. Those gigantic stone serpents alarm and prepare Harry and the reader not only for the great basilisk soon to appear, but for the death and resurrection that the many caducei promise. In Rowling's sealed chamber, her alembic, Harry is stabbed with vitriol through the fang of the poisonous green basilisk, breaking him down. Convinced that he is dying, Harry tears the fang from his flesh. "Even as he dropped the fang and watched his own blood soaking his robes, his vision went foggy. The Chamber was *dissolving* in a whirl of dull color" (320; emphasis added).

Dissolving. The pains of dissolution. Of alchemical death.

Resurrecting Through Fawkes' Tears

However, Harry is not alone. Imagine the flight of Fawkes in the Chamber and how the positioning of bird and serpent is described in the battle with the basilisk: "The enormous serpent, bright, poisonous green, thick as an oak trunk, had raised itself high in the air and its great blunt head was weaving drunkenly between the pillars.... Fawkes was soaring around its head, and the basilisk was snapping furiously at him with fangs long and thin as sabers—" (318). Like a great caduceus come to life, the basilisk weaves drunkenly among the pillars, striking at the bird flying overhead.

Then, with the healing phoenix tears, Fawkes utilizes the life-giving powers of the caduceus to restore Harry to life. Resigned to death, Harry wonders, "But was this dying? Instead of going black, the Chamber seemed to be coming back into focus. Harry gave his head a little shake and there was Fawkes, still resting his head on Harry's arm. A pearly patch of tears was shining all around the wound—except that there *was* no wound—" (321).

Alchemists used an alembic for their experiments in order to catch the vapors released from the heated solution. These vapors were believed to be the purified forms, or spirits, from the elements heated below. And due to the shapes of these stills, they were often symbolized with bird imagery, such as pelicans, herons, and phoenixes. Flying high overhead, Fawkes performs the final act of Rowling's alchemical experiment. Acting as the collector of vapors from Harry's dissolution below, Fawkes channels this purified spirit through his tears back into Harry. Harry is resurrected via his own sacrifice, the essence of which has been collected and transformed inside the alchemical alembic of the phoenix.

Spilling the Ink

Like torn muscle that has healed, Harry is stronger than before. Wounded, he knows what to do:

> Then, without thinking, without considering, as though he had meant to do it all along, Harry seized the basilisk fang on the floor next to him and plunged it straight into the heart of the book.
> There was a long, dreadful, piercing scream. Ink spurted out of the diary in torrents, streaming over Harry's hands, flooding the floor. (322)

Harry has been dissolved and purified. With his new strength and instinctual insight, he acts. He stabs Riddle's diary, spilling the ink in black streams. The experiment done, the alembic's dirty waters are drained and the feminine is revived. Ginny awakes. Thus this stage of the alchemical process is complete.

Although a shadow, Tom Riddle's dark blood is symbolically spilled, Harry has drunk in the knowledge that his book contained. Over the next years, Harry's knowledge of Tom Riddle's life and choices will increase. His sixth-year journeys with Dumbledore into the memories of those who knew Tom Riddle personally will give Harry, Hermione, and Ron the information they need to hunt Horcruxes in *Deathly Hallows*.

The Missing Element

Alchemy is basically the same process repeated over and over, with slight alterations, to refine and purify an element progressively. In *Chamber of Secrets*, Rowling sets the pattern for the rest of the series to come. Each year there is a challenge presented that tears away at Harry. Each choice he makes as he confronts these trials defines him and refines him, until that final decision in the Great Hall battle of *Deathly Hallows*—the choice to cast *Expelliarmus* rather than *Avada Kedavra*, like his Shadow. And so, a question remains: why could Harry achieve this alchemical transformation and Voldemort not? After all, the Dark Lord is more skilled, more mature, more powerful, and the one most desirous of the promise of eternal life.

Alchemy was never an exact recipe anyone could follow. The Flamels, after all, possessed *"the only Stone currently in existence"* (*Stone* 220). If it were a simple matter of combining the best ingredients in the precise process, even Voldemort could have accomplished it. There was, however, something more, something infinitesimal, but something on which the whole Great Work balanced: the missing element.

As mentioned earlier, the Eye of Horus, torn from Horus in his battle with Seth, became a symbol of resurrection and held a powerful charm. The Eye was an apotropaic amulet that provided protection for its bearer; it would turn back any evil directed its way—much as Lily's charm did for Harry. Metaphorically speaking, Lily pinned an Eye of Horus on her

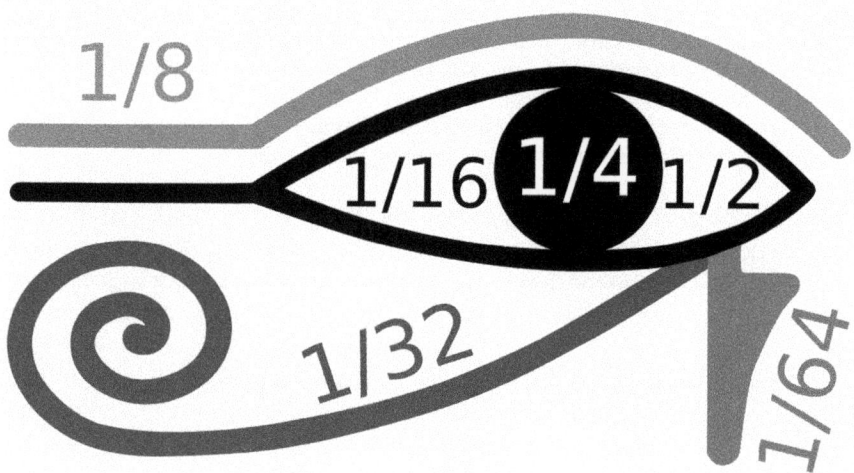

An illustration of the Eye of Horus fractions as derived from the ancient Egyptian *Rhind Mathematical Papyrus*.

beloved son, just as mothers in Turkey still do today (though they tend to pin a blue-eyed glass bead to their children's clothes rather than to their skin). Furthermore, it was long thought, though now academically disputed, that the symbols of the Eye of Horus served as an ancient mathematical calculator. Each stylized segment of the Eye was considered to be a fraction, that when added together equaled one. Here is an image that shows each part of the Eye with its fraction:

The six parts represented decreasing fractions progressively halved (½, ¼, ⅛, 1/16, 1/32, 1/64). Each of these Eye symbols also represented a sense that can be linked to one of Rowling's Horcruxes, as noted in the chart below. The six parts together embodied a whole, a complete—except that they total 63/64, missing one small fraction, 1/64, the seventh missing magical element ("Eye of Horus").

	Eye of Horus Part	**Sense It Represents**	**Corresponding Horcrux**	**Fraction**
1	Left side of eye (points to ear)	Hearing	Tom Riddle's voice (through his diary)	1/16
2	Teardrop	Touch	Peverell's ring	1/64
3	Pupil	Sight	Slytherin's locket	1/4
4	Sprout	Taste	Hufflepuff's cup	1/32
5	Eyebrow	Thought	Ravenclaw's diadem (wit beyond measure)	1/8
6	Right side of eye	Smell	Nagini	1/2
7				1/64 (missing)

Table 1 (Source: S.P. Şipal)

Among early twentieth-century Egyptologists, there was a secret meaning associated with this missing fraction (Robins 14). "The eye is the part of the body able to perceive light, and is therefore the symbol for spiritual ability" ("Eye of Horus"). The missing fraction of the eye represented a magical element supplied by Thoth, which cannot be quantified, but without which nothing, and no one, is complete ("Eye of Horus/Eye of Ra").

In *Harry Potter and the Half-Blood Prince*, Rowling left us two direct clues regarding this crucial, missing magical element: Golpalott's Third Law, a lesson in Slughorn's potions class; and *Quintessence: A Quest*, a book Harry reads to avoid Ron's grumblings against Hermione. To no one's surprise, "Hermione recited at top speed: 'Golpalott's-Third-Law-states-that-the-antidote-for-a-blended-poison-will-be-equal-to-more-than-the-sum-of-the-antidotes-for-each-of-the-separate-components.'"

Clarifying, Slughorn explains that the difficult task of determining antidotes, then, will be "to find that added component that will, by an almost alchemical process, transform these disparate elements—" (374–75).

This blink-and-you-miss-it exchange is a clever method for Rowling to drive home one of the central themes of her Great Work: the creation of the Philosopher's Stone requires the missing element, an intuitive, almost alchemical knowledge which the witch or wizard must master to create an antidote to a blended potion. The Half-Blood Prince was filled with this intuition for improving potions and creating spells. And, as Harry realizes in horror when he uses one of the Prince's Spells, Sectumsempra, on Draco to near fatal effect, this "added component" hints at the nature of the wizard who created it.

In alchemy, quintessence refers to the mystical fifth element. Earth, air, water, and fire are the traditional four elements which make up everything that exists. Rowling has confirmed that each Hogwarts House represents one of these elements: Earth = Hufflepuff, Air = Ravenclaw, Water = Slytherin, and Fire = Gryffindor (*Mugglenet*). Each of these elements is also represented in the Founders' corresponding Horcruxes, with Gryffindor's sword being the fiery item of destruction. In alchemy, the fifth element, quintessence, plays an even stronger role in the series, indeed *is* the embodiment of Harry's personal quest.

The Quintessence is the fifth element with which the alchemists could work. It was the

> essential presence of something or someone, the living thing itself that animated or gave something its deepest characteristics. The Quintessence partakes of both the Above and the Below, the mental as well as the material. It can be thought of as the ethereal embodiment of the life force that we encounter in dreams and altered states of consciousness. It is the purest individual essence of something that we must unveil and understand in order to transform it. (*Alchemy Lab*)

Essentially, quintessence is spirit, it is soul. Quintessence, for J.K. Rowling, is embodied in Harry. Voldemort didn't intend to make Harry a Horcrux. But he did. Harry *is* the surprise seventh Horcrux. He is the missing fifth element which Voldemort could not comprehend, and thus did not take into account in his quest to secure eternal life. Harry's noble nature and spiritual intuition, his heart, is what makes the Eye complete. Harry's love is what conquers Voldemort's dark magic.

We can now fill in the last line of our earlier Eye of Horus chart. That last line, the missing 1/64th, is love. The crucial alchemical element that Harry has in abundance, but Voldemort knows not at all.

	Eye of Horus Part	Sense It Represents	Corresponding Horcrux	Fraction
1	Left side of eye (points to ear)	Hearing	Tom Riddle's voice (through his diary)	1/16
2	Teardrop	Touch	Peverell's ring	1/64
3	Pupil	Sight	Slytherin's locket	1/4
4	Sprout	Taste	Hufflepuff's cup	1/32
5	Eyebrow	Thought	Ravenclaw's diadem (wit beyond measure)	1/8
6	Right side of eye	Smell	Nagini	1/2
7		Heart	Harry	1/64 (missing)

Table 2 (Source: S.P. Şipal)

On the Tail of the Phoenix

Devoid of love, Riddle will never soar on the tail of a phoenix with those he has saved. For love always involves a community. When Harry calls out for help in the Chamber, knowing he cannot survive alone, "Fawkes the phoenix ... swooped past Harry and was now fluttering in front of him, his beady eyes bright in the dark. He was waving his long golden tail feathers" (*Chamber* 325). After escaping the Chamber, Fawkes' alchemically golden tail feathers transport Harry, Ron, Ginny, and even Lockhart, who has betrayed them, upward through the pipes to rejoin their Hogwarts family. The sacrifice made, the community is restored.

Because Voldemort will never know, refuses to know, community, he will never achieve the eternal transformation Harry undergoes in his dissolution in the Chamber-alembic. Consistently choosing to sacrifice others so that he may live, Voldemort has shaped his soul into the denatured, repulsive object revealed in King's Cross. By contrast, Harry has sacrificed himself to save those he loves and has shaped his soul into something radiant. A radiance that merges with the rising sun at the moment of his final face-off with Riddle.

Although Harry faces his shadow by himself at the end of each book, he is never truly alone. Through the powerful love that he feels not only for his friends, but for a community that includes even his antagonists, Harry builds a magical network of support that comes to him in his time of need. Voldemort, on the other hand, the man who has no true friends, only people he uses, who never knows love, does not have this magical amulet at his disposal. His Horcruxes are his faux-friends, meant to serve only him. Once these faux-friends are gone, he has nothing left to sustain him. No remorse to make things right. No concept of the true magic of alchemy. It is Harry, a young wizard of lesser technical skill, who unites his true friends to defeat the darkest wizard of the century, precisely because he possesses an abundance of that missing mystery element.

Perhaps in the truest alchemy of this seven-book series, Rowling pours her reader into Harry's alembic along with him. Through the transformative power of a story told through myth and metaphor, her readers are provided the opportunity to turn themselves into their own Philosopher's Stone. Book by book, year after Hogwarts' year, they may experience their own alchemical journey and discover the hidden knowledge to defeat their own personal Voldemorts. However, the enlightenment of quintessence only arises from the steps that have come before. That transformation must involve dissolution, a breaking-down of self, of confronting one's own Shadow and fears. But for challenging oneself through this inner reflection, the reward of a real-life basilisk fang awaits. The knowledge and power to spill your problems and start anew.

Works Cited

Accio Quote. accio-quote.org/articles/2003/0626-alberthall-fry.htm. Accessed Apr. 2019.
Alchemy Lab. alchemylab.com/dictionary.htm. Accessed Apr. 2019.
Blavatsky, H.P. *Isis Unveiled*. J.W. Bouton, 1877.
Budge, E.A. Wallis. *The Book of the Dead*, translation of the Papyrus of Ani in the British Museum, 1895.
Doty, William G., editor. *World Mythology*. Barnes & Noble, 2002.
"The Eye of Horus." *San Graal*, sangraal.com/library/eyesofhorus.htm. Accessed Apr. 2019.
"Eye of Horus/Eye of Ra." *Ancient Egypt Online*, Ancientegyptonline.co.uk/eye.html. Accessed Apr. 2019.
Fowden, Garth. *The Egyptian Hermes*. Cambridge UP, 1987.
Gahlin, Lucia. *Egyptian Religion: The Beliefs of Ancient Egypt Explored and Explained*. Southwater, 2002.
Hauck, Dennis William. "The AZoth Ritual." *Azoth Alchemy*, 9 March 2008, azothalchemy.org/azoth_ritual.htm.
_____. *The Emerald Tablet*. Penguin, 1999.
_____. "A Hyper-History of the Emerald Table." *Alchemy Lab*, www.alchemylab.com/hyper_history.htm. Accessed Apr. 2019.
_____. *Sorcerer's Stone: A Beginner's Guide to Alchemy*. Citadel, 2004.
Jupiter (Les Trois Oiseaux). Plate 13 from *Splendor Solis*. upload.wikimedia.org/wikipedia/commons/d/d9/Splendor_Solis._Image_13_-_Jupiter_-_Les_trois_oiseaux.jpg. Accessed 20 Feb. 2019.
"New Interview with JK Rowling." *Mugglenet*, mugglenet.com/2008/03/new-interview-with-jk-rowling/. Accessed Apr. 2019.
Ophiolatreia, Chapter VII. *Internet Sacred Text Archives*, sacred-texts.com/etc/oph/oph07.htm. Accessed Apr. 2019.
Petrie, W.M. Flinders, editor. *Ancient Egypt: Part I*. Macmillan and Co. and British School of Archaeology in Egypt, 1916.
_____. *Egyptian Tales,* 2nd series. Methuen, 1913.
Robins, Gaye, and Charles Shute. *The Rhind Mathematical Papyrus: An Ancient Egyptian Text*. British Museum Press, 1987.

Rowling, J.K. *Harry Potter and the Chamber of Secrets*. Scholastic, 1999.
_____. *Harry Potter and the Deathly Hallows*. Scholastic, 2007.
_____. *Harry Potter and the Goblet of Fire*. Scholastic, 2000.
_____. *Harry Potter and the Half-Blood Prince*. Scholastic, 2005
_____. *Harry Potter and the Order of the Phoenix*. Bloomsbury, 2003.
_____. *Harry Potter and the Prisoner of Azkaban*. Scholastic, 1999.
_____. *Harry Potter and the Sorcerer's Stone*. Scholastic, 1997.
Stella, Benoît. *Eye of Horus Fractions*. s3.media.squarespace.com/production/434499/4823639/_IKrAmLHxEgc/RhpSMTK0qKI/AAAAAAAAAM/WDKfmkhizXE/s320/fraction_eye.jpg. Accessed 5 Feb. 2019.
Trismosin, Salomon. *Splendor Solis*. 1582.

On the Transmutation of Voldemort's Love of Power into Harry Potter's Power of Love

Lawrence W. Farris

The twentieth-century Trappist monk Thomas Merton is said to have been asked which of three monastic vows—of poverty, chastity, and obedience—was the most challenging to remain faithful to over a lifetime. Merton replied that the vow of poverty, having to do with one's relationship to material goods, was relatively easy, since most people seeking a deeper spiritual life easily recognize the need—and indeed desire—for greater simplicity through freedom from anxiety about material possessions. Chastity, he said, having to do with one's relationship to sexuality, was a greater challenge, but if pursued in a supportive community was not as difficult as might be supposed by those living outside a community that is not constantly focused on sexual issues. But obedience, having to do with one's relationship to power, that, Merton said, was a challenge that endured for a lifetime, and it rarely eased its demands.

How telling that in a time when issues surrounding materialism and sexuality loom large in social awareness, Joanne K. Rowling offers in her Harry Potter novels the villainous Lord Voldemort, obsessed not at all with the good things of life or sex, but with nothing but power—power not only over all other beings, wizards and Muggles alike, not only over the boy wizard Harry with whom he shares so much, but even over death. Voldemort's answer for his relationship to power is to pursue and amass it relentlessly and to overcome any form of authority or power that could compel his behavior. Absolute power seems to him the path to absolute freedom, even, finally, from death. He capriciously uses the power of death against others even as he seeks to overcome death through his own immortality. "You know my goal," says Voldemort to his Death Eaters and Harry, "to conquer death" (*Goblet* 653). Throughout the seven novels, Voldemort's obsession with power grows and grows, seemingly without end. Indeed, it is an end in itself, and perhaps only Rowling herself has the imagination to conjure a world as it would be if Voldemort had succeeded in killing Harry. What would he have to live for?

Voldemort makes his second assault on Harry—the first having been when Harry was an infant—by possessing the body of Hogwarts Professor Quirrell and attempting to secure the alchemical Philosopher's Stone, the source of the Elixir of Life, a substance that defers death so long as it continues to be consumed. As Harry battles Quirrell, the latter spews out Voldemort's philosophy: "A foolish young man I was ... full of ridiculous ideas about good and evil. Lord Voldemort showed me how wrong I was. There is no good and evil, there is only power, and those too weak to seek it" (*Stone* 291).

Unto the very end of the saga, Voldemort ridicules Dumbledore's countervailing philosophy, that love, not death, is the greatest of all powers. Death does not end Dumbledore's influence upon nor his relationship with Harry, for love renders it as proximate rather than ultimate. After the encounter with Quirrell, Dumbledore explains to Harry that Lily loved Harry so much that she gave her life so that he might live, a sacrifice leaving a powerful mark of protection on Harry. It is a mark utterly beyond Voldemort's comprehension. Sharing Voldemort's utter lack of empathy, Quirrell could not bear contact with Harry's skin, marked as it was by his mother's sacrificial love (*Stone* 299).

Because he was never loved as deeply as Harry, Voldemort has no curiosity about anything which does not enhance his accumulation of power—be it love or the one third of the Deathly Hallows that is the Invisibility Cloak. Harry, on the other hand, is curious to learn about his wizarding powers, about the various forms of love in human relationships, and finally about how his powers might serve the cause of love while thwarting evil.

The two wizards choose two astonishingly different paths and destinies, in spite of their many similarities in background and ability—both are orphans, both are taught by Dumbledore, both depart Hogwarts before their education is complete, both speak Parseltongue, both have wands with a feather core from the same phoenix (though Harry's is made of holly, a wood said to repel evil). Harry has a portion of Voldemort's soul; Voldemort gains a portion of Harry's blood. But they end up antagonists, even unto death: Harry committed to the power of love, Voldemort to the love of power. How so? Examining how they each understand alchemy and experience the several forms of love will shed light on that question.

On Alchemy

Any doubt about Rowling's interest in and familiarity with the subject of alchemy is put to rest by her inclusion of the historical figure Nicolas Flamel in her work. Flamel lived in Paris in the late fourteenth century, and, although he did not die at the age of 665 only because of the destruction of the Philosopher's Stone, there is historical evidence of his interest in alchemy and that his reputation as an alchemist increased in the centuries after his death (Hall 490–502). Dumbledore is described as Flamel's partner in "work on alchemy" (*Stone* 103).

Several elements of the alchemical tradition figure prominently in the Harry Potter novels. Popularly conceived and on the physical level, alchemy is the attempt to convert base metals, such as lead, into gold. But this transformation is better understood as descriptive of the process of growth from ignorance to wisdom, more metaphysical than physical. Philosopher, mystic, and astrologer Manley P. Hall explains: "Through *art* (the process of learning) the whole mass of base metals (the mental body of ignorance) was transmuted into pure gold (wisdom), for it was *tinctured* with understanding.... [T]he base metals of mental ignorance can, through proper endeavor and training, be transmuted into transcendent genius and wisdom" (499). Here the difference between Harry and Voldemort begins to come clear. The "gold" for Voldemort is not wisdom but raw power gained by using his training solely for that end, whereas Harry seeks understanding of his own journey and abilities. Although both were sought out by Dumbledore to be trained, they have chosen to understand alchemy at two different levels leading to two very different outcomes.

Likewise, the Magnum Opus of alchemy—the development of a Philosopher's Stone—can also be understood as functioning on a material as well as on a philosophical level. Voldemort is driven early on in the narrative to acquire two physical objects, the Stone and the Elder wand, as tools to be used in his obsessive quest for power, whereas Harry comes to understand their impermanence. The Stone is destroyed (but not its lessons) and the Wand set aside with the hope that its power will be destroyed if Harry dies a natural death (it is destroyed in the film version of *The Deathly Hallows*), confirming that their value is far more than intrinsic and extends to the worldview into which Harry grows. As Hall emphasizes, "The reader must bear in mind at all times that the formulae and emblems of alchemy are to be taken primarily as allegorical symbols; for until their esoteric significance has been comprehended, their interpretation is valueless" (512–13). Precisely there do Harry and Voldemort part ways.

As Harry moves through the physical, emotional, and intellectual transformation from boyhood through adolescence towards adulthood, he engages the metaphysical questions of identity and purpose with which that period of life is beset, even fraught. The much older Voldemort, in his maniacal drive to overcome physical death, dismisses such metaphysical concerns as irrelevant (even Tom Riddle had little interest in them). Thus, Harry's journey is grounded in both the physical and the metaphysical, whereas Voldemort's reduction of life to the merely physical means, ironically, that he has already succumbed partially to the death he so ardently seeks to overcome. While yet alive, he has surrendered a crucial part of what it is to be human.

Dumbledore, their discoverer, teacher, and would-be mentor, stands very much within the tradition of alchemical philosopher-sages who "made their way from place to place throughout Europe, appearing and disappearing at will" (Hall 512). Apparating and Disapparating! But more, such a philosopher-sage "sought for some younger [person] worthy to be entrusted with the formulae. To this one, and to this one only, as a rule, the philosopher was permitted to disclose the Arcanum [secret or mystery]. The younger man became the 'philosophical son' of the old sage, and to him the latter bequeathed his secrets" (Hall 512). While Voldemort seeks out others—such as Professor Slughorn—to gain from them the practical knowledge he needs (such as how to make a Horcrux), Harry binds himself to Dumbledore. As much as he learns, however, he is again and again frustrated that Dumbledore is not telling him everything he (Dumbledore) knows, or that he needs to know, to go forward in his pursuit of his own Magnum Opus, the work of becoming the person who can end Voldemort's pursuit. This, too, is in accord with alchemical tradition in that not everything needed by the student was disclosed by the teacher. Hall explains that "medieval philosophers [decided] that those who could not with their own intelligence discover the missing substance or process were not qualified to be entrusted with secrets which could give them control" (513). Part of Harry's apprenticeship, his artful training, must include finding his way forward with incomplete knowledge, so that the path he finds may be his own.

Harry is thus initiated into the alchemical vision, while Voldemort short circuits the process by believing he can find his way forward on his own. Ironically, through his faithful devotion to his alchemical tutelage with Dumbledore, Harry undergoes the necessary transmutation to come to a power greater than that pursued so relentlessly by Voldemort. As Hall writes:

> If two persons, one an initiate and the other unilluminated in the supreme art, were to set to work, side by side, using the same vessels, the same substances, and exactly the same *modus operandi*, the initiate would produce his "gold" and the uninitiated would not. Unless the greater alchemy has taken place within the soul, ... [a person] cannot perform the lesser alchemy of the retort.... Unless a [person] be "born again" he [or

she] cannot accomplish the *Great Work*, and if the student of alchemical formulae will remember this, it will save ... much sorrow and disappointment. (509)

Both Harry and Voldemort know much "sorrow and disappointment" in their lives, but Voldemort is determined, above all else, not to die. Both have the tools and techniques of wizardry. But in dividing his soul among the Horcruxes, damage is done to Voldemort that prevents the transformation, the "greater alchemy," that is the goal of this tradition. His humanity deteriorates and erodes. Harry, on the other hand, keeps enlarging his soul under Dumbledore's mentoring, so that his humanity is broadened and deepened.

Harry and Voldemort end up with two very different souls. In *Harry Potter and the Half-Blood Prince,* Dumbledore illuminates the contrast when he explains to Harry that, in his murderous, Horcrux-filled quest for immortality, Voldemort maimed and rent his soul, making himself less and less human (469). By contrast, Dumbledore explains his philosophy of love's power, which he insists is Harry's shield against Voldemort's sort of power. He tells Harry, "You remain [just as] pure in heart ... as you were at the age of eleven, when you stared into the mirror that reflected your heart's desire, and it showed you only the way to thwart Lord Voldemort, and not immortality and riches...." He reminds Harry that Voldemort has so mangled his soul that "he has never paused to understand the incomparable power of a soul that is untarnished and whole" (478–79). Where Voldemort splinters his soul (leaving him more broken than he knows), Harry's soul enlarges. And he comes to be able to share that soul in love with others, sometimes in joy and sometimes at the cost of suffering. He comes even to have great power, though it is not what he seeks. And Harry does indeed die and is "born again," and thereby passes through the death Voldemort so fears, to be able to do his Great Work, the work of a soul that is whole and given to love.

In her fine 2008 commencement speech at Harvard University, Rowling noted:

> I am not dull enough to suppose that because you are young, gifted, and well-educated, you have never known hardship or heartache. Talent and intelligence never yet inoculated anyone against the caprice of the Fates, and I do not for a moment suppose that everyone here has enjoyed an existence of unruffled privilege and contentment. (*Very Good Lives* 24–25)

Harry and Voldemort are, like those Harvard graduates, gifted and well educated. And talent and intelligence, which both also have, have not insulated them from suffering. But Voldemort labors under the illusion that these gifts can be honed and refined purely for the service of the self, that they can indeed protect him from suffering, that they can be used primarily to inflict the very suffering he, himself, would avoid.

In that same address, Rowling says further:

Unlike any other creature on the planet, human beings can learn and understand without having experienced. They can think themselves into other people's places.
 Of course, this is a power, like my brand of fictional magic, that is morally neutral. One might use such an ability to manipulate or control just as much as to understand or sympathise.
 And many prefer not to exercise their imaginations at all. They choose to remain comfortably within the bounds of their own experience, never troubling to wonder how it would feel to have been born other than they are. They can refuse to hear the screams or peer inside the cages; they can close their minds and hearts to any suffering that does not touch them personally; they can refuse to know. (56–59)

Imagination, developed and used aright, thus becomes the foundation of compassion, of becoming capable of being moved by the suffering of others. Harry is well familiar with the lack of imagination through his time under the Dursleys' roof (and staircase). Voldemort takes his corrupted imagination to a frighteningly higher level and explicitly chooses to use his highly developed wizarding powers to manipulate and control, wound and kill. This is a moral choice. His imagination is so distorted that he has moved far past merely hearing others' screams of agony to positively enjoying them. He hears the screams of those he wounds, but these bring him neither remorse nor compassion, but rather pleasure, because of the moral choice he has made. As Dumbledore puts it, "It is our choices, Harry, that show what we truly are, far more than our abilities" (*Chamber* 333).

Out of his long and deep familiarity with hurt and loss, Harry chooses not only to hear, but to share, others' suffering as he journeys ever more surely towards compassion and love—not only for his closest companions Hermione and Ron, but for Hagrid, Sirius, Dobby, Ginny, and even Snape. His heart's desire—the loving family he could imagine and even see in the Mirror of Erised—is realized through his relationships. The journey Harry makes in each individual novel through trials and challenges moves him ever onward in the larger, alchemical journey to fullness of person.

On Love

In his work on alchemy, Hall cites an unknown alchemical adept who said, "Wisdom is as a flower from which the bee its honey makes and the spider its poison, each according to its own nature" (512). How might Harry and Voldemort come to have such different natures and to have made such different choices? Theologian and writer C.S. Lewis wrote often on the subject of love, both in fiction and nonfiction. In *The Four Loves*, Lewis explicates the four classical Greek terms for love—*Storge* (affection), *Philia* (friendship), *Eros* (erotic love or being in love), and *Agape* (charity or "a love which desires the good of the object as such")—in order to come to a fuller understanding of love (76).

Affection is that love most commonly and naturally found amidst familial relationships, the reciprocal bond between parents and children. Lewis is clear that the lack of affection is an extreme deprivation and that, on the other hand, its presence "is responsible for nine-tenths of whatever solid and durable happiness there is in our natural lives" (80). As orphans, both Harry and Voldemort had limited exposure to affection. Voldemort's willingness to slay both his father and his grandparents is cruel evidence of his lack of experience of affection. Harry spends the first eleven years of his life with a family, the Dursleys—his aunt, uncle, and cousin. His presence among them is barely tolerated, but even a negative experience of affection—unlike its utter absence for Voldemort—can evoke a sense of its possibilities.

Writes Lewis:

> How many ... "happy homes" really exist? Worse still; are all the unhappy ones unhappy because Affection is absent? I believe not. It can be present, causing the unhappiness. Nearly all the characteristics of this love are ambivalent. They may work for ill as well as good. By itself, left simply to follow its own bent, it can darken and degrade human life. The debunkers and anti-sentimentalists have not said all the truth about it, but all they have said is true. (62)

Home for the Dursleys has what seems at best a shallow form of affection, which they constantly exalt even as it reveals its insipid character; and yet Harry is excluded even from that. Perhaps his later sympathy for house-elves is born of having been treated like one for many years by the Dursleys. Yet, even a negative example can teach. A bad family at least evokes the category of "family" as having potential, whereas having no family at all cannot. Even as Harry learns of his father's imperfections—his pettiness bordering on cruelty, for example, towards Snape—he still has something concrete to ponder, not the void that is Voldemort's.

Harry has the great good fortune to be befriended by Ron and his large and very affectionate family. The affection they share is expansive and welcoming, affording Harry a place not only to receive love, but also to experience giving it. He finds himself welcome at their table, the recipient of birthday and Christmas gifts, valued as a source of information about the Muggle world, and even the butt of some of their jokes, a sure sign of inclusion. Thus, on the brink of adolescence—and the new understandings of love it will bring—Harry is given a second chance to experience a happy childhood, one shaped by affection. He finds himself seen, accepted, even cherished; he receives the gifts affection is meant to bear.

Abandoned at an orphanage soon after birth, Voldemort finds none of this. He copes with the absence of affection through the use of his newly discovered gifts, even before Dumbledore finds him. Dumbledore and Harry note the contrast in Harry's and Tom Riddle's reactions to being told they were wizards and that their names were down for Hogwarts. While Harry was skeptical, the young Tom "was perfectly ready to believe that he was—to use his word—'special.'" Dumbledore was concerned for a young orphan going to school alone, but he also tells Harry of his concern for Riddle's classmates at Hogwarts, because Tom "was already using magic against other people, to frighten, to punish, to control. The little stories of the strangled rabbit and the young boy and girl he lured into a cave were most suggestive ... *I can make them hurt if I want to...*" (*Prince* 258–59). Having had no experience of affection, Voldemort turns his gifts to the service of love's opposite: power.

The affection Harry experiences from those outside his primary relationships with Hermione and Ron is also empowering. Neville's dogged, unflagging determination to resist Voldemort in the Battle of Hogwarts is the embodiment of Luna's affirmation, "We're all still here.... We're still fighting. Come on, now" (*Hallows* 649). Both encourage Harry, enabling him to produce a timely and much needed Patronus.

Lest the importance of affection be underestimated, it should be noted that it is affection that empowers the otherwise despicable Narcissa Malfoy to lie to Voldemort at the story's end. She declares the yet-alive Harry—having been subjected to the *Avada Kedavra* curse—to be dead, so that she may try to save her son Draco amidst the fighting at Hogwarts. Affection, if once known, can propel even the evil toward a moment of goodness.

Lewis is much taken with the second category of love, love as friendship—in part, no doubt, because of his long and fruitful association with that group of thinkers and writers called "The Inklings"—and laments its rarity in his world. Were he alive, he might well rejoice that Rowling also clearly cherishes it and senses its importance and power. Perhaps her work may even give birth to its renaissance. Says Lewis, "to the Ancients, Friendship seemed the happiest and most fully human of all loves, the crown of life and school of virtue. The modern world, in comparison, ignores it" (87). Part of Lewis' enthrallment with friendship is that it is a choice, and that a crucial one. He explains:

> I have no duty to be anyone's Friend and no [one] in the world has a duty to be mine. Friendship is unnecessary, like philosophy, like art, like the universe itself.... It has no survival value; rather it is one of those things which give value to survival. When I spoke of Friends as side by side ... I was pointing a necessary contrast between that posture and that of the lovers whom we picture face to face.... The common quest or vision which unites Friends does not absorb them in such a way that they remain ignorant or oblivious of one another. On the contrary it is the very medium in which their

mutual love and knowledge exists. One knows nobody so well as one's "fellow." Every step of the common journey tests [one's] metal and the tests are tests we fully understand because we are undergoing them ourselves. Hence, as he rings true time after time, our reliance, our respect, and our admiration blossom into an Appreciative love of a singularly robust and well-informed kind. (103–04)

Lewis could almost be describing the relationship among Harry, Hermione, and Ron that so shapes Rowling's tale. For example, the two boys have an uneasy friendship with Hermione until the interrupted Halloween feast when they first lock her in a bathroom with and then rescue her from a troll, and she rescues them from Professor McGonagall's threatened punishment. At the feast relocated to the Gryffindor Common Room, the three share an awkward moment and become friends when they mutter embarrassed gratitude and dash off for food. "There are some things you can't share without ending up liking each other, and knocking out a twelve-foot mountain troll is one of them" (*Stone* 179).

The three great friends come to understand one another profoundly. Indeed, Hermione and Ron can be understood as alchemical companions essential to Harry's harrowing, transformational journey through the cauldron of suffering that shapes each novel's plot (Granger 61–64). As friendship grows, Harry "liked it best when he was with Ron and Hermione and they were talking about other things, or else letting him sit in silence while they played chess. He felt as though all three of them had reached an understanding they didn't need to put into words; that each of them was waiting for some sign, some word, of what was going on outside Hogwarts" (*Goblet* 717).

As the story unfolds, Harry's friendship-love for Hermione and Ron becomes such that he doesn't want to expose them to the potentially fatal dangers that await him in the quest for the Horcruxes. But their friendship is such that Ron and Hermione will have none of his "go-it-alone" leanings. When he contemplates setting out on his own and asks if they are sure they want to leave school for this most dangerous of journeys, an exasperated Ron and Hermione show him all the preparations they have made and insist that they are sticking with Harry as they have for years (*Hallows* 96).

Their journey will sorely test their friendship as the stress of it intensifies, but their bonds do not permanently break. And at the end of it all, another friend, weird and wonderful Luna Lovegood—whose name and demeanor suggest she comes almost from another realm (perhaps she has completed her own alchemical journey) and who knows the value of love—recognizes that Harry's deepest need is to escape all the commotion in the aftermath of the Battle of Hogwarts. She creates a distraction so that he can be alone with his two best friends (*Hallows* 746). Notably, Harry has known the first stirrings of *Eros* at this point, in his feelings for Ginny, but these are set aside temporarily for the sake of that other love: friendship, his with Ron and Hermione.

This category of love is unknown to Voldemort. Unlike Harry who was happy to have Hagrid's help and company on his first trip to Diagon Alley, Tom Riddle insists on going it alone both as a child and as an adult. To be sure, he has followers, minions, a gaggle of students during his time at Hogwarts who want to think themselves part of his inner circle. He has those drawn to him by fear and a craven desire both to save themselves, and to perhaps share in the exercise of raw power, but no friends. Dumbledore affirms that those—like the repugnant Bellatrix Lestrange and Lucius Malfoy—who fancy themselves Voldemort's intimates are caught in a dangerous delusion. Dumbledore says to Harry, "Lord Voldemort has never had a friend, nor do I believe he has ever wanted one" (*Prince* 260). And, true to form, Voldemort "shows just as little mercy to his followers as to his enemies" (*Stone* 298).

The power of the love that is friendship is a "power with" that is able to endure many demands and trials, even those born of the folly and ego of friends. But Voldemort knows nothing of this, for his is always a "power over." Friendship empowers those enfolded in its bonds, calls forth their best selves. Voldemort's power does precisely the opposite—overpowering, oppressing those who edge near to him, and drawing forth their darkest instincts.

That Rowling knows the value of friendship is evident not only through Harry, Hermione, and Ron's thoroughly developed relationship but also through her words at Harvard. She sent the graduates on their way, saying:

> I have one last hope for you, which is something that I already had at twenty-one. The friends with whom I sat on graduation day have been my friends for life. They are my children's godparents, the people to whom I've been able to turn in times of real trouble, people who have been kind enough not to sue me when I took their names for Death Eaters. At our graduation, we were bound by enormous affection, by our shared experience of a time that could never come again, and, of course, by the knowledge that we held certain photographic evidence that would be exceptionally valuable if any of us ran for Prime Minister. (*Very Good Lives* 69)

Eros, being in love, is Lewis' third classical category of love. Lewis makes clear his (heterosexual) understanding of the relationship between *Eros* and sexuality, when he writes:

> Sexuality makes part of our subject only when it becomes an ingredient in the complex state of "being in love." That sexual experience can occur without Eros, without being "in love," and that Eros includes other things besides sexual activity, I take for granted....
> We use a most unfortunate idiom when we say, of a lustful man ... that he "wants a

woman." Strictly speaking, a woman is just what he does not want. He wants a pleasure for which a woman happens to be the necessary piece of apparatus.... Now Eros makes a man really want, not a woman, but one particular woman. In some mysterious, but quite indisputable fashion, the lover desires the Beloved herself. (131; 134–35)

Voldemort ridicules Snape's love for Lily Potter as mere desire. He dismisses Snape's pining for her, saying that there are other women: illustrating Lewis' distinction. Confined to the merely physical, he cannot conceive that Snape's love went far beyond physical longing to the sacred realm of true *Eros* (and even *Agape*). For Voldemort's lust is reserved for power, the only reality for which he has anything resembling love, as lust sometimes does.

As the young wizards come into adolescence, stirrings of physical attraction begin, and perplex. Who is kissing—"snogging" in Harry's world—whom becomes a matter of pressing concern and, at times, of jealousy, anger, and misunderstanding, even among great friends such as Harry, Hermione, and Ron. After some expected fits and starts in the world of dating, Harry finds himself drawn to Ron's sister Ginny, somewhat to Ron's consternation and Harry's anxiety over damaging his friendship with Ron. When Ginny joins the Quidditch team, Harry has a ready excuse to spend time with her, despite some pangs of conscience. And soon thereafter, when Gryffindor has won the Quidditch Cup:

> There was Ginny running towards him; she had a hard, blazing look in her face as she threw her arms around him. And without thinking, without planning it, ... Harry kissed her. After several long moments—or it might have been half an hour—or possibly several sunlit days—they broke apart. ... Hermione was beaming, but Harry's eyes sought Ron.... [Ron and Harry] looked at each other, then Ron gave a tiny jerk of the head that Harry understood to mean, "Well—if you must." (*Prince* 499)

In the end, Harry and Ginny are married, have children, and know healthy affection and *Eros*. And so do Ron and Hermione. *Eros* needs an object that is an equal. And since Voldemort suffers no equals, he cannot know the love that is *Eros*. Perhaps he knows something of sexual lust, of sex without love, although nothing is said on that score.

Lewis makes an interesting observation about the role of kissing in love, writing:

> This blending and overlapping of the loves is well kept before us by the fact that at most times and places all three of them [affection, friendship, and *eros*] had in common, as their expression, the kiss. In modern England friendship no longer uses it, but Affection and Eros do. It belongs so fully to both that we cannot now tell which borrowed it from the other or whether there were borrowing at all. To be sure, you may say that the kiss of Affection differs from the kiss of Eros. Yes; but not all kisses between lovers are lovers' kisses. (58)

Kissing finds its intended place among Harry and his friends. But kissing is absent from Voldemort's world save for a single manifestation—the

Dementor's Kiss, wherein a soul is taken from a person. Instead of binding two souls, a soul is stolen, and with it, personhood. The purpose of the kiss has been utterly perverted, to serve power instead of love.

Lewis calls the fourth classical form of love "charity," an older—and now somewhat freighted—translation of the Greek *"Agape,"* and he views it through a quite orthodox Christian perspective. While that perspective's place in the story of Harry Potter has been widely debated (and will not be here), Lewis' understanding of *Agape* as "a love that desires the good of the object as such" is certainly to be found in his story, for this is a love that places other before self, even unto death, that does not let fear of death determine actions, that is willing to sacrifice self for others' wellbeing, if need be. Lewis considers that the real wonder of the other three loves is in their coming to fullness and fruition in the fourth (163).

The house-elf Dobby is among those in whom such love is seen. Freed from a service where he would have been compelled to give his life if so ordered, Dobby freely chooses to do so to save Harry and his friends. Even at their first meeting early in the tale, Dobby shows evidence of his wisdom about love when he says, "Harry Potter asks if he can help Dobby ... Dobby has heard of your greatness, sir, but of your goodness, Dobby never knew..." (*Chamber* 15). When Dobby continues to describe Harry's character using the adjectives "humble," "modest," "valiant," and "bold," he is also describing this fourth love, charity or *Agape*. And as grief is the measure of love, Harry's love for Dobby also comes up to this high standard, for Dobby's sacrificial death evokes in Harry a deep sadness.

Even the ever-so-complicated character of Severus Snape knows something of *Agape*. A very long time is needed to reveal him as anything more than a Hogwarts teacher overflowing with anger, especially at Harry. But he loved Harry's mother, Lily, and loved her deeply. During his final confrontation with Voldemort, Harry makes this clear when he explains to Voldemort that Snape urged him to let her live, because he had loved her since childhood and that his silver doe Patronus took the same shape as Lily's (*Hallows* 740). In his long and crushing grief, born of such love, Snape becomes wary of emotion and warns Harry of it, thereby sharing the choice he has made to protect himself from Voldemort and to be faithful to Dumbledore. During his efforts to teach Harry Occlumency comes this exchange:

> "I told you to empty yourself of emotion!"
> "Yeah? Well, I'm finding that hard at the moment," Harry snarled.
> "Then you will find yourself easy prey for the Dark Lord!" said Snape savagely. "Fools who wear their hearts proudly on their sleeves, who cannot control their emotions, who wallow in sad memories and allow themselves to be provoked this easily—weak people, in other words—they stand no chance against his powers! He will penetrate your mind with absurd ease, Potter!" (*Phoenix* 536)

It could be argued that Snape has no love for Potter at all (and often he is deeply annoyed by and even cruel to the boy wizard), that he is merely training him as Dumbledore requested in order that Potter may have a chance to kill the one who killed Snape's beloved, which might give him a measure of healing for his grief. Perhaps. But when Snape learned of Voldemort's intention to kill James, Lily, and Harry, he promised to do anything to save not just Lily, but all of them. Snape wishes he could have died in their stead. Of this is his loyalty to Dumbledore born. And he does save Dumbledore, temporarily, from the curse of Marvolo Gaunt's ring, and finally from an ignominious death. He saves Draco Malfoy from the act of killing Dumbledore, an act that would have deformed Draco beyond any hope of being saved from Voldemort. These are acts of more than duty. Surely, even Snape knows of this fourth love (*Hallows* 663–87). Rowling's emphasis on the crucial importance of choice pertains even in the realm of love, especially as regards *Agape*, as it often involves sacrifice of one's own wellbeing for that of the beloved. This Snape does, for Lily, as he surrenders personal happiness, communion with others, and anyone's, save Dumbledore's, understanding to save Harry, about whom he so often has such negative feelings.

On Narrative and Conviction

In his foundational essay, "The Narrative Quality of Experience," philosopher and theologian Stephen Crites argues compellingly for the truth named in his title: that life is, by definition, best experienced as a story. His truth intersects Rowling's work in at least two ways. First, Harry and Dumbledore spend a great deal of time using the Pensieve to reconstruct the narrative of Voldemort's life, not only to solve problems like the identity of the Horcruxes but also to comprehend Voldemort's experience of reality. Understanding that dark story allows Harry to write his own narrative differently. Dumbledore shares his own narrative not only so that Harry will know him better but also so that Harry might learn from his mentor's failures as well as his successes. And when Harry uses the Pensieve to learn about Snape's life, the result is compassion for Snape, after years of revulsion. Understanding Dumbledore's and Snape's rich life stories allows Harry to make sense of the astonishing complexities amidst which he lives.

There is, on the other hand, little evidence that Voldemort is as curious about Harry's life story, and not just because the charms Dumbledore placed around the Dursley residence kept Voldemort at a distance for the ten years Harry lived with them. This lack of curiosity causes him not only to reduce Harry to a set of facts but also to underestimate him as they meet again and again. His only interest is in whether Harry has sufficient power to defeat him, for power is the only criterion by which he judges anyone. The power of narrative, like the power of love, eludes him utterly.

Outside the books themselves is the question of their enormous popularity. Why has this narrative taken hold of so many so strongly? Crites observes:

> There is a beautiful paradox in the peculiar intensity with which a person responds to music which is "his own": Even if he has not heard it before it is familiar, as though something is sounding in it that he has always felt in his bones; and yet it is really new. It is his own style, revealed to him at an otherwise unimaginable level of clarity and intensity.... [S]tories have a similar resonance for us. (294)

Certainly, Rowling's story has such resonance. Perhaps that is so because it not only provides a splendid mirror in which to reflect on the trials and joys of navigating adolescence but also because in Harry's profound valuing of friendship is an antidote to radical individualism and self-determination; in his steadfast determination to find meaning based on love rather than power is a hopeful alternative to seeking to control life; and in his imaginative and "magical" persistence is an encouragement to possibilities not always readily evident in a frightening world.

Harry's owl is named, fittingly, for St. Hedwig, the patron saint of orphans. Rowling also founded a charity called Lumos (wearelumos.org) which is dedicated to improving the lives of the eight million institutionalized children worldwide. Her tale of two orphans, one institutionalized during many of his formative years, one not, reflects her commitment to end the damage that institutionalization can do, especially when so much of it is unnecessary. Of course, if Tom Riddle had not been institutionalized, the world would lack her rich narrative. But if others can be spared that trauma, perhaps many a child can be given the opportunity to find the way towards love.

So many of those Harry has loved die—his parents, his godfather Sirius Black, his alchemical mentor Dumbledore, the freed elf Dobby who bound himself to Harry, even Snape, whose immense courage Harry comes to recognize in the end—that it would be understandable if Harry despaired and succumbed to the belief that all ends in death (*Hallows* 758). But all these deaths come to have purpose and meaning as Harry comes to understand them as born of love, a love that endures even unto, and beyond, death. This is his Magnum Opus, to become a person who doesn't fear death, who defeats it—and those who would make its power absolute—by surrendering to it. Voldemort seeks immortality, freedom from death; Harry finds *Agape*, love that transcends death's power. As Dumbledore says to Harry, "You are the true master of death, because the true master does not seek to run away from Death" (*Hallows* 720).

None of this can Voldemort understand, much less accept, for he believes that his power to inflict death trumps all else. He does not know any of the loves; he only knows death as the final arbiter of all conflict. Voldemort scoffs at the very idea that love overpowers death, since it seems not to have prevented Dumbledore's death, did not save Harry's parents, and seems to the sneering snake-like Voldemort not likely to save Harry from his building Curse (*Hallows* 739). Early in life, Dumbledore, too, learned the dangers of power when he pursued the Deathly Hallows. He is, therefore, uniquely suited to mentor Harry in his pursuit of his Magnum Opus. Other wizards were puzzled when he refused repeated requests to become the Minister of Magic. When Harry insists that Dumbledore would have been an excellent Minister, Dumbledore demurs, reminding Harry of his youthful abuses of power. The Headmaster suggests that it is precisely because Harry takes on a position of leadership out of a sense of obligation that he rises so well to the occasion (*Hallows* 718).

Perhaps his Merton-like acknowledgment of power's challenges, coupled with his turning away from its pursuit, led Dumbledore to have time and space within which to explore the nature of the love he came to believe in so firmly. The headmaster says to Harry:

> I cared about you too much.... I cared more for your happiness than for your knowing the truth, more for your peace of mind than my plan, more for your life than the lives that might be lost if the plan failed. In other words, I acted exactly as Voldemort expects we fools who love to act.
> Is there a defense? I defy anyone who has watched you as I have—and I have watched you more closely than you can have imagined—not to want to save you more pain than you had already suffered. (*Phoenix* 838–39)

In the end, it is not Harry who kills Voldemort. Death is its own destruction. Harry casts a spell to disarm Voldemort, and Voldemort's death spell rebounds against himself. The power of the fourth love—*Agape*—prevails. Harry has prevailed by coming to learn and live all four kinds of love. This is how he is saved from becoming the person he has reviled, even though the learning is convoluted and has brought him much puzzlement and pain. Voldemort's choices leave him in an altogether different reality—homeless, friendless, without a lover, without something finally for which to live. Lewis rightly concludes, "The only place outside Heaven where you can be perfectly safe from all the dangers and perturbations of love is Hell" (169). This, metaphorically and existentially, Voldemort knows all too well.

Harry has just enough experience of affection to begin his journey, under Dumbledore's loving alchemical tutelage, to do his great work of becoming a whole person capable of all the kinds of love. He chooses wisely, most of the time, to step towards love rather than power, towards community rather than isolation, towards ultimate matters rather than proximate, towards distinguishing between means and ends, towards knowing the difference between tools and the ideals they are meant to serve. Through this journey, he finds himself transformed, from powerless orphan into an adult—empowered and empowering—by love.

WORKS CITED

Crites, Stephen. "The Narrative Quality of Experience." *Journal of the American Academy of Religion*, vol. 39, no. 3, 1971, pp. 291–311.
Granger, John. *Unlocking Harry Potter: Five Keys for the Serious Reader*. Zossima, 2007.
Hall, Manly P. *The Secret Teachings of All Ages*. Jeremy P. Tarcher/Penguin, 2003.
Lewis, C.S. *The Four Loves*. Harcourt, Brace, Jovanovich, 1960.
Lumos Foundation USA, Inc. www.wearelumos.org. Accessed 28 Aug. 2016.
Rowling, J.K. *Harry Potter and the Chamber of Secrets*. Scholastic, 1999.
_____. *Harry Potter and the Deathly Hallows*. Scholastic, 2007.
_____. *Harry Potter and the Goblet of Fire*. Scholastic, 2000.
_____. *Harry Potter and the Half-Blood Prince*. Bloomsbury, 2005.
_____. *Harry Potter and the Order of the Phoenix*. Scholastic, 2003.
_____. *Harry Potter and the Sorcerer's Stone*. Scholastic, 1998.
_____. *Very Good Lives*. Little, Brown Book Group, 2015.

Auror Magic

An Almost Alchemical Process

LORRIE KIM

Three times before he died, without knowing what he did, Voldemort produced gold.

That wasn't his intention. Voldemort sought immortality, but through the Dark Arts, not through alchemy. His great magical ambition was to render himself unkillable by killing others, tearing his soul into pieces, and ensuring that those pieces could never reintegrate. He did not seek immortality as alchemists did, through learning to transform base metal into gold and purifying their souls in the process.

But on three occasions, when Voldemort cast a Killing Curse at Harry Potter, the magic from Harry's wand connected with his curse to transform that murderous intent into gold: once into golden light and phoenix song, twice into golden flames.

Harry did not set forth to learn alchemy either. With his momentous decision between "Horcruxes and Hallows," choosing to hunt the repositories of a Dark Wizard's destructive power rather than seek greater magical power for himself, Harry pursued a different sort of soul magic (*Hallows* 484). His quest was not to transmute base metals into gold but to transmute an unnaturally debased soul, Voldemort's soul, back to its own humanity. His aim was to reverse the damage done by Dark Magic and put an end to the evil. Harry chose to use his gifts to become not an alchemist, but an Auror. With the coined term, "Auror," which calls to mind "dawn" (*aurora*, Latin for dawn) and "gold" (*aurum*, Latin for gold), Rowling indicates that doing the work of an Auror, "Dark wizard catcher," is another way to produce gold (*Goblet* 161).

The *Harry Potter* books are heavily influenced by alchemy, but there are remarkably few direct mentions of alchemical process itself. There are references to Nicolas and Perenelle Flamel, other alchemical scholars, and the Sorcerer's (Philosopher's) Stone. Other than that, the *only* time the term appears is when Professor Slughorn teaches a way to reverse the effects of magical damage.

During his Potions lesson, Hermione rattles off a basic principle of antidotes to the class: "Golpalott's-Third-Law-states-that-the-antidote-for-a-blended-poison-will-be-equal-to-more-than-the-sum-of-the-antidotes-for-each-of-the-separate-components" (*Prince* 374). This means, as Slughorn explains, that "our primary aim is not the relatively simple one of selecting antidotes to those ingredients in and of themselves, but to find that added component that will, **by an almost alchemical process**, transform these disparate elements—" (*Prince* 374, emphasis added). Through this principle, Rowling defines what it takes to defend against the Dark Arts: knowledge of every component of the original destructive magic plus "an added component" that will not only fight but overpower and reverse the effects of that Dark Magic.

Voldemort experienced this effect when his Killing Curses connected with Harry's magic to produce gold, encountering the power of an opponent whom he had created uniquely into his equal—someone he had forced to share blood and harbor a portion of his soul—but who possessed the "added component" of protective love.

The first time this happened, at the end of *Goblet of Fire*, he cast *Avada Kedavra*, the Killing Curse, against Harry's *Expelliarmus* and the magic from the two wands connected into threads of golden light that resonated with phoenix song. Harry controlled this light to force Voldemort to see and hear his most recent murder victims. Voldemort wielded his yew and phoenix feather wand; Harry wielded his holly and phoenix feather wand, the "brother" wand to Voldemort's (*Goblet* 697).

The second time, at the beginning of *Deathly Hallows*, Voldemort cast *Avada Kedavra* using Lucius Malfoy's wand, elm and dragon heartstring. Harry did not respond, but his holly wand acted of its own accord to counter this curse with "a spurt of golden fire" that connected to Lucius Malfoy's wand and destroyed it (*Hallows* 61).

The third time, in the last act of his life, Voldemort cast *Avada Kedavra* at Harry using the Elder Wand. Harry countered again with *Expelliarmus*, using the hawthorn and unicorn hair wand he had won from Draco. The two spells collided and burst into "golden flames" before Voldemort's curse rebounded upon him and Harry ended up holding both wands (*Hallows* 743).

That wasn't how Voldemort expected things to go.

The Killing Curse is usually foolproof, as long as the caster has sufficient power and intention. As Barty Crouch, Jr. explained while impersonating Mad-Eye Moody, "There's no counter curse. There's no blocking it. Only one known person has ever survived it" (*Goblet* 216). Until he failed to kill baby Harry, the Killing Curse had never failed Voldemort. He spent the rest of his life trying to understand what made Harry the single exception.

He wondered if Harry was a powerful wizard, but he was unable to see any unusual power in Harry, and Snape frequently assured him that Harry "had no extraordinary talent at all" (*Prince* 31). He rejected the notion that Harry's exceptional power could be "Dumbledore's favorite solution, *love*, which he claimed conquered death," since Voldemort had been able to kill other people who had known love (*Hallows* 739). Instead, he spent a year in vain pursuit of a prophecy that he hoped might yield a different answer. He tortured Ollivander into revealing that "brother" wands that share cores, such as the phoenix feathers shared by his yew wand and Harry's holly wand, "will not work properly against each other" (*Goblet* 697). That sounded like promising information, but when switching to Lucius Malfoy's wand didn't work, he set his sights on a supposedly unbeatable wand, a strategy that ended up backfiring on him.

It never occurred to Voldemort that the only reason he couldn't kill Harry was because at a crucial point in his life, Voldemort identified with him. He was not equipped to recognize that his spontaneous production of gold was related to the mundane experience of *connecting* with a fellow human.

Until he heard a prophecy foretelling the approach of "the one with the power to vanquish the Dark Lord," Voldemort had never identified with another person, preferring to think himself "different, separate, notorious" (*Prince* 277), "much, much more than a man" (*Goblet* 15).

Voldemort heard only the first two sentences of the full prophecy:

THE ONE WITH THE POWER TO VANQUISH THE DARK LORD APPROACHES.... BORN TO THOSE WHO HAVE THRICE DEFIED HIM, BORN AS THE SEVENTH MONTH DIES ... AND THE DARK LORD WILL MARK HIM AS HIS EQUAL, BUT HE WILL HAVE POWER THE DARK LORD KNOWS NOT ... AND EITHER MUST DIE AT THE HAND OF THE OTHER FOR NEITHER CAN LIVE WHILE THE OTHER SURVIVES.... (*Phoenix* 841)

According to the portion of the prophecy that Voldemort heard, the one person with the power to vanquish him would be either Harry Potter or Neville Longbottom. Voldemort had to *choose* which one he thought it would be. He had to picture what type of person could have powers that would match and overcome his own, taking into account what he knew of each child — more thought than he usually gave to other people, whom he generally despised as weaker than himself.

As Dumbledore explains to Harry, Voldemort's choice mirrored his fears, for tyrants everywhere ... realize that, one day, amongst their many victims, there is sure to be one who rises against them and strikes back! Voldemort ... heard the prophecy and he leapt into action, with the result that he not only handpicked the man most likely to finish him, he handed him uniquely deadly weapons! (*Prince* 510)

Dumbledore pointed out that Voldemort targeted the boy with whom he could identify. Despite his pureblood rhetoric, Voldemort pursued "the half-blood, like himself. **He saw himself in you** before he had ever seen you, and in marking you with that scar, he did not kill you, as he intended, but gave you powers, and a future, which have fitted you to escape him" (*Phoenix* 842, emphasis added).

Professor Quirrell described learning from Voldemort that "There is no good and evil, there is only power, and those too weak to seek it..." (*Stone* 291). Voldemort did not compare himself with fellow humans in most respects, but he did value power and continually sought new powers to master. Anytime he pictured someone great enough to vanquish him, he could only imagine someone *like himself*—directly challenging his self-image as "the greatest wizard of them all" (*Hallows* 550). He could only understand greatness and power as the ability to wield magic strong enough to kill anyone who got in his way, whether through minor irritation or through direct challenges, such as Dumbledore's to his murderous regime.

In scarring baby Harry for life by murdering his parents and mounting a near-fatal attack on him, Voldemort was making Harry into *someone who would understand how Voldemort felt*.

Voldemort once tried to do something similar with the mysterious, unnamed crime he committed against two Muggle children, Amy Benson and Dennis Bishop, when they were all living in the orphanage. Mrs. Cole, the orphanage director, told Dumbledore that Tom had lured them into a cave and that they "were never quite right afterwards.... He swore they'd just gone exploring, but *something* happened in there, I'm sure of it" (*Prince* 268). Though exactly what happens in the cave remains a mystery, we get a hint when Harry saw Voldemort remembering the moment after he killed Harry's parents: "*He did not like it crying, he had never been able to stomach the small ones whining in the orphanage—*" (*Hallows* 345).

Mrs. Cole told Dumbledore that Tom Riddle had been "a funny baby" who "hardly ever cried" (*Prince* 267). As Harry saw, Tom Riddle, as a child, could not bear the crying of the other orphans; he had never formed any attachments to lose, had never received attention and care by crying, and had not felt enough love to feel grief. He may have stopped their crying by removing their memories of attachments and love. This would have had the effect, intentional or not, of making them *more like himself*, even if he would never have seen anything of himself in children he would have considered weak.

He had the urge to silence the crying of baby Harry, as well, but it backfired on him because unlike the children at the orphanage, he thought of Harry as someone similar to himself—an orphaned wizard with significant power, a trait that he recognized and valued in himself. Preparing the Killing Curse, Voldemort relished not only the elimination of the infant Harry's threat to Voldemort's power, but witnessing the moment of Harry's fear and death as well. Yet, the Curse rebounded upon Voldemort instead, both breaking and highlighting the two wizards' connection: "*He had killed the boy, and yet he* was *the boy…*" (*Hallows* 345).

Voldemort looked closely at the frightened face of a baby whose parents he had just killed, and then moved to kill the child as well. But unlike every other time he ever cast the Killing Curse, Voldemort had selected the victim for having traits he saw in himself: he had felt *identification*. Seeing Harry's "pain and terror," for the first time, Voldemort had the terrifying and incapacitating experience of a moment of *empathy* ("he had killed the boy, and yet he *was* the boy"). Knowing that Voldemort's own deliberate actions had caused this pain could have led Voldemort to experience *remorse*, a potent and terrible magic that Voldemort might not have survived.

Remorse can be painful for anyone, but it poses a potentially fatal risk for people who have split their souls through murder. As Hermione said, deep and genuine remorse, which is also profoundly painful, is the only way to reintegrate a split soul after making a Horcrux. She doubts Voldemort would make the effort (*Hallows* 103). If reintegrating a soul split only once might kill a person, then the agony of trying to integrate a soul split seven times would be beyond endurance.

For most of his life, pain had not concerned Voldemort. When he cast *Avada Kedavra* at baby Harry, that was the first time, in his empathy-starved life, that he had thought enough about his victim to "really feel" what he had done. His pain was compounded by near-fatal levels of jealousy at the sight of Harry having been loved enough by his parents to have reason to grieve. Voldemort's usual response to love and grief was mockery, but in his moment of witnessing Harry's loss of parental love, he recalled his own existence as a terrified baby in need of care. Voldemort described to his Death Eaters his bleak existence after the curse rebounded:

> Aaah … pain beyond pain, my friends; nothing could have prepared me for it. I was ripped from my body, I was less than spirit, less than the meanest ghost … but still, I was alive. What I was, even I do not know … I, who have gone further than anybody along the path that leads to immortality. You know my goal—to conquer death. And now, I was tested, and it appeared that one or more of my experiments had worked … for I had not been killed, though the curse should have done it. (*Goblet* 653)

The pain of realizing how he had made baby Harry feel would have been enough to destroy a normal person. To put it another way: this realization, and the superhuman degree of pain it caused Voldemort during his years without a body, is what it means to say that Voldemort's Killing Curse rebounded upon him. That degree of pain should have killed him, but because of the unnatural magic Voldemort had performed, *he could not die*. He had removed any upper limit to how much pain he could experience, although he had not dulled his sensitivity to pain. His suffering, potentially, could be infinite.

In exchange for the Dark Magic power he gained through his Horcruxes, Voldemort had altered himself to sacrifice the safeguard and mercy of a pain threshold that would kill a mortal human. As Dumbledore described it, this tampered with "the deepest laws of magic" (*Hallows* 711). Surviving the destruction of one's body by hiding part of the soul in a Horcrux, according to Slughorn, leads to an existence so unnatural that "death would be preferable": "You must understand that the soul is supposed to remain intact and whole. Splitting it is an act of violation, it is against nature" (*Prince* 498).

As long as Voldemort retained a fragment of his original soul, he was still subject to the natural human yearning to become whole again—but after fragmenting himself to such an extreme degree, he had destroyed his ability to fulfill this yearning. The pain of becoming whole again would be too great for him to withstand, yet he would be unable to die of it. As Hagrid said of Voldemort on Harry's eleventh birthday, "Dunno if he had enough human in him left to die" (*Stone* 57).

When Harry saw Voldemort drinking unicorn blood, the centaur Firenze confirmed that Voldemort existed in a form so unnatural that death would be preferable: "Only one who has nothing to lose, and everything to gain, would commit such a crime. The blood of a unicorn will keep you alive, even if you are an inch from death, but at a terrible price. You have slain something pure and defenseless to save yourself, and you will have but a half-life, a cursed life, from the moment the blood touches your lips" (*Stone* 258).

Meanwhile, Voldemort had scarred Harry Potter for life, so that Harry, orphaned and traumatized, with a piece of Voldemort's soul taking shelter in his forehead, would always know *how Voldemort felt*. He had made Harry more like himself. As long as Harry was alive, Voldemort was less alone in the world and a small part of his soul was kept alive.

For thirteen years, Voldemort lived life as less than a ghost, "forcing [him]self, sleeplessly, endlessly, second by second, to exist..." (*Goblet* 653). Confronting his followers for never coming to his aid during those years of torment that would have killed anyone else, Voldemort said ominously, "I smell guilt. There is a stench of guilt upon the air" (*Hallows* 647).

Voldemort felt closer to Harry than to his Death Eaters at that moment. Harry, the boy whom Voldemort had scarred into someone who would be his "equal," would have known what it was to spend those exact same thirteen years in pain. When Harry is forty years old, he dreams of Voldemort's words again in a nightmare about the Dursleys and Dumbledore: "I smell guilt. There is a stench of guilt upon the air" (*Child* 202). Had he been inclined, he might have spoken the same words to his supposed caregivers for abusing and abandoning him during his childhood.

After Wormtail helped him regain a rudimentary body through Dark Magic, Voldemort found that he remained infantile and weak throughout Harry's fourth year at Hogwarts. Voldemort, despite all his genius, had no power to self-generate magic great enough to make his tiny rudimentary body grow to his former adult size. This magic would be dependent on outside assistance, the blood of a foe. Wormtail gave perfectly sound counsel against using the blood of Harry Potter, which Voldemort disregarded. This would turn out to have mortally significant consequences, but from Voldemort's point of view, this decision make sense. For one thing, Harry was the only person Voldemort thought might be powerful enough to be his equal and therefore worthwhile. But for another, Voldemort knew with certainty that Harry could put nurturing love into Voldemort's blood, "for the lingering protection his mother once gave him would then reside in my veins too…" (*Goblet* 657).

It seems that Voldemort did not understand how the surges of love in the blood, known as oxytocin to Muggles and as "blood magic" to the wizarding world, enable infants to grow and thrive but also encourage interpersonal connection, love, empathy, grief, and remorse. Until he reconstituted himself using Harry's love-rich blood, Voldemort had been unable to touch Harry without unendurable pain (*Goblet* 652–53). As Slughorn put it, he had taken into his own blood an "added component" that could enable someone opposing his Dark Magic, "by an almost alchemical process," to actually reverse the Dark Magic's effects.

Dumbledore explained to Harry: "To have been loved so deeply, even though the person who loved us is gone, will give us some protection forever. It is in your very skin. Quirrell, full of hatred, greed, and ambition, sharing his soul with Voldemort, could not touch you for this reason. It was agony to touch a person marked by something so good" (*Stone* 299).

The agony was the feeling of mortal jealousy about the gulf between Harry's love-rich infancy and Tom Riddle's loveless one. Taking Harry's blood into his own body overcame the barrier of Harry's skin so that Voldemort could touch him, but Voldemort did not realize that the agony and jealousy had not changed; he had simply moved the barrier from Harry's skin to Harry's mind.

When Voldemort unintentionally put some of his soul into Harry's scar, he also gave Harry one-way insight into his attacker's mind and emotions. In wandlore terms, Harry was chosen by a wand that was "brother" to Voldemort's wand, the only other wand to have a phoenix feather from Fawkes at its core, because the holly wand recognized this one-sided kinship.

But once Voldemort made the deliberate choice to take some of Harry's blood protection into himself, the insight was no longer one-way. Voldemort didn't realize that love transforms those it protects. Once Voldemort admitted that Harry had a power that Voldemort wanted, admitted his lack and admitted Harry's and Lily's love into his blood, he was sensitized to near-fatal levels of agony and jealousy whenever he could sense Harry feeling love, whether or not he was touching Harry's skin. This sensitivity was beyond his control or comprehension; he was undefended against it.

At the end of Harry's fifth year, after possessing Harry meant that Voldemort experienced Harry's grief for Sirius, Voldemort took measures to protect himself from ever again feeling Harry's emotions. Even though he had gained the power to see into Harry's mind, he found that he could not risk using this power. He had needed Harry's ability to love and to feel in order to grow from his stunted rudimentary body to his adult form, but once he was capable of that degree of feeling, he found that his soul was too unstable to withstand it. He had not foreseen that obstacle and could not overcome it.

As Dumbledore told Harry in King's Cross, instead of destroying his connection with Harry the night he took Harry's blood in the graveyard to regain a body, Voldemort redoubled the bond he created with Harry the night he murdered Lily (*Hallows* 710). This doubling intensified the effect when the magic from Voldemort's wand connected with the magic from Harry's wand and produced unexpected gold. According to the wands that chose them, the two wizards were similar at the core, brothers. When they forced their brother wands to duel, Voldemort *connected* with Harry, the first time in his life he had ever experienced an emotional connection with another person: "a narrow beam of light **connected** the two wands, neither red nor green, but bright, deep gold" (*Goblet* 663, emphasis added).

In Rowling's fictional universe, gold often symbolizes emotional connection. The wedding between Bill and Fleur was suffused with gold colors, from the décor to the bridesmaids' dresses to the dance floor of molten gold. Gold lines of embroidery connected the names on the Black family tree. Most poignantly, Luna used golden ink to connect the beloved faces she painted on her bedroom ceiling with the repeated word "*friends ... friends ... friends ...,*" and the sight created a change in Harry, filling him with tenderness for Luna (*Hallows* 417).

Voldemort assembled all his Death Eaters to witness what he thought would be his moment of triumph, his ascent to immortality upon the murder of the only wizard with the power to vanquish him. Instead, they witnessed his loss of control as Voldemort experienced his first emotional connection with another person. His *Avada Kedavra* connected with Harry's *Expelliarmus* with a golden light that caused both wizards' hands to seize up around their wands, then splintered into "a thousand more beams" that crisscrossed into a golden dome forming "a cage of light." The two connected phoenix feather cores resonated to emit phoenix song (*Goblet* 663–64).

Voldemort had inadvertently created gold by connecting with Harry.

Once the phoenix song started, the beam of gold between Voldemort and Harry changed, "as though large beads of light were sliding up and down the thread connecting the wands" (*Goblet* 664). Harry focused on pushing the beads of light toward Voldemort. When they connected with Voldemort's wand, the wand emitted the moving, speaking images of Voldemort's last several victims: *Priori Incantatem*, a rare effect in which one wand forces another "to regurgitate spells it has performed—in reverse" (*Goblet* 697).

With his blood newly infused with love, strengthened further by the unintended new sensation of connection with another person, strengthened further still by connecting with a piece of his own soul within that person, Voldemort was seeing the consequences of his crimes and hearing the voices of his victims. Even after Harry broke their wand connection, the shades of Voldemort's victims continued to crowd around and accuse him, giving Harry cover to escape. The shades were coming not from Harry, nor even from the connection between Harry and Voldemort, but from Voldemort's newly expanded awareness. Unlike Harry, Voldemort had no basis to understand what was happening to him and so he experienced fear even greater than Harry's rather than the exultation in victory he had expected (*Hallows* 711).

A year later, determined not to repeat the terrifying humiliation of that evening, Voldemort forced Ollivander, under torture, to explain why his wand and Harry's connected. On Ollivander's advice, he used a wand without a phoenix feather core when he next cast *Avada Kedavra* at Harry, thinking this would circumvent the emotional connection between his magic and Harry's. It didn't occur to Voldemort that Harry's wand would recognize Voldemort's magic, no matter whose wand conducted it. He didn't know, either, that part of his soul resided in Harry and would be drawn to reconnect with him.

This led to the second time that Voldemort inadvertently produced gold.

Voldemort used Lucius Malfoy's wand to cast the Killing Curse during the Flight of the Seven Harrys. Neither he nor Harry expected what happened next. His scar searing, Harry could not act, but his wand could. Harry "felt it drag his hand around like some great magnet, saw a spurt of golden fire through his half-closed eyelids, heard a crack and a scream of fury" (*Hallows* 61). As Harry told the Order later, he had never heard of such a spell or made gold flames appear before.

The wording of the wand's autonomous action is significant. It occurred when the part of Voldemort's soul in Harry's scar was unusually active and painful while Voldemort was sending the Killing Curse through Lucius Malfoy's wand. Harry "saw a spurt of golden fire" and heard a crack, but he didn't know which wand issued the fire or caused the crack; he only knew it was not a spell of his casting. There was no phoenix song since there was no connection between phoenix feather cores, but connections of different sorts were creating gold.

As Slughorn said, souls are meant to remain "intact and whole," and splitting a soul is "against nature." Still-living soul fragments, then, would be drawn, by nature, to reintegrate. We see hints of this pull when Harry's scar pain intensifies around the presence of Voldemort or one of his Horcruxes. Horcruxes can only remain effectively separate if stored within magical containers powerful enough to hold the soul fragments fast despite their natural tendency to rejoin their sources. Harry hears the Slughorn in the recovered memory explain to Tom Riddle that Horcruxes are objects containing a bit of the creator's soul torn off in the act of murder. Pressed for instructions, Slughorn protests, "'Do I look as though I have tried it—do I look like a killer?'" (*Prince* 498).

Hermione found, in her research, that soul fragments enclosed within magical containers "can flit in and out of someone" and become a threat to that person if they become too emotionally close to the object, as Ginny did with the diary Horcrux (*Hallows* 105). According to this explanation, then, Voldemort's obsession with Harry would have increased the natural urge of his soul fragments to reunite into a whole. As Harry destroyed more Horcruxes, Harry's influence on the ever-diminishing remainder of Voldemort's soul would have grown only stronger. The soul fragment in Harry exercised greater pull on Voldemort than the other fragments, because Harry was not an intentional Horcrux. Voldemort was unaware that part of his soul resided in Harry and had not performed the spell to encase it safely. As Dumbledore told Snape, when Voldemort first tried to kill Harry, the curse rebounded, ripping away a piece of Voldemort's soul, which attached itself to Harry, making Harry Voldemort's protection against death (*Hallows* 686).

A fragment of soul can "act and think for itself" independently of the rest of the same soul, as demonstrated by the diary Horcrux (*Prince* 500). At a moment of mortal peril, when Voldemort was unable to fight the yearning, one soul fragment betrayed Voldemort's human desire for nurturing and sheltered with Harry in the hopes of absorbing some of the protection that Harry's soul had known. When Voldemort's magic connected with Harry and this soul fragment during the Flight of the Seven Harrys, that moment of increased soulfulness for Voldemort, after decades of relentless self-harm and privation, contributed to the manifestation of golden flames.

By the third and final time Voldemort produced gold, he had barely any of his soul remaining. With the destruction of each Horcrux, Harry had found it easier and easier to look into Voldemort's mind, and Voldemort had no awareness of Harry's mental presence at all. When Voldemort cast his last *Avada Kedavra* to meet Harry's *Expelliarmus*, he and Harry both used wands that Harry had won from Draco. Voldemort held the Elder Wand, Harry the hawthorn wand that had once been Draco's. The same two wands had dueled a year earlier when Draco's *Expelliarmus* disarmed Dumbledore and won the Elder Wand for Draco. After that battle, both wands recognized disarmament as more powerful than attack.

By this moment, following Dumbledore's lead, Harry had destroyed the parts of Voldemort's soul that he had debased with Dark Magic, leaving only the portion of soul that remained in its natural state. Harry had done something humble and beautiful for Voldemort: he had restored Voldemort to humanity.

With all the Horcruxes gone, Voldemort would no longer subsist in limitless, bodiless agony if a curse rebounded upon him. When Voldemort chose to cast a final *Avada Kedavra*, the curse collided with Harry's *Expelliarmus* to produce "golden flames" as it rebounded (*Hallows* 743). With that connection, Harry completed Voldemort's transformation back to his final, mortal form, finishing the work begun by Regulus Black and recorded in his message: "I have stolen the real Horcrux and intend to destroy it.... I face death in the hope that when you meet your match, you will be mortal once more" (*Prince* 609).

Voldemort rejected Harry's offer to try to save his own soul through remorse, a process that would have undoubtedly overwhelmed the unstable sliver of soul he had remaining. But Harry's labors as an Auror, a wizard who can reverse and destroy Dark Magic, released him from the self-inflicted, unnatural limitlessness of his pain.

Works Cited

Rowling, J.K., et al. *Harry Potter and the Cursed Child*. Scholastic, 2016.
Rowling, J.K. *Harry Potter and the Deathly Hallows*. Scholastic, 2007.
_____. *Harry Potter and the Goblet of Fire*. Scholastic, 2000.
_____. *Harry Potter and the Half-Blood Prince*. Scholastic, 2005.
_____. *Harry Potter and the Order of the Phoenix*. Scholastic, 2002.
_____. *Harry Potter and the Prisoner of Azkaban*. Scholastic, 1999.
_____. *Harry Potter and the Sorcerer's Stone*. Scholastic, 1997.

Tapping on Just Another Brick in the Wall

Sean Paulsgrove

> We don't need magic to change the world; we have the power to imagine better.
> —J.K. Rowling

> All alone, or in twos
> The ones who really love you
> Walk up and down, outside the wall
> Some hand in hand
> Some gathering together in bands
> The bleeding hearts and the artists
> Make their stand
> And when they've given you their all
> Some stagger and fall, after all it's not easy
> Banging your heart against some mad bugger's wall.
> —Roger Waters ("Outside the Wall")

A simple brick wall may convey or conceal much. While for some a wall is a barrier and nothing more, for others it is cause to wonder. What could be behind it? Why was it built? What could be painted on it? The imagination can run wild when given such a blank yet unyielding canvas. For young, first-time readers of *Harry Potter and the Sorcerer's Stone*, walls evoke even more of the same imaginative magic. Tapped in the right order, the bricks in the wall in an alley behind the Leaky Cauldron give way to the portal to Diagon Alley, marking both Harry's and the readers' first entrance into the magical world.

Not all walls hold such pleasant surprises, though. For Pink, the central character of Pink Floyd's album and movie, both titled *The Wall*, a certain Wall is instead a crushing adversary. While Pink's Wall is made of many different metaphoric bricks, a great deal of its foundation is built solidly during his childhood in his interactions in classes with the Schoolmaster, a hand of oppressing conformity and suffocating obedience to societal norms. Similarly, in J.K. Rowling's *Harry Potter and the Order of the Phoenix*, Ministry of Magic plant Dolores Umbridge uses her powers as an educator to oppress freedom of thought and to crush reflectivity and critical thinking among the students at Hogwarts.

On the face of it, the two teachers seem quite different. Professor Umbridge comes to Hogwarts with the express purpose of spreading the Ministry's dogmatic no-Voldemort narrative in particular and obedience to the Ministry's self-serving agenda in general. The Schoolmaster simply mirrors and maintains implicit adherence to socially held norms and is not acting in direct service to any explicitly stated agenda. Yet, both Dolores Umbridge and the Schoolmaster attempt to build walls in the minds of their students. Whether the barriers are obvious from the start or just take the form of ordinary cultural assumptions, it is when someone puts a toe over the line (or risks a glance over the wall) that the similarities between the two teachers become apparent. They both react with the utmost animosity when a student dares to imagine beyond these walls. Whether this be in the form of direct, calculated resistance from Dumbledore's Army, or the then-child Pink expressing his sorrow through poetry and thus unintentionally challenging dogmas of gendered self-expression, the response is the same: heavy-handed and cruel, so as to scare any other possible offenders back into marching lock-step with the dogmas that both the Ministry of Magic or society in general build, brick by brick, around their respective citizens.

In "On a Certain Blindness in Human Beings," American Pragmatist William James gives us tools to understand and resist Umbridge's overt repression and the Schoolmaster's equally threatening but less obvious version. At the same time, James suggests that everyone, even ordinary and generally good people, might impose repressive beliefs on others simply because those beliefs might be held without reflection as universally true, when beliefs might, indeed must, be locally formed. It takes immense courage and imagination to resist external oppression; it takes an equally large dose of each to examine and transform oneself in order both to root out bricks of internalized oppression and to try to see the world through others' eyes. Although often difficult and sometimes frightening, tapping on just another brick in the wall can be transformative and liberating.

Defining a kind of perspectival blindness* inherent to human beings,

---

*It is important to note that the usage of the "blindness" language is not to suggest that blindness is inherently a negative trait. This language was chosen as it aligns with William James' work and is not meant to suggest any level of negativity towards those differently abled. The usage of "blindness" utilizes the same meaning of James' "blindness," which could be alternatively worded as "non-perceiving" or "unperceived."

James writes, "we are but finite.... Each one of us has some single specialized vocation of his [or her] own" (3). When a person devotes energy, study, and practice to one profession, hobby, or interest, some other possible pursuits are left behind. An automotive mechanic, for example, would no doubt notice issues in a car more skillfully than an accountant. And though Ron admits with some reluctance that there is a distant accountant cousin in his family of witches and wizards, he might come to appreciate that accountants have their uses now and then (*Stone* 99). We are also acculturated to liking certain things more than others based on our own life experiences. For example, someone who grew up near a sunny beach may enjoy the sea more or at least in a different way than someone who grew up near a cold and rocky shore. Rowena Ravenclaw might prefer her native glen to Helga Hufflepuff's broad valley home (*Goblet* 176).

On a very practical level, people close some doors when they open others. It takes hours and years and decades to become, for example, a skilled Seeker on a Quidditch team or to hone the writer's craft. If one should devote one's energy to one skill or another, one must leave other possible skills undeveloped. James continues, bleakly, "It seems as if energy in the service of [one's vocation's] particular duties might be got only by hardening the heart toward everything unlike them." He adds, "Our deadness toward all but one particular kind of joy would thus be the price we inevitably have to pay for being practical creatures" (3). Yet, James is not content to settle for such a hardening of the heart or a deadness toward many sorts of joy. The price is too high.

We are not only practical creatures, and the difficulties of perceiving and understanding the world move well beyond making this choice or that. The choices we make are not only personal. What seems valuable or pleasurable depends on the underlying culturally created assumptions and preconceptions that give us an ability both to make certain choices and also to "make sense" of the world. If a culture devalues the arts, so that music and art classes are cut first from stressed school budgets, children would have a more difficult time "choosing" to pick up a violin or a paintbrush. People also need a lens through which to see the world in order to make sense of new information and to interpret our experiences. About this, we have no choice. At the same time, it is often terribly difficult to be aware of those interpretive lenses, as they are imbibed like the air as one breathes in one's cultural assumptions. It is as difficult, then, to imagine that another person might have a different set of assumptions and preconceptions which might work as well for them as a kind of roadmap of life as surely as one's own set does.

James does not suggest that any person, any limited, finite person, can ever see from a universal point of view. But he does suggest that we might become aware of our necessarily limited perspectives to avoid the ossification of those frameworks. Disagreements, even profound ones, are not in themselves problematic or to be avoided. Disagreements and those who disagree can be transformed if we can overcome barricading our views and perceptions behind utterly unyielding, dogmatic walls. Dogmatic thought is an adherence to a certain code of beliefs or perception so intense that the person holding it refuses to admit that the position both cannot possibly take into account all factors and is not necessarily the superior way of perceiving the world. These attitudes lead to an unwillingness to engage in reflection on one's positions and their underlying assumptions. Having strong convictions, preferences, and commitments is not the problem; dogmatic thinking—the unwillingness to be open and listen to others' perspectives, others' equally finite versions of the truth—is the problem.

Describing an outing in rural North Carolina, the affluent, formally educated, Boston-born and -bred James uses his own experiences as an example of how dogmatic thinking works and how it might be avoided with a little courage and a great deal of imagination. James' first reaction to a farmhouse he and his mountaineer companion encounter is that it was a hovel made piecemeal of log and clay, a place of "unmitigated squalor." He very nearly fell into a class- and urban-based dogmatic condemnation of what he saw as disorganized fields strewn with charred stumps and corn growing among the shattered remains of the once-beautiful forest that a farmer had cleared (2). James thought the farmers must also be squalid and disorganized, until his traveling companion helped him to see from another angle of vision. The mountaineer explains, "Why, we ain't happy here, unless we are getting one of these coves under cultivation" (3).

It is at this moment that James has an epiphany—the judgment he made of this farm was entirely relative to his own personal and cultural experiences, expectations, and perspectives. This mountaineer and the people of this farming community in North Carolina found the farmstead beautiful, because it symbolized the final reward of months, if not years, of toil and effort and of the security and sustenance that a home would provide them (3). The difference in perspective here is stark. While James' initial reaction to seeing this farmstead was disgust, as it was so different from his pre-conceived notions of idyllic farm living and the beauty of the natural world, the unnamed mountaineer (and likely the owners of the farmstead through him) reacts to this familiar site with respect for the toil that such a feat took, respect for the motivations that lead to the toil, and almost a sense of reverence.

James realizes, "I had been as blind to the peculiar ideality of their conditions as they certainly would also have been to the ideality of mine, had they a peep at my strange indoor academic ways of life at Cambridge"

(2). In his Gryffindor dormitory, Ron has not yet had this realization when he describes Dean's Muggle poster of the completely and utterly stationary players of the West Ham football team as "Mental" (*Goblet* 191). When confronted with a clear-cut farmstead like James or by a stationary soccer poster like Ron, one stands at a metaphorical, possibly metaphysical, crossroads. Two routes can be taken. One could choose to attempt to understand better what one has confronted by approaching it from a perspective of openness, free from the assumption that one's perspective and experience are in some way a definitive account that cannot be challenged. James caught a glimpse of the beauty, even reverence, in the clear-cut fields; Ron might yet learn his father's endearing curiosity about all things Muggle and begin to understand and come to value Seamus' world of which he, at present, knows very little.

Taking the other route, one could stay barricaded within one's own supposedly superior perception—behind their Wall, so to speak. Of course a Quidditch poster with animate characters swooping across it is more exciting than an ordinary, Muggle football poster; to say differently must be self-deception. Of course a deforested, clear-cut, and disorganized farmstead is an eyesore. To think such, without willingness to consider other perspectives, is precisely dogmatic thought. In "Heroic Hermione: Celebrating the Love of Learning," Patrick Shade writes, "Just as we should not forget the context that purposes give our achievements and [blindnesses], so too should we not ignore the generative context of our interests and desires" (Shade 90). The refusal to be open to new ways of thinking, to listen to the story behind the football poster or the farm, means that one is refusing to participate in the inherently self-reflective process of comparing and contrasting such perspectives. Walls of dogmatic thought hurt both the self and the other, diminishing the generative power of both one's own frameworks of perception and those of one's interlocutor.

James' epiphany might become our own if it helps us to understand that we cannot claim a monopoly on how something should be considered. If it helps us to avoid the dangers of dogmatic thinking, it helps to lay the framework for traveling through the wall to Platform 9¾ to start our journey on the Hogwarts Express or to ride on the psychedelic waves of sound to the top of Pink's Wall. In giving us "the power to imagine better," James makes us theoretical alchemists, concerned with bettering both human society and ourselves. In the cases of both Dumbledore's Army and Pink's riot, we see the power of imagination to tear down The Wall—and all brick walls of oppression—or to transform those walls into magical passageways to and through worlds of liberating imagination.

The members of Dumbledore's Army use their imaginations to subvert

Umbridge's agenda. When they practice spells in secret, they are not only learning practical skills. Through honing those skills, they also empower themselves for physical resistance and as creative and open thinkers. Able and devoted members of the D.A., Fred and George Weasley also illustrate how one's vocation can either limit one's range of vision or expand it. While one might see the twins' aspiration to open a joke shop only as a lark or a business opportunity, Fred and George's last flight from Hogwarts shows how their practical skills allow their classmates' imaginations to soar while also empowering them to keep up the resistance. More important than literally supplying the resistance with magical spy gadgets, they represent the idea that those who have relatively little power can still resist dogmatic, oppressive regimes. As Adam-Troy Castro points out in "From Azkaban to Abu Ghraib: Fear and Fascism in *Harry Potter and the Order of the Phoenix*," "nothing hurts an established power figure more than being made to look ridiculous," and this is primarily the case because it frees others under the regime from at least a little of their fear, empowering them to rise up (129–30). The grand nature of Fred and George's exit creates a spectacle which dazzles and inspires the other students. Promised a discount on Weasleys' Wizard Wheezes products if they'll use them "to get rid of this old bat," the students follow through with a vengeance (*Phoenix* 675). Not only do the students undermine Umbridge's lessons when they use Skiving Snackboxes to break out in boils, faint, and swoon with "Umbridge-itis," they also realize that they have allies in the faculty and in Peeves, the Poltergeist, who keep Umbridge flying from one emergency to another (678). In their resistance, they turn education from Umbridge and the Ministry's "thought control" into empowerment (Roger Waters).

In the opening sequence for "Just Another Brick in the Wall, Part 2," Pink responds to being oppressed and openly mocked by the Schoolmaster like the D.A. responds to Umbridge's regime. Pink represents the oppression of a dogmatic educational system as a nightmarish factory in which students are molded into a uniform mob of clones, all walking lockstep in silence towards an enormous meat grinder where they are rendered indistinguishable as humans (*Wall*). Most people would not walk to their own destruction with such docility. Dogmatic education, however, prepares them not to notice. Castro writes, "More dangerous fascist movements proceed with caution, instituting their abuses incrementally … as a series of nested abuses, each one couched in the most beneficial language possible" (125). The students go to class, take exams, wear school uniforms, and participate in what seem to be perfectly ordinary activities, so many may not be aware that their "education" serves another purpose. Castro explains, "The agenda has less to do with educating students than with raising a class of obedient little functionaries. The dangerous thing, of course, is that there is no bottom line ... the more repressive a society becomes, the more repressive it becomes" (127).

As if to represent Pink's imagination arriving and acting as a liberating force, we hear the opening of Roger Waters' chords and lyrics, "We don't need no education / We don't need no thought control" (*The Wall*). Pink instigates the students to riot and to vandalize the school before setting it aflame in a display strikingly reminiscent of the disruptively grandiose last flight of Fred and George in *Order of the Phoenix*. Pink's resistance is imagined, and, while the resistance in the Harry Potter series "really" takes place, it does so in the pages of Rowling's novels. That is, it, too, is imagined. Both take place "in our heads." But, as Dumbledore says to Harry in the "in-between" place of King's Cross Station in *Deathly Hallows*, "why on earth should that mean it is not real?" (723). This resistance, although entirely internal, allows Pink to keep the embers of hope and resistance to the status quo alive, even in the face of the Schoolmaster's overwhelming oppression. In fact, if the Schoolmaster's task is to put critical engagement to sleep, Pink's reawakening of those powers in both his classmates and his audience (and Rowling's in hers) is one antidote to dogmatic thinking.

It is one thing to use the imagination to inspire resistance to externally imposed dogma. Sometimes, though, the things that are happening "in our heads" are self-imposed walls, keeping people imprisoned in dogmatic thinking that either hurts us or empowers us to hurt others. Rowling not only invites her readers to resist oppression, she invites us to understand why some are oppressors. She invites us to examine our own beliefs, too, to see our own blindness and to see when it might cross into dogmatism. If readers can have a look into the minds of even the most bitterly dogmatic characters, we might be empowered both to be more patient with, more sympathetic to, and more self-reflective on the ordinary blindnesses in our own ordinary lives, and, therefore, more strategic in resisting dogmatic oppression.

Where is a better place to start our examinations than with Tom Riddle or Lord Voldemort? Voldemort is a constant victim of his own ignorance and prejudice. While it may be difficult for some to imagine Voldemort being a victim, Shade points out that "Voldemort's plan to purge the Wizarding World of impure blood, for instance, stems from his hatred of his Muggle father" (90). As Harry learns in studying the memories in the Pensieve in *Harry Potter and the Half-Blood Prince*, Voldemort's father leaves his mother, Merope Gaunt, after discovering he had been bound to her by a love potion and was thus in a relationship with her under false pretenses (Shade 91). To make matters worse, Merope dies shortly after Voldemort is born, leaving him essentially alone in the world. It comes as no surprise, then, when Shade writes that "[t]he absence of a mother's love and the hatred of a muggle father who abandoned him leave Voldemort consumed with disdain for others" (91).

Voldemort never understood that his mother, abused lifelong by both her father and her brother, dared to hope for love. He never understood that Merope misused a love potion to ensnare his father and then recognized the flaws in her own thinking and actions. She loved Tom Riddle, Sr., enough to stop giving him the potion, hoping he might love her and their coming child enough to stay. Surely she was torn both by the abuses she suffered in childhood and the abuse she inflicted on Tom Riddle, Sr. In her remorse, she put her soul back together, but the pain of it was more than she could bear (*Hallows* 741). In "Love Potion No. 9¾," Gregory Bassham suggests that Tom Riddle, Jr. was who he became precisely because he was *not* his mother's son (73). While she recognized the mistake in her use of the potion and died of grief rather than continuing to misuse magic, her son hardened his heart and used his considerable magical power to manipulate, control, and murder. As Shade points out, Voldemort's distrust of others and his learned tendency to rely only on himself leads Voldemort to be "blind to the power of love and also the unique gifts of others, especially non-wizards" (Shade 91). Merope's broken heart, ironically, made her more whole. Ripping his soul in his efforts to avoid what he perceived to be the weaknesses of both love and death, Merope's son became less and less whole.

Time and time again, Voldemort's blindness to love's power and blindness to the gifts and contributions of others lead to his failure—both to kill Harry and to redeem himself. When he tried to kill the infant Harry, he both turned Harry into an unintended Horcrux and transfigured him into the Boy Who Lived. The house-elf, Kreacher, succeeded in retrieving Voldemort's locket Horcrux from the island in the center of the lake in the cave where Regulus Black drowned, pulled into the water by Voldemort's army of Inferi. Kreacher succeeded, because Voldemort never understood that elves operate by different magical rules than his and because Regulus was willing to sacrifice his own life for the good of the community. Dobby was able to save Harry, Ron, Hermione, and Griphook from Malfoy Manor because neither Voldemort nor the Malfoys expected an elf to act with Dobby's courage and love, freely given. As Dumbledore says, "Of house-elves and children's tales, of love, loyalty and innocence, Voldemort knows and understands nothing. *Nothing*" (*Hallows* 709).

Voldemort fails to understand Professor Trelawney's prophecy, too. Given his intelligence, Voldemort could quite easily see the flaws in his own plans were he willing to admit that he might be wrong or might not have fully (and fairly) considered a situation. He was utterly and dogmatically blind to the prophecy, which told him "THE ONE WITH THE POWER

TO VANQUISH THE DARK LORD ... WILL HAVE POWER THE DARK LORD KNOWS NOT" (*Phoenix* 841). He might have learned that he had to become Harry's equal, as the prophecy suggests, not the other way around. To make this transformation, Voldemort would have had to understand that Lily's sacrifice gave Harry the power that he, Riddle, knows not. Voldemort consistently and stubbornly fails to think differently, no matter how many times others try to show him another way. He dilutes his humanity with dogma further and further, hurting innumerable others as he does so.

As Dumbledore says to Harry as they listen to the whimpers of the pathetic, agonized bit of Voldemort's soul which had been accidentally placed within Harry, Voldemort could not comprehend the profound magic of Lily's sacrifice for her son, never considered that there might be danger for him in taking Harry's blood. "But then, if he had been able to understand, he could not be Lord Voldemort, and might never have murdered at all" (*Hallows* 710). If Voldemort had been capable of thinking differently, he might not have perished behind his wall, dying broken, alone, and totally unable to do what his mother had done and what Harry asked him to do: "Try for some remorse" (*Hallows* 741).

Even to the end, Rowling leaves the possibility for Voldemort to imagine that he may be wrong and to reflect upon the roots of, and responses to, his dogmatic thinking. Although Voldemort fails to redeem himself, other characters such as Albus Dumbledore and Hermione Granger do manage to take the chance provided to them. Because of these examples, I feel, contrary to what Pink affirms in "Hey You," we may begin to see that the Wall of dogma is not so high that its defeat could be "only fantasy" (Roger Waters).

In the context of Harry Potter, "ignorance" and "Dumbledore" seem an odd pairing of words. However, Dumbledore is so adept at strategizing against Voldemort during his initial reign of terror as well as after Voldemort's resurrection precisely because he has suffered from his own forms of blindness in the past. As Voldemort never learned, love can be the greatest magic, the greatest power. But Dumbledore's friendship with Grindelwald led him not only to seek equality for the magical community but to seek domination over Muggles. In the duel over Ariana's future, Dumbledore was never sure if it was he, in his youthful foolishness, who struck his sister dead (*Hallows* 718). Anti-Magic bigotry had caused her to be damaged and revenge his father to be imprisoned, but Dumbledore's resulting brief quest not only for equality with, but for domination over, Muggles led to her death and his terrible grief.

In his grief, though, Dumbledore does learn something about himself. He tells Harry, "Reality returned in the form of my rough, unlettered, and infinitely more admirable brother" (*Hallows* 717). Describing Aberforth this way, Albus is already shifting away from his love of power.

It matters not if someone has a formal education or a title. Using power responsibly matters; care for the community matters; introspection matters. When Dumbledore says, "[P]ower was my weakness and my temptation" (*Hallows* 718) and tells Harry that he has spent most of his adult life avoiding positions of power, we see something of Dumbledore's epiphany, his pivotal realization of falling prey to, examining, and then working beyond his own blindness. While Dumbledore's caring and compassionate nature towards others leads him to judge that his harmful actions and thus his perception must be corrected, Voldemort's learned distrust of others leads him never to examine his own perspectives critically. As Shade notes, while Voldemort's blindness "only seems to grow, Dumbledore learns from his tragedy. Because he cares for others, especially his sister, his acts' negative consequences to others matter and produce a profound effect on him" (91). Dumbledore understands that his actions are wrong, because his perspective values others, whom his actions have harmed. Precisely because he is able to imagine how someone else thinks and feels, Dumbledore is able to examine his own blindness, to begin to see the world differently, and to "learn to live with [his] guilt and [his] terrible grief, the price of [his] shame" (*Hallows* 717).

Like Dumbledore, Hermione has a keen sense of justice. A Muggle-born witch, she only gradually learns something of the dogmatic blindness in some wizards. Malfoy calls her "Mudblood," and it is Ron's and Hagrid's outraged reactions that show her the cruelty behind the epithet (*Chamber* 112, 115). But, she is also open to seeing the world through more than one set of lenses, precisely because she was raised in one context and goes through the magical barrier at Platform 9¾ to learn about another world, which is also her birthright. Her parents, too, demonstrate this openness to cultures that are unfamiliar to them when they eagerly meet with the Weasleys in Diagon Alley and then head back to the Muggle world through the wall into the Leaky Cauldron (*Chamber* 59, 63). Although the pub is supposedly invisible to Muggle eyes, maybe Stan Shunpike reveals that the problem is more lack of attention—a certain blindness—rather than any particular magical barrier. When Harry wonders why Muggles do not notice whole houses jumping out of the way of the Knight Bus, Stan explains, "Them! ... Don' look properly, do they? ... Never notice nuffink, they don'" (*Azkaban* 36).

Hermione's parents and Mr. Weasley show that there are other worlds to see, if only one looks properly. Hermione herself undertakes the even-more-difficult task of attending to her own birth culture from the point of view of her perspective in the magical world. She demonstrates the best sort of education in her love for learning about the world through different perspectives. Though Muggle-born and thus heavily acclimated to life in a non-magical world, Hermione opts to enroll in a Muggle Studies course. When met with skepticism from Ron, Hermione responds "it'll be fascinating to study them from the wizarding point of view" (*Azkaban* 57). Hermione's willingness to be open to new perspectives and her eagerness to learn about them allow her to work through her own blindnesses. She is not only able to see when she is on the receiving end of an injustice, she is also able to see injustice that works to her benefit. She undertakes the tremendously difficult task of trying to see and overcome both her own oppression and her own unearned privilege.

Hermione's own care for others and her strong sense of justice both allow her to imagine and work for a more fair world and allow her to stand up for herself when she faces anti-Muggle discrimination. It gives her the clear-headed insight to imagine and then to implement Dumbledore's Army, including helping Harry to believe he can teach his friends Defense and empower them to fight against the Ministry's dogmatic, crushing policies. At the same time, these very same and admirable commitments cloud her vision when she takes up the cause of house-elf liberation. For one summer "of insanity, of cruel dreams, and neglect of the only two members of [his] family left to [him]" (*Hallows* 717), Dumbledore was blinded by "the greater good" in his pursuit of power with Grindelwald. Even Voldemort almost assuredly believes that his cause is justified, believing as he does that he is "special" (*Prince* 271). This is not to say that Hermione was ever guided by cruelty or a sense of superiority. Hers is an example of something harder to see. Because she was not able, at least at first, to try to imagine the elves' position through their eyes, she was not as effective an ally to them as she might have been. This is an especially vital consideration, as it shows that even the most well-intentioned actions may in reality be harmful if they are coming from a person hindered by blindness.

At the Quidditch World Cup in *Goblet of Fire*, Hermione is outraged by Barty Crouch's treatment of Winky, the house-elf whom he has enslaved and then dismisses. As young as she is, Hermione responds in a remarkably sophisticated way when she decides to form the Society for the Promotion of Elfish Welfare, a group with the unfortunate acronym, S.P.E.W. Hermione writes admirable goals in the Society's manifesto: "Our short-term aims … are to secure house-elves fair wages and working conditions. Our long-term aims include changing the law about non-wand use, and trying to get an elf into the Department for the Regulation and Control of Magical Creatures, because they are shockingly underrepresented" (*Goblet* 224–25). In response, she faces a certain blindness from some in the wizarding world. Ron, taking for granted the status of the elves, argues that "[t]hey *like* being enslaved!" while Fred and George protest "we've met them, and they're *happy*. They think they've got the best job in the world—" (*Goblet*

224; 239). Even our beloved Hagrid, who so often faces discrimination himself, says Hermione would "be makin' 'em unhappy ter take away their work, an' insultin' 'em if yeh tried ter pay 'em." When Hermione points out how happy Dobby is to be free, Hagrid responds, "yeh get weirdos in every breed" (265).

When I was reading the series for the first time as a child, I was inspired by Hermione's efforts to free the elves. As I came back to the series later as a young adult, I realized that Hermione and, at least in my case, the reader alongside her were eager to lead this crusade for elfish welfare without taking time to see the house-elves' lives through elves' eyes and to listen to their stories, hopes, and fears. We were in some ways guilty of Stan Shunpike's observations about Muggles who "never notice nuffink" about the actual culture or opinions of the house-elves in the magical world in general or at Hogwarts in particular. Neither Hermione nor I would argue that the elves' enslavement can be justified, even if the elves themselves cannot see any other way. As Bryccan Carey explains in "Hermione and the House-Elves," part of the elves' enslavement is an internalization of the very ideology used to keep them in thrall (104). It is as if Umbridge's and the Schoolmaster's campaign to create what Castro called "obedient little functionaries" has been carried to the extreme. But the remedy to this oppression cannot exclude the elves themselves, even if they are unable to see the unfair conditions of their lives or to imagine other possibilities.

Among her classmates who are willing to fight and risk punishment for a change on the social and political level for the magical world, only Hermione takes this political activism to the lives of the elves (Carey 105). Yet no one, not even Hermione, sees Winky for Winky, at least not at first. Imagine if someone could recognize her skill and diplomacy as she kept both Crouch's home and his secrets (*Goblet* 381–82). Imagine if someone could understand how accomplished she was and that she deserved praise and respect for her achievements. At the same time, were we able to accomplish this shift in vision, we might be able to see how clothes might not seem like liberation for all or even many elves. They might take clothes as a signal that their work is not understood or appreciated. At the same time, the "liberated" elf might face homelessness, hunger, and isolation. If only witches and wizards could begin to see the elves' work this way, they might, then, revalue that work and start to value those lives as much as they value their own. The elves, too, might, then, see such things as a voice in government and fair wages as a recognition of their value and as a sense of security, rather than as an insult.

Carey argues that while Ron has internalized the "status quo" position of the wizarding world, Harry has a "sympathetic and personal" response to Dobby's particular enslavement rather than looking at the larger political picture as Hermione does (104). As a child who was hidden away under the stairs and neglected or abused by his aunt, uncle, and cousin, Harry knows something of the conditions in which Dobby lives. At their first meeting in *Chamber of Secrets*, Harry, who is "in [his] room, making no noise and pretending [he is] not there," asks Dobby to sit down, "like an *equal*—" (6, 13). To Harry's horror, the elf bursts into tears and says, "Dobby has heard of your greatness, sir, but of your goodness, Dobby never knew..." (15). At the beginning of the novel, Dobby is trying to protect Harry both from the Malfoys and from Voldemort. By the end of the novel, Harry has tricked Lucius Malfoy into freeing Dobby. Carey is right that Harry, at this point, acts from personal connection to one elf in particular. Although Harry and Dobby have helped each other out, individual to individual, the corrupt system of elf enslavement needs the kind of systemic attention Hermione suggests. Although her supporters are at first few, she does have them. Mr. Weasley agrees that the house-elves are poorly treated (*Goblet* 139). Dumbledore hires both Winky and Dobby when they cannot find employment anywhere else and offers them a salary, time off, and permission to call him "a barmy old codger"—without having to punish themselves, of course (380).

Harry and Hermione, though, might both benefit if they could combine their points of view, the personal and the political. Ironically, even Ron's, Hagrid's, and the twins' perspectives are useful in trying to see the situation more clearly and to act more effectively. When Hermione, Ron, and Harry go to visit Dobby in the Hogwarts' kitchens, they discover that Winky is mortified by her new employment. She is disheveled and drinks too much Butterbeer. Once proud of her work for Crouch, she is now despondent. Even Dobby has to set some limits. He is proud to be a free house-elf, and he insists that, because he is free, he "can obey anyone he likes and Dobby will do whatever Harry Potter wants him to do!" (*Prince* 421). And he proudly tells Hermione that "Professor Dumbledore offered Dobby ten Galleons a week, and weekends off ... but Dobby beat him down, miss.... Dobby likes freedom, miss, but he isn't wanting too much, miss, he likes work better" (*Goblet* 379). The other elves make their wishes known, too, scornfully escorting the students out of their domain.

But, even though Hermione brings a certain human blindness to her elf-liberation campaign, she is not dogmatic. She has a passion for learning—both about particular facts and skills and about other people's points of view. She studies the nuances of even difficult situations and plans strategically. Her thinking about the elves shifts and grows as she gets to know some of them. Ron, too, "takes a liking to Dobby" once he actually talks with him (*Goblet* 382). With her growing ability to respect the elves' agency, Hermione also learns more about internalized oppression and how difficult it is to overcome. When she, Ron, and Harry are hiding out at twelve, Grimmauld Place, Harry summons Kreacher, the house-elf he inherited from Sirius along with the hated House of Black. Even though Kreacher calls her "Mudblood," Hermione cries out, "Oh, don't you see now how sick it is, the way they've got to obey?" (*Hallows* 197).

And then she puts the blame squarely back on wizards, again calling attention both to her position of privilege and to her desire for change on a political, systemic level. She explains to Ron and Harry how it was that Kreacher could betray Sirius to Voldemort even after Voldemort killed Kreacher's much-loved Regulus, saying that kindness was the most important motivating factor for Kreacher. Even though Sirius was admirable in so many ways, he was never kind to Kreacher, who reminded him of the family whose beliefs he despised (198). Harry has grown from being an abused child forced to work for an aunt and uncle who seemed to despise him into a young-adult owner of a house-elf, something he never desired but which, nevertheless, gave him power over another living creature's life. After listening to Kreacher's tale and to Hermione's shifting analysis, Harry has a kind of epiphany. He changes his tone toward Kreacher and begins to treat him as he treated Dobby, with some sort of recognition and empathy. Offering Kreacher Regulus' locket is also an offer of a partnership, or as close to one as is possible while the system of enslavement persists. Kreacher takes pride in his work, and Harry's simple recognition that it is important work done well goes some small way toward making a needed change. Even Ron has a revelation of sorts, which he demonstrates during the Battle of Hogwarts when he insists the elves should be moved to safety, saying "We can't order them to die for us—" (*Hallows* 625).

Albus Dumbledore, Ron, Harry, and, perhaps especially, Hermione, stand in contrast with Voldemort for sure. But Pink, too, falls short. Pink Floyd's movie and album, *The Wall*, provides a heavily internal narrative, focusing more on what Pink feels and imagines rather than what he actually does. Yet, feeling and imagining are also doing, just as poring over books and appreciating other people's ideas are doing, as Hermione shows us over and over. Pink's life in *The Wall* illustrates resistance to dogma, but in "Hey You," one of the biggest turning points in the film, Pink seems unable or unwilling to self-reflect or care. Until this point, Pink uses his imagination to resist the pressing dogmas and traumas he faces. Pink, the poet and musician, the one who dares to dream and imagine better and who so pounds against the Wall, fails to see it living inside of himself. There is a risk in making one's identity only in resistance, for then the power of the thing resisted is reified and amplified; the Wall without might well become the Wall within.

Like Voldemort's, Pink's home situation is less than ideal. After his father's untimely death during World War II, his mother becomes increasingly doting and suffocating to him, going to pains to shelter him from both the benefits of connecting with others and from the pain of being hurt by others (Roger Waters). The bricks in Pink's Wall include his grief and his mother's misguided protection, include the Schoolmaster, include "education" in unthinking obedience to cultural convention, and include a refusal to connect with others precisely because he sees connection as complicity in the numb walk to the meat grinder of crushing conformity—or as just another risk of more loss and grief. Between "Another Brick in The Wall, Part 2" and "Hey You," Pink has grown into an adult rock star, still tormented by the blindness he holds to the value of connecting with others. He has public adulation but no human connection, the very kind of "relationship" Voldemort has with at least some of his followers.

Unlike Voldemort, though, Pink understands that he is struggling to make connections with others as he sits behind his Wall. At this point, however, he does not understand that his inability to connect with others stems from his personal blindness to the value of these connections, caused initially by his childhood trauma; instead, he believes that making connections with others means acquiescing to the dogmatic social norms impressed upon him (*The Wall*). In roughly the first thirty seconds of the scene in which "Hey You" plays, Pink struggles futilely against an endlessly long, hopelessly solid brick wall. He can see the wall, and is, in fact, painfully aware of it, but he cannot do more than claw and pound against it. "Hey You" displays Pink's realization that, despite his best efforts, the very same society that harmed him both with its dogmatic status quo and for his resistance to it has also conditioned him to uphold it, whether he is willing or not (*The Wall*). His Wall is built by bricks of trauma and oppression and is mortared together by his personal blindness.

Shortly after "Hey You" plays in the movie, a riot unfolds. Rioters struggle in the streets as riot police form an impenetrable shield wall and drive them back, symbolizing Pink's last embers of resistance being crushed. As the rioters clash with police and the violence escalates, the song's lyrics take on the form of an inner monologue between Pink's exhaustion and his will to continue to pound against his Wall. Since the Wall lives in his head, it is especially real for him. As Pink struggles against the Wall, the song suggests something of the futility of that struggle when it says, "it was only fantasy" and that "[t]he wall was too high …/He could not break free." Another, silent, entity representing his conscious mind urges him on: "Hey you, don't help them to bury the light/Don't give in without a fight," symbolizing Pink's will to resist, to be drawn once again into action against the Wall (Roger Waters).

If anything is made clear during "Hey You," it is that Pink wants desperately to tear down his Wall. Yet, while the riot does represent Pink's rage against his Wall, it seems that the riot itself represents that he is going about doing so in a fundamentally wrong way. As the riot police bear down on the protestors with their wall of shields, the protestors in turn create a barricade—a wall of debris to shield them from the advance of the police. Because of his fundamental misunderstanding of, and blindness to, the value of forming emotional connections with others, Pink is essentially trying to hate himself into being able to make connections with others. The Wall proves too high for him to scale, because he has internalized dogmas of prejudice and hate, brought to creepy, crawling, ubiquitous light in the "And the worms ate into his brain" line in "Hey You" (Roger Waters). Steeped in self-hate, Pink becomes more like Voldemort when he changes from being blind to the value of emotional connection with others to being blind to the value of others entirely. When "the worms [eat] into his brain," he finally succumbs to the hateful dogmas of racism, sexism, and homophobia impressed upon him by the culture in which he lives and has, at least for the moment, lost any reason to resist (Roger Waters).

In "Waiting for the Worms," Pink assumes a leadership position in a hate group and uses his charisma as a rock star to recruit new members, mirroring Voldemort's descent from a troubled and violent youth to an outright icon of hate and violence. In this song, Pink spreads the "worms" (or dogmas) and attempts to draw racists and homophobes to the group in much the same way Voldemort draws in his own Death Eaters. From refusing human connection, precisely because he mistook it for giving in to corrupt socialization, Pink embraces that worry with a vengeance, when he—like Voldemort and his Death Eaters, Umbridge and her Ministry propaganda, or the Schoolmaster and his rigid adherence to the status quo—tells his followers that if they desire the fulfillment of their hate-filled dogma, "All [they] have to do is follow the worms" (Roger Waters).

Thankfully, though, Pink differs from Voldemort; in the end, he finds redemption. In "Stop," the very next track on the album, we see Pink's epiphany. Pink comes to his senses as the chaos reaches a peak, and he looks outward to the violence he has caused in his delusional state. He then realizes that this cannot be the result he sought, mirroring Albus Dumbledore's lifelong remorse over his role in Ariana's death. The shortest track on the album, "Stop" aches with Pink's longing:

> I wanna go home
> Take off this uniform and leave the show
> And I'm waiting in this cell because I have to know
> Have I been guilty all this time? [Roger Waters]

Finally, we see Pink critically engage with his blindness in a way that is not through self-hate or hatred of others. When Pink questions his own guilt, he questions his own role as the architect of his Wall for the first time in the entire film and album. Instead of following Voldemort's example of blaming his failures on others and subsequently building his Wall higher, Pink begins to "try for some remorse," which, as Hermione predicted, is terribly painful but liberating at the same time (*Hallows* 103). He, like Dumbledore, is able to recognize that he has done wrong when he knew (or thought he knew) no better way. He recognizes that he is not seeing the entire picture—that he is blind to something.

In a climactic scene aptly named "The Trial," Pink journeys within himself and uses his imagination to reflect critically upon himself in a grand-scale inquisition before his memories, feelings, and childhood traumas. The defendant, Pink is being prosecuted for "showing feelings of an almost human nature" (Roger Waters & Bob Erzin). Presiding over the trial is the Judge, whom the Prosecutor addresses officially as "Worm your honor." Since Pink's perspective is now heavily infested by worms, or, in other words, corrupted by dogmatic thinking, the dogma-worms morph and form not only the Judge himself, but everything and everyone else that appears in "The Trial" aside from Pink and his Wall (*The Wall*).

Pink's choice to imagine himself on trial by his own dogma-infested mind shows that he has realized that his judgment is fundamentally hampered by his blindness. Thus, Pink uses his imagination in a curiously backwards way—he judges himself by the only standards he possesses, even though he knows that they are corrupted. Because of his new-found awareness (or alleviated blindness) regarding the harmful nature of his Wall-bound thought, he knows that being "guilty" of "showing feelings of an almost human nature" must actually be an exoneration and a turn toward a different, more open sort of life (Roger Waters & Bob Erzin). "The Trial" concludes with Pink being found overwhelmingly, incontrovertibly guilty of this crime, and his greatest desire and fear are simultaneously realized. The judge screams "Tear down The Wall!," and Pink's Wall comes thundering down (Roger Waters & Bob Erzin).

Even so, Pink screams in terror as his Wall is blown to pieces (*The Wall*). These "feelings of an almost human nature" are exactly what Harry pushes Voldemort to try for at the end of *Deathly Hallows*, something which he, unlike Pink, cannot bear (Roger Waters & Bob Erzin). Voldemort never "tries for some remorse," perhaps because he cannot see his wall but also maybe because he does sense its presence and fears its climactic fall and the responsibility he would then have to adopt for the harm he had caused by his own dogmatic blindness (*Hallows* 741). And so, we finally see the great challenge that comes with reflecting on blindness—it inevitably requires an admission of ignorance and responsibility for the resulting harm.

Ron learned something about his ignorance from Dobby's heroic sacrifice. After Harry's insistence on honoring Dobby by digging the grave with a spade, Ron and Dean join Harry in swaddling Dobby in socks, a hat, and a jacket (*Hallows* 478–79). Harry insists, too, on carving the headstone by hand. "HERE LIES DOBBY, A FREE ELF," who gave his life with his eyes wide open as Lily had done and as Harry tried to do (481). Hermione has helped herself and her friends to imagine potential antidotes to their blindness. She is the very reverse of the sort of learner Umbridge or the Schoolmaster wanted her to be as she "amply demonstrates joy and fascination in learning itself," which allows her to understand that there is some vague wall in the dark that she is not seeing and which she brings to light (Shade 101).

Hermione sees through many perspectives to understand both her own privilege and her oppression and to work against both. When she is able to say "Mudblood, and proud of it" after being tortured at Malfoy Manor, she shatters the idea that simply the name for who she is by birth is somehow shameful. When she reminds Griphook that she is hunted just as much as he or any elf under the present regime and makes "Ron fidget … uncomfortably on the arm of [her] chair" into the bargain, she shifts from merely banging her head against someone else's wall to becoming an ally to the oppressed—whether people of her heritage or house-elves—rather than a human savior (*Hallows* 489). She tears down walls of oppression as she works against human blindness and avoids becoming dogmatic. She shows that

> The ones who really love you
> Walk up and down outside The Wall
> Some hand in hand
> And some gathered together in bands
> The bleeding hearts and the artists
> Make their stand. (Roger Waters, "Outside the Wall")

Hermione shows the power of imagining better in order to make an alchemical transfiguration both in individuals and in communities. When one knows how to tap on the correct bricks in a Wall, however tall, a portal opens into the magical world beyond it in which blindness is cured and dogma destroyed. Contrary to what parts of The Wall may tell us, a door can be found or made in the Wall, provided one taps on just the right bricks. The doorway we make using imagination is not where we came in but is, instead, how we get out.

Works Cited

Ackermann, Zeno. "Rocking the Culture Industry/Performing Breakdown: Pink Floyd's *The Wall* and the Termination of the Postwar Era." *Popular Music and Society*, vol. 35, no. 1, Taylor and Francis Online, 22 Feb. 2012, pp. 1–23, doi/abs/10.1080/03007766.2010.522830.
"Another Brick in The Wall, Part 2." Music and lyrics by Roger Waters. *Pink Floyd The Wall*. Columbia Records 1979. Vinyl LP.
Bassham, Gregory. "Love Potion No. 9¾." *The Ultimate Harry Potter and Philosophy: Hogwarts for Muggles*, edited by Gregory Bassham, Wiley, 2010, pp. 66–79. Blackwell Philosophy and Pop-Culture Series.
Carey, Brycchan. "Hermione and the House Elves: The Literary and Historical Contexts of J.K. Rowling's Antislavery Campaign." *Reading Harry Potter: Critical Essays*, edited by Giselle Liza Anatol, Greenwood, 2003, pp. 103–15. Contributions to the Study of Popular Culture Series.
Castro, Adam-Troy. "From Azkaban to Abu Ghraib: Fear and Facism in *Harry Potter and the Order of the Phoenix*." *Mapping the World of the Sorcerer's Apprentice: An Unauthorized Exploration of the Harry Potter Series*, edited by Mercedes Lackey, BenBella, 2005, pp. 125–29. Smart Pop Books.
"Hey You." Music and lyrics by Roger Waters. *Pink Floyd The Wall*. Columbia Records, 1979. Vinyl LP.
James, William. "On a Certain Blindness in Human Beings." *On Some of Life's Ideals*, Henry Holt, 1899, archive.org/details/onsomeoflifeside001778mbp. Accessed 14 Feb. 2018.
"Mother." Music and lyrics by Roger Waters. *Pink Floyd The Wall*, Columbia Records, 1979. Vinyl LP.
Pink Floyd The Wall. Columbia Records, 1979. Vinyl LP.
Pink Floyd The Wall. Directed by Alan Parker, Goldcrest Films International, 1982.
Rowling, J.K. *Harry Potter and the Chamber of Secrets*. Scholastic, 1998
_____. *Harry Potter and the Deathly Hallows*. Scholastic, 2007.
_____. *Harry Potter and the Goblet of Fire*. Scholastic, 2000.
_____. *Harry Potter and the Half-Blood Prince*. Scholastic, 2005.
_____. *Harry Potter and the Order of the Phoenix*. Scholastic, 2002.
_____. *Harry Potter and the Prisoner of Azkaban*. Scholastic, 1999.
_____. *Harry Potter and the Sorcerer's Stone*. Scholastic, 1997.
Shade, Patrick. "Heroic Hermione: Celebrating the Love of Learning." *Reason Papers*, vol. 34, no. 1, pp. 89–108, June 2012. reasonpapers.com/pdf/341/rp_341_7.pdf.
"The Trial." Written by Roger Waters, and Bob Erzin. *Pink Floyd The Wall*. Columbia Records, 1979. Vinyl LP.
"Waiting for the Worms." Music and lyrics by Roger Waters. *Pink Floyd The Wall*. Columbia Records, 1979. Vinyl LP.

III
The Cloak of Invisibility and the Transfiguration of Self and Community

And All Was Well

TAMYRA DIXON-RANKIN, DEPUTY
HEADMISTRESS, DUMBLEDORE'S ACADEMY

I teach in a small rural school district in the heart of the Corn Belt with a total K–12 enrollment of under nine hundred. My introduction to the Potter books came in the late 1990s, when I began to notice the same book appearing on the desks of my middle school science students. It was *Harry Potter and the Sorcerer's Stone*. I was often asked, "If I get my lab done can I read my book?" How can you say no to a student who wants to read?

Soon, I began seeing this book on more desks and discovered it was the most requested book in our school library. Since it seemed always to be checked out, I ordered a few copies for my classroom and they, too, vanished quickly. I decided I had better read the book myself so I could not only understand the Harry Potter phenomenon, but perhaps also better communicate with my students. From my years of teaching, I had learned that a good way to engage students is to talk about their reading: what they like in a book, what keeps them turning pages, and what stimulates their imaginations.

So I read *Harry Potter and the Sorcerer's Stone* and I understood immediately—this was a book about them.

I realized that Harry's experience going to Hogwarts and leaving all he knows behind, being an eleven-year-old in a strange new building with older students, bullies, complex rules and expectations, increasing social and academic pressures, lost in the hallways, looking for rooms and new teachers—these are the experiences our eleven-year-old sixth graders are having when they leave the elementary campus eight miles away and join us at our middle school in a totally different town, with new bus schedules and new teachers and new hallways to learn and navigate, big eighth graders, and mean kids.

Harry's story is their story—at precisely the time they need to hear it. They need to understand that friends do come through for you, that you can handle a bully in many ways, that people will talk about you and you will be OK, that some understanding adult has your back, and that you will find your way to art class.

To help address pressing family and social needs in our district, in 2012 we created an after-school program. During the development of that program, a sixth grader came to me and asked if he could start a Harry Potter book club. I was delighted by both the idea and his exuberant "pitching" of his plan, and so Dumbledore's Academy was born.

It was all Conner—I was just there to be the adult in the room and see that no potions went wrong, and that dueling did not get out of hand. I sometimes facilitated the discussions of the reading as they progressed through the books that year. Conner—or "Headmaster," as the kids called him—occasionally asked me for advice on the day's discussion of the books, and I would walk him through some vocabulary and guide him to discuss themes and symbolism. It was a remarkable year.

Like J.K. Rowling's books, our Harry Potter Reading Club has become an institution in our school: a place for safety, a place for friendship and solidarity, protection, and wonder. The books have changed how I teach, how I respond to student needs, how I see reluctant readers, how I see the voracious readers progress through the series, and how I listen to their conversations and comparisons of the Harry Potter themes and the similar but also different themes in other literature they are consuming. I have been a better teacher for reading Harry Potter, and my students have become better readers and better people. I have seen it; I have heard them use Potter examples and metaphors when they advise or comfort other students. I have even experienced the most moving and profound exchange of my career.

A cancer diagnosis caused me to be absent from the classroom for nearly a semester. Within a few weeks of my return, one of my seventh graders lost a brother in a car accident. We spent many moments in silent understanding, tears, a hand pat, words of support and comfort. On the last day of school, he came to me with big wet eyes and handed me a small piece of paper. He told me not to look until he was gone. As I watched this small boy depart for the summer, to a house one brother short now, I opened the paper and on it was written "And All Was Well." I took that to mean "We made it, Mrs. R.—you and I made it through this terrible year." That is framed and propped on my desk and reminds me of the power of literature in a child's life, and the influence the morals and themes in the Harry Potter books have had on me and my students.

The Snitch, the Stone, and the Sword

Harry Potter the Alchemical Seeker

B.L. Purdom

Alchemy's goal is to produce the Philosopher's Stone, which can be the catalyst for converting base metals into gold or brewing the Elixir of Life. Metaphorical alchemical transformations occur throughout the seven-book *Harry Potter* series, and many that prove most significant in later books occur in the first, whose original title refers to the result of a process of alchemical transformation: *Harry Potter and the Philosopher's Stone*. Alchemy is based upon the idea that all objects—and people—are constantly engaged in a gradual process of "improvement," of becoming the best or most-exalted forms of themselves. Despite what seems to be abundant evidence to the contrary, this philosophy maintains that all metals will eventually become gold over long periods and that humans will come close to divinity, which includes immortality and overcoming the corruption of the physical body. Historian of Religion Mircea Eliade calls the alchemist, the person who works to hurry these human or metallurgical transformations toward perfection, *homo faber*, a human creator or *smith* (52, 100–01).

Bernard Snits defines a game as "the voluntary attempt to overcome unnecessary obstacles" (McGonigal 22). Alchemy, then, could be called, at its core, a *game*. Speeding up an "inevitable" process certainly seems unnecessary, as is overcoming obstacles to achieving its ends more quickly. One does it because one *chooses* it; one opts for the difficult path, rather than letting nature take its course. As Dumbledore reminds a frightened eleven-year-old boy who has just killed a basilisk, "It is our choices, Harry, that show what we truly are, far more than our abilities," and Harry has made his choice (*Chamber* 245).

Rowling rounds out her creation of an enchanted British boarding school with Quidditch, a game played on broomsticks. Three "Chasers" try to put the Quaffle through three hoops, guarded by "Keepers" at opposite ends of the pitch. Two "Beaters" hit cannonball-like "Bludgers" at opposing players, making it more difficult for them to play without coming to grievous bodily harm. The seventh position is the Seeker, whose sole job is to catch the Golden Snitch, the tiny winged ball whose capture ends the game and scores 150 points for the Seeker's team. Curiously, even if a team has 140 points from goals and the opposing team has zero, if the Seeker on the team with no goals catches the Snitch, that team receives 150 points and wins. If the difference in points between the teams is greater than 150 and the trailing team's Seeker catches the Snitch, the Seeker who caught the Snitch is *not* on the winning team; that Seeker has won the game for the "enemy." In *Harry Potter and the Goblet of Fire*, Viktor Krum, Bulgaria's Seeker, catches the Snitch to end the Quidditch World Cup, which goes to Ireland (113). His actions foreshadow Ginny Weasley's in her first match as a Seeker in *Order of the Phoenix*. That this is possible—a Seeker pursuing a Snitch may not be trying to win for their side but could be pursuing a higher purpose—distinguishes Quidditch from all other games, even ones like soccer, rugby, or basketball, in which players can score "own goals"—usually accidentally—that benefit the opposing team.

It is striking that Rowling chose the title of "Seeker" for this key seventh position. In the early seventeenth century, English religious dissenters known as Seekers believed that a person should be open to direct revelation from God, rather than relying upon an intermediary, a belief also common to Baptists and Quakers; many Seekers joined Quaker meetings (Hill 71–76). Rowling's choice to begin the seventh book of the series with Quaker William Penn's words, "Death is but crossing the world, as friends do the seas…" (*Hallows* xvii), reinforces the link between the Seekers and Quakers, and the alchemical philosophy of death being an illusion (Place, *Magic and Alchemy* 47). The alchemical belief in nature's essential goodness and inevitable perfection along with the Seekers' credo of direct communion with God or the sacred in the world ran counter to Calvin's theology of the world being irretrievably corrupted by the Fall in Eden (Allen 41–42).

Harry's Quidditch position becomes not just a sports role but a metaphysical title pointing to his inherently liminal nature as an *axis mundi*, a link between worlds. As an alchemical "Seeker" he is like a shaman crossing thresholds into forbidden or hidden realms, returning with a boon or the solution for removing a curse from the world, transforming Quidditch from an inter-house rivalry into an alchemical journey with mystical overtones. If the alchemical transformations of Rowling's series, then, take the form of a metaphorical Quidditch match, Harry is at times the catalyst for change, while at other times he is the one transformed. The youngest Seeker in a century, Harry excels in that role, yet sometimes he is the metaphorical Snitch, the flying golden ball pursued across the skies. Gryffindor Quidditch captain, Oliver Wood, calls Harry the team's "secret weapon" (*Stone* 133), and Harry is sometimes like the Sword of Gryffindor coming to the aid of others, while at other times, the literal sword or a metaphorical sword comes to him in his hour of need. That is, sometimes Harry is the intercessor and sometimes the one in need of intercession. He is Seeker and Snitch, the Philosopher's Stone and the Elixir created from the Stone, the Sword of Gryffindor and the beneficiary of the Sword.

The night Voldemort kills Harry's parents, Harry becomes the Boy Who Lived and an accidental Horcrux, a vessel containing/protecting part of Voldemort's soul, which Voldemort has ripped apart by committing murder. Harry's mother's love leads her to sacrifice her life, giving him protection "in his very skin"; when Voldemort attempts to murder Harry next, the infant survives the "fatal" curse and becomes something like a human Philosopher's Stone—both a thing to make someone immortal and someone who seems immortal himself (*Stone* 299). Lily's protection causes the curse to rebound, destroying the Dark Lord's body and lodging part of his soul in the infant Harry. In attempting to make six Horcruxes and a seven-part soul, Voldemort had thought this added to his power, as "seven [is] the most powerfully magical number" (*Prince* 466). Along with his other Horcruxes, Harry tethers Voldemort to life (*Hallows* 686); though without a body, he is not truly dead or even a ghost (*Prince* 497). Harry, by contrast, is not only intact but *augmented* by his scar and by becoming a Horcrux. This is the paradox of Harry—he *begins* as whole, a complete soul, yet pieces added to him augment him throughout his journey to wholeness, though *he is already whole*. His Hogwarts letter is a piece of that journey as well, making him someone who *knows* he is a wizard. His wand is a piece, *choosing him*, augmenting him again. Throughout his Seeker's journey, Harry repeatedly becomes *more complete*, while Voldemort is the epitome of incompletion.

The Snitch

The catalyst for Harry's and Voldemort's contrasting transformations at the beginning of *Harry Potter and the Philosopher's Stone* is the prophecy Severus Snape overhears during Sybill Trelawney's job interview, preserved at the Ministry of Magic in a Prophecy Orb (*Prince* 677). Rowling does not reveal the existence of the Orb until *Harry Potter and the Order of the Phoenix*; in *Philosopher's Stone*, its stand-in is Neville Longbottom's Remembrall.

The Prophecy Orb preserves the memory of Professor Trelawney's prediction; the Remembrall glows red to remind Neville of what he has forgotten. The two "memory orbs" link Harry and Neville as surely as their parents' fates do. Dumbledore later suggests that Neville, also born at the end of July, was another possible candidate for "Prophecy Boy" (*Phoenix* 842).

When Professor McGonagall sees Harry catch the Snitch-like Remembrall, she recognizes him as a natural Seeker, takes him to Oliver Wood straight away, and transfigures him (she *is* the Transfiguration professor) into the Gryffindor Seeker. When Harry recovers Neville's orb from Draco in a spectacular airborne chase on his broom, the size and red color of the Remembrall make it a doppelgänger to the Philosopher's Stone, and Harry protects it from a Slytherin, like the real Stone and like the Prophecy Orb later. In all three cases, Harry rescues the Remembrall, the Stone, and the Orb to protect others and himself, not for self-aggrandizement. In contrast, Draco steals the Remembrall to humiliate Neville and show off. Harry is not trying to win accolades or even a spot on the Quidditch team, though he gets both (he expected to be expelled). By acting the Seeker he already is, Harry is transfigured into one.

After Harry is transformed into a Seeker he is transformed again by catching the Snitch in his mouth and spitting it out. It is now *of* him, part of him; he is a human Snitch, symbolically giving birth to the ball and to his transfigured self, in a reversal of Voldemort's transformations. Before Harry and Hermione go to Godric's Hollow in the final book, Hermione reads a passage from *A History of Magic* by Bathilda Bagshot about Godric's Hollow being where "*Godric Gryffindor was born, and where Bowman Wright, Wizarding smith, forged the first Golden Snitch*" (*Hallows* 319). This small detail links Quidditch to Godric's Hollow and again suggests that Harry is both Seeker and Snitch; the birthplace of all Snitches is *his* birthplace, and he and Hermione are going there to "Seek" answers. In Bathilda Bagshot's house they battle Nagini and Voldemort, barely escaping with their lives; Rowling provides a clue that they will be in a Quidditch-like battle in which Harry is again a Snitch by prefacing the battle with a reference to Godric's Hollow being home to the creator of the Golden Snitch.

Throughout the series, Harry is either the Seeker or the Sought. Playing Seeker in Quidditch is an alchemy whose allegorical goal is wholeness, which Harry achieves when he reunites with the Snitch, and whose literal goal is gold, also achieved by catching a *Golden* Snitch. In *Order of the Phoenix*, Harry holds a struggling Snitch at the end of the year's first match, after Umbridge bans him from Quidditch for life. The struggling Snitch is clearly *Harry*, feeling as trapped as the golden ball in his fist, after having been banned from the game that is an act of spiritual completion for him. During the remainder of the school year, his future spouse, Ginny

Weasley, is Seeker on the Gryffindor Quidditch team, and when she catches the Snitch "from under Cho's nose," she is catching Harry, symbolically taking him from his ex-girlfriend (621).

When Harry Seeks a Snitch, it can be seen as his pursuing a piece of himself, as if Snitches are Philosopher's Stones to him, strengthening and completing himself by doing this and making his already whole soul more so, in stark contrast to Voldemort, whose Horcruxes are a more sinister version of Harry's Golden Snitches, seen "through a glass, darkly" (*King James Bible* 1 Corinthians 13:12). Voldemort diminishes himself when he splits his soul, seeking a corrupted form of immortality, neither human nor divine.

Harry's transfiguration into a virtual Snitch colors the entire series, in which his battles often have game-like qualities. The Order moves Harry out of Privet Drive in a chaotic operation analogous to a more-dangerous-than-usual Quidditch match. Rather than seven players, Harry's side has fourteen, six impersonating him. Many times that number are on Voldemort's side. Each pair on Harry's side is a unit: a Harry and a partner. Like his mother Lily, they are also willing to die for him as they escort him across three counties (*Hallows* 130). Instead of two teams with two Seekers both pursuing a Snitch, Voldemort and the Death Eaters try to catch Harry, while the Order tries to keep him. On the eve of his seventeenth birthday, Harry is about to lose the protection his mother's sacrifice gave him as long as he was in the Dursleys' care. While he might have traveled to a remote location with the Dursleys and taken Muggle transportation to the Burrow, he is now fully of the Magical world, his world. If the Ministry of Magic had had its eyes wide open, Harry and his friends would not have had to play this game; it is in that way unnecessary. Though a matter of life and death, Harry's departure is structured like a virtual Quidditch match, a *game* of the highest possible stakes.

The Stone

In his will, Dumbledore leaves Harry the Snitch from his first match. The Snitch-like Horcruxes each contain a bit of Voldemort's soul, but this Snitch, a symbolic Philosopher's Stone caught in an alchemical game, hides the ring Horcrux with the Resurrection Stone. It no longer has a piece of his enemy's soul; instead, Harry uses it to summon the shades of Lily, James, Sirius, and Remus, who give him an invisible honor guard as he walks to his death (*Hallows* 698–700). Voldemort's Horcruxes splinter him, separating him from others; the pieces steadily added to Harry augment him and connect him to others, living or dead, repeatedly confirming his status as a complete, integrated soul.

When the series begins, Harry is literally closeted in the cupboard beneath the stairs at number four, Privet Drive, and when he finally reads his Hogwarts letter, the true nature of his Otherness is revealed: he is a wizard. His uncle, Vernon Dursley, wants him to be what he is not: "normal." His metaphorical queerness/liminality, however, is not just because he is a wizard in the Muggle world. Rather, he is able to bridge the "real" and numinous worlds, and his letter from Hogwarts simply makes plain the journey on which he is already bound. The letter is a kind of initiation for young Harry as he prepares to board the Hogwarts Express for his journey to a new world not only physically but metaphysically.

"Liminality" refers to a moment during a rite of passage when the one being initiated is neither in their original state nor in the post-ritual, transformed state. During the moment of initiation, they are on the threshold. Bernadette Lynn Bosky wrote in the *New York Review of Science Fiction* about "Liminal Places and Liminal States" in *Little, Big* by John Crowley, but what she says can be applied to many stories with liminal characters. She explains:

> One of the goals of ritual is to turn boundaries into thresholds, as when a shaman crosses the barrier between our world and the other world and then personally forms a bridge between them.... Roads and paths can be liminal also; they lead from one place to another, joining them, but also help define, for instance, what is safe versus what is not. (Bosky)

The *Rebis*, another term for the end-product of alchemy, the Philosopher's Stone, also implies liminality. The word comes from the Latin *res + bina*, "binary thing," and is sometimes called the Great Hermaphrodite (DiBernard 71). It is not about a binary or neutral gender identity but a symbolic union of opposites. Like all liminal beings, it is an *axis mundi*, a link between worlds—heaven and earth, male and female, life and death— because the *"prima materia,"* the material to make the Stone, is a combination of opposites, contradictions. This aspect of the "prime substance" does not change during the process that produces the Stone. As artist and Tarot scholar Robert M. Place wrote, "The prime substance is often described as something that is very common and of unrecognized value—the stone rejected by the builder and trodden underfoot, yet more valuable than gold" (Place, *The Tarot* 34). Harry is not only a human version of the prime substance from which the Stone is made but also the Stone itself. When he "catches" it from the Mirror of Erised it is another symbolic Snitch for a Seeker who recognizes the Stone as a transcendent object. Professor McGonagall sees in Harry a natural Seeker, while Dumbledore recognizes Harry's selfless instinct to protect but not exploit the Stone. This is the truth Harry already knows in his first year: he believes it is worth giving up his life to

Heinrich Nollius' seventeenth-century depiction of the Rebis shows a binary figure standing on a fire-breathing dragon, which in turn stands atop a winged orb—like a Snitch. With its vertical and triangular lines, the orb also resembles the sign of the Deathly Hallows.

keep the Stone from Voldemort. He is prepared to make this sacrifice *as an eleven-year-old*.

In Harry's first match in *Prisoner of Azkaban*, dementors make him fall from his broom (*Azkaban* 178). Harry asks Remus Lupin, the new Defense Against the Dark Arts teacher, for dementor-fighting lessons, framing it as what he needs *to succeed at Quidditch* (*Azkaban* 239). He hopes to conjure a Patronus to succeed at allegorical alchemy, symbolically keeping his self/soul intact when he reunites with a Snitch, a metaphorical piece of himself.

After winning the Cup, Harry is filled with such euphoria that he "felt like he could have produced the world's best Patronus" (*Azkaban* 313). Harry saves his soul/self literally when he conjures a Patronus to protect himself, Sirius, and Hermione from the Dementor's Kiss—a violation, an act of splintering and incompletion, like Voldemort ripping his own soul. Harry grows to regard Quidditch and conjuring a Patronus as interchangeable. Keeping his soul intact is presented as equivalent to catching a Snitch, a moment of sublime completion since his first match, and to achieve this he must stop wishing to hear his parents' voices, especially his mother's, just before their deaths, which is what he hears when dementors are nearby. He must stop clinging to his only conscious memory of his parents. When he does, his parents live on in him. Dumbledore asks, "You think the dead we have loved ever truly leave us?" and tells Harry that his father being alive in him is why his Patronus takes the form of a stag, the form of James Potter's Animagus, Prongs (*Azkaban* 312).

Harry repeatedly draws on his innate wholeness to create a protective force for good. He shares power or is given power he does not pursue, as when he "catches" the Stone from the Mirror, saves the Remembrall from Draco, or uses the Patronus he learned to conjure for Quidditch to repel dementors. This puts the lie to Quirrell's assertion that those who do not seek power are weak; the dogged pursuit of power is weakness writ large (*Stone* 211). Harry instinctively knows that true strength lies in resisting the pursuit and abuse of power. As a result, he becomes a human Philosopher's Stone with the ability to convert base metal into gold (metallurgically or metaphorically) and death into life.

Whenever Harry does this, he is offering a mercy—a grace—that does not discriminate; for instance, when he spares Peter Pettigrew, it is not because of anything Peter has done to earn Harry's mercy. It is instead an offering of grace to his father's two best friends, Sirius and Lupin, whom Harry spares from becoming killers (*Azkaban* 275). The same is true when Harry frees the Muggle-born wizards waiting outside Umbridge's courtroom in *Deathly Hallows* (265–66). No conditions are placed on receiving these gifts. Harry acts from his liminality as an intercessor and an *axis mundi*. Rowling gives Harry the title of an intercessor in *every game he plays*. His role in the life-sized chess game that is an obstacle to the Philosopher's Stone is that of a bishop, a conduit between heaven and earth. The title of Champion in the Triwizard Tournament is also that of an intercessor: a champion does "battle" on behalf of someone else, which the Champions do in the tournament as representatives of their schools.

In *Harry Potter and the Goblet of Fire*, Rowling temporarily replaces Quidditch with another game of allegorical alchemy: the Triwizard Tournament. The Tournament's tasks are rife with symbolism related to fire, air, water, and earth, the four "elements" alchemists associated with the Great Work of creating a Philosopher's Stone. The sixteenth-century Swiss alchemist Paracelsus named salamanders as the elemental being linked to fire (222), while Carl Jung notes that other alchemists placed fire-breathing dragons in that role (13). Rowling includes both fire-loving creatures in the series. In *Harry Potter and the Chamber of Secrets*, Fred and George Weasley remove a salamander from its home in a fire in their Care of Magical Creatures class to learn what will happen if they feed it a Filibuster Firework. To their delight, it "suddenly whizzed into the air, emitting loud sparks and bangs as it whirled wildly around the room" before escaping into the fire, where it evidently feels at home (*Chamber* 100). In *Harry Potter and the Goblet of Fire*, recovering a golden egg from fire-breathing dragons is the first task of the Triwizard Tournament.

Rowling also associates each champion with a Hogwarts house, as well as linking each champion and house with a task and element. Gryffindor, aligned with fire, has for its mascot a lion. The constellation Leo symbolizes the lion and gives its name to this astrological fire sign (Harry's, Neville's, and Rowling's birth sign). Gryffindor's heraldic colors are the fiery red and gold. Harry, the Gryffindor Champion, "catches" his gold egg as if it is a Golden Snitch.

Air is the element for "the Unexpected Task" of the Yule Ball, which makes four tasks, not three, just as Harry is the fourth Champion. The elemental being linked to air and thus to the Yule Ball is the sylph, which Paracelsus describes as "an invisible spirit of the air" (222). He believed each elemental being could move easily only through its own element, so in fire, sylphs burn; in water, they drown; and in earth, they get stuck. Fleur Delacour, a part-veela witch, is like a sylph or part-sylph herself, and excels here.

Air is linked to Ravenclaw, whose emblem is an eagle. Its common room is in a tower with a ceiling of blue—Ravenclaw's color (*Hallows* 587). Fleur is the virtual Ravenclaw Champion and Viktor Krum, of Durmstrang, is the virtual Slytherin Champion, because they sit at the Ravenclaw and Slytherin tables respectively, and the way the students and teachers from their schools arrive at Hogwarts reflects the colors and elements for Ravenclaw and Slytherin. The Beauxbatons delegation descends from the air in a blue carriage—the element and color of Ravenclaw—while the Durmstrang ship rises up from the greenish lake waters—Slytherin's chief color and element (*Goblet* 213, 216–17).

Water is linked to the task of retrieving the hostages from the lake; this task's elemental being is the undine, a water creature often treated as interchangeable with sirens, selkies, and mermaids, and the Champions do indeed meet merpeople in the lake (*Goblet* 432–36). The "Slytherin" Champion, Viktor Krum, partially transfigures into a shark for the task. He is also a virtual Slytherin in the World Cup final, when he catches the Snitch and gives the victory to the Irish team, whose color is green, like Slytherin.

Earth is aligned with the last task, which begins in a maze on the Quidditch pitch but ends, for Harry and Cedric, in a graveyard. The elemental being for this task is introduced in *Chamber of Secrets*, when Harry throws garden gnomes over the hedge at the Burrow (*Chamber* 33). Paracelsus associated gnomes with earth; the Champions must navigate a maze growing from the earth. At the Burrow, the gnomes' underground homes seem rather maze-like; the tournament maze is of hedges, and the Champions become virtual gnomes. The element of earth is aligned with Hufflepuff, and Cedric is that house's Champion. Herbology Professor Pomona Sprout specializes in plants grown from the earth and is head of Hufflepuff, whose colors are black and yellow, called "sable" and "gold" in heraldry. The heraldic meaning linked to sable is "constancy or grief," which is fitting for the house that loses its favorite son, Cedric Diggory (American College of Heraldry). The badger, Hufflepuff's mascot, also digs complicated, maze-like tunnels.

The Seekers Harry and Cedric "catch" the tournament cup together, fairness and justice more important to them than a solitary victory. The cup, too, is another symbolic Snitch (they *are* on the Quidditch pitch), which transports Cedric and Harry to a graveyard—to Cedric's death and Voldemort's pale imitation of rebirth. As Harry is a human Philosopher's Stone, his blood is an Elixir of Life integral to Voldemort's resurrection, doubling the link between them (*Goblet* 557). Attempting to kill the infant Harry, Voldemort had unwittingly sent a part of his soul to lodge in the child; conversely, Harry's blood in Voldemort tethers Harry to the earth in the same way Horcruxes tether Voldemort to life. But unlike the Horcruxes that make Voldemort splintered and incomplete, Harry's blood in Voldemort again augments Harry, making him *more* complete. Voldemort gains a new body, but Harry gains a Horcrux-like relationship with the blood in his enemy, allowing the liminal Harry to return to life after death.

When Harry duels Voldemort in the graveyard where the Riddles are interred, he has another virtual Philosopher's Stone: his phoenix-feather-and-holly wand, which links to Voldemort's to create a *golden* cage of light (*Goblet* 576). Their spells are inherently opposed: Killing Curse and Disarming Charm. Thus the cage of light is another manifestation of the *rebis*: opposites united in one entity. Voldemort's wand then emits vestiges of previous spells; it is as if the liminal joining of the wands has "thinned" the barrier between life and death, allowing the shades of Frank Bryce, Cedric, and Harry's parents to intercede for him with Voldemort, foreshadowing Harry using the Resurrection Stone.

Harry is awarded a thousand gold Galleons for winning the

tournament, but it will not make up for seeing Cedric killed in a re-enactment of James Potter's murder (*Goblet* 616). He gives the gold to the Weasley twins. Harry is an adept metaphorical alchemist, easily acquiring gold (his bank vault, Snitches, the tournament), and as the only survivor of the Killing Curse, the Elixir of Life seems redundant for Harry. Gold and immortality are temptations with no power over him. Instead, he transforms them into golden, immortal friendship when he insists on returning to Hogwarts with Cedric's body and helps bring the twins' dream to life.

The Sword

Harry Potter embodies more than one paradox. The chief transfigurations Harry undergoes in *Chamber of Secrets* are his spiritual coming-of-age and his symbolic transfiguration into an object linked to his being a symbolic Snitch and Philosopher's Stone and literal Horcrux. When Harry voices his belief in Dumbledore to Tom Riddle in the Chamber, Fawkes the phoenix comes to him (*Chamber* 232). This statement of faith and the response can be considered Harry's Pentecostal moment, his symbolic confirmation or bar mitzvah, his spiritual coming-of-age. Phoenixes burn up when they die but are reborn from the ashes, and the Pentecost story says that Jesus' disciples saw the Holy Spirit appear as *tongues of fire* on their heads. When this occurs, the story says that they received the ability to speak in other tongues (Acts 2:1–20), the flip side of the Babel story (Lubac 127). Pentecost later becomes the feast marking the Church's "birthday" and is the preferred time in the Church calendar for the confirmation of young people, marking their spiritual maturation (Murphy 71). Fawkes, intimately linked to fire, by which he both dies and is reborn, serves as the Holy Spirit here. This spiritual milestone for Harry is necessary before he destroys the basilisk and the diary.

Three of Harry's allies undergo spiritual coming-of-age rituals *that are an echo of Harry's* before they each destroy a Horcrux. Rowling first presents these four as a group—Harry plus Ron Weasley, Hermione Granger, and Neville Longbottom—when they cross the lake in the same boat as first-years (*Stone* 83). This water-crossing that all first-year Hogwarts students undergo might be seen as a symbolic baptism representing the start of their new lives. It is fitting that Hagrid, a threshold guardian, accompanies the children as they cross the lake. Rowling gives her threshold guardian a very Christian title: "Keeper of the Keys," also St. Peter's title, though for Peter the "keys" are to the gates of heaven. Not coincidentally, to guard the entrance to the underground hiding place for the Philosopher's

Stone, Hagrid also gives Dumbledore "Fluffy," the three-headed dog clearly related to the three-headed dog Cerberus in Greek mythology, guardian of the entrance to the Realm of the Dead. One threshold guardian provides another. Harry, Ron, Hermione, and Neville encounter Fluffy together when they stumble into the wrong corridor, foreshadowing the roles all four will play in the protection of the Philosopher's Stone in the climax of the first book (*Stone* 119).

Ron is the first to have a coming-of-age experience in *Deathly Hallows*, one that echoes Harry's in *Chamber of Secrets*. Instead of Fawkes delivering the sword to Harry in the Chamber of Secrets, Snape's doe Patronus leads Harry to the sword in *Hallows* (689). As Ginny unwisely trusted Tom Riddle while writing in the diary, Harry unwisely wears the locket Horcrux while attempting to retrieve the sword from the pool in the Forest of Dean. This time the locket plays the role of the basilisk, a snaky, Tom Riddle-controlled attacker attempting to kill Harry. Like Harry killing the basilisk in the Chamber, Ron uses the sword to cut the chain strangling Harry and pulls him from the pool. Harry instinctively knows that because Ron took the sword from the pool and saved him, he should destroy the locket. Harry must speak in Parseltongue to open the locket but otherwise delegates this task to Ron, like a mentor inculcating an initiate.

Hermione undergoes a truncated coming-of-age before destroying the cup Horcrux, perhaps because, as a Muggle-born witch, she is already liminal. The part of Harry's ritual that she echoes is entering the Chamber of Secrets, with the help of Ron, now serving as the mentor to her initiate. She uses a basilisk fang, the original weapon Harry used to "kill" the diary, to destroy the cup Horcrux. The fang would not have been available if Harry had not slain the basilisk, just as Ron could not have accessed the Chamber without learning the word for "open" in Parseltongue from Harry.

Together Harry, Ron, and Hermione seek the diadem Horcrux in the Room of Requirement. In a re-enactment of Harry Seeking the Remembrall during the first book's flying lesson, Harry again competes on a broomstick with Draco Malfoy, and, as in the first tournament task, Harry must contend with fire while Seeking the Horcrux. Fiendfyre destroys the diadem as Harry pursues it through the chaotic air, catching it on his outstretched arm. This fiery imitation of a Quidditch match foreshadows Voldemort's rebounding curse during his final duel with Harry; this magical fire is meant as a weapon against Harry and his comrades, but instead kills its creator—Crabbe—and the diadem holding a portion of Voldemort's soul.

Even when he is absent, Harry still has a role to play in the destruction of *every Horcrux*, including the Peverell ring, since Harry slew the basilisk with Gryffindor's Sword and it imbibed the great snake's venom, which allowed Dumbledore to use it to destroy the Horcrux whose curse is slowly killing him.

Neville, the fourth member of the quartet, is the final initiate. His coming-of-age echoes Harry's yet again when he defiantly makes a statement of faith in Dumbledore with his cry of "Dumbledore's Army!" Voldemort summons the Sorting Hat, making it light on Neville's head before setting it on fire (*Hallows* 731). When Fawkes lands on Harry in the Chamber it is the equivalent of *symbolic* flames, an echo of the Pentecost story; Neville *literally* has flames on his head here, and, like Harry, it is his Pentecostal moment. He breaks free of the spell binding him, removes the Sword of Gryffindor from the hat, which has delivered itself to him in a true moment of need, and slays Nagini, the final Horcrux and another basilisk stand-in. Before this, Rowling initiates Neville as she did Harry: he makes a statement of faith, flames appear on his head, and the weapon of salvation is delivered to him. Thus, even though his friends destroy the locket, cup, and snake, they must undergo symbolic transfigurations that make them *like Harry*, and they must either use the same weapon he used to destroy the diary, a basilisk fang, or the weapon he transfigured into a *virtual* basilisk fang: the sword.

Harry is entangled with Snitches in his first year, and in his second with the item Dumbledore later bequeaths to him and that Minister of Magic, Rufus Scrimgeour withholds: the Sword of Gryffindor. Voldemort made Horcruxes from Ravenclaw's diadem, Hufflepuff's cup, and Slytherin's locket. He failed to make one of Gryffindor's sword, and the Gryffindor artifact Voldemort sought becomes a destroyer of Horcruxes (*Prince* 505). Harry becomes a *human* sword, as a Horcrux *and* a hunter/destroyer of them, even when not directly responsible for destroying a Horcrux, since those doing this must become *like him* and/or use a weapon he made into a Horcrux-destroyer.

Harry's scar marks him as a human sword from the start; Joseph Campbell calls the sword "the counterpart of the thunderbolt"—a jagged lightning-bolt, like Harry's scar (198). Voldemort accidentally makes him a Horcrux, and in turn Harry becomes a *symbolic* Sword of Gryffindor, rather than the *literal* sword becoming a Horcrux. When Harry slays the basilisk, he is simultaneously pierced by a fang; this is similar to the Norse saga of Ragnarök, in which Thor, god of thunder, kills "the world-enveloping serpent of the cosmic ocean" before falling dead from the serpent's venom (Campbell 347). Thor's emblem is the lightning-bolt, like Harry's scar. Unlike Thor, phoenix tears save Harry; the symbolic Holy Spirit heals him (*Chamber* 237).

Had Voldemort never targeted Harry, making him a Horcrux *and* the perfect Horcrux-destruction machine, a human Sword of Gryffindor, Harry, Ron, Hermione, Neville, and Dumbledore would have been unable

Kampf der untergehenden Götter (*Battle of the Doomed Gods*), showing Odin battling Fenrir from horseback and Thor fighting the serpent Jörmungandr.

to find and destroy the diary, locket, cup, ring, diadem and snake, and Voldemort would have been immortal.

The Seeker

The first spell Harry teaches Dumbledore's Army is the Disarming Charm. Some D.A. members scoff at this, but he reminds them that it helped him to survive a duel with Voldemort. Remus Lupin criticizes *Expelliarmus* as Harry's "signature move," when Harry uses it against Stan Shunpike during the flight from Surrey (*Hallows* 71). Harry embraces it as his signature move. Rather than using offensive attack spells, Harry often confers mercy and grace indiscriminately even on foes, such as saving Dudley from dementors, sparing the Confunded Stan, and showing mercy to Peter Pettigrew in *Prisoner of Azkaban*.

Disarming is, for Harry, as integral to his nature as catching Snitches; he thinks of its opposite as anathema, something that could tear his soul and make him incomplete. This is how Harry wields the love his mother bequeathed to him. Thus, despite Quidditch being presented as mock-war, Harry's status as metaphysical Seeker reminds us that his position is not truly a warrior in a mock-war, but an intermediary, an intercessor, an anti-soldier in an alchemical game of transfiguration. Lupin wants him to attack; Harry-the-anti-soldier objects, even when his life is threatened (*Hallows* 70–71). He is the bridge, not the ordnance that blows up the bridge. His liminality again comes to the fore, and his choice to disarm, not harm, also brings us back to the link between the seventeenth-century Seekers and the pacifist Quakers.

Harry is entangled with a variety of objects: Snitches, the Philosopher's Stone, the Sword of Gryffindor, the other Horcruxes, and his wand, which is an experience all wizards share. When a wand chooses its wizard, they are bound to each other, but in *Deathly Hallows* Rowling reveals that disarming breaks that bond. If the disarming occurs in earnest, a new relationship forms between the disarmer and the wand previously bound to the disarmed wizard. The disarmer catching a wand is like a Seeker catching a Snitch, a similarity that blossoms with new meaning in Rowling's use of one Quidditch metaphor after another in the passages about Harry's death and final confrontation with Voldemort.

It is clearly significant that Draco Malfoy *disarms* Dumbledore in *Half-Blood Prince*, rather than killing him, as he was ordered to; if he had not chosen Harry's "signature move" Voldemort might not have been defeated. Like Ron, Hermione, and Neville, Draco also follows in Harry's footsteps and has the potential for redemption if he chooses it. Before the Death Eaters arrive, Dumbledore tells Draco that he is not a murderer, and wants Draco to believe this as well. Like Harry, Draco wants to protect those he loves; Dumbledore does not blame him for this but offers a way out. Draco takes the first step: he disarms rather than kills (*Prince* 584). Though the Elder Wand sails over the ramparts of the tower, not into Draco's hand (he never was as skilled a Seeker as Harry), we later learn that Disarming Dumbledore makes him Master of the Elder Wand. Like the initiation rites Harry's friends undergo that make them like him, this also makes Draco like Harry, and is one of the final steps toward Voldemort's defeat.

Dumbledore's Chocolate Frog card credits him with *defeating* Grindelwald, not killing him (*Stone* 77, emphasis added). When Dumbledore *disarmed* Grindelwald, he became Master of the Elder Wand. Harry's wand "imbibes" power from Voldemort's when the brother wands duel in the graveyard, as Harry had "imbibed" part of Voldemort's soul as a baby, during another murder attempt. This power turns against Voldemort during the flight from Surrey, just as Harry's Parseltongue ability, received the first time Voldemort tries to kill him, is also turned against Voldemort. This is consistent with what Rowling has revealed about innate magical ability rising up when the need is great, because the wand *is* an extension of its master's magical power.

Rowling confirms this theory in the commentaries "authored" by Albus Dumbledore in *The Tales of Beedle the Bard*, specifically the commentary on "The Tale of the Three Brothers." Rowling-as-Dumbledore writes:

> [W]ands do indeed absorb the expertise of those who use them, though this is an unpredictable and imperfect business.... Nevertheless, a hypothetical wand that had passed through the hands of many Dark wizards would be likely to have, at the very least, a marked affinity for the most dangerous kinds of magic. (*Beedle* 103–04)

A hypothetical wand that had passed through the hands of good wizards would likely have a similar affinity for the most powerfully good kinds of magic. If Voldemort had thought about it, he would have realized that Dumbledore defeating Grindelwald had made *Dumbledore* the wand's master, but Voldemort does not consider a spell like the Disarming Charm for a moment. It is anathema to him, as much as stunning someone who could fall to his death is to Harry. Despite knowing that Dumbledore became the wand's master without killing Grindelwald, he believes that the only way to transfer mastery of the wand from Snape (who killed Dumbledore at his own request) is to murder Snape, whom he believes to be both Master of the Elder Wand and a loyal Death Eater. He is so focused on *his* signature move—*Avada Kedavra*—that he sacrifices a perceived ally, never considering a less violent approach. In Voldemort's world, every problem is a nail, and the Killing Curse is his hammer.

Wizards catching wands like Snitches is not the only metaphorical Quidditch in *Deathly Hallows*, which has no *literal* matches. When Harry pursues Horcruxes in the final book he plays *virtual* Quidditch. These Horcruxes resemble Snitches—the locket, cup, and diadem are all round and golden—and the process of capturing and/or destroying each resembles a match, which for Harry is an act of completion, metaphorically reuniting with a missing piece of himself and achieving wholeness again. He also reunites "his" Voldemort soul-bit with the one in each Horcrux every time he "catches" a Horcrux. Wholeness is also a goal of alchemy: accepting that all is one and death is an illusion, which is the purview of the Master of Death as well (Place, *Magic and Alchemy* 47). Birth, life, and death make a complete life cycle, and so one who never dies is forever incomplete. Harry is completed by catching Snitches/Horcruxes and by presenting himself to Voldemort to die.

Each year, Gryffindor plays Quidditch against Slytherin, Hufflepuff, and Ravenclaw. In his sixth year Harry is captain of the Gryffindor team; in the seventh book, Harry, captain of the "team" that includes him, Ron, and Hermione (and eventually all of the Order and Dumbledore's Army) plays virtual matches to rescue Slytherin's locket from Umbridge in the "arena" of a courtroom; steal Hufflepuff's cup from Gringotts (Hermione even levitates Harry at the end, as if he is flying); and acquire/destroy Ravenclaw's diadem in the Room of Requirement.

The Battle of Hogwarts itself is an elaborate mock-Quidditch game;

everyone must keep Voldemort and the Death Eaters at bay until Harry finds Rowena Ravenclaw's diadem. Scores of metaphorical Chasers, Beaters, and Keepers play; they occupy the other side's players while their Seeker, Harry, tries to catch the diadem-Snitch. They must also keep the other Seeker—Voldemort—from catching the Snitch he wants: Harry. Draco, another Seeker, also tries to catch the Harry-Snitch, but is thwarted by the Slytherin Beaters, Crabbe and Goyle (*Hallows* 628–34). Despite Draco again being his opponent, Harry saves him (and Goyle) from death-by-Fiendfyre, conferring his mercy, his grace, on someone in need of it regardless of whether that person "deserves" it. In the end, though Draco is a Seeker attempting to catch a Harry-Snitch, the liminal Harry is the victorious Seeker and intercessor who catches a Draco-Snitch, saving his life.

After Voldemort has Nagini kill Snape, Harry sees Snape's full story (*Hallows* 659–90), at last learning the truth: Harry is a Horcrux. With this knowledge, he makes the agonizing decision to present himself for death. As with the Horcruxes destroyed by people other than Harry, his contribution is key to the destruction of the soul-bit inside him; he must *choose* to make this sacrifice. Like the other Horcrux missions, this sacrifice is a Quidditch match, but a specific type: it is like the World Cup in which Viktor gave up victory, and the first match Ginny played as a Seeker. They each caught a Snitch to help others, all the while knowing they would lose.

As Harry enters the forest, the Quidditch metaphor appears again: "The long game was ended, the Snitch had been caught, it was time to leave the air…" (*Hallows* 698). When Harry thinks of the end of his life, he thinks of it as the end of *a Quidditch match*. He instinctively knows now the meaning of the legend on the Snitch Dumbledore left him in his will, that the golden ball hiding the Resurrection Stone will open for him now as he walks toward his own death (*Hallows* 698).

In the end, *every single Horcrux,* including Harry, resembles a Snitch in some way, no matter how minor or symbolic. The first Horcrux destroyed, the diary, is not Snitch-like until Ginny, who is eventually a Seeker, throws it in Myrtle's toilet and Harry "catches" it, which Myrtle specifically compares to a game, talking about "points" earned for throwing it at different parts of her (*Chamber* 230). Though all of the Horcruxes diminish Voldemort, created as they are from his mutilated soul, Harry is augmented, more complete with each interaction. Harry is entangled with Snitches, and he and Voldemort are entangled with each other; like the yin-yang symbol, each has a piece of the other in him. Nagini, the last Horcrux destroyed, does not usually resemble anything round or golden, but now, because of the "glittering, charmed cage" of protection Voldemort gives her, the snake *does* have these attributes (*Hallows* 702).

Harry encounters Dumbledore in an amorphous "afterlife," a version of King's Cross, where they speak before the liminal Harry returns to life, tethered to the earth by the blood taken from him that Voldemort used to regain his body, a virtual Horcrux for Harry. This is likely to explain why Harry sees "a gleam of something like triumph in Dumbledore's eyes" at the end of *Goblet of Fire*, when Dumbledore learns that Voldemort took Harry's blood (604); he sees a way for Harry-the-Horcrux to be destroyed, breaking another link between Voldemort and life, while also making it possible for "the Boy Who Lived" to continue to do so.

When Harry reveals himself to Voldemort after returning to life, they are in a virtual arena/pitch with those who fought on both sides as spectators. Harry offers his grace, his mercy, to Voldemort, telling him that he (Harry) is very likely the Master of the Elder Wand, but Voldemort disregards this and attacks (*Hallows* 739–43). Harry again makes his signature move, the Disarming Charm, but this time the Snitch he catches is the Elder Wand, which recognizes *only Harry* as its master. Like Harry reuniting with a piece of himself when he catches Snitches, he does the same by reuniting with the Elder Wand. In the forest, Voldemort could only kill Harry with it because it was Harry's will to die. This is why Harry's is the key contribution to his own destruction; without his *intent* to die, it is likely that the Elder Wand *would not have killed him*. If he had not chosen to remove his Cloak of Invisibility and embrace Death "as an old friend" (*Beedle* 93), Voldemort would have remained invulnerable. Now Harry's will is to live, and the Elder Wand again obeys. In the final face-off:

> Harry saw Voldemort's green jet meet his own spell, saw the Elder Wand fly high, dark against the sunrise, spinning across the enchanted ceiling... spinning through the air toward the master it would not kill.... And Harry, with the unerring skill of the Seeker, caught the wand in his free hand as Voldemort fell.... (*Hallows* 743–44)

The Boy Who Lived and Master of Death again catches the Golden Snitch. In the end, Harry is Snitch, Stone, and Sword, three in one. He is one of the Horcruxes, all of which resemble Golden Snitches; he is the Philosopher's Stone, transcending life and death by being Master of Death; and he is a human Sword of Gryffindor, the ultimate destroyer of Horcruxes, having "imbibed" the power meant to destroy him that also marked him with the sign of the sword, a lightning bolt. But Harry is, most enduringly, the youngest Seeker in a hundred years, who communes directly with a higher power as a Seeker should, interceding on behalf of the entire wizarding world and making it whole again.

Works Cited

Allen, R. Michael. *Reformed Theology.* T & T Clark, 2010.
American College of Heraldry. *Heraldic "Meanings."* www.americancollegeofheraldry.org/achsymbols.html.
American-Israeli Cooperative Enterprise. "Bar Mitzvah, Bat Mitzvah and Confirmation." *Jewish Virtual Library,* www.jewishvirtuallibrary.org/jsource/Judaism/barmitz.html.
The Bible. Authorized King James Version, Oxford UP, 1998.
Biblica. New International Version, BibleGateway.com, 2011, www.biblegateway.com/versions/New-International-Version-NIV-Bible/#booklist.
Bosky, Bernadette Lynn. "Liminal Places and Liminal States in John Crowley's *Little, Big.*" *The New York Review of Science Fiction* 292, vol. 25, no. 3, Nov. 2012, www.nyrsf.com/2012/12/liminal-places-and-liminal-states-in-john-crowleys-little-big-by-bernadette-lynn-bosky.html.
Campbell, Joseph. *Hero with a Thousand Faces.* New World Library, 1979.
DiBernard, Barbara. *Alchemy and Finnegans Wake.* SUNY, 1980.
Eliade, Mircea. *The Forge and the Crucible.* Harper, 1978.
Heine, Friedrich Wilhelm. *Kampf Der Untergehenden Götter (Battle of the Doomed Gods). Nordisch-germanische Götter Und Helden,* Wägner, Wilhelm, Otto Spamer, 1882, p. 317. upload.wikimedia.org/wikipedia/commons/f/fd/Kampf_der_untergehenden_G%C3%B6tter_by_F._W._Heine.jpg. Accessed 15 Feb. 2019.
Hill, Christopher. *Milton and the English Revolution.* Faber & Faber, 1977.
Jung, Carl G. *Alchemical Studies.* Translated by R.F.C. Hull, Princeton UP, 1967.
Lubac, Henri. *Scripture in the Tradition.* Crossroads Publishing Company, 2001.
McGonigal, Jane. *Reality Is Broken: Why Games Make Us Better and How They Can Change the World.* Penguin, 2011.
Murphy, G. Ronald. *The Owl, the Raven, and the Dove: The Religious Meaning of Grimms' Magic Fairy Tales.* Oxford UP, 2000.
Nollius, Heinrich. "Rebis." *Theoria Philosophiae Hermeticae,* 1617. commons.wikimedia.org/wiki/File:Rebis_Theoria_Philosophiae_Hermeticae_1617.jpg. Accessed 15 Feb. 2019.
Paracelsus. *Four Treatises of Theophrastus von Hohenheim.* 1941. Edited by Henry E. Sigerist, translated by C. Lilian Temkin, George Rosen, Gregory Zilboorg, and Henry E. Sigerist, Johns Hopkins UP, 1996.
Place, Robert M. *Magic and Alchemy: Mysteries, Legends, and Unexplained Phenomena.* Chelsea House Publications, 2009.
_____. *The Tarot: History, Symbolism and Divination.* Jeremy P. Tarcher/Penguin, 2005.
Rowling, J.K. *Harry Potter and the Chamber of Secrets.* Bloomsbury, 1998.
_____. *Harry Potter and the Deathly Hallows.* Scholastic, 2007.
_____. *Harry Potter and the Goblet of Fire.* Scholastic, 2000.
_____. *Harry Potter and the Half-Blood Prince.* Scholastic, 2005.
_____. *Harry Potter and the Order of the Phoenix.* Scholastic, 2003.
_____. *Harry Potter and the Philosopher's Stone.* Bloomsbury, 1997.
_____. *Harry Potter and the Prisoner of Azkaban.* Bloomsbury, 1999.
_____. *The Tales of Beedle the Bard.* Arthur A. Levine Books, 2007, 2008.

Alchemy as a Metaphor for Learning

MARY PYLE

> I've never wanted to be a witch, but an alchemist, now that's a different matter.... To invent this wizard world, I've learned a ridiculous amount about alchemy. Perhaps much of it I'll never use in the books, but I have to know in detail what magic can and cannot do in order to set the parameters and establish the stories' internal logic.
> —J.K. Rowling (*The Herald*)

Rowling's statement poses the question: what part does alchemy play in the Harry Potter series? The title of the first novel, *Harry Potter and the Philosopher's Stone,* emphatically introduces the topic of alchemy in the context that people most commonly associate with it: the search for the Philosopher's Stone, which is reputed to grant wealth because it can be used as a means of transforming base metal into gold. The Stone can also be used to produce an elixir which will grant immortality to the possessor; and so for both reasons, possession of it has always been seen as something desirable and enviable. As a result, the search for the Stone very often comes at a high price.

The origins of alchemy lie in Egypt, where the belief in life after death and an impressive chemical knowledge enabled their practice of mummification. The alchemists' ideas and search for knowledge came to Spain in the eighth century and spread across Europe, incurring the displeasure of the powerful Christian Church. Long before this, it seems that the Church felt threatened by the alchemists' freedom of thought: it was Christians who burned the great library at Alexandria in the fourth century. The Church preferred to rely on authoritative writings rather than to be challenged with new discoveries. Knowledge not sanctioned by Church doctrine was forbidden as being of the devil. The fifteenth-century physician and surgeon

Paracelsus, for one, showed his opposition to this ideal by publically burning the works of Galen, a physician of the first century, arguing that medicine must be based on what is observed rather than on unchallenged beliefs.

In the legend of Faust, versions of which go back to the Middle Ages, and which Goethe retold as a long dramatic poem, Faust sells his soul to the devil, Mephistopheles, for all knowledge and time enough to enjoy it. Metaphorically, Faust represents the seeker after knowledge, one who is prepared to pay the ultimate price for it. As psychiatrist and literary scholar Iain McGilchrist observes, Goethe's Faust was also:

> an essentially good man who has already done much for others through his skills as a physician before his lust for power and knowledge lead him to do many destructive things.... He is brought back ... to an awareness of the good his knowledge can bring to others ... [and a] realisation of what he can do for humanity, not for himself. (233)

There is an echo of this at the end of *Philosopher's Stone* when Dumbledore explains to Harry that the reason the Stone had dropped out of the Mirror and into his pocket was because he, Dumbledore, had arranged it so that "[o]nly one who wanted to *find* the Stone—find it, but not use it—would be able to get it, otherwise they'd just see themselves making gold or drinking Elixir of Life" (217).

Knowledge, whether from magic or from alchemy, is a source of power for those who possess it, and can be used for good or for evil. This is a theme which runs through Rowling's series, epitomized by the rivalry between Harry and Draco Malfoy, and the greater struggle between Dumbledore and Voldemort. Like the alchemists, the students acquire their power gradually, much of it experientially, leading to failures as well as successes. Writing about the alchemists, sociologist of religion David Barrett says:

> Alchemists, or the Hermetic Philosophers, while searching for enlightenment, were actually chemists—and physicists, and astronomers, and mathematicians, physicians, botanists and biologists.... They were the ones to discover that a polished lens of glass could focus the light of the sun to a hot, burning point, or could magnify what is seen through it. They were the ones who ... worked out ... how the human body worked, ... who studied plants, and learned which were poisonous and which beneficial, and which lethal ones could, in tiny doses, heal. (67)

This pragmatism was the basis of the work of the Alchemists, who referred to their study as the Royal Art, or the Great Work, and which, as well as the scientific studies, included a spiritual dimension whereby practitioners were to move from the base material of ignorance to the gold of enlightenment and perfection.

David Goddard, who teaches esoteric topics including Spiritual Alchemy, introduces his manual for modern day alchemists as

> a manual to the science of Hermes, the Thrice-great, ... that Sacred and Royal Art.... It presents the specific teachings and guided practices ... that can culminate in the completion, the Great Work.... For this work is ... the true Alchemy ... [which] leads to the attainment of the Philosopher's Stone, whereby the personal consciousness and the Primordial consciousness unite as one. That Stone—the Jewel of Eternity—overcomes all limitation, heals all disease, and brings an end to the need for death itself. (xi)

This spiritual dimension is the focus for contemporary alchemists, as the experimental aspects have been taken over by modern scientific studies. Writers on the subject make the point that it is no longer about physically turning base metal into gold, but a symbolic transmutation of base humans to a more godly state, or the moving from ignorance to knowledge.

Alchemy in the Series

Rowling introduces the subject of alchemy in the title of her first novel and with the inclusion of two historical fourteenth-century figures, the husband-wife team of Nicolas and Perenelle Flamel. They were reputed to have created a Philosopher's Stone and to have become very wealthy as a result. In Rowling's narrative, in accordance with a long established myth, they are still alive. After the destruction of the Stone, Harry is dismayed when Dumbledore tells him that the Flamels are accepting the need to prepare for death. Dumbledore reassures an incredulous Harry, saying:

> To ... Nicolas and Perenelle, it really is like going to bed after a very, *very* long day. After all, to the well-organised mind, death is but the next great adventure. You know, the Stone was really not such a wonderful thing. As much money and life as you could want! The two things most human beings would choose above all—the trouble is, humans do have a knack of choosing precisely those things which are worst for them. (215)

Dumbledore suggests that death is an inevitable part of life, rather than something to be feared. Learning to accept the fact of physical death, and to see it as a transformation, is an important part of the alchemist's journey. Each of the novels involves a conversation between Harry and Dumbledore on the subject, growing in intensity to the final transformation in *Deathly Hallows*. Dumbledore, then, is expressing the alchemical and ethical core of the series: teaching Harry and the readers that alchemy is more than desire for the Stone, a lesson that Voldemort has never learned. Voldemort will stop at nothing to gain immortality and power. In a bid to ensure that he will not die, he divides his soul into eight parts, seven of which he hides in Horcruxes, feeling confident that not all will be destroyed.

Despite these alchemical overtones and Rowling's professed interest in the topic, "Alchemy" is not a course on the Hogwarts curriculum.

Rowling says: "There are books [on alchemy] in the library at Hogwarts, and I always imagined that it would be studied by very clever students in their sixth and seventh years..." ("Alchemy"). However, the young witches and wizards at Hogwarts do study topics which formed the basis of alchemical knowledge, including Potions, Divination, Herbology, Transfiguration, Astronomy, and Care of Magical Creatures. Rowling's world starts in the late twentieth century, and to get to Hogwarts in the wizard world, a fantasy medieval world, they travel in an old-fashioned steam train which belongs in neither time. Once at Hogwarts the studies are similar to those of the medieval alchemists. This is clear in the British Library book *Harry Potter: A History of Magic*, which takes all the topics on the Hogwarts curriculum and addresses the medieval beliefs underlying them. Rowling often weaves classical and mythological beliefs into the novels, thus hinting at the background alchemical logic of the series without having to name it explicitly.

Hagrid is responsible for the magical creatures through the series, first as gamekeeper and from the third novel as teacher of Care of Magical Creatures. Some of these creatures are versions of mythical or classical beasts, among them the savage three-headed dog, Cerberus, who in Greek mythology guards the gates of the Underworld, in this case guarding a trapdoor and with the unlikely name of Fluffy. As part of his game-keeping duties, Hagrid also pays attention to what goes on in the forest and cares for the creatures who live there. He is concerned because something has been attacking Unicorns, a symbol of purity, and of which the twelfth-century *Book of Beasts* comments: "Not a single one has ever come alive into the hands of man, and although it is possible to kill them, it is not possible to capture them" (White 44).

During a detention with Hagrid, Harry and Draco come across a sinister cloaked figure drinking the blood of a dead unicorn. After Draco runs away in fear, the centaur, Firenze, explains the terrible and desperate act of killing a unicorn. He tells Harry: "You have slain something pure and defenceless to save yourself, and you will have but a half-life, a cursed life, from the moment the blood touches your lips" (*Stone* 188). This is true of Voldemort, who, although he grows in strength and power through the series, lives a life which is totally focused on domination and immortality. It is a life very different from that of the alchemists, which is based on cooperation and has as its goals enlightenment and perfection. Voldemort is not capable of love or friendship, as Dumbledore often reminds Harry, and as he put it to Voldemort when Voldemort came seeking a teaching post at Hogwarts (*Prince* 416).

Firenze is one of a herd of centaurs who live in the Forbidden Forest. They study the movements of the planets for their particular form of Divination, a branch of Alchemy, but, as Hagrid complains, they will never give a straight answer. Hagrid's query about what evil creature might be in the forest elicits the reply "Mars is bright tonight" (*Stone* 185). It is possible, however, that Hagrid did not understand the response: the alchemists regarded the planets as living beings influencing human behavior, and Mars was "the impetus to battle" (Harpur 121).

Other creatures, such as the merpeople who live in the lake, owe their origins to the belief that "[e]verything on the earth had its counterpart in the sea. The horse and the sea-horse, the dog and the dog-fish, the snake and the eel.... Why should there not be men in both? Mermen?" (White 250–51). The lake at Hogwarts is an integral part of the community. The merpeople have their part to play in the underwater challenge of the Triwizard Tournament, trying to thwart Harry but also telling Dumbledore what had transpired, and so adding to Harry's score (*Goblet* 433–40).

In Harry's second confrontation with Voldemort, which takes place in the Chamber of Secrets, Voldemort's weapon is a basilisk; likely based on Sir Thomas Browne's 1646 *Pseudodoxia Epidemica*, the basilisk is a giant serpent who, it was believed, could kill with a look. In *Harry Potter and the Chamber of Secrets*, those whom it attacked were Petrified rather than killed as they saw its reflection in water, a mirror, or through the ghost Nearly Headless Nick, rather than seeing the creature itself. When Harry confronts the snake, he avoids looking at it so as not to meet its gaze, stumbling around blindly, until Dumbledore's phoenix, Fawkes, comes to the rescue and puts out the creature's eyes so that it can no longer look at Harry (234–37).

A special feature of the phoenix is that when it dies, traditionally in the flames of its own funeral pyre, it is reborn from the ashes, and so for the Philosophers it was a symbol of rebirth (White 125–27). In Rowling's text, Phoenix tears had healing powers and when Harry is apparently fatally wounded by basilisk venom, Fawkes lays its "beautiful head on the spot where the serpent's fang had pierced him ... Thick pearly tears were trickling down the glossy feathers ... A pearly patch of tears was shining all around the wound—except that there *was* no wound" (*Chamber* 236–37). The pearly tears and the silvery unicorn blood both have healing properties, but while Fawkes' tears are offered as a gift to Harry, Voldemort kills the unicorn, thus taking its blood by force.

Rowling develops the theme of the relationship between animals and people when Hagrid brings along a herd of hippogriffs to his first Care of Magical Creatures class in *Prisoner of Azkaban*. This legendary creature was the offspring of a mare and a griffin, the latter also a legendary animal, with an eagle's head and wings and the body of a lion. The hippogriff had the body, hind legs, and tail of a horse but with the head, front legs, and wings of a giant eagle. It was said to be so powerful that it was able to fly around the moon. Rowling gives the hippogriff some additional characteristics. Mutual respect is necessary, and Hagrid tells the class, "Now, firs' thing yeh gotta know abou' hippogriffs is they're proud.... Yeh always wait for the hippogriff to make the firs' move.... Yeh walk towards him, and yeh bow, an' yeh wait. If he bows back, yeh're allowed ter touch him..." (*Azkaban* 88–90). Harry, although full of misgivings, wants the lesson to be a success for Hagrid and so steps forward. Harry bows respectfully, and so does Buckbeak, the hippogriff, which then permits Harry to ride him. Malfoy, on the other hand, an arrogant Pure-Blood who despises Hagrid for being half-giant, and is determined to spoil Hagrid's class, refuses to perform the required ritual and is slashed "in a flash of steely talons" (90). While it is a nasty injury, Madam Pomfrey heals it at once. Malfoy, however, exaggerates the extent of the wound, hoping that his influential father will insist on Hagrid being dismissed. While Malfoy's malevolence has some early gratification, as Buckbeak is condemned to death, the outcome is more benevolent for Harry. In respecting and trusting the animal, and eventually saving its life, Harry forges a relationship with it, thereby saving Sirius (302–03).

In addition to the magical creatures, Rowling also turns her attention to plants with mythical powers, giving particular attention to the Mandrake. The Mandrake, Anna Pavord writes, "is a powerful plant—hallucinogenic and widely recommended in early herbals as a painkiller. And an aphrodisiac..." (72). The plant was assumed to have human characteristics, in part because of its forked roots which resembled legs and which was said to have a male or female appearance, although Culpeper (1616–1654), on whose *Herbal* Rowling based her descriptions of herbs and potions, asserts that "it really resembles a carrot or a parsnip"(76). The perceived resemblance to a human led some alchemists to hope to discover a homunculus, or miniature human, from which it was believed a fetus developed. The Mandrake was reputed to scream when it was dug up, and anyone hearing it would die. In *Chamber of Secrets* Rowling develops the traditions around Mandrakes as being almost human. In the first Herbology lesson, Professor Sprout issues the students with earmuffs, telling them to be careful to block out all sound, because although "our Mandrakes are only seedlings [and] their cries won't kill yet, ... they will knock you out for several hours" (73). The Mandrake she pulls from the pot is "a small, muddy and extremely ugly baby ... the leaves were growing right out of his head. He had pale green mottled skin, and was clearly bawling at the top of his lungs" (73).

Besides the traditional characteristics of the mandrake, Rowling gives it an added use: it can be made into a potion to bring back to life those who have been Petrified by the basilisk's glance. First the cat, Mrs. Norris, who belongs to the caretaker, Filch, and, later, several students, including Hermione, are found stiff and Petrified. Dumbledore explains that as soon as the Mandrakes reach their full size a potion can be made which will restore those who have been attacked. Rowling continues the fantasy of Mandrakes sharing human characteristics by giving regular updates on their development: "the moment their acne clears up, they'll be ready for re-potting again," and "the moment they start trying to move into each other's pots, we'll know they're fully mature, then we'll be able to revive those poor people in the hospital wing" (186).

Secrets

Alchemy's reputation for secrecy is based only partly on the fact that historically any knowledge which was not in the hands of the authorities was likely to be regarded as heretical. We see an echo of such expediency in Rowling's novels when the magical community takes care to hide the fact of its existence. In answer to Harry's question of why this needs to be kept secret from the Muggle world, Hagrid says, "*Why?* Blimey, Harry, everyone'd be wantin' magic solutions to their problems. Nah, we're best left alone" (*Stone* 51).

In *Goblet of Fire*, the Ministry of Magic works for months to conceal the Quidditch World Cup, so the wizarding community can enjoy the spectacle in peace. Rowling plays with the secrecy when she describes meetings between Fudge, the Minister of Magic, and the Muggle Prime Minister. Fudge, having proved that he was really a wizard by turning the Prime Minister's teacup into a gerbil, explains that he makes it his business to keep the Prime Minister of the day up to date with Wizarding matters. To the Prime Minister's question as to why no previous Prime Minister had warned him, Fudge laughs, "'My dear Prime Minister, are *you* ever going to tell anybody?' … The Prime Minister … realised that he would never … dare mention this encounter to a living soul, for who in the wide world would believe him?" (*Prince* 12).

Beyond the expediency of social or political survival, education itself contains an element of a pleasurable secrecy. Psychologically this desire for secrecy goes back to the sense of Us and Them: originally They, the parents, are the powerful "in" group who make decisions. In the secret group, the favored ones are in the group and the others are kept outside. Rowling offers the reader the possibility of becoming a member of the secret society of Wizardry. As her readers, actually Muggles, learn Hogwarts' many secrets along with Harry, we become as it were, honorary Wizards. In addition to the ordinary "mysteries" of the castle, such as learning how to find the Great Hall and the Divination classroom, there are also "staircases that led somewhere different on a Friday" (*Stone* 98), and students find that access to Gryffindor tower is possible only by giving the secret password to the portrait of the fat lady, who would then swing open to allow the students through, unless she happened to be visiting someone in another picture (*Stone* 96).

Among other secrets at Hogwarts there is the Room of Requirement, which can only be found when it is actually needed and then will appear equipped appropriately (*Phoenix* 234–37). Harry receives gifts from unknown donors: at his first Christmas he unwraps a mysterious Invisibility Cloak, "fluid and silvery grey ... like water woven into material," which he is told had belonged to his father (*Stone* 148). The cloak, big enough to hide all three friends at times, enables Harry to move around the castle and visit Hogsmeade undetected, and plays an essential part in many of the stories. Two years later, again at Christmas, he receives an anonymous gift of his dream broomstick, a Firebolt, the best model on the market (*Azkaban* 165).

Harry is overjoyed, but Hermione is suspicious that there might be a secret jinx on it and informs Professor McGonagall, who confiscates it until it can be thoroughly checked. There is the precious Marauder's Map given to Harry by the Weasley twins, Fred and George, which had been drawn up by the unknown "Messrs. Moony, Wormtail, Padfoot and Prongs..." and which shows not only every corner of Hogwarts and the whereabouts of everyone in it, but also secret passages from the castle to the nearby village of Hogsmeade (*Azkaban* 143–44). Harry and Ron are puzzled as to how Hermione seems to be taking so many extra classes, and the secret is revealed to be a small crystal hourglass which could alter time. In addition to understanding why Hermione is so exhausted, we learn about the dangers of altering time later, when Dumbledore sends Hermione and Harry to take the enormous risk of using the Time-Turner to save Sirius and Buckbeak.

Given secrecy's many purposes, it is no wonder that it can be used well or used poorly. While Dumbledore is nearly always trustworthy, able to keep confidences to protect Hogwarts students and staff, he has also misused secrecy. His brother, Aberforth, tells Harry, Ron, and Hermione that the Dumbledore boys were raised on "secrets and lies" and that Albus was an especially able practitioner (*Hallows* 453). Harry, like Aberforth, is hurt by Dumbledore's lack of openness. This instinct for secrecy is perhaps the biggest flaw in Dumbledore's character. He admits to Harry that if he had been fully open with him Sirius might not have died (*Phoenix* 727–28); and again, when they meet in the in-between space of King's Cross Station, Dumbledore asks Harry's forgiveness for not trusting him (*Hallows* 571). It seems that the secrecy that Dumbledore and his siblings grew up with in order to protect the youngest child, Ariana, had become a fixed pattern, one that haunts Dumbledore even after his death.

In the King's Cross meeting, Dumbledore describes his short alliance with Gellert Grindelwald. What started out, perhaps, as a strategy of expediency to protect wizards and witches from oppression and to bring the community into the open turned out to be, as Dumbledore described it: "Two months of insanity, of cruel dreams, and neglect of the only two members of my family left to me" (*Hallows* 574). Of all the things one might admire about Dumbledore, his ability to search his own soul and to admit his errors might be among the most admirable. Not only is he able to admit to Harry that he bore responsibility for the death of his sister, but he is also quite clear that Aberforth is his "rough, unlettered, and infinitely more admirable brother" (574). Albus has learned from his mistakes about secrecy when it moves from the empowerment of learning to the tendency toward the power of domination. He has turned from those cruel dreams and tried to "learn to live with [his] guilt and [his] terrible grief, the price of [his] shame" (575).

One of the greatest secrets of the series is whether Snape is on the side of Dumbledore and the Order of the Phoenix or on the side of Voldemort. In novel after novel Rowling keeps her readers guessing, wanting to believe Dumbledore, who trusts Snape, but seeing his actions as working for Voldemort, until finally his act of killing Dumbledore and his subsequent flight appear to confirm that he was in thrall to Voldemort all along (*Prince* 556). Only near the end of the final novel does Rowling let Harry and her readers learn the truth, as Harry sees Snape's memories in the Pensieve (*Hallows* 529–53).

Order of the Phoenix begins with resentment about secrets. Harry is furious at having been left at Privet Drive with no knowledge of what is happening in the wizard world and finds that it is no better at Grimmauld Place. All of the children are frustrated at not knowing what the members of the Order are discussing, despite using Fred and George's Extendable Ears. In the chapter "The Order of the Phoenix," tensions emerge between Mrs. Weasley and Sirius as to how much information Harry should be given (*Phoenix* 84–91). There is talk of a secret weapon, "Something he didn't have last time." Although Rowling describes Sirius and Lupin as exchanging a fleeting look, she does not divulge what this weapon might be, thus keeping her characters and her readers in the dark (91).

Introducing the "true matter" or secret fire of the Philosophers, one of the essential ingredients for making the Philosopher's Stone, Patrick Harpur writes:

> The secret fire ... was a secret that was passed down from antiquity—some say, from Orpheus; others from Moses; most, from Hermes Trismegistus—in a long series of links which constituted what the Philosophers called the Golden Chain. This august

succession of philosophers embodied a tradition which we have either ignored or labelled "esoteric", even "occult"; but it continues to run like a vein of quicksilver beneath Western culture... (xiii).

Significantly, Harpur continues, "It is not a piece of information; nor is it a code to be cracked or a riddle to be solved" (xiii). To begin the work of alchemy the one thing necessary is the *Prima Materia*, Harpur says, but, like the Philosopher's Stone as it will later be known, no two people can agree on what exactly it is. Citing the sixteenth-century *Gloria Mundi*, Harpur writes that it is:

> found in the country, in the village, in the town, in all things created by God; yet it is despised by all. Rich and poor handle it every day. It is cast into the street by servant maids. Children play with it. Yet no one prizes it, though, next to the human soul, it is ... the most precious thing upon earth and has the power to pull down kings and princes. (151)

It is as elusive as the "secret fire," which, he says "was *the* secret of alchemy," again with contradictions: "Fire which does not burn.... Water ... which does not wet the hands" (152). Given that the sub-title of Harpur's book is *A History of the Imagination*, I suggest that this precious element might *be* imagination, without which no ideas, philosophical or alchemical, can be conceived.

Harpur also makes the point that the church authorities liked beliefs to be rigidly defined (31), thereby limiting experimentation and forbidding any discoveries which might contradict their edicts. The secret fire, I suggest, is also the questioning spirit, which is open to ideas of all kinds. As such, it is a threat to power and therefore inimical to authority and has to be kept secret. In Rowling's series this is made particularly clear in the character of Professor Umbridge, for whom knowledge in the students presents a threat. Although ostensibly teaching the topic of Defence Against the Dark Arts, she attempts to teach unthinking obedience as she tries to silence not only inquiry and learning but the truth of Voldemort's return (*Phoenix* 216–25).

As a result, a group of students takes matters into its own hands and, as with the early alchemists, pursues learning in enforced secrecy. Calling itself "Dumbledore's Army," the group, under Harry's tuition, succeeds really well in mastering defensive skills (*Phoenix* 534–35). Working together has also created a bond between the members: the two outsiders who have fought with Harry at the Ministry, Neville and Luna, in particular, are disappointed to think that the group might not need to continue. Neville tells Harry, "I liked the DA! I learned loads with you!" The dreamy Luna says, "I enjoyed the meetings, too.... It was like having friends." (*Prince* 132). A shared secret creates a bond.

Moving from Ignorance to Enlightenment

Rowling commented on *Pottermore* that "[o]ne interpretation of the 'instructions' left by the alchemists is that they are symbolic of a spiritual journey, leading the alchemist from ignorance (base metal) to enlightenment (gold)" ("Alchemy"). Harry, like the reader, begins with no knowledge of magic or of its existence, although strange things do happen around him: when chased by Dudley and his friends at school he finds himself on a roof without knowing how he got there; when Aunt Petunia cuts his hair it grows again overnight; and most memorably when at the zoo he discovers he can converse with a snake which he then releases, again without knowing how he has done so (*Stone* 23–26). To the best of his knowledge, his parents had been killed in a car crash when he was an infant and he himself got the lightning shaped scar on his forehead. Only when Hagrid, shocked at his ignorance about his magical heritage, informs him about his parents and his magical history does the journey of learning about Hogwarts and magic begin for Harry and for the reader.

For the young child, learning is an esoteric exercise, an initiation into secret knowledge which will grant power. Donald Meltzer, a Kleinian psychoanalyst, writes about the inherent desire for learning and knowledge. Among the tokens of rank is information; thus, "[t]he school books of the next higher class appear to be so many holy tablets mysteriously inscribed by the gods" (Meltzer 157–59). In children's fantasy literature, too, this growing knowledge helps the characters as they undertake ever more demanding tasks. In Susan Cooper's series *The Dark is Rising*, the seemingly hidden structures of the universe are revealed to the young protagonist, Will Stanton, in *The Book of Gramarye*, "the oldest book in the world." In its poetic and magical description, Will experiences the magical in the world. As he reads, Will flies with the eagles, swims with the fishes, learns how to "control wind and storm, sky and air," everything in the universe past and present becomes part of him (118–22).

By contrast, in Rowling's series Harry's education takes place in a school setting more typical of the gradual ordered learning of the alchemists and also more familiar to the readers. Yet, through that gradual learning, Rowling's characters—and through them her readers—learn something of how the universe is present in them and how to understand the importance of transforming their lives, both emotionally and academically, as they move through their years in school and grow from prepubescent eleven-year-olds to seventeen-year-olds who are of age in the Wizard world. This gradual learning, building from what has gone before as well as practical experimentation, is similar to the ways in which the alchemists learned, and as with them, there are sometimes failures. In Rowling's series, one such dramatic failure is when Hermione, having painstakingly made Polyjuice Potion for herself, Harry, and Ron, accidentally turns herself into a cat (*Chamber* 168).

In the first novel, Rowling introduces her protagonists and her readers to the Wizard World. Using a characteristic trope of the school story genre, she uses the train as a link between the Muggle World, including the normality of King's Cross Station, and the Wizarding World of Hogwarts. Rowling uses this to introduce the three who will eventually become friends, all from different backgrounds: Ron, a Pure-Blood wizard from an old Wizarding family who takes the magic world for granted; Hermione, Muggle-born but who has already read all the books for the year ahead, and Harry, a Half-Blood who knows nothing at all about magic apart from what Hagrid has recently introduced him to (*Stone* 74–82). Harry is totally ignorant of everything in the Wizard World, and on the train it is all magical: the moving pictures on collectable cards contained in the Chocolate Frogs, and the information that he gleans from them about Dumbledore; Bertie Bott's Every-Flavor Beans, Cauldron Cakes, and Pumpkin Pasties. Harry worries about his lack of knowledge: "I bet I'm the worst in the class." Ron reassures Harry that many people come to Hogwarts from a Muggle background, "and they learn quick enough" (*Stone* 76).

For Harry the contact with Ron on the train is a completely new experience. For the first time, he has a friend with whom he can share things, and money with which to buy treats to share. Rowling writes, "Harry ... had never had anything to share before or, indeed, anyone to share it with. It was a nice feeling, sitting there with Ron, eating their way through all Harry's pasties and cakes..." (76). In this first novel the focus of the emotional development is about learning how to relate both to friends and to enemies. Harry and Ron dislike the bossy Hermione intensely until all three find themselves locked in a toilet with a troll, and, to their amazement, Hermione lies to Professor McGonagall to get the other two out of trouble. "From that moment on, Hermione Granger became their friend. There are some things you can't share without ending up liking each other, and knocking out a twelve-foot mountain troll is one of them" (*Stone* 129–32).

This incident not only marks the beginning of friendship among the three but is also the beginning of Rowling showing how they need what each can bring to the solving of problems. Later in the novel, trying to save the Philosopher's Stone from Voldemort, their combined skills are required to work out how to get through the various spells protecting the trapdoor: the academic Hermione solves the problem of which potion it is safe to drink, and how to deal with the killer plant, Devil's Snare, which is about to strangle them; Ron, brought up in Wizard traditions, plays the game of Wizard chess; and Harry, the Quidditch Seeker, finds and catches the flying key (200–08). This pattern of co-operation continues throughout the series as the three friends grow in knowledge and skill and also respect for each other's capabilities.

Each of the novels has as its climax a terrifying encounter between Harry and Voldemort, and through each, Harry learns something important, usually about death. In an interview in *Tatler Magazine*, Rowling says: "My books are largely about death. They open with the death of Harry's parents. There is Voldemort's obsession with conquering death and his quest for immortality at any price, the goal of anyone with magic. I so understand why Voldemort wants to conquer death. We're all frightened of it." One of the greatest challenges in life is learning to accept the fact of our own death and that of those we love. Rowling's skill lies in her ability to introduce the topic of death in a way that is accessible to a young audience but not too simplistic for the adult reader. She neither presents it in a specifically Christian way, as C.S. Lewis does in the Narnia series, nor does she insist that death is the end. Her emphasis is on facing the truth in a way that renders it acceptable. In the first novel, in which Harry learns that the Stone has been destroyed, he becomes aware that as a consequence of this, Nicolas and Perenelle Flamel will die. Although this novel, and indeed the series as a whole, begins with the significant fact of the death of Harry's parents, this is the first occasion that Rowling invites Harry, and therefore her readers, to reflect on the topic. It is, however, at a safe remove, as we do not know the Flamels and at their age, death is appropriate.

In the next novel, *Chamber of Secrets*, only the basilisk dies, but the topic comes closer as several students, including Hermione, are Petrified, a state which could be regarded as a temporary death, and Ginny Weasley is very close to actual death when Harry rescues her. In the concluding chapters of *Prisoner of Azkaban*, Harry and his friends learn some very important lessons. One is that Dumbledore, although clever and wise, is not omnipotent. He cannot intervene, by magic or otherwise, to save the lives of Sirius and the hippogriff, Buckbeak. What he can and does do is to point out to Hermione that she and Harry have the means to do so by using a Time-Turner. It is they, the younger generation, on whom the task depends (287–303). Similarly, Harry realizes that the person who sent the powerful Patronus to save his life and those of Sirius and Hermione was not, as he had thought, his father but himself. Both situations show the teenagers no longer being able to rely on the adults to deal with the situation but finding the power to do so within themselves, a hugely significant step on the way to maturity.

It is in *Azkaban*, too, that Harry learns the value of compassion. Although ready to kill Sirius Black in order, as he thinks at first, to avenge his father's death, when Sirius and Lupin are about to kill the man who informed Voldemort about the whereabouts of Lily and James, Harry stops them, telling Pettigrew, "I'm not doing this for you. I'm doing it because I don't reckon my dad would've wanted his best friends to become killers—just for you" (275). This is the first time that Harry finds himself with the power of life or death over another person, and he chooses not to kill, a choice which becomes his hallmark. This nearly leads to disaster when Harry's use of *Expelliarmus* results in his being recognized among seven lookalikes as they escape from Privet Drive (*Goblet* 552–58).

With the death of Cedric, a character we know and have come to like, at the end of *Goblet of Fire*, Rowling brings the topic of death close up, and from that point the novels become much darker. This death is followed by those of Sirius, Dumbledore, and Harry's owl, Hedwig. Each loss brings its unique pain: that of Sirius brings guilt and rage at the loss of the person who had come to represent his father and with whom he hoped to have a new life away from the Dursleys; that of Dumbledore, not only the leader in the battle of good against evil, but the one who "always had the answers"; and that of Hedwig, the first creature he had loved, his link with Hogwarts during the summer holidays at Privet Drive, and his companion through the series. Learning how to cope with grief is a major and painful aspect of gaining maturity, and death and resurrection are important aspects of alchemy. David Goddard writes: "That Stone—the Jewel of Eternity—overcomes all limitation, heals all disease, and brings an end to the need for death itself" (xi).

Throughout the series Rowling insists that love is stronger than death and can survive it in some form. She expands this idea into a mechanism whereby she has Harry's parents emerge from Voldemort's wand in the graveyard to help Harry escape and bring Cedric's body back to Hogwarts. Again when Harry, having apparently been killed by Voldemort, meets Dumbledore at King's Cross, Rowling suggests a place between worlds, where Harry has a choice to go back or "On." This is a particularly complex scene in which Dumbledore elucidates many of the puzzles that have occurred through the series. But there is a third creature in that place in the form of "a small naked child … its skin raw and rough, flayed-looking … unwanted, stuffed out of sight, struggling for breath." In killing Harry, Voldemort has killed the fragment of his soul that he had unwittingly put into Harry (*Hallows* 566). In terms of alchemy, all three had achieved enlightenment but used it differently. Dumbledore, by his own admission, had been tempted to abuse his power and knowledge, but turned from that temptation and decided to use his power for good. He has completed his task and is ready to move on. Harry, although reluctant to leave the peacefulness of this place, recognizes that he has to return to take part in the struggle against evil. The miserable fragment of Voldemort's soul, we are left to assume, has to remain where it is, as Dumbledore says, "there is no help possible" (568).

Emotional learning is not only about exploring the extreme edges of life, nor is it confined to serious and painful moments. It is also about growing more fully into life, and Rowling describes the confusions and difficulties of adolescence with a mixture of poignancy and humor. Relations between men and women were important to the alchemists, and early prints show both at work. The spiritual link between the sexes was essential for the alchemical work to go forward, and Rowling suggests that such a link is gradually forged between Harry and Ginny. After Dumbledore's death, relationships become more real. It is Ginny who is able to reach out to the shocked and distraught Harry. Fleur Delacour proves to be made of sterner stuff than the arrogant and contemptuous beauty that she seemed to be. The protagonists have come through a shattering experience—the death of Dumbledore, who had seemed invincible; the first Battle of Hogwarts; Bill Weasley badly injured. Nothing can ever be the same. The young protagonists have come through the darkness of death and betrayal to stand with the remaining adults ready to play an equal part in fighting the ultimate battle against Voldemort, whenever and wherever that should take place.

In alchemy, two of the important symbols of spiritual growth are marriage and death with resurrection. Rowling addresses these issues in the final novel, *Deathly Hallows*. In the early chapters, a large group of familiar and unfamiliar Wizards gather for the wedding of Bill Weasley and Fleur Delacour. Towards the end of the novel Harry is called upon by Voldemort to sacrifice himself to save his companions, and walks to his anticipated death with the support and reassurance of those who have loved him and who are already dead. Rowling shows Harry moving from one world to another; this is a journey he has to go alone. As he walks towards Voldemort, the spirits of his parents, Sirius, and Lupin join him, and seem much more substantial than his living friends at Hogwarts, "who felt like ghosts as he stumbled and slipped towards the end of his life…" (562).

Alchemy is about transformation: transformation of base metal into gold, transformation from ignorance to enlightenment, from incompetence to skill. The Battle of Hogwarts, a metaphor for the struggle of good against evil, light against dark, knowledge against ignorance, show the skills that the protagonists have learned over their years at the school being put into action. Not merely fighting skills, the battles also demonstrate how the individual protagonists have been transformed in stature. Clumsy Neville, mocked by Voldemort, is the one who kills the snake, Nagini, who holds the last piece of Voldemort's soul. Ginny, once lured to danger by Riddle's diary, is helping an injured girl to safety. Luna inspires them all to continue, saying "We're all still here.... We're still fighting. Come on, now..." (*Hallows* 522). In the Pensieve Harry learns the truth about Snape with all his conflicted feelings, and how he, too, was transformed and ultimately did all he could for the side of Good against Evil.

The alchemists saw knowledge as enlightenment leading to the transformation of base humanity to a more godly state. Rowling, more realistically, recognizes that this does not necessarily happen. It can only offer choice. The two most powerful wizards, Dumbledore and Voldemort, chose very different paths, and for each the result is shown at King's Cross Station: Dumbledore transformed into a whole and radiant version of himself, Voldemort's part-soul pathetic and tragic. Harry's symbolic death and resurrection have resulted in an alchemy that offers victory to those fighting for truth and justice.

WORKS CITED

Barrett, David V. *Secret Societies: From the Ancient and Arcane to the Modern and Clandestine*. Blandford, 1997.
British Library Board and Bloomsbury Publishing. *Harry Potter: A History of Magic*. Bloomsbury, 2017.
Cooper, Susan. *The Dark Is Rising*. Puffin Books, 1976.
Culpeper, Nicholas. *Culpeper's Complete Herbal: Consisting of a Comprehensive Description of Nearly All Herbs with Their Medicinal Properties and Directions for Compounding the Medicines Extracted from Them*. W. Foulsham, 1994.
Goddard, David. *The Tower of Alchemy: An Advanced Guide to the Great Work*. Samuel Weiser, 1999.
Goethe, Johann Wolfgang von. *Faust*. Translated by Albert G. Latham, J.M. Dent, 1948.
Greig, Geordie. Interview with J.K. Rowling. *Tatler Magazine*. 10 Jan. 2006. www.the-leaky-cauldron.org/2006/01/09/new-j-k-rowling-interview-in-tatler-magazine/.
Harpur, Patrick. *The Philosophers' Secret Fire: A History of the Imagination*. Squeeze Press, 2009.
McGilchrist, Iain. *The Master and His Emissary*. Yale UP, 2009.
Meltzer, Donald. *Sexual States of Mind*. Clunie Press, 1979.
Pavord, Anna. "Herbology." *Harry Potter: A History of Magic*, British Library Board and Bloomsbury Publishing, 2017, pp. 70–98.
Rowling, J.K. "Alchemy." *Pottermore*, www.pottermore.com/writing-by-jk-rowling/alchemy. Accessed 15 Sept. 2018.
_____. *Harry Potter and the Chamber of Secrets*. Bloomsbury, 1998.
_____. *Harry Potter and the Deathly Hallows*. Bloomsbury, 2007.
_____. *Harry Potter and the Goblet of Fire*. Bloomsbury, 2000.
_____. *Harry Potter and the Half-Blood Prince*. Bloomsbury, 2005.
_____. *Harry Potter and the Order of the Phoenix*. Bloomsbury, 2003.
_____. *Harry Potter and the Philosopher's Stone*. Bloomsbury, 1997.
_____. *Harry Potter and the Prisoner of Azkaban*. Bloomsbury, 1999.
_____. *The Tales of Beedle the Bard*. Bloomsbury, 2008.
Simpson, Anne. "Casting a Spell Over Young Minds; Anne Simpson FACE TO FACE with J K Rowling." *The Herald*, 6 Dec. 1998, www.heraldscotland.com/news/12012592.casting-spell-over-young-minds-anne-simpson-face-to-face-with-j-k-rowling/.
White, T.H. *The Book of Beasts, Being a Translation from a Latin Bestiary of the Twelfth Century*. Jonathan Cape, 1956.

Harry Potter and the Root of All Evil

CHARLES M. RUPERT

In the allegorical world of J.K. Rowling's *Harry Potter* series, the mindscape comes alive. Rowling performs a kind of mental alchemy as she weaves a complex morality, magically endowing a level of reality to what otherwise might be purely psychological phenomena. In Harry Potter's world, not unlike our own, right and wrong are subjective, pluralistic, and infinitely open to interpretation, thus requiring work on the part of the characters to achieve and sustain an ethical status. The degrees separating good from evil are presented as contextual and shifting. Actions are often not what they appear. Rowling offers no objective authority for moral guidance, but instead places the burden for moral responsibility on her characters (children included) and allows them the freedom of interpretation for their own actions. That is not to say she allows unguided morality to play, but that characters, through discourse, observation, and reflection on experiences, hammer out for themselves their own justifications for their actions.

With Rowling's emphasis on character and context in mind, I have chosen to highlight the moral themes of the series by a psychoanalysis of Lord Voldemort, the series' arch-villain, and Albus Dumbledore, the series' moral epitome. Rowling's morality is subjective and existential, and it is neither given nor is it even discoverable. Morality is earned in the flesh, through the process of trial and error. Dumbledore is no monster of virtue. His errors reassure us of his humanity; because the other characters and readers can relate to him: he is a respectable moral figure, making his character stronger and more complete through his admissions of failure and work to change. Similarly, Voldemort is never beyond redemption. Moral choice perpetually remains before him despite the tunnel vision of his ethical certitude, which, ironically, diminishes him, makes him less whole, less human. Other characters in the series are to be seen as either fixed somewhere on the spectrum between these two ideals, or they may be moral apprentices, such as Harry, shifting about between the two.

To conduct this analysis, I've employed the work of Erich Fromm, whose perspective of social psychology presents surprising insight into Rowling's text. Fromm's psycho-analysis offers us a largely existential moral perspective, broad enough to capture psycho-social phenomena. Despite their access to magic, Rowling's characters must traverse the same shifting and confusing world we inhabit. Subjectivism, isolation, individuality, interpersonal connection, self-control, love, and most importantly, the struggle for self-determination against society and nature or authenticity are the key moral themes. Authenticity has grown progressively more difficult since the rise of global capitalism. This mindset, developed in the twentieth century, remains the current Western personality, and is embodied, albeit in an exaggerated manner, by the series' antagonists.

After a brief overview of Fromm's psychology, I will examine the authoritarian psycho-social perspective where the individual is isolated, afraid, and powerless, and wishing desperately to escape these feelings, manifests a life aimed at self-possession through the domination of everything and everyone in their lives. I will then argue that although the authoritarian type sees submission as the only alternative, the existentialist humanitarian view provides a way out of the supposed dilemma. The existential alternative emphasizes freedom, individuality, self-recognition in the relation to others, and the need for human connection to create meaning and foster happiness. These ideologies are not figments of Rowling's gifted imagination. Her allegorical world brings our own moral struggles into sharper relief with a dash of magic through her storyteller's craft.

An Overview of Fromm's Existential Psychology

Fromm saw morality through a conflict between two orientations toward the world and the self (*To Have* 20). The first of these orientations assumes that healthy human beings are mentally whole in and of themselves; they are intact, and that which makes up the completed self, though a construct of one's environs, may neither be divided nor subtracted from the whole, whether or not one is aware of such a state. Fromm labels this view as *being*. A "being" person relates to the world through authenticity, seeks truth, and develops relationships with people and things based upon sober need (*To Have* 21). The alternative view imagines humans as loosely cohesive fragments that may intertwine into other objects via psychic forces. Bits of the self in other objects form a unique relationship with them, a type of psychological joining to other bodies. In this perspective, which Fromm labels *having*, a person's relationship to the world is one of possessing and owning, where the person seeks to make everybody and everything—including one's self—property, and relationships, which are all based only on cultivated dependency as a means of domination.

"Being," by its very nature as participatory in experience, is more difficult to explain and comprehend than "having," which seeks to create an objective, observable world (Fromm, *To Have* 71). As a psychoanalyst, Fromm finds his model in the language his patients employ: "instead of 'I *have* a problem,' the patient [may as well] have said, 'I *am* troubled'; instead of 'I *have* insomnia,' 'I *cannot* sleep'; instead of 'I *have* a happy marriage,' 'I *am* happily married,'" (*To Have* 18). We are either in a state of something or we possess that something. Fromm explains that being is not to be confused with asceticism, which he describes as "the negation of strong desires for having and consuming" (69). He sees asceticism not as the mode of being but as the mode of *not* having. In asceticism the locus of the self remains on the external rather than the internal, and so it is simply a negative variation of the having mode. Being is a state of existing as both collective and individual, seen as a figure/ground relationship. Being, as Fromm sees it, is the fulfillment of an individual human's potential through activity, a sense of reality disabused of projection; it is giving, sharing, sacrifice, and ultimately solidarity (71–87).

"Having," on the other hand, is foundational in humans; for example, the nursling understands the relation of its self to its world through "having" the breast. Freud suggested links between infant psychological possessiveness and adult narcissism (Schwartz 266). The infant is wholly incapable of self-gratification because, as Freud understood it, there is not yet any awareness of a self (Crockatt 7). Mahler suggests that the infant has no defined sense of self and is unable to distinguish between itself and its mother (Zerin and Zerin 63), a view suggestive of the pre-imaginary views of Lacan, where the undifferentiated infant exists, as in Klein's Phantasy, as so-many fragmented needs (Lacan 55). A young child's locus of identification (its ego) is outside the self, with an emphasis on immediate gratification of its needs. Indeed, the child views itself only as those needs, or at best infers itself from them. This is the essence of the having mode; the boundaries between the self and the external objects are diffuse, with a preserved emphasis on possession and consumption to satisfy the "needs" of the person (Fromm, *To Have* 63–64). As Fromm explains, "having" obscures the true relationship between one's possessions and one's self. He writes, "[i]t and I have become things, and I have *it*, because I have the force to make it mine. But there is also a reverse relationship: *it has me*, because my sense of identity, i.e., of sanity, rests upon my having *it* (and as many things as possible)" (*To Have* 63–64). Having is not mere custody of a thing but a psychic entanglement of possessor and the possessed.

Movement away from the having mode is considered necessary for healthy psychological development. The child is not merely transfigured into an adult, but must be transfigured by some experiential process. Freud referred to the hoarding phase of the child as the "anal-erotic" and held that, while it is a normal part of development in the young, it is pathological when seen in adults. "For Freud," suggests Fromm, "the person exclusively concerned with having and possession is a neurotic, [a] mentally sick person" (*To Have* 68). Fromm saw the having mode as prevailing in western culture and developing into a habitual social norm. This is not to say that he viewed the having mode as something inherently bad. Rather, in Western modernity, reductionist thinking and logical positivism—which tend to ignore (and so devalue) the unobservable—along with the Reformation—which removed man from his place within the ecosystem and set him above it—have elevated a moral deficit into a virtue. Today, humanity is left unsure, and that state has given rise to anxiety, from which we are compelled to "escape" by seeking a sense (albeit a false one) of security in the things around us. Here the two orientations through which morality is obtained can be seen as a motivation for our actions. The "being" person progresses from one position to another on the search for truth in an ever-shifting world of contexts. Alternately, the "having" person flees a position only when they can no longer deny its untenability. They rush desperately into the nearest position that seems to offer permanence and wholly submit to whatever tenets it imposes upon them (*Escape* xx). It is these two notions that separate true freedom from false freedom, with the implication being that only the truly free have the opportunity to choose a moral script, while the remainder must follow any available scripts or, if at the pinnacle of society, their own uninformed and arbitrary desires.

In sum, the "having" person confuses isolation for independence. These people seek domination before cooperation with others. They fear intimacy because they cannot bear its costs. They construct a living fantasy where they and their property are one and the same, where they are the undiscovered heir-apparent of history, and where existential impossibility is a hindrance only of the weak-willed. They relate better to inanimate things than to people, personifying objects of affection and then trusting in those things' fidelity and imperishability the way a child believes in the safety of a blanket. Greed in fact defines them, because their logic assumes objective values for property and money. By seeking companionship in objects and things, the "havers" inadvertently and quite ironically become absolutely dependent on society to tell them who they are, what they should value, and how they should live their lives. But this fantasy does not really obtain. Thus, they live lives of great anxiety. The dependency on their things leaves them struggling desperately to be autonomous.

Meanwhile, the "being" person accepts the reality of interdependence with others. Such people relate authentically to those around them, revealing to those others their true selves as the expression of love. They seek the truth in-between phenomenal facts. They dig beneath the external and get to the heart of a matter, and know that doing so very likely changes the matter itself. They think of themselves as whole and require only existential needs, not immanent ones. They accept what they cannot be and cannot change. They live both for themselves and for others, varying as necessity dictates. They are beholden to nothing. They cultivate understanding rather than attempting to possess a bank of knowledge. They feel in a living way all the connections of being, even unto an abstract oneness with all. They alone can sacrifice, and so they alone can love. That the mode of being is not rendered into magical allegory in Rowling's work says something important about it: being is not "like something"; it merely is that thing. Thus, to speak of it in metaphor is to confound its haecceity—the qualities that make being itself, its "thisness"—and destroy the last, best hope of a sincere conveyance of its authenticity.

He-Who-Must-Not-Be-Named

With Fromm's framework in mind, we begin with an exploration of the most rational, logical, and gifted wizard who ever lived in Rowling's world: The Dark Lord Voldemort. Significantly, Rowling begins the series with the occasion of this main villain's "death." His own murderous spell has reflected back on him by the love of a mother's sacrifice for her child. Seven books and nearly eighteen story-years later, it ends almost exactly as it began, with the death of the same villain, killed again by his own spell reflected back from that very same boy. Lord Voldemort has, since his initial failure, seemingly remained the same, despite a host of existential transformations. He is morally and mentally identical at the time of both of his "deaths," whereas Harry has been transmuted physically, emotionally, mentally, and spiritually. Indeed, as we'll see, in their first quarrel the two are, morally speaking, quite alike, whereas in the final confrontation they could hardly be more different.

At that first meeting, when Harry lost his parents, he and Voldemort were both operating on a similar moral level, namely a narcissistic one. Freud's quip, "His Majesty the Baby," deliciously describes children's worldview, in which they see themselves as the center of all consequence (Schwartz 266). His Majesty's moral development is thus limited, at least according to Kohlberg's model, to "might makes right" (Whited and Grimes 185). In the case of Lord Voldemort, the introduction of early childhood trauma is required. Distress could arrest development precisely at this early stage, crystalizing the foundational *Weltanschauung* and transforming it into an adult pathology. We learn in *Half-Blood Prince* that just such a trauma took place in young Tom Riddle's life: his orphaning. The trauma of that abandonment may have led to stunted moral growth, locking him in a pre-conventional ethic.

Rowling expresses this view in imagery, when she depicts the Dark Lord as a wounded child. At Voldemort's return to a body in the graveyard in *Goblet of Fire*, Rowling describes him as a "thing ... [which] had the shape of a crouched human child, except that Harry had never seen anything less like a child. It was hairless and scaly-looking, a dark, raw, reddish black. Its arms and legs were thin and feeble, and its face—no child alive ever had a face like that—flat and snakelike, with gleaming red eyes" (*Goblet* 640). Again in *Deathly Hallows*, the remains of Voldemort's Horcrux appear as "a small, naked child, curled on the ground, its skin raw and rough, flayed-looking, ... shuddering under a seat where it had been left, unwanted, stuffed out of sight, struggling for breath" (*Hallows* 706–07). These depictions when viewed allegorically suggest Voldemort's "inner" child, revealed by Rowling, as a helpless, mutilated babe, abandoned and alone, struggling, malnourished, and abused. Abused as a child, Tom Riddle is both vulnerable and afraid, and the unbearable anxiety of his situation will drive him through a series of coping strategies over the course of his life, which in their own right determine his moral identity, making him Lord Voldemort.

Hoarding becomes an occupation for Voldemort from an early age, as we see in *Half-Blood Prince*, when the eleven-year-old Riddle collects trophies from his victims, and he continues it throughout his life, for example when he collects relics from the Hogwarts' founders (*Prince* 273). It is important to note that he is not collecting these items for their practical use, such as Harry does with his Invisibility Cloak and the Marauder's Map, but simply to bolster his own sense of self-worth by proxy. Hoarding seems a component of many wizards and witches associated with Slytherin House, from Marvolo Gaunt's fixation on his family's heirlooms, to Professor Snape's obsession with the past, to Professor Slughorn's collection of promising students, to the Malfoys' obscene wealth, to Crabbe and Goyle's gluttony. Salazar Slytherin's eventual obsession with power broke his friendship with Gryffindor, moving him from a pillar of Hogwarts to a threat to its existence. The Sorting Hat, created in the wake of that rift, urges a return to "being" one of the Hogwarts four from a mistaken sense of "having" power over others (*Phoenix* 204–07). The predilection is not exclusive to Slytherins or fallen witches or wizards: Harry's Muggle relatives illustrate this hoarding behavior as well. At his eleventh birthday, Dudley Dursley moves away from the moral world Harry is about to enter when he, with his father's support, declares that it is the number of presents and not their contents that matters (*Stone* 21).

The most immediate explanation for such a tendency toward hoarding would be simply to employ Freud's "anal character," where the youthful fear of loss is arrested and manifests itself as a compulsion to hoard in the adult (Fromm, *To Have* 68). Trauma might arrest development in a young Tom Riddle, but few if any of the others seem to have suffered such a loss or injury. We may see a bit more clearly if we look through the lens of Adorno and Horkheimer's principle of quantity over quality as it plays out in the status-conscious middle-class of Western civilization (xiv). Capitalism expands Fromm's "having" identity into a culture that inflicts mass trauma on the majority of the population. Dumbledore, who is capable of seeing the injury, perplexes the Dursleys when he accuses them of having done "appalling damage" to their beloved son (*Prince* 55).

What is at stake here is the metaphysical stance regarding human nature, or more precisely, whether or not human beings are inherently capable of rising above their own worst tendencies. Salazar Slytherin was an elitist when he turned away from his brave friend, Godric Gryffindor, and from the Hogwarts community. He reserved the resources that provide a full and flourishing life, like magical education, for those few who, like himself, were from "all-magic families. He disliked taking students of Muggle parentage, believing them to be untrustworthy" (*Chamber* 150). In Slytherin's hands, the "having" mode, as an ethic, blossoms into a full political ideology, where the right of the strong to rule the weak is insisted upon, and if this results in greater benefits for the strong, so be it. This philosophy of "might makes right" holds that when the strong lead it is the best of all worlds, even for the weak who are held to be the primary beneficiaries of the rule of their betters. The political ideology of the "having" ethic, then, is authoritarianism.

Authoritarianism, however, is myopic, insisting that power is only obtained in the demonstrated obedience of those below. Without domination, one can hardly justify the claim to being an elite. Thus, with this world view, the virtues are valued for their ability to produce the strength to control and dominate others, which is believed to be synonymous with power. Money, magic, relics, know-how, etc. are each proofs (and tools) in the service of self-exaltation. The will to dominate everything becomes the singular focus of authoritarianism. In a "having" culture, politics are morally relative, after all. Thus, there is no light and dark, "no good and evil, there is only power, and those too weak to seek it," as Quirrell learned from Voldemort (*Stone* 291).

The Slytherin tendency to authoritarianism might be juxtaposed to the worldview shared, more or less, by the other three houses, those remaining after Slytherin's failure of friendship. Both views seek to use possessions as social means to individual aims. However, the aims of this latter group are not so one-sided. Here the goal is mutual beneficence and not self-exaltation. We see this early in Harry, who first experiences it on the Hogwarts Express, when he shares his glut of comestible goodies with the impoverished Ron. The feeling that sharing elicits in him is described by Rowling simply as "nice" (*Stone* 102). Hardly a ringing endorsement, but, nevertheless, the seed of "being" is there. However, the inclination to have is there as well, in the collecting of the Chocolate Frog cards. If being is to sprout, it must be cultivated, and that is the mission of the Hogwartian education. As we see by book seven, the Chocolate Frog card collection has long been forgotten. By book seven, we also learn that the Slytherin, Regulus Black, has sacrificed himself for the good of the whole magical world as he moves from owning and a sense of superiority simply because of the accident of his birth. He is transfigured at this moment of sacrifice into "being." The brave Regulus has transformed the very meaning of power and weakness—and brings Slytherin back to Hogwarts, at least partly redeemed.

Owning, to subscribers of the having mode, is more than simple possession; it is to possess in the demonic sense or *incorporation*, to use Fromm's term (*To Have* 22). By contrast, Voldemort embodies this idea best, in both a figurative and literal sense. Literally, when the reader first encounters him as a spirit possessing the body of Professor Quirrell, and figuratively, in his employment of the Horcruxes. A Horcrux (an object endowed with a piece of soul) is the ideal relationship for a "haver" and his possessions. Voldemort believes he is immortal because he places his "self" in objects he feels are everlasting. Fromm, in describing the having mode, foresaw this tendency: "possession of property constitutes the fulfillment of the craving for immortality.... If my *self* is constituted by what I *have*, then I am immortal if the things I have are indestructible" (*To Have* 67). This relationship (a divided, separable self) leaves Voldemort vulnerable, "for where your treasure is, there will your heart be also" (*King James Bible* Matthew 6.21; *Hallows* 326). Magically separated from his "heart," he may not always be around to protect it. Voldemort's understanding of this situation causes him great anxiety, which compels the elaborate measures he takes to protect his treasure: namely, the parts of his soul hidden in Horcruxes.

The reciprocal desire of the "having" relationship is the complete devaluation of anything the self does not want to possess. Dumbledore, in describing Voldemort's arrogance to Harry, says, "That which Voldemort does not value, he takes no trouble to comprehend" (*Hallows* 709). Voldemort, like all in the having mode, sees power as external to the self; it is for him an object to be sought and obtained from the world, not a state cultivated from within. Voldemort sees his values as measurable and objective, and so he dismisses qualitative ideas, like love, as metaphysical nonsense because he cannot quantify them (*Prince* 444). In this way, emotions, even hate, rage, and fear, do not factor into behavioral decisions. Voldemort believes himself to be as a force of nature, beyond emotion, beyond good and evil, merely acting a certain way because he has the power to act that way.

Although, in truth, his actions are no more rationally cool than anyone else's, and in fact, Voldemort suffers the irony of all those in the having mode: *his* values are finally and wholly dependent on society's values, or at least his perceptions of them. In short, they are immanently determined. His sense of what is worthy may not be self-determined but is instead designated by his society, which leaves even his self-worth beyond his control. This is the control, the "power," he truly seeks and will do anything to gain. We can see that Voldemort, despite his impressive abilities, is in fact dependent on his victims and followers to provide him the satisfaction he needs. So, naturally, he has mistaken control of others for self-control, possession of objects of power for internal fortitude, and domination of nature (or magic in his case) for serenity. In short, Voldemort has confused internal states of being with external possessions. We will expand on these mistakes in a moment, but first I want to say a word about the supposed goal of all this domination and authority.

The ultimate aim of "having," as Fromm points out, is to possess the self, or "self-ownership" (*To Have* 59). This is unquestionably the case for Voldemort. In rechristening himself as Lord Voldemort, Tom Riddle is in fact trying to lay claim on himself. He starts on a lifelong quest to reinvent himself and by so doing to prove once and for all that he alone is master of his fate. Unhappily for him, possessing the self, like the snake swallowing its own tail, is mere paradox. Owning the self is self-delusion, and prolonged pursuit of an impossible desire leads to madness. Voldemort's attempt at self-possession takes the form of immortality. He states this explicitly, saying to his followers, "You know my goal—to conquer death" (*Goblet* 653). Even his name for these followers, "Death Eaters," when taken literally, suggests the consumption of death, by doing so making it one with the self; to consume death is to conquer it. Voldemort's worst fear then, it may be inferred, is death. He states as much one book later: "There is nothing worse than death, Dumbledore!" (*Phoenix* 814). We can further surmise that killing holds crucial significance for the narcissist Voldemort, where he is, in his mind, delivering the ultimate blow. The foundations of his death obsession are revealed during Dumbledore's recollected first encounter with the boy Tom Riddle. We learn that, although she was a witch, his mother was unable to prevent her own death, at least from his childish perspective (*Prince* 275). Riddle's abandonment, his prime trauma, is attributed to death, hence its great power over him. Vulnerable and afraid, Riddle would seek any and all means to defeat death, the "shameful human weakness" (*Prince* 363).

Because Voldemort needs others to provide his sense of worth, he depends on them either to fear or exalt him. It really does not matter which is chosen, for it is his unquestioned dependency that leaves him feeling ceaselessly insecure. While the being person cultivates love, he or she does not depend on others to provide it in a forced and unilateral way. Voldemort, ever with an eye to self-possession, attempts not independence from these others, but domination over them, in hopes of gaining a measure of security and self-assurance. But to dominate these others, the having person must first objectify them. Voldemort does this many times in the series, as when in *Goblet of Fire*, he explains to his Death Eaters, more servants than friends, that after kidnapping the witch Bertha Jorkins and torturing her for information, she became useless. In his words: "She had now served her purpose. I could not possess her. I disposed of her" (*Goblet* 655). He is hardly more sympathetic to his devotees. As Dumbledore explains in *Sorcerer's Stone*, "He left Quirrell to die; he shows just as little mercy to his followers as his enemies" (*Stone* 298). Thus objectified, all people become either instruments to employ or impediments to destroy.

But all objects are not equal. Subscribers of the having mode reason that the more powerful the object, the more power it confers to its possessor or destroyer (though this again leaves them open to the customs of society). The mistake here is to misplace the source of "power" in the object—say, the wand—and not in the wizard who wields it. To obtain objects, be they followers or weapons or wealth or even friends, then, lends resilience to the "haver" of these objects. Strengthened by the envied objects, the possessor feels more in control of his or her situation. It is for this reason that Voldemort collects deadly spells, fashions his Horcruxes out of renowned objects, and pursues what he believes to be the greatest weapon he can obtain, the first of the three "Deathly Hallows," the Elder Wand. This pursuit of powerful objects, as well as the emphasis he places on death, leads directly to his downfall. Voldemort pursues a more powerful object with which he would vanquish his rival, all the while trusting in the indestructibility of his Horcruxes. Harry, along with Dumbledore, Hermione, Ron, and Neville each destroy a piece of Voldemort, but in the end, it is Voldemort who destroys himself.

Acting on misunderstandings brings Voldemort to his doom. In this case the misunderstanding rests on his supposed possession of the Elder Wand. Voldemort believes it to now be his, both because he has murdered

Severus Snape, whom he believes to be the wand's owner after Snape has delivered the death blow to Dumbledore, and because the wand is now in his immediate possession (literally *in his hand*). It is Voldemort's emphasis on death and control that clouds his judgment of who really owns the wand. Confident of his ownership of the powerful weapon, he is unwilling to change his reasoning. Harry tries to correct him, explaining that simply having the wand in hand does not mean the wand has given Voldemort its allegiance (*Hallows* 742). But Voldemort cannot see the truth of his relationships, and this disadvantage precipitates his defeat. Harry knows it is he, and not Voldemort, who is the rightful owner of the Elder Wand, and to his credit tells the Dark Lord as much. Voldemort's narcissism leaves him unable to comprehend his own internal weakness, and so, trusting blindly in the superiority of his possessions, he attacks and destroys himself. His contentment that his enemy has become secured under his thumb, thanks to his powerful possessions, shows that he has not learned from his mistake nearly two decades earlier, but instead applies merely *more* of the same faulty logic to his life.

What the Headmaster Taught

Of Harry Potter, a child, we may ask how he came to grasp a concept beyond the reach of the most talented dark wizard ever. To answer that question, we must evaluate his Hogwartian education, and to do so demands a close scrutiny of its champion, Headmaster Albus Dumbledore. Harry's pre-Hogwarts foundations are squarely middle-class suburban. The Durselys' world, according to Karin Westman, "revolves around the fear of appearing different from their middle-class neighbors" (309). In her view, the Dursleys' attitude toward their foundling nephew forces Harry to bear witness to the blood bath that is the modern materialistic competition for social status, and at the same time prohibits his participation in its advantages. His exclusion from materialism not only preserves him from becoming Dudley Dursley, his greedy cousin, it also sharpens his senses to its many forms of oppression. Westman confirms this sense by showing that, although Harry readily joins the delights of consumerism as soon as he is able, he quickly realizes that consuming "goods only pays off emotionally when items are needed or are given to others as gifts" (309–11). De-emphasizing materialism, Dumbledore stations Harry at Privet Drive, because the gift of his mother's sacrifice—his mother's blood—resides there.

As Lisa Hopkins points out, in his first year "ignorance becomes Harry's defining condition..." (25). Learning that he and his parents are magical and that his parents were murdered by and brought about the fall of the mysterious Dark Lord are unknown histories that launch Harry on a journey of self-discovery, which become not only the main plot line of the series but an education in the art of being. The key to understanding Harry's Hogwartian education is to view it in terms of personal development rather than only measurable scholastic achievement. Farah Mendlesohn, who describes Harry as "the gentleman scholar," a "natural," who "rarely needs to exert himself," fails to recognize the ethical and conceptual struggles in which Harry engages (169). Mendlesohn writes, "We know Harry is bright because we are told he is," and "Harry's important magical adventures focus on his talents and not his learning" (169). The critical oversight of Mendlesohn's view is that it assumes a single relevant kind of education, viz. scholastics. But Dumbledore, whom we can imagine saying, with Socrates, "a man who is any good at all should [not] take into account the risk of life or death; he should look to this only in his actions, whether what he does is right or wrong, whether he is acting like a good or bad man," understands the difference between teaching students what to think and teaching them that they ought to think (*Apol.* 28b–c). If Dumbledore's goal is not for his students to *have* knowledge but to *be* both knowledgeable and good people, then again we look to Socrates, whose dialectic method, in essence, is Dumbledore's method. Harry himself observes at the end of *Stone*: "I think [Dumbledore] ... wanted to give me a chance. I think he knows more or less everything that goes on here, you know. I reckon he had a pretty good idea we were going to try, and instead of stopping us, he just taught us enough to help" (*Stone* 302). From this perspective it is Harry's internal development at which we must look for signs of his education, and not only the skills and knowledge presented in his classes.

Many instances of this kind of learning can be drawn from the series, and nearly all of them occur outside the classroom. An early example is Harry's "lesson" with Dumbledore, at the Mirror of Erised. Taija Piippo sees the Mirror as "giving unconscious wishes a possibility to come into sight of the consciousness" (75). In other words, the observer gets a glimpse of what he or she craves, whether or not they are aware that they crave it. This is an internal insight, a growing of the self; more specifically, it marks the limitations of the self. Knowing oneself is the first step on the path to being, but when Harry first encounters the mirror he fails to realize its function. As Piippo puts it, Harry "keeps feeding an unconscious desire with conscious activity, receiving nothing in return" (75). For Harry, the mirror is not a tool revealing his inner desire but an external thing that fulfills it. In this way, Harry is representing the having mode: he wants something, but he does not perceive that the fulfillment of this desire must come from within. Harry is unable to deviate from this perception by himself, or even at the urging of his friend, Ron. So here it is, after observing Harry's inability to extricate himself from the mirror, that Dumbledore intervenes, instructing him in the proper use of this tool.

With a gentle hand, Dumbledore guides Harry away from the mirror, not by forbidding his access to it, although we are led to believe this at first, but by explaining away its essential lure. "The happiest man on earth would be able to use the Mirror of Erised like a normal mirror, that is, he would look into it and see himself exactly as he is" (*Stone* 213). Contentment, Dumbledore explains to Harry in an almost Buddha-like manner, is to recognize the self in frank disillusionment and to understand that *eudaimonia*, the Greek idea of contentment over a lifetime, is the state of being oneself (Fromm, *To Have* 140). At the same time, he tells Harry that he must seek truth wherever it is, saying "It does not do to dwell on dreams and forget to live" (*Stone* 214). Fromm says as much when speaking of being, demanding that we not only develop a healthy respect for reality but that we are active and not passive in our pursuits (*To Have* 75–81). In the end, an object, just like the magical mirror, only reflects back to us what we share with it. It is not alive and has no soul to reveal to us in an authentic act of love. Thus, to share yourself with things is inauthentic, a neurotic form of love, in a word, narcissism.

Harry spends most of his second year questioning his identity. After several similarities are revealed between him and Lord Voldemort, Harry is again lost, unable to see where his ego stops and Voldemort's begins. Just as before, Dumbledore intervenes after Harry has stalled in his progress. Harry, at his darkest, believes himself misplaced in Gryffindor House and consults Dumbledore, who explains, "You happened to have many qualities Salazar Slytherin prized.... His own very rare gift, Parseltongue—resourcefulness—determination—a certain disregard for the rules.... Yet the Sorting Hat placed you in Gryffindor. You know why that was. Think." Harry then admits that he asked not to be sorted into Slytherin. "*Exactly*," Dumbledore continues, "Which makes you *very different* from Tom Riddle. It is our choices, Harry, that show what we truly are, far more than our abilities" (*Chamber* 333). Years later, Dumbledore suffers his own identity crisis, and it is Harry who insists that it was his choice of "Hallows, not Horcruxes" that made all the difference (*Hallows* 713). This emphasis on action (choice) over aspect (ability) is reflective of our capacity to love. As Fromm says, "Love is an activity, not a passive affect" (*Loving* 18). For Dumbledore, just as in Fromm, it is through love that we come to truly know others, and it is by truly knowing others (through the opposition of the Other) that we come to truly know ourselves (*Loving* 25–26).

The fourth and fifth books deal to some extent with image. Appearance, as a mask of behavior that conceals the true self, is contrasted with an existential reality, which, according to Fromm, is undeniable but it can be and often is repressed. For Fromm, the conscious mind is a mixed soup of reality and illusion, while the unconscious mind shows us who we truly are (*To Have* 79–80). Examples of the repression of reality abound in the series. Harry's time before the Mirror of Erised indicates that his unconscious is more aware of his desires than his conscious mind. But more than any other book, *Goblet of Fire* is littered with intentional deceptions, from Harry's mistaken entrance into the Triwizard Tournament to Rita Skeeter's secret eavesdropping ability to the questionable loyalties of Bagman, Krum, Snape, Karkaroff, and others to the concept of the Imperious Curse, which complicates any judgment of character almost beyond any rational capability. The dastardliness of these deceptions varies, but all pale in comparison with the impersonation of Professor Moody by Barty Crouch Junior. This cunning sham succeeds not only in returning the Dark Lord to body but costs the life of Harry's classmate, Cedric Diggory.

While the danger of external deception is very real, it is the subtle danger of self-deception, prevalent in the *Order of the Phoenix*, which is closer to Fromm's intention. Dolores Umbridge, whose righteous zealotry and moral certitude, rather strikingly, provide her the liberty to torture children, is a prime example of what Fromm calls the "authoritarian character" (*Phoenix* 266). She "admires authority and tends to submit to it," as her zeal toward the ministry demonstrates, "but at the same time [she] wants to be an authority [herself] and have others submit to [her]" (*Escape* 164). Professor Umbridge's teaching is not based on guided understanding but on eliciting compliance. She is not an authority because people respect her, as is Dumbledore or McGonagall, but because she submits herself to the "rules" of those in power, as we see in the seventh book when she has successfully transitioned from Fudge's administration to Voldemort's. Her vile actions lead Harry to suspect her of affiliation with Voldemort, but Sirius broadens Harry's narrow view by telling him, "the world isn't split into good people and Death Eaters" (*Phoenix* 302). Harry's confusion orbits Umbridge's duality. She is simultaneously a respected agent of the established order and a bad person. Harry struggles to transmogrify his perspective from the simple one where only good people are allowed to occupy positions of power. Fromm holds that society breaks a person's will without his or her awareness by "a complicated process of indoctrination, rewards, punishments, and fitting ideology" (*To Have* 64). The understanding that this technique is not simply evil escapes Harry for the better part of the book.

But it is from no less a personage than Dumbledore that we get the best example of self-deception. Aware of the link between Harry and Voldemort, Dumbledore distances himself from his pupil in the hopes that Voldemort will be less tempted to use the boy as a spy. This costly "old man's mistake," as he calls it later, is a brief reversion to the having mode (*Phoenix* 828). Denying the student counsel and instruction, unwilling to trust in Harry, Dumbledore has acted not as mentor but as censor, educating extraneously via ignorance and neglect. Dumbledore has remained distant in order to be close and has acted wrongly in order to be right. But without his guide, Harry misreads the situation (falling for Voldemort's deception), with the result measured in peril and death. We may only "be" when we are being honest with ourselves.

At the end of book five, having been returned to safety after witnessing his godfather Sirius Black's death, Harry feels uncomfortable as himself. "[Harry] had never felt more trapped inside his own head and body, never wished so intensely that he could be somebody—anybody—else." Harry is confused, irritated at his pain, and annoyed with the burden of authentic existence, when he finds his anger roused by Dumbledore's sympathy. He rages, when the elder claims to understand his feelings and declares them to be human. "'THEN – I – DON'T – WANT – TO – BE – HUMAN!' Harry roared, and he seized one of the delicate silver instruments from the spindle-legged table beside him and flung it across the room." Harry tries to incite Dumbledore by smashing his office, but the wily professor transfigures his provocation into yet another lesson, saying, "By all means continue destroying my possessions.... I daresay I have too many." Harry, realizing the painful lesson that the wisest of us are only human and can fail terribly, attacks Dumbledore's property because he cannot attack the man himself. He assumes that possessions are tied to an objectified sense of self. But Dumbledore is no "haver," and he deflects Harry's rage not safely away but back directly on himself, where it justly belongs (*Phoenix* 820–24).

Harry's instincts tell him to hide, to become someone else, to flee into fantasy, to repress and deny his pain, but Dumbledore helps him to face it and continue being. "This pain is part of being human," Dumbledore tells him (*Phoenix* 824). In the chapter entitled "Mechanisms of Escape," Fromm lays out the desires of the masochist, for whom suffering, submission, and the loss of self, become the means, albeit a fictitious one, of escape (*Escape* 152–57). The masochist, Fromm writes, "is saved from making decisions …, the final responsibility of the fate of his self, and thereby saved from the doubt of what decision to make" (*Escape* 156). This masochist does not seek to suffer domination but chooses it over the unbearable pain of uncertainty. This is the essence of Dumbledore's lesson: being brings hard choices with dire consequences, and the uncertainty of choice brings pain in decision-making. But being human entails facing doubt, accepting the woes of error, and finding meaning even in suffering. And, as long as you can love, you don't have to do it alone.

Love is the subtle art of revealing our authentic self to another, not necessarily our best self or the one we'd like to present, but our true self, warts and all. Nor does it mean imbuing yourself in another thing or person, as it does with Voldemort. Love is a skill, the practiced art of exposing our souls to others. It is in this way that we develop ourselves authentically and help others develop themselves. Doing this, it is not hard to understand, demands a good deal of courage, even for a Gryffindor.

The last two books deal with Harry's relations to others. Now that Harry knows and accepts who he is, he must continue to learn who others are and how to relate to them, as he did on the first train ride with Ron. *Half-Blood Prince* marks Harry's special education on the history of Lord Voldemort. These private lessons with Dumbledore illustrate to Harry an understanding of the *modus operandi* of the "having" neurosis. An understanding that will prove crucial to his victory over Voldemort, but it is not the only understanding Harry needs to defeat Voldemort. He must also understand the motives of his defenders—his parents, and Dumbledore, among others. Fromm believes that sacrifice is a "deep-seated human desire" (*To Have* 83) that allows us to give of ourselves and in doing so to "overcome [our] isolation by oneness with others" (*To Have* 86). Love then is a powerful motivator for sacrifice. Dumbledore explains this to Harry, very early in the series, saying, "Your mother died to save you. If there is one thing Voldemort cannot understand, it is love. He didn't realize that love as powerful as your mother's for you leaves its own mark.... [T]o have been loved so deeply, even though the person who loved us is gone, will give us some protection forever" (*Stone* 299). Harry's youthful fear of death clouds this sense of sacrifice, as seen by his reaction to the Stone's destruction. The Flamels' choice of death to prevent the return of Voldemort equally confounds Harry. But Dumbledore explains, "After all, to the well-organized mind, death is but the next great adventure. You know, the Stone was really not such a wonderful thing. As much money and life as you could want! The two things most human beings would choose above all—the trouble is, humans do have a knack of choosing precisely those things that are worst for them" (*Stone* 297).

This lesson is the core of Dumbledore's position: as Neil Postman observed, "what we love will ruin us" (xx). Love in this sense is inauthentic, pure desire, and not the mature love we truly need. Dumbledore reveals that he rebuked power (such as refusing the position of Minister and giving up his quest for the Hallows) after the tragic death of his sister (*Hallows* 717–18). Through this "sacrifice" he achieved authority through "being," which Fromm describes as "grounded not only in the individual's competence to fulfill certain social functions, but equally so in the very essence of a personality that has achieved a high degree of growth and integration. Such persons radiate authority.... They are highly developed individuals who demonstrate by what they are ... what human beings can be" (*To Have* 31). Dumbledore in the end attempts to make the final sacrifice in true Socratic fashion: to die by his own choosing. By doing so, he hopes to leave his wand, the so-called "Death Stick," without a successor, although things do not go as he planned (*Prince* 595).

By the end of *Deathly Hallows*, the message that sacrifice is a form of love has stuck. Harry, realizing that he, himself, is a Horcrux, walks into the Forbidden Forest to allow Voldemort to destroy him and so bring Voldemort one step closer to mortality (*Hallows* 693). His act of devotion to his friends, he later informs Voldemort, protects them from harm. Harry has, like Christ and his mother, sacrificed himself for another because of his great love for them. And like Christ, he is reborn, a whole human being, aware of his reality and disabused of his own prejudices. In their final confrontation, Harry can now see both himself for who he is, and Voldemort not as "Dark Lord," but as the abandoned and scared man-child, Tom Riddle.

But the clearest sign of Harry's transformation into authentic being is that he retains compassion for his enemy. He does not attack Voldemort from behind the Cloak of Invisibility in a surprise blitz, but instead he reveals himself honorably, explains to Voldemort that he has the upper hand, and offers him a final chance at redemption. That Voldemort strikes and dies is a fact of the book, but whether he does so because he still believes he is superior and would slay Harry, or whether he does so because he cannot face the uncertainty of authentic life and so allows himself to be destroyed, creates an intriguing question.

Rowling's description of Riddle's final demise is revealing: "Voldemort fell backwards, arms splayed, the slit pupils of the scarlet eyes rolling upward. Tom Riddle hit the floor with a mundane finality, his body feeble and shrunken, the white hands empty, the snakelike face vacant and unknowing" (*Hallows* 744). Voldemort was only ever an illusion, an appearance, performed by the existential actor, Tom Riddle, who died empty-handed, emotionally vacant, and woefully devoid of wisdom. He who fled from death was still made to submit to it, while he who would willingly give up his life is conclusively "the boy who lived."

The greatest irony lies here then, for Harry has achieved exactly what Voldemort desired, to tame death and become its master. Harry is exceptional, as Dumbledore tells him, for his capacity to love, despite everything he's been through (*Prince* 509). Everything being markedly similar to what Voldemort went through. With his Horcruxes Voldemort saw to it that he could not die, but then neither could he live, in the authentic sense. Harry too has survived his own vanquishing on many separate occasions. Harry's continued survival should not be interpreted as luck or skill, but as an allegorical expression of his inner mastery over death, and so the transmutation of mere survival into genuine living. He has mastered his being, accepted death, and is being-towards-death; this and only this is able to affirm life. After all it is our choices that define us. The Deathly Hallows themselves confirm this, for they truly belong to Harry, in the same sense that the wand chooses the wizard.

The Most Powerful Magic

Daniel Moloney suggests that this power of being that allows Harry to conquer death goes by another name in Rowling's series: love (15). I do not think Fromm would have disagreed with his assessment. Fromm wrote, "Love is the only sane and satisfactory answer to the problem of human existence" (*Loving* 111–12). Love is the name by which we surrender our self to something greater than ourselves. Moloney suggests that the only love Voldemort possesses is self-love (16). However, this love is self-defeating in that, when taken by itself, it is meaningless. That we are all born without meaning, as the existentialists claim, may be taken to mean that we are born with only self-love. The transfiguration of the self from that initial state into a full human being, capable of love and sacrifice, is a rare feat of the most difficult alchemy. Harry achieves it, but not alone, for love can only come from love, and one who is loved is never alone.

Works Cited

Adorno, Theodor, and Max Horkheimer. *Dialectic of Enlightenment.* Translated by John Cumming, Verso, 1997.
Crockatt, Philip. "Freud's 'On Narcissism: An Introduction.'" *Journal of Child Psychotherapy* vol. 32, no. 1, 2006, pp. 4–20. doi:10.1080/00754170600563638.
Fromm, Erich. *The Art of Loving.* Harper, 1967.
_____. *Escape from Freedom.* Rinehart, 1960.
_____. *To Have or to Be?* Continuum, 1997.
Hopkins, Lisa. "Harry Potter and the Acquisition of Knowledge." *Reading Harry Potter: Critical Essays,* edited by Giselle Liza Anatol, Praeger, 2003, pp. 25–34.
Lacan, Jacques. *Écrits: The First Complete Edition in English.* Translated by Bruce Fink, Norton, 2006.
King James Bible. Benjamin Blayney edition. Electronic Text. Germany. www.academic-bible.com/en/online-bibles/king-james-version/read-the-bible-text/bibel/text/lesen/stelle/50/60001/69999/ch/ 767a58a45b5eeeac084e5c2fe2ec20b6/.
Mendlesohn, Farah. "Crowning the King: Harry Potter and the Construction of Authority." *The Ivory Tower and Harry Potter: Perspectives on a Literary Phenomenon,* edited by Lana A. Whited, U of Missouri P, 2002, pp. 159–81.
Moloney, Daniel P. "Harry Potter and the Young Man's Mistake: The Illusion of Innocence

and the Temptation of Power." *Mapping the World of the Sorcerer's Apprentice: An Unauthorized Exploration of the Harry Potter Series*, edited by Mercedes Lackey, BenBella, 2006, pp. 7–26.
Piippo, Taija. "Is Desire Beneficial or Harmful in the Harry Potter Series?" *Critical Perspectives on Harry Potter*, edited by Elizabeth E. Heilman, 2nd ed., Routledge-Taylor & Francis, 2009, pp. 65–82.
Plato. *Five Dialogues: Euthyphro, Apology, Crito, Meno, Phaedo.* 2nd ed., Translated by George M.A. Grube and Revised by John M. Cooper, Hackett, 2002.
Postman, Neil. *Amusing Ourselves to Death: Public Discourse in the Age of Show Business*, Penguin, 2006.
Rowling, J.K. *Harry Potter and the Chamber of Secrets.* Scholastic, 2000.
_____. *Harry Potter and the Deathly Hallows.* Scholastic, 2009.
_____. *Harry Potter and the Goblet of Fire.* Scholastic, 2002.
_____. *Harry Potter and the Half-Blood Prince.* Scholastic, 2006.
_____. *Harry Potter and the Order of the Phoenix.* Scholastic, 2004.
_____. *Harry Potter and the Prisoner of Azkaban.* Scholastic, 2001.
_____. *Harry Potter and the Sorcerer's Stone.* Scholastic, 1999.
Schwartz, Peter Hammond. "'His Majesty the Baby': Narcissism and Royal Authority." *Political Theory*, vol. 17, no. 2, 1989, pp. 266–90. doi.org/10.1177/00905917002006.
Sheltrown, Nicholas. "Harry Potter's World as a Morality Tale of Technology and Media." *Critical Perspectives on Harry Potter*, edited by Elizabeth E. Heilman, 2nd ed., Routledge-Talyor & Francis, 2009, pp. 47–64.
Westman, Karin E. "Specters of Thatcherism: Contemporary British Culture in J.K. Rowling's Harry Potter Series." *The Ivory Tower and Harry Potter: Perspectives on a Literary Phenomenon*, edited by Lana A. Whited, U of Missouri P, 2002, pp. 305–28.
Whited, Lana A., with M. Katherine Grimes. "What Would Harry Do? J.K. Rowling and Lawrence Kohlberg's Theories of Moral Development." *The Ivory Tower and Harry Potter: Perspectives on a Literary Phenomenon*, edited by Lana A. Whited, U of Missouri P, 2002, pp. 182–208.
Zerin, Edward, and Marjory Zerin. "A Meta Model for the Unifying of Psychological Theories." *Pastoral Psychology*, vol. 46, no. 1, 1997, pp. 55–75.

Soul Making and Soul Splitting
Alchemy of the Soul in Harry Potter

JULIE LOVELAND SWANSTROM

Alchemy is most closely associated with the manipulation of metal, purifying "base metals into gold or other precious metals" (Whitney 33). With its attempts to "understand and master the hidden powers within the earth," however, alchemy goes beyond manipulating elements for mundane human gain to provide a "map of how the energy of creation moves" (Hughes 15; Cotnoir 25, 40). The thirteenth-century German Dominican friar, Albertus Magnus, sought efficient causes "existing in the material and transmuting it," which means that the alchemist is utilizing something inherent in the substance to initiate change (Kibre 188).

Alchemy is based on a systematic worldview of a fundamentally unified universe in which transmutation is possible because of the qualities elements have in common (Fabricius 8). Mercury, or the *prima materia*, was understood to be the purest metal, "the first principle of all matter" or the "original prime matter that was regarded as the origin of all life" and the catalyst for alchemical transformations (Hughes 41–42; Fabricius 12). This prime matter "from which all bodies were formed and into which they might again be dissolved" provides the theoretical underpinnings of the "unity of nature" in alchemy (Fabricius 8). The qualities that physical elements share are based on the standard division of elements into earth, air, fire, and water, and the shared qualities that cross these elemental boundaries are dry, cold, wet, and heat (Fabricius 8).

The alchemists also understood the terrestrial and the heavenly (whether in a Christian sense of God's active work in the world or in the sense of the enchanted cosmos) to be interrelated. Transmutation is possible not only because of the basic shared properties and interrelatedness of existing things, including human physiology, but also because the root of those shared properties is God's active work in the world. Andreas

Libavius, a German alchemist living from 1555 to 1616 CE, wrote that "chymists" deal with "genuine mixts that supply the essential being to all things [that] descend from the heavens as *semina*." These *semina*, once deposited in matter, "act on it to produce the myriad generations and corruptions of the physical world." The *semina* are what "determine essential characteristics, and supply particular qualities to physical things" (Newman 316). In short, for Libavius, the *semina* bridge the spiritual and physical worlds. Fourteenth-century British alchemist John Dastin explained the transmutation in terms of the spirit—Mercury—being joined to the body through the soul (Hughes 49). In the seventeenth century, British alchemist, Thomas Browne, saw alchemy as a "way of learning about the mysterious operation of the soul in the body" (Hughes 4).

Cotnoir reminds us that the "interlocking worldview is the framework of the practice" and that it is based on the Platonic notion that humans are a microcosm of the universe (48). The *semina* of Libavius, the spirit of mercury of Dastin, and the soul-in-body of Browne are all medieval (Neo) Platonic reflections on God's active work in the world. Because the "transmogrification" of metal ultimately depends upon God's activity in creating, the alchemist must herself undergo transformation (*Chamber* 141; Cotnoir 48). According to Fabricius, "the purgation and transformation of metals were 'translated' into symbolic procedures concerned with the purgation and transformation of *souls*" (12). Hughes notes that in the "holistic view of the universe the [human] was seen to be at the center, mirroring the alchemical process" (46). Human beings are understood as spirit first, then soul, and then body (Granger 50). The spiritual aspect of alchemy cannot be distilled away, because God created (a) elements with common properties and (b) human beings, as substances, who are subject to the alchemical process as well.

The purpose of such transmutations is to purify oneself. Changes to the alchemist would necessarily occur, as Hughes notes, because, since God (or the heavenly) and mercury are in nature, the "divine principle could also be found in the mind and soul of the artificer." The quest for the Philosopher's Stone, therefore, becomes "a search for the buried self, the spirit bound up in the *prima materia*, with the object of releasing the spirit from the unconscious to the light of the consciousness" (Hughes 60). In short, alchemy purifies and perfects the soul as the alchemist purifies base metal into gold (Granger 52; Burns 35; Burckhardt 23; Highfield 244, 250).

The purification of the soul by purifying metal should not give the impression that matter is not important or that the alchemist seeks to leave the body behind. Instead, "the material world is appropriated toward an inner, more spiritual world. To this end, the material world or the human body is not denied, tortured, or abused. It is kept strong and healthy"

(Cotnoir 52). The purification of both soul and matter elevates them both rather than implicitly denigrating the body in favor of the soul. The alchemist becomes "a transformed person who is the conjunction of opposites, the resolution of contraries" (Granger 53). The alchemist is, by her own personal change, able to resolve natural divisions, including such natural divisions as "life and death and the supernatural divisions between God and [humans]" (Granger 53). The life-giving capacity of the Philosopher's Stone, then, resolves the division between body and soul, between life and death, by extending life indefinitely.

Along with reconciling divisions, the practice of alchemy changes the alchemist by purifying him morally. As James Hannam explains, alchemy "should always be approached with a good heart" and moral integrity (131). Without "a life of purity and spiritual discipline," without a "steady mind" in pursuit of alchemy's delicate balance, the scientific insights of alchemy could not be attained (Hughes 60; Cotnoir 52). The immortality attainable through the alchemical arts is different in circumstance but not in kind from the immortality available to the believers granted eternal life by God; the alchemist is able, now, in this physical form, to enjoy the gift of eternal life. It is no accident that Christian alchemists linked their practice to the "Passion and the Redemption of the flesh" and to Jesus' teaching that love and mercy for all is the means to following God (Hughes 48; *The Harper-Collins Study Bible*, Luke 10.25–37; St. Hilaire 272).

Alchemy works to alleviate suffering both by improving the practitioner and by using the riches gained to "care for the poor and sick" (Cotnoir 54). An alchemist's work, then, is an expression of love: love toward God, the creator, shown by imitating God's actions; love toward created things, shown by learning and exposing the interconnectedness present in nature; and love toward fellow humans, shown by caring for the physical and emotional needs of all. The moral element of alchemy means that alchemy had to be hidden from the wicked (Hughes 50). If someone lacking the proper character has the knowledge of the alchemical sciences, harm would ensue. People who are greedy or evil would exploit the natural harmony in nature for their own gain, and they would not respect God, God's creation, or fellow humans. The wicked might pervert these sacred arts to their own ends, thereby not actually performing true alchemy at all.

To review, alchemy is never a solely metallurgical enterprise, for it is an attempt to reach the divine presence in the world through the *prima materia* out of which the universe is constructed. The spiritual component of alchemy cannot be stripped away, and doing alchemy properly entails that the alchemist operate on herself as a substance as well as on the metals with which she works. The transmutation in alchemy, then, is global, applying to all involved in the alchemical process. A true alchemist performing proper alchemy will be disciplined, balanced, and moral; the purity of the alchemist is exhibited by a reconciling nature and moral uprightness, and those traits—along with appropriate secrecy—ensure success in the alchemical pursuits. Alchemy simply is alchemy of the soul.

In the Harry Potter heptalogy, Harry and Tom Riddle have a number of similar life experiences: rough childhoods rife with abusive situations; the feeling of belonging at school; a relationship to fame; a search for companions; and an exploration of eternal life. Their very different reactions to those experiences allow for an examination of how they do (in Harry's case) or do not (in Tom's) perform alchemy on their own souls. The evils Harry suffers feed his soul making; the more he refuses to replicate those evils, the more he drains them of their power and purifies his soul, making it more whole, more golden. By contrast, Voldemort, né Tom, returns evil for evil as he splits his soul in his quest to overcome what he sees as the weakness of human mortality. In the process, he amplifies and strengthens evils. Embracing opportunities to unify people, to become more moral, and to respect magic through appropriate secrecy, Harry discovers the divine cosmos in himself. Spurning those same opportunities, Voldemort remains lonely, selfish, and fractured.

Harry Potter, Alchemist of the Soul

No single character in the *Harry Potter* heptalogy more clearly illustrates how alchemy involves the soul than its titular character. At Privet Drive, Harry's cousin, aunt, and uncle do not attend to his basic needs, all the while regularly berating and verbally abusing him. When we meet soon-to-be-eleven-year-old Harry, he is living in a cupboard under the stairs (*Stone* 19). He is expected to contribute to the household in terms of chores but is never welcomed as part of the household (*Stone* 19, 26). He suffers from general neglect while his cousin is spoiled outrageously (*Stone* 27, 33–43; *Hallows* 43–44). Love seems missing, distorted by the Dursleys toward their son and their nephew: Dudley is given too many things, which do not replace love and affection; Harry is given too few things as a sign of lack of affection. Both boys suffer (*Prince* 55). Verbal abuse and emotional abuse are deeply negative experiences (Keith-Oaks 131). Love is a basic human need.

The Dursleys perhaps do not deserve Harry's care or kindness, and a teenaged Harry aptly expresses anger and angst toward them and their treatment of him, notably in the case of Aunt Marge's visit (*Azkaban* 20–21). Harry transcends these responses to a remarkable degree. When Harry is set upon by dementors, he works to save not only himself but also Dudley

(*Phoenix* 16–19). Knowing that he is doing something for which he can face steep consequences, Harry acts anyway. Whether Dudley would have done the same is questionable.

As he faces his likely final separation with the Dursleys, Harry acknowledges that he does not want to go with them, but he does not want them harmed, either. Dudley unexpectedly shows some fondness (of a sort) to Harry on their last day together, setting tea outside his door and insisting that Harry is not a "waste of space." Harry thanks him and acknowledges the depth of these sentiments, which are shallow for others but quite deep from Dudley (*Hallows* 40, 33–42). Harry and Dudley shake hands—a rare nonviolent physical interaction. Harry and Dudley are able to unite, however briefly. Their parting is not an overwhelming display of love, but it shows a willingness to find the good in each other and respect it. An alchemist must find the unity in the disparate qualities in substances, and Harry's and Dudley's history shows them to bear different qualities. Despite this difference, Harry is able to see and accept Dudley's care. The peace between different qualities is an expression of the unity in the cosmos. Harry *almost* connects with his Aunt Petunia (*Hallows* 42). While perhaps Harry and Dudley—or the other Durselys—are not producing gold, it is still precious; Harry is able to work as an alchemist by bridging these divides with the Dursleys.

In the family he builds with Ginny, Harry does not replicate the neglectful behaviors he experienced or the harmful overindulgence Dudley experienced. When his child is hesitant to leave for Hogwarts for the first time, Harry could channel Vernon Dursley and tell him to hurry up or get over it. Instead, Harry takes his child's concerns seriously, giving him time and space to express himself. He responds kindly, helping young Albus Severus process information in an emotionally healthy manner (*Hallows* 758). This short interaction is revelatory of Harry's family and parenting style. The large, interconnected family that Harry has constructed for himself—the connection to Ron and Hermione's children, the other Weasley in-laws and cousins, and young Teddy Lupin—also shows the healthy human bonding he has fostered over the years (*Hallows* 755–58). Harry is able to find balance and avoid the evil twins of neglect and overindulgence. He has seen their evils, and the alchemist must use his power to work for good. Harry unites the best qualities of the opposites of neglect and overindulgence—care measured by attention but not suffocation, met needs but not excess—and transforms them with the love he has for his family.

Harry truly has wrought gold in his family, coaxing the value out of his own terrible experiences. He has transformed the loathing and neglect he experienced into genuine care and love. Harry has accomplished a number of unifications of disparate entities: he builds a bond with Dudley, and he unites himself to Ginny and the Weasleys in love. Harry has purified himself of the toxic elements of his youth, transforming those elements into the best human emotion of all: love.

Harry's ability to love reveals him to be "pure of heart," a true alchemist (*Prince* 511). The alchemy of Harry's soul is *love*. Love imbued him with the ability to survive as a baby, and the love he fosters for and in those around him saves him time and again. His love of Sirius Black drives out Voldemort when Voldemort tries to possess him in the Ministry (*Phoenix* 816, 844). Harry remains determined to love despite his losses, fiercely asserting his will to fight Voldemort and refusing to "shut [himself] away" (*Prince* 77). Love is the pure element that revives, restores, and resurrects. It is love that flows through Harry's soul, connecting and uniting Harry's world.

The next shared life experience to consider is the sense of belonging at Hogwarts. Harry moves from being an outsider at Hogwarts who does not understand the oddities of the school to being an insider who overcomes his lack of knowledge to view it as home (*Hallows* 697). The castle seems to feel similarly, for Harry is able to coax it into providing for several of his wants and needs. Harry's felicity with the Room of Requirement is of note; Professor Trelawney is surprised to find that Harry knows of it (*Prince* 541). Harry is able to use the Room with consistent success, and he shares this knowledge with his friends (*Phoenix* 386–87; 389).

These gentle, cooperative uses of magic are correlated to alchemy. When faced with strangeness and the clear lack of control he has in such a place, Harry's response is to learn of it and cooperate with it. He comes to feel a sense of belonging, but that sense of belonging does not translate into behaviors of ownership. Harry asks rather than demands. Of the Room of Requirement, he clarifies his needs and asks for help (*Phoenix* 389). To the Sorting Hat (before experiencing its power), he desperately pleads not to be sorted into Slytherin without knowing if this request would be effective (*Stone* 121). Gentle asking—even imploring—shows respect to the order of things; Harry is able to acknowledge that while he may influence, he does not command. The same is true of alchemy: the alchemist learns and works within the system, acknowledging that everything has a relation to other things. When in great peril, Harry cries out rather blindly for help; help is provided in terms of Fawkes the Phoenix—beak glittering gold— and the Sorting Hat, out of which Harry pulls Godric Gryffindor's sword after thinking, *"please help me"* (*Chamber* 319, 322). Harry makes precious metal and gemstone—the sword—out of the provision. Harry transforms himself as he transforms his environment to the best end by working in it and with it. Instead of seeking to exert undue control, Harry unites himself to his environment through his humility and willingness to learn. Harry asks for help, which marks him as someone who hopes for unity in the world.

Harry's maturity and soul-work can be clearly seen in his shifting views of Slytherin House. Despite the Sorting Hat repeatedly reminding students of the importance of Slytherin House, Harry does not like it or its members (*Stone* 118; *Goblet* 176–77; *Phoenix* 204–07; *Prince* 163). He initially views it with suspicion and shows prejudice against its members and leaders (*Stone* 80, 121; *Prince* 545, 549). He makes headway to overcome his prejudices, however, when he saves Draco and Ron and Hermione save Goyle from the Fiendfyre in the Room of Requirement (*Hallows* 633). Upon seeing Snape's memories, Harry finally recognizes in Snape the qualities he prizes, such as bravery, and comes to appreciate his cunning as well. Naming his son after a Slytherin who was head of Slytherin House shows how far he has come, but he goes further when he tells young Albus Severus that it would be Slytherin's gain should Albus be sorted into that house (*Hallows* 758).

The four houses mirror the four qualities, and just as substances need those qualities, Hogwarts needs its houses. By rejecting Slytherin House as evil, Harry rejects one element making up the school. This unbalanced approach causes problems, chief among them Harry's fixation on Snape (*Prince* 545, 549). Harry grows and learns, coming to realize the value and importance of the qualities embodied by Snape and Regulus Black (*Hallows* 199). The houses, like elemental qualities, share commonalities, and removing one diminishes all. The true alchemist knows the unity in the diverse qualities, and Harry now knows it of the Hogwarts houses.

The third shared life experience of Harry and Voldemort is a relationship to fame. Harry's status as the "Boy Who Lived" bestows fame upon him, and Dumbledore argues that exposure to such fame would be deeply harmful to him (*Stone* 13). Harry is repeatedly recognized by other wizards (*Stone* 69; *Chamber* 54, 61). Harry fights not just Voldemort but his own fame as he works to defeat Voldemort. Hermione's Hex upon the Dumbledore's Army sign-up sheet illustrates this (Dumbledore's not Potter's, as the Headmaster points out when Umbridge and Fudge haul Harry in once the DA is betrayed), as does Romilda Vane hunting Harry with love potion (*Phoenix* 340–41, 618; *Prince* 305). Everyone recognizes Harry on sight. His anonymity is impossible, which may help explain his affinity for his Invisibility Cloak.

Yet Harry's response to fame is tempered. Like many teenagers, he dreams of success at Quidditch and the fame that follows (*Stone* 152–53; *Prince* 528). But the fame Harry has thrust upon him stems from tragedy. His fame requires him to question the motives of those around him, sometimes of those closest to him. He cannot manage to pick up his school books without causing a stir when Gilderoy Lockhart tries to piggyback on Harry's fame (*Chamber* 60–61). His own teacher, Horace Slughorn, harangues him about a book deal for Harry's autobiography (*Prince* 316). The young women, like Romilda Vane, who seek to ensnare Harry with love potion, are likely trying to land a wealthy, famous individual; they are not interested in Harry for himself (*Prince* 305). Harry, though, is not happy to be known *of*; Harry wants to be known.

Harry's distaste of fame born of Voldemort's murderous intent shows alchemy of his soul in several ways. First, fame is contrary to knowledge. Famous, well known things are sometimes false—the idea that air, not water vapor, is what is in bubbles in boiling water, for example (Stein 2–3). Alchemy requires diligent study, and fame depends on widely held information that often lacks depth, as Gilderoy Lockhart repeatedly makes clear (*Chamber* 297–98). Second, fame is contrary to the alchemical commitment to secrecy. Secrecy is necessary in alchemy so that the knowledge of alchemy does not fall into the hands of those who lack the particular spiritual and moral preparation to be able to act on it (Cotnoir 54; Hannam 131; Hughes 50). The *Harry Potter* heptalogy makes it clear that a little knowledge is a dangerous thing: Harry is easy to locate because he is so well known, and Voldemort repeatedly presses this advantage, observing Harry at school through Professor Quirrell, kidnapping Harry from school in the Goblet of Fire competition, and staking out his aunt and uncle's home (*Stone* 290–94; *Goblet* 12; *Hallows* 55). People have a sense that they understand Harry, but a little knowledge of Harry can be used for harm.

Though Harry chafes at Voldemort being the reason for his fame, he also, early on, chafes at the secrecy imposed on the resistance. Secrecy is difficult to manage, for there are a number of concerns that must be balanced. Harry's youth and his link to Voldemort lead Dumbledore to exclude him from the Order of the Phoenix (*Phoenix* 833). If Voldemort had information about the Order, he would use it for great harm; keeping the Order's information secret is alchemical, but not all secrets are. Dumbledore acknowledges his own errors—his own brother calls him a master of "secrets and lies," and he accepts blame for Sirius' death—and says he has struggled with when and what to tell Harry (*Hallows* 562; *Phoenix* 826). But once Voldemort and Harry's psychic bond is blocked, Dumbledore shares all he knows with Harry and enlists Harry's help. Dumbledore encourages Harry to share what he knows with Ron and Hermione about the prophecy and Horcruxes (*Prince* 78).

Dumbledore's sharing and his encouragement to Harry to share with his best friends follows the strictures of alchemy because it is only those who have the proper moral growth who share in the secret of how to defeat Voldemort. Dumbledore sees the need to keep this information from

Voldemort in order to allow the trio to right Voldemort's wrongs. If Voldemort's Horcruxes were common knowledge, then the trio would be unable to complete their mission. The secrecy enables victory, and it entrusts the secret to those who have purified themselves. Harry learns to share what he can: after persuasion, he allows his friends to help him find the Diadem, and, without persuasion, tells Neville what he can about Nagini (*Hallows* 583; 695–96). Despite the secrecy, Harry works to unite the elements: he tries to bring together the different houses at Hogwarts; he supports Hagrid's outreach to the giants; he builds bonds with students at other wizarding schools; and Harry even reaches out to Voldemort in Voldemort's final moments (*Phoenix* 338, 693–94; *Goblet* 724–25; *Hallows* 741).

Harry preserves the alchemical pattern of secrecy, a pattern that he is still working to master in *Hallows*. Those who have done the work to understand share with those others who have also done similar work. Because the information being widely known would cause harm, it must be secret. Even as it is kept secret, though, the Secret-Keepers use the secret to promote good. Marietta Edgecombe fails at alchemical secrecy, betraying the D.A. to promote her mother's work at the Ministry of Magic and endangering those who are fighting for what is good (*Phoenix* 395, 611–12). Harry follows Dumbledore in working toward unity with information yet under the blanket of secrecy. Harry could have tried to leverage his fame for personal gain, but instead he works for good, often quietly, and often while deemed a villain (*Phoenix* 217–19). What Harry learns is that the alchemical secrecy is not an impediment to unity, and he learns to be more open with his friends even when he cannot reveal all. Harry may be a master of secrets, but he works so as to not be a master of lies. When done rightly, such secrecy enhances the good and can promote unity.

The fourth shared experience is the pursuit of friendship. Harry heads to Hogwarts a deeply lonely child. Loneliness can be debilitating. The same way Harry could have been embittered by his family experiences, he could have become caustic. Instead, Harry exhibits a longing for companionship to replace the loneliness and enhance his life (*Stone* 99).

Despite the unfamiliar experience of traveling to Hogwarts, Harry reaches out toward others and accepts it when others reach out toward him. Harry delights in the budding friendship with Ron. Pulling gold from his pocket, Harry provides what they desire: Ron to be treated as special, and Harry to be treated as a worthwhile companion (*Stone* 99–110, 242–43). Harry collects friends despite differences, sharing a deep and platonic love with Hermione and a strong connection with Neville (*Stone* 173–79; Chan 20). As Granger notes, Hermione represents Mercury—her initials, her name, and her parents' employment—and Ron represents Sulphur—red hair, fiery personality (61, 63). Dumbledore strongly encourages Harry to unburden himself to his friends, and Harry feels a sense of warmth spread through him after he tells Ron and Hermione about the prophecy (*Prince* 78, 99). Harry is able to unite with Ron and Hermione to defeat Voldemort, and he needs them in order to complete the task. When Harry's friends volunteer to protect him from Voldemort by using Polyjuice Potion to appear as Harry, they drink a potion that is gold (*Hallows* 50). Most importantly, Harry and his friends make and imbibe gold in their friendships.

The friends Harry makes are not merely those who reach out to him or happen to fall into his path. Harry repeatedly reaches out to those who face exclusion or derision. When given the opportunity to invite someone to Slughorn's Christmas party, Harry asks Luna Lovegood (*Prince* 311; *Hallows* 417). Shunned by others for her unique perspective, Luna had not been welcomed at Hogwarts the same way Harry had been. Harry's willingness to reach out to her, particularly, shows that Harry is trying not only to alleviate his *own* loneliness but also to alleviate the loneliness of others. Harry befriends and frees Dobby from the abusive Malfoy family; Harry loves Dobby and hand-digs Dobby's grave after Dobby dies while saving Harry's life (*Chamber* 337–38; *Hallows* 480–81).

Harry gathers people around him and treasures them, treating his friends with the respect and dignity they deserve. The respect for others shows a strong and healthy individual. While alchemy involves the call to care for the poor or the sick, Harry has broadened that to care for those found unlovely by others. When Ron feels overlooked and useless, Harry's friendship helps Ron grow to become a prefect (and Harry to overcome his own jealousy at not having been chosen), a Quidditch star, and an excellent magician (*Stone* 99–101; *Phoenix* 161; *Prince* 298–99). Harry keeps Dobby in a steady supply of socks, helps find him a job, and supports him (*Azkaban* 375–83; *Phoenix* 148). Upon visiting Luna's home and being shown into her room, Harry sees painted portraits of "Harry, Ron, Hermione, Ginny, and Neville" on Luna's ceiling. "[F]ine golden chains" made of "one word, repeated a thousand times in golden ink: *friends ... friends ... friends...*" link the portraits (*Hallows* 417). Harry's own soul-work bolsters the work of others. By forming such bonds, Harry betters himself and others. He builds a community out of those lacking one, which shows his alchemical commitment to unity. He shows unity with, and compassion toward, those on the journey with him. And, as Luna makes clear, friends are as good as gold.

The final similar life experience is linked to Harry's own fame. The promise of eternal life is extended to Harry in two quite distinct ways, once in terms of his own fame garnered from Voldemort, and the other in terms of actual power over death. As previously discussed, Harry sought to reject fame from Voldemort's actions; the "eternal life" Harry would be granted for his repeated tangles with Voldemort was not something that he sought or desired, and it was thrust upon him by Voldemort's own decision (*Hallows* 677).

Harry's power over death as related to the Deathly Hallows is another matter. The complicated history of the Deathly Hallows, the locations of which were manipulated by Dumbledore, leaves Harry in control of all three Hallows insofar as he possesses the Invisibility Cloak and the Resurrection Stone but is master of the Elder Wand (*Hallows* 703). Combined, they allow victory over death (*Hallows* 401). As Harry approaches what he thinks is his final confrontation with Voldemort, he could possibly wield the power of the Deathly Hallows to avoid death, but he makes no such attempt. Harry has, some time before, decided that he would trust Dumbledore and pursue the death of Voldemort—hunting and destroying Horcruxes—instead of pursuing his own eternal life (*Hallows* 484). Harry makes no move to defend himself, to preserve his own life (*Hallows* 704). It is this self-sacrificial act, this giving of himself out of love for his friends, that allows Harry's triumph over death (St. Hilaire 285).

When Harry has the tools to be, as Dumbledore says, "master of death," Harry does not use them to defeat death (*Hallows* 713). Harry is "master of death," able to unite the Hallows because he wants them—but wants them *not* to use them. Harry's mastery of death is like Ignotus, who hides from Death, lives a fulfilling life, and greets Death like an old friend and an equal; Harry does not force his survival even when he is able, because Harry is selfless. He has lived his life well in preparation for a good death (*Hallows* 409, 716). The alchemist understands himself as a microcosm of the universe, and Harry's ability to see the importance of his submission to death and act accordingly while he has the means to master death shows him to be an alchemist: he uses understanding to produce good, and his own death would produce the most good. Harry "masters" death by removing the fear from it, accepting it as a part of life, and making sure his own death matters. He neutralizes the evil of death, instead turning his own death to good. Death cannot conquer him, because he understands and accepts death under the proper conditions—such as accepting his own death in order to ensure Voldemort's demise (*Hallows* 691).

In the world of *Harry Potter*, there are two known ways to conquer death. The first is Horcruxes, which Harry and Dumbledore both refuse due to the morally despicable nature of their formation. The second is Hallows, which are extraordinarily powerful—and dangerous if used in the wrong way for the wrong reasons. Dumbledore despises himself for his single-minded and misguided pursuit of the Hallows in his youth that brought about his family's ruin (*Hallows* 715). He calls himself selfish, and that seems true. Dumbledore was seeking power, ostensibly for the benefit of all witches and wizards, but, as he later came to understand, for his and Grindelwald's own power of domination. Harry approaches power differently, actually using it for the benefit of all. Since Harry's death would bring that benefit, he does not opt to wield his power, or rather he transfigures power. Harry chooses to live for his community, rather than going peacefully "On," even though returning to the chaos and noise of the castle will surely mean pain and loss (*Hallows* 722). Harry sees himself in relation to others, whom he deems equally important. Harry shows his power by refraining, precisely where the young Dumbledore would have acted (*Hallows* 716, 720).

Contrast those two ways of maintaining life with the Philosopher's Stone. One cannot produce the stone without intense study, study that itself purifies the alchemist and brings about moral growth. For the alchemist to produce the Philosopher's Stone, personal goodness is required (Cotnoir 54). No such strictures lie upon Horcruxes; in fact, creating Horcruxes requires moral badness. Similarly, no such strictures lay upon the Hallows, for one need not put any work into producing the Hallows. One must procure them, but there is no craft, no method, for how one goes about doing so; young Dumbledore and Grindelwald show this (*Hallows* 716–17). Harry has done the alchemical work on his own soul, which enables him to unite them (*Hallows* 720). It is clear that the only moral way to pursue eternal life is through alchemy, and the alchemist's own moral advancement is the primary reason why alchemy can lead to an appropriate extension of one's life. Moral use of the Hallows seems to depend on the soul work of alchemy, which provides the potential user with restraint.

Yet even when Harry holds the Philosopher's Stone, he does not wish to use it (*Stone* 291–92, 300). Even this most moral approach to extending one's life is beyond Harry's wish. As he has done with the Philosopher's Stone, Harry does not attempt to use the Hallows to preserve his life, because he does not wish it. Harry shows a balanced attachment to his life, desiring for his life and death to be worth something. He gauges that worth in terms of whom he can save, not by showing the power of a conqueror but instead by showing the power of love (*Hallows* 693). Harry values the lives of others as much as he values his own life, which shows a lack of *ego* and a lack of selfishness. If his death can save lives, he will submit; if his death can protect his friends, he will go to it boldly. And then, because of the power of his mother's love and sacrifice, Harry survives (*Hallows* 709–10; St. Hilaire 278). In this self-sacrificial act, Harry unites life and death. His willingness to die for those he loves is a possibility precisely because of his mother's self-sacrificial act. Harry's selfless love, passed down to him from his mother, allows him to live in death, to rise again, and to flourish. Harry performs the perfect alchemical reaction, resolving "the great natural divisions in life and death" by his love (Granger 53). Love "transcends death" in every way, and Harry rides a wave of love to survive (Granger 81). When his task with Voldemort is completed, Harry refuses to reunite the Hallows, allowing them to pass into history (*Hallows* 748–49). With this act, Harry ensures that love alone—which can be the underlying motivation for alchemy—is the path to eternal life.

Harry Potter is a great alchemist. He has drawn family from abuse. He has built a home in an unfamiliar place. He has withdrawn from the fame thrust upon him. He has surrounded himself with a wealth of friends, despite his lonely beginnings. And he has bridged the gap between life and death through the power of his and his mother's love. Harry unites these contraries because of the alchemical work he has performed upon his own soul.

Voldemort, né Tom Riddle, Failed Alchemist of the Soul

Inauspicious beginnings need not herald a life like Voldemort's, but the young Tom Riddle takes the elements of his own experiences and reproduces abuse. Born at an orphanage and full of anger, he uses that anger to torture his classmates (*Prince* 262–75). The eleven-year-old who arrives at Hogwarts uses his skills in manipulation to gain position, and then he uses the respect afforded to him by his trusting professors not only to unleash the basilisk of the xenophobic Salazar Slytherin, killing young Myrtle, but also to blame Rubeus Hagrid for Tom's own crimes (*Chamber* 292, 299, 311–12). He manipulates his professors into providing him with information necessary to make Horcruxes (*Prince* 494–99). He even tricks Helena Ravenclaw into revealing the location of her mother's Diadem (*Hallows* 617). As an adult, he is eager to use magic to bend others to his will: he tortures Bertha Jorkins, kills Frank the gardener, makes Hokey the elf poison Hepzibah Smith, among many other instances of such unethical use of magic (*Goblet* 10–12, 14–15; *Prince* 438).

A common misconception about alchemy is that it is about manipulation. Alchemy does involve change, but alchemical change works with and through the natures of the things being changed; it is because of the specific mixtures in things that alchemy is able to work. As Firenze explains, divination is an attempt to understand the "impersonal and impartial" truths of the universe, induced from careful observation (*Phoenix* 603). Even such knowledge is not "foolproof." Alchemy involves recognizing the interconnectedness of all things and the limitations of the alchemist, and, even so, alchemical attempts may or may not be successful (*Phoenix* 604).

Voldemort's response to the prophecy shows that he does not grasp this interconnectedness or his own limitations. As Dumbledore explains, the prophecy referred to a boy born at the end of July, but it could have meant Harry or Neville. Contextualizing the prophecy, Dumbledore reminds Harry that Voldemort's own actions themselves launched the prophecy. The prophecy itself is not set, as though simply knowing it gives one the ability to control the future (*Phoenix* 842–44; *Prince* 509). Voldemort responds to the prophecy by trying to destroy the child, and doing so moves the claims of the prophecy toward truth. The prophecy shows how things are interconnected, and asserting control has important unintended consequences. Had Voldemort refrained, Harry would not have been Voldemort's undoing. The alchemist, like the divination expert, explores possibilities through the unity in the cosmos. That unity is not about someone controlling the order and the universe, as Voldemort seeks to do.

At almost every turn, Tom Riddle refuses to respect entities and artificially attempts to influence or exert undue control over agents and items. Merope Gaunt Riddle repented of the manipulation tactics she used on Tom Riddle, Sr., yet the young Riddle does not learn from her mistakes (*Prince* 213–15). When Merope stopped using the potion to secure love for herself, she accepted and suffered the consequences when Tom, Sr., left (*Prince* 201–15). Her son did not follow her remorseful footsteps. He did not learn the properties that others had in order to work with them; he made no move toward respecting others. He shows no movement toward reconciliation or morality, and thus he has made no move toward alchemy. Out of the abusive situation he endured, he simply manufactured more abuse.

Tom also has the seeming sense of belonging at the school. Finding out that he is magical helps Tom make sense of some of his own life experiences, and Tom seems wary about, but excited by, the prospect of school (*Prince* 271–77). Identifying strongly with his house—perhaps unsurprising given that he is one of Salazar Slytherin's descendants—Tom embraces house politics as a way to gain authority (*Chamber* 311; *Prince* 495–96). Tom's well-researched obsession with Salazar Slytherin leads him to the Chamber of Secrets, to release the basilisk, and to seek further fame, yet Tom blames Hagrid and closes the Chamber to avoid detection and to gain commendation at school (*Chamber* 311–12). Tom even applies for a job as a professor of Defense Against the Dark Arts shortly after his graduation (*Prince* 432). The chief lasting manifestation for Tom's attachment to Hogwarts is the curse he places on the Defense Against the Dark Arts position, preventing any other professor from holding the position longer than a year (*Prince* 446). Tom leaves his mark on Hogwarts, and he calls it "the beloved castle, his first kingdom, his birthright" (*Hallows* 500).

The connections between Tom and Hogwarts do not fit nicely with the practice of alchemy. If the Hogwarts houses are akin to the different qualities of elements, then Tom's zealous adherence to Slytherin shows him to lack balance; unlike Harry, Tom never seems to grow out of this. He embraces not only the good qualities of Slytherin but also the bad. Tom enthusiastically adopts the totality of Salazar Slytherin's xenophobia seemingly as an obvious component of being the Heir of Slytherin (*Chamber* 312–14). In elevating his own house and pushing pure-blood status, Tom rejects the necessity of different qualities and the unity of these distinct elements. Upon his return to conquer Hogwarts, Voldemort tells Neville that Slytherin will be the only house (*Hallows* 732). He fails to see how these different parts form a larger whole and how these component parts are each a microcosm of that whole. Exclusion, particularly exclusion based on kind, shows a lack of comprehension of the alchemical view of interconnectedness.

Once again, Tom consistently exerts control by any measure he deems necessary. Tom treats the school not like its own entity or even its own place. Instead, he treats it as an item over which he can exert his own control for his own wishes. Tom treats the school as his own, altering his own actions only when others like Dumbledore intervene and he is unable to control the circumstances. Tom's "rules are made to be broken" attitude, shown to Professor Slughorn when Tom enquires about Horcruxes, exemplifies Tom's attitude about the school: it exists for him, and he is special as Slytherin's descendant, not subject to the strictures as others are (*Chamber* 311–12; *Hallows* 500). But that very attitude is contrary to alchemy, for Tom's desire for control and his perception of himself as better than others shows that he does not place himself within the same united universe as the other elements. Tom sees himself as outside the regular order rather than a part of it; Tom does not seek to understand or to provide balance. Instead, he seeks to exert his own power and control despite the cost.

Regarding the characteristic of fame, which stalks Harry and which Tom seeks, Tom's relentless pursuit transforms his fame into infamy. As Tom's Diary-Horcrux makes clear, he has long sought great fame. His obsession with people knowing his chosen name illustrates this. Diary-Riddle seems disappointed that it is not widely known that Tom himself opened the Chamber of Secrets as Slytherin's heir (*Chamber* 311–12). He marks his followers and delights in making his Dark Mark widely known (*Goblet* 119–29; *Prince* 581–92).

Though fame itself is neither good nor bad, Voldemort's pursuit of fame does not conform to the strictures of alchemy. Consider the radical difference between Nicolas Flamel and Voldemort. The best alchemist—for centuries!—alive, Flamel lives a happy yet largely retiring existence, so retiring that Hermione has a difficult time locating appropriate information about him (*Stone* 219). Flamel is holding to the alchemical practice of secrecy and silence, ensuring that his own work does not fall into inappropriate hands. Voldemort wants to be known *of* rather than known. He wants to frighten and intimidate, to manipulate and cajole. His desire for fame is tied to his desire to control, for the more famous he becomes, the more feared he can be (*Stone* 298; *Chamber* 314). Yet again, Voldemort shows that he privileges himself over others, pursues his own ends to the exclusion of others' ends, and places himself so that he can manipulate others. A true alchemist would not seek to bend the world to himself, but fame is one way Voldemort attempts to do exactly that.

Voldemort's quest for fame necessarily involves some elements of secrecy, but this secrecy is not alchemical. The Death Eaters' identities are secret (*Goblet* 587–96). They pursue secret projects for the larger, publicly known goal of elevating pure-blood witches and wizards and harming Muggles and their sympathizers. Voldemort runs the Ministry in secret (*Hallows* 208). The point of their secrecy is not to prevent harm; it is to promote it. Some prerequisite work may be required to join the Death Eaters, but it will be an evil act or an act in service of evil. Dumbledore experienced similar temptations to use power for his own selfish ends and kept his quest secret, but Dumbledore repented, because that sort of secrecy led to evil (*Hallows* 562–67; 718–19). Dumbledore expresses difficulties determining the right amount of secrecy, but Voldemort defaults to secrecy as a tool for manipulation and increasing fear. Sharing Voldemort's information would bring harm to Voldemort but would save others, and the secrecy does not promote good.

The fourth shared element is companionship, which means to have followers who obey Voldemort's dictates. They exist to follow and serve, branded like slaves (*Hallows* 453). The Death Eaters' tattooed "pagers" cause them pain if they delay after Voldemort calls them; they obey him, even unto their own capture, like Bellatrix, or pain, like Wormtail; they face his mockery and abuse, like Lucius and Draco Malfoy (*Goblet* 641; *Hallows* 456–61, 471). Voldemort's followers are not his friends or confidants. Even Bellatrix, arguably his most devoted follower, is tolerated but not trusted or confided in (*Hallows* 491). Voldemort views himself as peerless; Dumbledore declares that Voldemort deigns to befriend no one (*Prince* 277). Despite insisting that the Death Eaters are his friends, no such gold is produced by his so-called friendships as is produced by Harry's genuine ones (*Prince* 444–45).

A skilled alchemist will set himself apart in a manner quite distinct from Voldemort's. Voldemort separates himself out of haughtiness and pride, out of a desire to reinforce his manufactured notion of purity. Flamel, however, distinguishes himself by his actions. The skills necessary to perform alchemy do not involve viewing himself as superior to others; instead, alchemy depends on embracing the interconnectedness of all elements. Further, alchemy depends upon a person refining his own soul in moral pursuits (Sweeney 174). According to Cotnoir, Nicolas Flamel—the historical figure on whom Rowling's character is likely based—supposedly donated money to many charitable enterprises, including founding and funding fourteen hospitals and three chapels (Cotnoir 54). Clearly Flamel has the requisite moral character to succeed as an alchemist, and Voldemort does not.

Moreover, Voldemort has the wrong relationship to the universe. His belief in his peerlessness means that he does not understand himself and others each to be a microcosm of the universe. He may view himself alone as such a microcosm, given his sense of self-importance, but alchemy involves the view that each human has that relationship to the cosmos. Peerlessness would set Voldemort apart in a way contrary to alchemy, for all things are composed of different mixes of elements that themselves share mixes of common qualities. Were Voldemort to be peerless, he would not hold such basics in common. Voldemort's insistence on his own importance to the exclusion of others reveals that he does not understand deep alchemical truths.

The final similarity between Harry and Voldemort examined here is eternal life. A driving force in Voldemort's life was learning how to extend it and preserve it, primarily through Horcruxes. A Horcrux is intended to preserve a part of one's soul, should that person be mortally wounded. Voldemort combines his pursuit of Hogwarts memorabilia, fame, and eternal life by placing several of his soul fragments into objects known to have been owned by or to be significant to Hogwarts founders (*Prince* 503–04). Since Horcrux creation requires one to perform an evil act to be able to split one's soul, Voldemort's commitment to his own continued existence involves the deliberate snuffing out of the existence of others, including (if things had gone according to Voldemort's plan) a very young baby (*Prince* 496–502). His interest in unicorn blood and body sharing relate to his unanticipated failure to destroy baby Harry, as does his pursuit of a new physical body for the purpose of further pursuing immortality (*Goblet* 569).

Voldemort's quest for Horcruxes undermines each element of alchemy of the soul. Voldemort uses secrecy to guard his evil pursuit, not to protect and aid others. Splitting his soul violates the alchemical view of the unity and interrelatedness of the elements in the cosmos. In splitting his own soul, Voldemort fractures his moral and spiritual nature. The rending of the soul divides one unnaturally, whereas alchemy seeks and works through unity (*Prince* 496–502). Horcruxes make Voldemort less human (*Prince*

502). Contrition can possibly mend a rend in one's soul—such sorrow is the first step back toward humanity—but Voldemort shows no interest (*Hallows* 103). The disrupted unity of Voldemort's soul is best shown by one Horcrux being unaware of the others (*Prince* 507). Voldemort's Horcruxes behave as separate parts instead of one substance. The common element between them—Voldemort's very soul—is not enough to ensure psychic connection. The soul fragments do not behave as things sharing common traits, as alchemy emphasizes of the elements.

The universe is united in one whole, and Voldemort as a microcosm should be united in himself as well. Instead of embracing the richness of his soul, he parcels it out. He does not understand the value he has or the opportunities he is given for growth in order to mirror the divine in the universe. Rochelle Deans argues that the creation of Horcruxes and Voldemort's re-instantiation of himself is a sort of reverse alchemy, moving from bodied to disembodied and back to embodied (111, 113). Voldemort is a "deluded adept" who has capabilities but does not yet fully understand, and his rush to divide himself in order to preserve his life shows this (Deans 106).

While Horcruxes require moral impurity, Voldemort expresses great concern over purity—blood purity. In his quest for an immoral and xenophobic outward purity, he obliterates any inward purity when he creates Horcruxes through murder to preserve his existence (Deans 109). Voldemort's motivation for Horcruxes is not knowledge or charity (either love or charitable giving); it is his own fear (Deans 114). Voldemort has the wrong motivation for his action, the wrong type of purity in mind, and the wrong method to achieve his end. Thus, Horcruxes work against alchemy.

By contrast, alchemy preserves, purifies, and enhances substances. As Granger notes, Horcruxes are not transcendence—they do not allow one to embrace duality and rise above it, as alchemy does—but are instead mimicry. The Horcruxes keep the ego at the center (Granger 81–82). By putting his soul into objects, Voldemort is attempting to preserve himself, but "death is a necessary part of the alchemical work; only in the death of one thing, from the alchemical perspective, is the greater thing born" (Granger 74). Voldemort's self-centered pursuit makes him less human (St. Hilaire 275). Voldemort's egotistical, self-involved approach to eternal life drives him further from understanding and embodying the divine work in the cosmos, which makes his pursuit directly contrary to alchemy.

Unlike Harry, Voldemort is unable to purify his experiences into something better. He does not bring together the contraries as Harry did, for he simply replicates his experiences. He continues the cycle of abuse; he treats all places as though they exist for him alone; he seeks fame for himself out of pride; he surrounds himself with followers but remains alone;

and he seeks eternal life in a manner that rids him of his own humanity, which hardly counts as living. Dumbledore's estimation of Voldemort, as a person who is ignorant, greedy, and cruel, rings true (*Hallows* 708). Without the remorse that might heal these character traits, Voldemort can never succeed at the alchemy of his soul (*Hallows* 741). If Voldemort could have felt remorse, then he would not be Voldemort.

Love: The Elixir of Life

Harry bears the marks of an alchemist in all of the ways that Voldemort does not. These orphaned, abandoned children experience neglect and mistreatment, yet one of them builds a family out of love. They each feel at home at Hogwarts, finding a sense of belonging there, but Tom treats the school like his own play thing while Harry enjoys the school for its own oddities. Fame is Tom's relentless pursuit while Harry prefers anonymity. Tom fashions himself a cabal of Death Eaters while Harry and his friends help each other learn to defend themselves. Voldemort obsesses over eternal life, while Harry, holding the keys to conquer death, deliberately misplaces them. Ironically, alchemically, this makes him "true master of death" (*Hallows* 720). The differences between Tom and Harry arise not in their circumstances, but, as Dumbledore emphasizes, in their *choices*, their actions, their responses to their situations (*Chamber* 333).

The growth that Harry shows in his movement toward love—a movement mirroring his mother's self-sacrifice, and a movement that also encompasses forgiving those, such as Snape and Dumbledore, who have done him wrong—is alchemical. Harry unites contraries in his growth, transforming himself into a morally upstanding, steady-minded person who is capable of facing fear and death for the sake of those he loves (Granger 53). The love, loyalty, and trust that Harry develops in his life are the products of the alchemy of his soul, and they glitter and gleam while revealing Harry's greatest glory: his love-laden soul, resplendent in its self-sacrifice. Harry does indeed "pity the living, and, above all, those who live without love" (*Hallows* 722).

Dumbledore, however, is confounded by his own desire for Harry's happiness, and he delays Harry's coming confrontation with Voldemort to spare Harry further pain (*Phoenix* 838–39). While Dumbledore laments the delay, for many have been harmed by Voldemort in the meantime, Harry has not been idle. He has sought deep knowledge and let it shape him, molding him into one who brings forth gold. Harry brings forth the wealth of family in his touching parting from Dudley and his own union with Ginny, resurrecting his parents' names in his children (*Hallows* 753).

Harry brings forth the gold of Fawkes the Phoenix, who uses his golden beak to fight the basilisk, because of his loyalty to Dumbledore (*Chamber* 322, 332). He brings forth gold sparks from his wand, unbidden, in his fight against Voldemort (*Hallows* 83). He is trusted by Griphook, the goblin, *not* to bring forth gold for *himself* while robbing the Lestrange vault in order to secure another Horcrux (*Hallows* 488).

Harry has been given much lead, and out of it, he has purified himself into pure gold. His journey is compelling because of his alchemical success; if Harry can do it in such awful circumstances, there is hope for anyone to be an alchemist, even Voldemort, a hope that Harry expresses in his last interaction with the man who brought Harry so much pain and took so much from him (*Hallows* 741). Harry seeks to disarm Voldemort, but in the light of the "golden flames," Harry watches Voldemort's Killing Curse rebound upon himself (*Hallows* 743–44). Harry defeats Voldemort without murder, which is surely a mark of a moral man. Harry then takes the riches gained in his quest—the Deathly Hallows—and distributes them, ensuring that their murderous legacy ends (*Hallows* 748–49). Harry's alchemy of the soul is complete: he understands that love will persevere and preserve, and he has made for himself a soul that glows in the golden light of *agape*, of universal, hallowed love.

Works Cited

Burckhardt, Titus. *Alchemy: Science of the Cosmos, Science of the Soul*. Penguin, 1972.
Burns, William E. *Knowledge and Power: Science in World History*. Pearson, 2011.
Chan, Deborah M. "Love Is the Strongest Family Tie." McDaniel and Prinzi, pp. 9–26.
Cotnoir, Brian. *Alchemy*. Weiser Books, 2006.
Deans, Rochelle. "The Dark Lord's Descent: How Voldemort Falls from Soul to Body Through Reverse Alchemy." McDaniel and Prinzi, pp. 103–14.
Fabricius, Johannes. *Alchemy: The Medieval Alchemists and Their Royal Art*. Rosenkilde and Bagger, 1976.
Granger, John. *Unlocking Harry Potter: Five Keys for the Serious Reader*. Zossima, 2007.
Hannam, James. *God's Philosophers: How the Medieval World Laid the Foundations of Modern Science*. Penguin, 2010.
The HarperCollins Study Bible. Edited by Harold W. Attridge, New Revised Standard Version, HarperOne, 2006.
Highfield, Roger. *The Science of Harry Potter: How Magic Really Works*. Penguin, 2003.
Hughes, Jonathan. *The Rise of Alchemy in Fourteenth-Century England: Plantagenet Kings and the Search for the Philosopher's Stone*. Continuum, 2012.
Kibre, Pearl. "Albertus Magnus on Alchemy." *Albertus Magnus and the Sciences: Commemorative Essays 1980*, edited by James A. Weisheipl, Pontifical Institute for Medieval Studies, 2000, pp. 187–202.
Keith-Oaks, Judy. "Emotional Abuse: Destruction of the Spirit and the Sense of Self." *The Clearing House*, vol. 64, no. 1, 1990, pp. 31–35. JSTOR, www.jstor.org/stable/30188557. Accessed 13 July 2019.
McDaniel, Kathryn N., and Travis Prinzi, editors. *Harry Potter for Nerds II: Essays for Fans, Academics, and Lit Geeks*. Unlocking Press, 2015.

Newman, William R. "Experimental Corpuscular Theory in Aristotelian Alchemy: From Geber to Sennert." *Late Medieval and Early Modern Corpuscular Matter Theories*, edited by Lüthy Christoph Herbert. et al., Brill, 2001, pp. 291–329.
Prinzi, Travis, editor. *Harry Potter for Nerds: Essays for Fans, Academics, and Lit Geeks*. Unlocking Press, 2011.
Rowling, J.K. *Harry Potter and the Chamber of Secrets*. Scholastic, 2002.
_____. *Harry Potter and the Deathly Hallows*. Scholastic, 2007.
_____. *Harry Potter and the Goblet of Fire*. Scholastic, 2000.
_____. *Harry Potter and the Half-Blood Prince*. Scholastic, 2005.
_____. *Harry Potter and the Order of the Phoenix*. Scholastic, 2003.
_____. *Harry Potter and the Prisoner of Azkaban*. Scholastic, 1999.
_____. *Harry Potter and the Sorcerer's Stone*. Scholastic, 1998.
St. Hilaire, Jenna. "Harry Potter and the Greatest Virtue." Prinzi, pp. 269–99.
Stein, Mary, et al. "A Study of Common Beliefs and Misconceptions in Physical Science." *Journal of Elementary Science Education*, vol. 20, no. 2, 9 Jan. 2007, pp. 1–11. doi:10.1007/bf03173666. Accessed 13 July 2019.
Sweeney, Erin. "Cracking the Planetary Code: Harry Potter, Alchemy and the Seven Book Series as a Whole." Prinzi, pp. 171–98.
Whitney, Elspeth. *Medieval Science and Technology*. Greenwood Press, 2004.

Ruddy Stargazers
Centaurs, Philosophers, and a Life Worth Living

ANNE J. MAMARY

> You are a star-gazer, my Aster: if only I were the sky, so that I could look at you with a multitude of eyes.
> —Plato (Diogenes Laërtius 3.29)

> In the end, it mattered not that you could not close your mind. It was your heart that saved you.
> —Albus Dumbledore (*Phoenix* 844)

I first read *Harry Potter and the Sorcerer's Stone* in my thirties, a year or two after it was published. By the time *Goblet of Fire* was released, I was standing in a bookstore line at midnight with a bunch of teenagers in Hogwarts robes waiting as if we were on Platform 9¾ for the scarlet steam engine to transport us to the world of magic. Plato, too, tells the story of a journey at the start of the *Republic* (*Politeia* in the Greek). Socrates says, "I went down ... to the Piraeus with Glaucon, son of Ariston" for the festival of Bendis, the Thracian moon goddess, newly introduced in Greece (327a). Plato invites readers to join in on the nightlong conversation that might well transport us to a whole new world.

Rowling and Plato are remarkable, nuanced story-tellers. Their stories follow me into "real life" and awaken in me new ways of engaging with other people and our shared world. They remind me of Maxine Hong Kingston's discussion of oral cultures' storytelling in *The Woman Warrior: Memoirs of a Girlhood Among Ghosts*. She recalls that her mother "would talk-story until we fell asleep. I couldn't tell where the stories left off and the dreams began, her voice the voice of the heroines in my sleep" (19). As Hong Kingston slept, she became Fa Mu Lan, the woman warrior who took her father's place in battle. She awoke empowered. What seems magical to me about both Rowling's and Plato's series (the *Politeia* is a dialogue in ten books), in addition to the sheer delight in learning Spells and discovering cloaks and rings of invisibility, is that as many times as I return to each, I emerge each time transformed. Like Hong Kingston's dreams inspired by ancient stories, Rowling and Plato transport readers to different worlds and spark our imaginations and senses of what is possible if only we love enough, are brave enough, are smart enough, try enough.

Rowling's novels are largely set at Hogwarts School of Witchcraft and Wizardry, and at the most obvious level are about education. The students go to classes, do homework, and take exams. Yet, like Plato, Rowling recognizes that "imitations, if continued from youth far into life, settle down into habits and (second) nature in the body, the speech, and the thought" (*Rep.* 395d). The novels, then, are also about an education in living, about what sort of person each is and will become. From the Sorting on the first night, to how the young students treat each other and what commitments they develop toward the school and the world beyond, Rowling invites readers to think about justice as we accompany her characters through the seven novels.

Plato's *Politeia*, too, reflects who his characters are and suggests who they might become in their conversation—in their education for living. Plato's dialogue recounts a moon- and torch-lit conversation on justice at Cephalus' house with Socrates and Glaucon and also Thrasymachus, Polemarchus, and Adeimantus. Though the *Politeia* is surely an examination of justice both in the person and in the community, it is, too, about education in the sense of what and how a person ought to study in order to become just and to build a just society. The Greek title, *Politeia*, means "constitution," in the sense of how a person and community are put together or constituted, and is built on the words, *polis* (city) and *polites* (citizen) (Sallis 313). As at Hogwarts, education is not only an external collection of subjects and examinations. Education is about shaping who one is at heart, about how the choices one makes (and in what context) constitute both character and community, and, at the same time, about how one's character and the often-invisible norms of one's community shape the choices one is able to make.

Harry and his classmates are welcomed to Hogwarts with a feast, ghosts bursting through the castle walls, and the Sorting, which reflects something of who they are, already, at the age of eleven. As Harry returns "home" to the Dursleys between academic years, he is more and more transformed. His education—both in his course subjects (what the ancients called the intellectual virtues) and in how those courses and his interactions with his classmates shape who he is and is becoming (the moral virtues)—makes four, Privet Drive more strange every year. Socrates and Glaucon are waylaid on their return to Athens from the festival for the "foreign" goddess when Polemarchus intercepts them with the promise of a feast of food and conversation and a torchlit race on horseback. When Socrates and Glaucon finally return to Athens, they and their friends have rethought who they and their society are at a foundational level. They, like Harry and his Hogwarts classmates, are transformed, and the Athens they thought they knew may well seem alien.

Both Harry and Plato's characters might seem like "stargazers" to their families and friends as the familiar becomes odd and the foreign ordinary. The Dursleys might think of Harry as a wizard with his head in the clouds. Hagrid describes the Hogwarts centaurs as "Ruddy stargazers" (*Stone* 254). Socrates, who, incidentally, is sometimes described as having a pig-like nose, was also sometimes dismissed as a "star-gazer, an idle babbler" (*Rep.* 488e). Yet the centaurs and the philosopher might be stargazers in another sense: Harry and his classmates study Astronomy at Hogwarts, and Plato's Socrates insists on the study of astronomy for all who will become lovers of wisdom. The ceiling of the Great Hall at Hogwarts is enchanted to look like the sky outside, and Plato emphasizes that the *Politeia*'s conversation happens at night.

Both Rowling and Plato suggest that we become stargazers like the half-human, half-horse centaurs at Hogwarts and like Socrates, who is described as the half-goat, half-human Satyr in Plato's *Symposium*, one of his dialogues on love (215b). Rowling's centaurs are able practitioners of Divination, able to read something in the stars woven in the fabric of the night sky on which best to pattern the lives of the person and the collective. Satyrs were consorts of the Greek god, Dionysus, known for "crossing and transgressing the border between the divine and the human world" (Näsström 139). Rowling's centaurs and Plato's philosophers are stargazers, who, like the alchemists, believe that our individual and collective lives are microcosms of the vast cosmos and that we might read patterns there to help us navigate the "ship of state" with care for the whole community, as "true pilots" (*Rep.* 529e, 488d).

Delightful and Useful

As his characters in the *Politeia* try to define justice, however, Plato shows that most have a more mundane focus, as if the human being were the whole of the universe rather than one part of an immense living cosmos. Early in the conversation, Thrasymachus insists that "injustice on a sufficiently large scale is a stronger, freer, and more masterful thing than justice.... [I]t is what profits a man's self and is for his advantage" (344c).

268　Part III—The Cloak of Invisibility and the Transfiguration of Self

Even better, if those who are "strong" enough to take whatever they want and do whatever they think is to their own advantage hold political office, whatever they do is, by definition, justice. Justice, Thrasymachus says, is "the advantage of the stronger" (344c). Voldemort operates by this definition. In *Sorcerer's Stone*, Professor Quirrell, who is host to the disembodied Voldemort, says that in his misguided youth, he was "full of ridiculous ideas about good and evil. Lord Voldemort showed [him] how wrong [he] was. There is no good and evil, there is only power, and those too weak to seek it" (*Stone* 291).

While Thrasymachus, Voldemort, and Quirrell may seem at first glance to have an unusually selfish view of justice or injustice, Plato's brother, Glaucon, explains what he sees to be the common view of justice, which is different in degree but not in kind from Thrasymachus' (and Voldemort's) view. Glaucon reports:

> By nature, they say, to commit injustice is a good and to suffer it an evil, but that the excess of evil in being wronged is greater than the excess of good in doing wrong.... [That is, most people think of justice as] a compromise between the best, which is to do wrong with impunity, and the worst, which is to be wronged and be impotent to get one's revenge.... Justice ... [is] a thing honoured in the lack of vigour to do injustice, since anyone who had the power to do it and was in reality a "man" would never make a compact with anybody neither to wrong nor to be wronged; for he would be mad. (358e, 359a–b)

It is a contract, bitterly accepted, to avoid doing harm in exchange for not being harmed.

Some of Rowling's characters enact Thrasymachus' idea of injustice as the best or justice as the advantage of the stronger, when they use power as the ability to manipulate other people and to get whatever they want without regard for the means of acquisition. And sometimes the very same people seem to (or do) follow the laws to avoid punishment or retribution. The Malfoys, for example, often abuse their wealth, status, and position when they can get away with it, and at least put on the appearance of following the laws of their community when they cannot. Lucius Malfoy uses his position as school governor and his ability to threaten and intimidate others to remove Dumbledore from Hogwarts in *Harry Potter and the Chamber of Secrets*, but also takes some of his more suspicious Dark artifacts to sell at Borgin and Burkes, trying to remove "items at home that might embarrass" him as the Ministry steps up raids (262–63, 51). Lucius teaches his son to assume that his pure-blood status and birth into a wealthy family with some political power make him stronger and worthy of advantage. He encourages a kind of class superiority when he ridicules his son, saying, "I would have thought you'd be ashamed that a girl of no wizard family [Hermione Granger] beat you in every exam" (*Chamber* 52). He also teaches Draco that he can buy or bully his way into whatever he wants when he ostentatiously supplies racing brooms for the Slytherin Quidditch team on the condition that Draco play Seeker (*Chamber* 111).

The Dursleys, too, seem to share something of Thrasymachus' view while settling for the common view of Glaucon's account. Although they did save Harry's life when they took him in as an infant, they also treat Harry abysmally while he is growing up, sometimes nearly starving him, keeping him from having any friends, belittling him, and allowing and even encouraging Dudley to bully his cousin. They also teach Dudley to have an attitude of superiority and entitlement: for example, rewarding him with praise for his greed when he whines about having fewer birthday presents as he turns eleven than he did at ten; ignoring or praising his bullying of younger neighborhood children; and cheering or excusing his excesses in the boxing ring or with his knobbly Smeltings stick (*Stone* 22, 31–32).

Most people do not have the access to power or the wealth to silence critics or to amass supporters. Even Draco and Dudley appear to follow the rules as much as they can to avoid detention or a scolding. Like Glaucon (or at least the majority about whom he says he is reporting), they and their families appear to abide by the contract of not harming in exchange for not being harmed. And, if they can catch someone else out of bounds, so much the better. Aunt Petunia spends a lot of time "spying on the boring, law abiding neighbors," for she would "love to be the one to call the hot line number" if Sirius Black should happen to stroll down Privet Drive (*Azkaban* 17). Yet, when Dumbledore visits with the Dursleys the night he and Harry set off to visit Horace Slughorn, Dumbledore chides the Dursleys for treating Harry badly. At the same time, he is downright harsh with them about how they have raised their son. Dumbledore's assessment of Dudley's abuse, however, shifts something of what it means to be powerful and just. Though Uncle Vernon and Aunt Petunia are utterly perplexed, Dumbledore suggests they have damaged their son, their precious son, precisely by giving him a sense of entitlement and superiority (*Prince* 55).

Similarly, Socrates suggests to his interlocutors that they have misunderstood justice and that the misunderstanding has impoverished them. Socrates suggests that there are three categories of goods and that his friends have put justice into the wrong one. Socrates explains that some things are chosen because they are good in themselves, like joy (357b). In a second class, there are things chosen, like medicine or physical training, not because they are good in themselves (and which may be downright unpleasant), but because they lead to good results, like health or skill. The final and highest class, Socrates explains, includes things "which are desirable both for their consequences and still more for their own sake, as sight, hearing, intelligence, and, yes, health, too" (367c). His friends have put justice into the class of bitter medicine, when, Socrates argues, it belongs in the class of things that are both good in themselves and good for their results—for the person and the community.

Gyges' Ring and the Cloak of Invisibility

In describing the common view of justice, Glaucon has shown a world in which people must always "be guarding against one another's injustice" (367a), not realizing, like Draco and Dudley, that they are making not only others but themselves miserable as well. They lack both empathy and simple delight in the company of friends. One of the things I admire most about both Rowling and Plato is that they seem to think that no one is beyond hope or redemption. Both authors leave open the possibility of learning different habits of behavior, or changing one's mind. Even Voldemort, whom Harry invites at the last moment to "[b]e a man ... try ... Try for some remorse" (*Hallows* 741). Even Draco, to whom Dumbledore says, "You are not a murderer," while the scared teenager intends to murder his headmaster on Voldemort's orders. Even Thrasymachus and the whole company, whom Socrates invites to reconsider the lesson each learned from childhood: that being a man means being able to abuse others without fear of punishment.

Both stories ask their characters and readers to consider how they (and we) would act if there were no possibility of detection—of either punishment or reward. In Plato, there is Gyges' Ring of invisibility and in Rowling, the Cloak. In Plato's tale, a shepherd climbs into a chasm in the earth that opened during an earthquake and discovers a bronze horse surrounding a corpse wearing a magnificent golden ring. The shepherd takes the ring from the corpse's hand, as Voldemort takes the Elder Wand from Dumbledore's tomb. Later, the shepherd discovers that the ring makes him invisible when he turns the stone toward his palm. The shepherd then acts exactly as Glaucon or Thrasymachus might have expected him to act. He uses the ring to seduce the queen, to overthrow the king, and to seize power for himself (359d–360b), just as Voldemort wants to use the Wand to give himself a kind of shield behind which to hide while attempting to secure power for himself.

Plato's story might, at first glance, tend to confirm the view of justice as second best to injustice if practiced undetected. If there were two such rings, one on the hand of the just person and the other on the hand of the unjust, Plato's men are convinced there would be little to distinguish between the two. They are convinced that no one with such a ring would "persevere in justice and endure to refrain his hands from the possessions of others and not touch them, though he might with impunity take what he wished ever from the marketplace, and enter into houses and lie with whom he pleased, and slay and loose from bonds whomsoever he would" (360b). Glaucon and Plato's brother, Adeimantus, suggests that fathers teach their sons to seem just rather than to be just. They "urge the necessity of being just, not by praising justice itself, but the good repute with mankind that accrues from it, the object that they hold before us being that by *seeming* to be just the man may get from the reputation office and alliances and all the good things that Glaucon just now enumerated as coming to the unjust man from his good name" (363a, emphasis added). That is, the seeming gives a kind of invisibility behind which to gain wealth or power without regard for others or for punishment. It might confirm Lucius Malfoy's warning to Draco "that it is not—prudent—to appear less than fond of Harry Potter, not when most of our kind regard him as the hero who made the Dark Lord disappear" (*Chamber* 50).

Yet Socrates asks his friends to accompany him on a thought experiment that might move their thinking in another direction. What if there were two such rings, he asks them again, one on the hand of the entirely just person and the other on the hand of the entirely unjust? The idea of invisibility might allow the company to examine justice and injustice without the complicating factor of public opinion. The ring, as Socrates suggests, "takes away the seeming" (361c) and reveals the wearer's true heart. Or, rather, it reveals the virtue (*arete*) or true function of the human being. Socrates is asking the men to do the near-impossible—to reconsider those lessons they learned at their parents' knees and to think about the virtue or function of the soul like the virtue of the craftsperson. If the physician's virtue, for example, is to heal as well as possible, and the pilot's the safe navigation of ships, is the soul's virtue not to be just? Is the soul's virtue not to provide for health and safe navigation through life, and its goal and "advantage [as in the other arts] to be as perfect as possible?" (340d–341e).

Even though he uses the same language as Thrasymachus—justice is the advantage of the stronger—what counts as advantage and what qualifies as strength have shifted nearly beyond recognition. If Socrates is right, people would have to be compelled to rule for the sake of the good of the community and for themselves, since the penalty for refusing would be "to be governed by someone worse" (347c). He suggests it would be best, then, to have a coincidence of being and seeming, to strive to perfect the excellence or virtue or function of the soul, which is "justice and [to avoid] its defect injustice." Socrates continues, and the men appear to agree, that the one "who lives well is blessed and happy, and he who does not the contrary.... Then the just is happy and the unjust miserable" (353e–354a). When justice moves from the lowest to the highest category, both individuals and communities are transformed from guarding against others' injustice to fostering and celebrating human growth.

The Cloak of Invisibility can work in the same two ways as the Ring. It can enable the best of behavior or the worst. It can be used for narrow self-interest, as Harry uses it to sneak into Hogsmeade even though "[e]veryone from the Minister of Magic downwards" has been trying to protect him from Sirius Black, whom we do not yet know is innocent of betraying Harry's parent. As Snape puts it, "Harry Potter is a law unto himself" (*Azkaban* 284). This is not generally true of Harry, and he is filled with genuine remorse when Lupin reminds him, "Your parents gave their lives to keep you alive, Harry. A poor way to repay them—gambling their sacrifice for a bag of magic tricks" (*Azkaban* 290). Though Harry learns from this abuse of invisibility, Glaucon and his friends would need more convincing to believe that Harry's problem was not getting caught in the act but the act itself. Most of the time, Harry is inclined to use the Cloak to protect himself and others, as Socrates' hypothetical entirely just person practices justice both because it is the right thing to do in itself and because it brings about the good both of the individual and of the whole community.

As Socrates presents this new (to his friends) way of thinking about justice as belonging to the class of goods chosen for themselves and for what they yield, he suggests that they look for justice in the *polis*, since, he says, justice in the city is like justice in the person, but "perhaps, there would be more justice in the larger object and more easy to apprehend" (368e). Socrates proposes a healthy city of artisans founded on human need rather than on greed. Its inhabitants "live together as partners and helpers ... and ... share things with one another, giving and taking" (369c). The city's inhabitants each contribute their skills, like making clothing or shoes or building houses or trading with other societies, and they live together in peace, with neither excess nor poverty (which is equally destructive) (372b–c).

Glaucon is not convinced, after hearing Socrates' proposal, that either he or the city might change as much as that, calling the healthy city a "city for pigs" (372d). He insists that people will want "relishes and myrrh and incense and girls and cakes—all sorts of all of them." They will want "gold and ivory and similar adornments" and to be able to have "a little Corinthian maid ... and the seeming delights of Attic pastry" (which, according to Professor Anthony Preus, were often shaped like phalluses) (373a, 404d). They want luxuries; they treat other people's sexuality as a commodity; they value wealth and prestige above mutual support. They echo (or perhaps presage) Voldemort's assessment of Snape's love for Lily Evans, when he says, "He desired her, that was all," reducing Snape's love to the basest sort of desire as Socrates' friends reduce what is important in their lives to luxuries (*Hallows* 740). They want, as Socrates says, a "fevered city," one which he tries to heal in the rest of the dialogue's books, much as Rowling tries to heal a world fevered with fear of Voldemort's greed and quest for dominance and an ordinary view of happiness tied to wealth and position.

Harry and Ron illustrate justice as both delightful and useful on their first trip to school on the Hogwarts Express. When Harry has both money and a friend for the first time in his life, he buys as much as he can carry from the lunch trolley and happily shares the treats with Ron. Ron and Harry's new friendship is like Socrates' description of justice in the healthy city or city of artisans on the smallest of scales. Ron and Harry enact justice as something good in itself as they enjoy each other's society, happily eat their way through a pile of goodies, Ron's corned-beef sandwiches abandoned on the seat nearby (*Stone* 102). It is a rare moment of sheer joy. At the same time, the two new friends practice justice for the good results it produces. Each gives the other something he craves: Harry the friendship and fun he has been denied for ten years, and Ron the singularity he rarely experiences with so many siblings. Rather than each taking whatever he can get, each gives what the other needs.

A Tale of Two Sortings: The Myth of the Metals and the Sorting Hat's Songs

Socrates makes an alchemical move in his attempt to heal the fever in both the *polis* and the person, just as Ron and Harry do on their first journey to school. It was an impoverished alchemist, indeed, who sought gold (or birthday presents or spots on the Quidditch team) only for personal gain. The caption to an engraving in Christoph Weigel's book of heraldry, now in the Wellcome Library of London, "depicts the double identity of the 'alchemist' who helps nature by preparing medicines but, when desirous of gold, watches 'honor, wit, money, and mercury' go up in smoke" (Moran 41).

Trying to help them to see that they are fevered with a desire for possessions and position, Socrates tells his friends the story of the metals in each of our souls precisely to help them heal their souls' acquisitiveness. Plato's story shows both that we are all kin and that we at the same time each have our own unique abilities. According to the tale, "the earth as being their mother delivered them, and now as if their land were their mother and their nurse they ought to take thought for her and defend her against any attack and regard the other citizens as their brothers and children of the self-same earth" (414e). Those with golden souls are wisest and fittest to leadership (they are not power-hungry but hungry for a society that meets human need rather than greed); those with souls of silver are "sorted" into the guardians of society—both gentle and courageous; and the ones with souls of brass or ivory are the farmers and craftspeople, who have the predominant virtue of *sophrosune*, which is often translated as moderation or temperance, but which has the wider connotation of being level-headed under pressure or having excellence of character. Socrates says the just person "regulates well what is really his own and rules himself. He puts himself in order, is his own friend, and harmonizes the three parts of himself like three limiting notes in a musical scale—high, low, and middle" (443d). By contrast, Socrates describes injustice as "a kind of civil war between the three parts..." acting without harmony (444b).

While some have interpreted the "myth" as evidence that Plato was an authoritarian, advocating a rigid class structure, another truth, the opposite truth, emerges from the story. We are mixed with the metals of the planet, and we are not born to follow our parents' lives. Instead, we are born to follow our own lives, which are a combination of our connection to the universe—in the *Timaeus*, the demiurge "assigned each soul to a star—and our own choices, some made so frequently that they seem to have come from nature" (41d). The story is a reversal of the commonly held idea that one is bound by one's parents' class and a reversal of the idea that rulers are the best (*aristos*) simply by accident of birth. Brothers Glaucon, Adeimantus, and Plato are sons of Ariston. Plato seems to be having some fun with his own name. He was born to the conventional aristocracy (*aristos* is the root of our English word) and was expected, because of his birth to wealth and power, to have a position of political power.

Yet Plato quit politics when Athens executed Socrates and made his life's work trying to reconfigure what qualifies as power and wealth in both his personal efforts to temper those with power and in his character, Socrates, who challenges social norms in every Platonic dialogue.* Plato urges his compatriots and his readers to rethink what qualifies as "the best." The best are those who, like Harry, "have leadership thrust upon them, and take up the mantle because they must, and find to their own surprise that they wear it well" (*Hallows* 718). Each group has a predominant virtue, yet they are all siblings, born of the earth and strongest standing together. A microcosm of the city, each person has all of these virtues as well, and justice,

---

*At the urging of his long-time partner, Dion, Plato traveled to Sicily in the early fourth century BCE as a tutor to the tyrant, Dionysius II, who was Dion's nephew. Plato tried to awaken the philosophical in the tyrant's soul, so "that those whom we now call our kings and rulers take to the pursuit of philosophy seriously and adequately..." (*Rep.* 473d). At first Dionysisus was receptive, but, when Plato somehow irritated him, sold him into slavery (at least according to some accounts). Fortunately, Plato's friends bought him and returned him to Athens (Diodurus Siculus xv.7).

both in the person and in the *polis*, is the harmony of wisdom, courage, and moderation or excellence of character (433e).

In Rowling's tale, the Hat prefaces each Sorting with a song, which operates something like Plato's "Myth of the Metals." The Sorting Hat can see something of the "heavenly imprint" in each student, that something that belongs to each alone. At the same time, the Hat recognizes the imprint of family and culture: that in the first eleven years of life, each student has already practiced some behaviors and attitudes long enough to have them become habitual. Socrates' story suggests that justice is based in each person's unique character in harmony with the others.*

This is also true of the Hogwarts sorting. Each student has a combination of the virtues represented by the four houses. In the first two versions of the song, one in *Sorcerer's Stone* and the other in *Goblet of Fire*, the Hat describes Gryffindors as courageous; Hufflepuffs as excelling in friendship, justice, and loyalty; Ravenclaws as those "of wit and learning"; and Slytherins as "cunning" and "having great ambition" (*Stone* 118; *Goblet* 177). The moderation of a virtuous Slytherin's ambition must also be in the other houses, for it takes effort and determination to make good choices. It also takes Gryffindor courage not to back down in the face of adversity and an ounce of Ravenclaw wit to know the difference. The friendship and loyalty of Hufflepuff is the justice or harmony of the whole.

Near the end of *Harry Potter and the Goblet of Fire*, Dumbledore asks the assembled school to raise a glass to Cedric Diggory, murdered by Voldemort, saying "Lord Voldemort's gift for spreading discord and enmity is very great. We can fight it only by showing an equally strong bond of friendship and trust" (*Goblet* 723). Cedric and Hufflepuff House represent the harmony—the friendship—of the person and the *polis*. The headmaster continues:

---

*Socrates calls the "Myth of the Metals" a Noble Lie, signaling that it is a story, a metaphor, a fiction. This does not mean it is a lie any more than the Sorting Hat in Rowling's fictional universe is a lie. That is, the story requires interpretation, just as the Sorting Hat story does. Both are fictions; neither is a lie in the conventional sense of being a falsehood. The *Daily Prophet* headline "The Boy Who Lies," in *Order of the Phoenix*, is a blatant untruth attempting to discredit Harry and his evidence that Voldemort is back. Dolores Umbridge forces Harry to engrave "I must not tell lies" into his own skin as punishment for his truth telling on the matter.

Even the newspaper's and Umbridge's deliberate concealing of the truth reveals a kind of truth. Umbridge wants to maintain her own power at Hogwarts and the power of the Ministry of Magic, for which she works. Hermione uncovers something of the motivation when she asks the "reporter," Rita Skeeter, if "the *Daily Prophet* exists to tell people what they want to hear," to which Skeeter responds, "The *Prophet* exists to sell itself, you silly girl" (*Phoenix* 567). Similarly, Socrates spends a good portion of his defense at his trial addressing false rumors the jury had likely heard for years, so that they might be able to listen without prejudice to his defense against the actual charges for which he was on trial. By contrast to the rumors and to Skeeter's "reporting," both Rowling's and Plato's sorting stories, though not literally true, nevertheless tell truths.

> Cedric was a person who exemplified many of the qualities that distinguish Hufflepuff house.... He was a good and loyal friend, a hard worker, he valued fair play. His death has affected you all, whether you knew him well or not.... Remember Cedric. Remember, if the time should come when you have to make a choice between what is right and what is easy, remember what happened to a boy who was good, and kind, and brave, because he strayed across the path of Lord Voldemort. Remember Cedric Diggory. (*Goblet* 721–22)

The death of one good person, Cedric, is a loss; the death of Hufflepuff's unifying qualities of friendship and loyalty, of persistence and hard work, is the loss of justice at Hogwarts and beyond.

The Hogwarts Houses can give their students a community in which to hone their unique talents, yet when those communities forget the bond of friendship that ties the whole together, like the friendships among the school's founders, Hogwarts might descend into injustice and civil war, as the Sorting Hat warns explicitly at the opening of the school year in *Harry Potter and the Order of the Phoenix*. It is only in this version of the Hat's song that the school's co-founder, Slytherin, is described as wanting students "whose ancestry is purest" in his house. In this version of the song, the Hat is not praising the shift in Slytherin's commitment to pure ancestry, describing it, instead, as the mistake that nearly tore the school apart. As long as the four founders remained friends, "Hogwarts worked in harmony / For several happy years, / But then discord crept among us / Feeding on our faults and fears" (205). While Slytherin's departure averted Hogwarts' collapse, it would have been better to have him stay and to think about what would be best for him, for his House, for Hogwarts.

Socrates' interlocutor, Thrasymachus, might have stormed out of the conversation in the *Politeia* after calling Socrates names and insisting that those with power (usually those from old and wealthy families) define justice simply as whatever is to their advantage (336b–338c). But, unlike Slytherin, Thrasymachus stayed and changed, at least a little, when he admitted, however unwillingly, that "justice is virtue and wisdom and injustice vice and ignorance" (350d). Slytherin's departure may have brought a temporary halt to hostilities but left the school and its students in peril still. The Hat worries that it is wrong to separate the students into Houses in the *Order of the Phoenix* version of the song, not, I think, because the Sorting itself is inherently troubling, but because they have forgotten Plato's reminder that we are all born from the earth, all siblings to each other. They are missing the "glue" of *sophrosune* and the unifying friendship of justice, which may make them "crumble from within" (207).

In his Aristotlean reading of the series, Stephen Patterson reminds readers to resist the prejudice against Slytherin we might have inherited from our beloved Hagrid, who tells Harry, "There's not a single witch or wizard who went bad who wasn't in Slytherin" (*Stone* 80). Patterson says that unless we are prepared to say that Slytherin is the house for "evil ones from old families," we will have to practice empathy and recognize the value in the virtue of ambition, which, like all of the virtues, is the mean between two vices—slacking, the deficiency of ambition, and social climbing, ambition's excess (122, 130). Patterson points out that Draco Malfoy seems to go between the two, sometimes thinking he deserves special treatment precisely because he comes from an old and wealthy pure-blood family, and sometimes seeking power and status through his own actions, such as in his assignment from Voldemort to kill Dumbledore, little caring who is harmed along the way.

Similarly, Susan Matthews writes, Draco "has been taught to confuse talent and success ... with strength and power" (137). They are not examples of what it means to be a virtuous Slytherin any more than Harry's occasional excess of courage, his rash behavior, exemplifies the Gryffindor virtue of courage. He has to live with the guilt of Sirius' death when he insists on leading his friends on a rescue mission at the Ministry when there was never anyone in danger. Gryffindor Peter Pettigrew demonstrated the other vice associated with courage, its deficiency of cowardice, when he betrayed Harry's parents to Voldemort. Bravery would have been doing anything, including dying, not to betray his innocent friends, as Sirius says he and Lupin would have died for James and Lily, and the four of them would have died for Peter (*Azkaban* 375). Ultimately Plato's Thrasymachus seems to have come to see his initial view of justice as mistaken when he blushes (350d). Even Pettigrew shows a move toward Gryffindor courage when he hesitates for one moment about giving away Harry and Ron's position in the basement of Malfoy Manor. He dies rather than betraying Lily and James' son and his best friend (*Hallows* 470).

Regulus Black, an extraordinarily brave Slytherin, uses his virtuous ambition in an attempt to destroy Voldemort's Horcrux locket, sacrificing himself in the process. Snape, too, practices a virtuous ambition, acting as spy for Dumbledore out of love, the life-long love he had for Lily Evans. An abused child, the son of an abused mother, Snape has no model for love or friendship along the Hufflepuff model of loyalty. He has no understanding of Socrates' idea of friendship, which Socrates values more "than all Darius's gold," as wanting what is best for one's friend, the one loved (and finding that that is also best for oneself) (*Lysis* 211e, 213a). Instead, in his youthful excitement over being freed from abuse, the teen-aged Snape re-creates that very abuse, calling Lily and her friends "Mudbloods" and joining the heartless Death Eaters. She refuses to be abused, and, though she says they are best friends, refuses to enable his behavior. He could have chosen vengeance and ripped his soul to pieces, but, instead, he chooses love. Making the nearly impossible choice to cut himself off from all human society except for Dumbledore and from any possibility of golden friendship, Snape chooses to spend the rest of his life atoning for those early experiences and choices (Deavel and Deavel 55).

Snape summons all of his Ravenclaw wit and his Gryffindor courage, which Dumbledore recognizes when he sighs, "I sometimes think we sort too soon" (*Hallows* 680). Snape, though, would have failed without Slytherin cunning, persistence, and ambition, which he uses to embody Hufflepuff loyalty and love. He is composed of all of the virtues, all of the human geniuses (Matthews 133). As if to prove Patterson's point, Harry names his first son Albus Severus and names Snape "probably the bravest man [he] ever knew." And when his son frets that he might be sorted into Slytherin, Harry tells him that he has a choice, and also that if he goes to Slytherin, "— then Slytherin House will have gained an excellent student" (*Hallows* 758).

Harry is only sorted into Gryffindor because he asks the Hat not to put him in Slytherin. Decades later, though, Harry's words of comfort to Albus Severus recognize the friendship between Godric Gryffindor and Salazar Slytherin at the heart of Hogwarts. Whatever happened later, the houses and the school were founded in friendship. The Hat asks "where were there such friends anywhere / As Slytherin and Gryffindor? / Unless it was the second pair / Of Hufflepuff and Ravenclaw?" (*Phoenix* 204). Ambition and courage, loyalty and wit need each other. The school is strongest if the four houses recognize their unique talents and understand that they are all siblings, to borrow Plato's language.

In both Plato's "sorting" and the Hat's "sorting," one truth readers might learn is that both tales encourage a shift in thinking about identity. Rather than "I am a Gryffindor, because I am not a Slytherin," one might understand that I am a Gryffindor precisely because you are a Slytherin.* I am who I am in partnership with you and who you are. Rather than a class hierarchy in Plato's tale, readers might understand that one is "gold" precisely because someone else is bronze or ivory or silver, the harmony of all the "parts," whether in the person or in the *polis* or at Hogwarts, creating justice.

Ruddy Stargazers: An Alchemical Education

In his image of prisoners in a subterranean cave, Socrates tries to shift his friends' attention from understanding who they are by being not someone else (usually not someone with less money and fewer resources) to understanding themselves as unique individuals and also as both a part

---

*Thanks to the students in the 2018 Monmouth College class, "Harry Potter and the Philosopher's Soul," for this insight.

of the whole and a reflection of it. The prisoners are chained at the neck and at the ankles and observe the images cast on the wall in front of them, thinking they are reality. When Glaucon remarks that they are "strange prisoners," Socrates responds, they "are like to us" (515a). That is, they are ordinary people, like the kids who arrive at Hogwarts are ordinary people. The image makers are "the stronger" in Thrasymachus' understanding of the word, and maintain their power not with physical force but with a constant display of images, with advertising that reinforces the worldview that wealth and power are best and that justice is only guarding against others' treachery.

All of the prisoners have the power to turn their heads around and to see another possible world. Their hands are free; they are not gagged. They have the power to undo their bonds physically and to free their minds in conversation with each other, but it is hard to make a bid for freedom if one does not realize one is not free in the first place. Though Socrates' friends say they really want to be convinced that justice is the best, Adeimantus articulates Glaucon's visceral reaction to the healthy city when he says that being truly convinced would require turning his world upside down, would require "justice and injustice, inverting their true potencies" (367a). The story of the cave works toward just such an inversion, but the prisoners react to the one who has broken free and comes back to report a world of basic fairness illuminated by the sun with the same confusion the Dursleys have when Dumbledore tells them they had abused Dudley.

Socrates says that the cave is an allegory of education and continues to explain that education is not about pouring "knowledge into a soul that does not possess it, as if they were inserting vision into blind eyes." Rather, education ought to be an awakening of the power already present in us, "the indwelling power of the soul" (518b–d). Sometimes known as Pythagoras' "ninth successor," Plato drew on the Pythagorean idea that the person is a microcosm of the community and that the human community is "a microcosm of the universe illuminated by the sun" (Joost-Gaugier 69). Paracelsus, too, drew on this idea "around at least since the time of Plato ... [and] applied the notion to nature in a new way viewing the human body as a condensation or synthesis of all the powers of the universe" (Moran 75).

In Socrates' view, the philosopher, the seeker after wisdom, is no longer "an idle babbler" (*Rep.* 488e). Instead, he or she is "captain of the ship of state," a stargazer who uses "the blazonry of the heavens as patterns to aid in the study of those realities.... He [or she] will be willing to concede that the artisan (demiurge) of heaven fashioned it and all that it contains in the best possible manner for such a fabric" (529e–530a). In the *Timaeus*, the demiurge, who is good, without any mean-spiritedness or jealousy (29e) fashioned the perfectly good cosmos as "a moving image of eternity" (37d) upon which we might model our lives. It is not that the heavens—the stars and the planets—are in one realm and that our lives are in another. Rather, when the students of astronomy become philosophers they are seeing and hearing the wisdom of the cosmos shining through our physical and temporal lives. In the tenth and eleventh centuries, just as Hogwarts was founded, Muslim and Christian scholars alike "recognized Pythagoras as an example of moral authority.... He knew the road to heaven because he knew, in essence, how to measure heaven" (Joost-Gaugier 69). That study of number, geometry, and astronomy was "adopted by practitioners of magic, medicine, and alchemy"—and the Hogwarts centaurs (Joost-Gaugier 116).

In *Harry Potter and the Sorcerer's Stone*, Hagrid shows that he has both an uncommonly close relationship with the centaurs and a bit of impatience with them when he asks them if they've seen anything unusual in the forest only to get "Mars is bright tonight" in response (*Stone* 253). "'Never,' said Hagrid irritably, 'try an' get a straight answer out of a centaur. Ruddy stargazers. Not interested in anythin' closer'n the moon'" (254). On the one hand, we can share Hagrid's frustration, since, as we find out soon enough, Voldemort is loose in the forest, killing unicorns, and trying to kill Harry. Hagrid could really use the centaurs' help. On the other hand, even in his irritation, when ruby red Rubeus Hagrid mentions the moon, he reminds us of Aristotle's sublunary world, the world of the four elements (earth, air, fire, and water), of changing nature, which operates by discernable scientific principles. Beyond the moon, in the ancient Greek imagination, was the world of the unchanging planets, the heavenly or Celestial sphere, made of what Plato called Aether (*Tim.* 58d) or the Quintessence (Moran 11). It is to the heavens that the centaurs cast their attention and about which Firenze tries to teach his students in his first-floor classroom, which has been enchanted to resemble the forest outside.

Firenze reminds us that, for the alchemist, the enchanted world, like his classroom, is not a resource for humans in the sense of providing raw materials to buy and sell or by which to navigate ships, or even as a causal factor for small human concerns. Rather, it is the whole of which we are part, and is a resource in that other sense of being mentor and guide. He tells the students:

In the past decade, the indications have been that Wizardkind is living through nothing

> more than a brief calm between two wars. Mars, bringer of battle, shines brightly above us, suggesting that the fight must soon break out again. How soon, centaurs may attempt to divine by the burning of certain herbs and leaves, by the observation of fume and flame. (*Phoenix* 603)

In addition to having the students burn Mallowsweet and other herbs on the classroom forest floor, he has them cast their eyes to the heavens emblazoned on their classroom ceiling.

While the students sprawl on the black, earthy floor* of their classroom (with a wastepaper basket next to a tree stump!), Firenze builds on what the students have learned about the night skies in Astronomy, saying the centaurs' studies of the heavens "teach us that the future may be glimpsed in the sky above us..." (*Phoenix* 602). When he tells the students about the centaurs' study of the planets, Firenze positions humans and our non-human compatriots in the world. We are all part of it and so can learn from it. He reminds his young human charges that the centaurs, while having a certain attitude of superiority to humans, recognize the superiority of the cosmos to any wisdom of those living on earth. As Socrates shifts his angle of vision from mundane human concerns, so, too, does Firenze when he dismisses Professor Trelawney's connection of Mars—the red planet, which the ancients sometimes called "ruddy"—in a certain angle to Saturn as causing accidents and burns as "human nonsense" (James 54; *Phoenix* 604).

While the stars and planets (things "further'n the moon") may have been seen as unchanging models, the Sublunary sphere—of which we and the centaurs, along with the herbs Firenze burns with his students, are a part—is an active agent from which we might learn. From gazing at the stars to attending to the smallest of plants, Firenze helps the students to recognize that they are a tiny part of the vast universe, neither insignificant nor overly significant in our own imaginations. They, the centaurs, and readers must make choices, even if they are unpopular within our cultures, like Firenze carrying a human being to safety on his broad back or Hagrid carrying the infant Harry across the star-strewn skies on the back of a flying motorbike.

The Myth of Er and the Tale of the Three Brothers: A Life Worth Living

With Socrates' and the centaurs' shifts in angle of vision comes risk. Socrates recognizes that the just person or the person who has broken free of competitions among images of gold and power will face resistance and possibly violence (*Rep.* 517a). The historical Socrates was tried and sentenced to death in Athens in 399 BCE for impiety and corrupting the young. At his trial, as he tried to sweep away decades of rumors and false beliefs, Socrates said many people believed that he busied himself "investigating the things beneath the earth and in the heavens" (*Apol.* 19b). That is, he is a

---

*In addition to alchemy's Arabic root "*kimia*" from the Coptic "*khem*" that alluded to the fertile black soil of the Nile delta, esoterically and hieroglyphically, the word refers to the dark mystery of the primordial or First Matter (the *Khem*).

stargazer of the most useless and dangerous sort in some of their minds. Socrates refused to propose exile at his trial or to escape from prison as he awaited execution, saying, a person "in whom there is even a little merit ought to consider danger of life or death, and not rather regard this only, when he does things, whether the things he does are right or wrong and the acts of a good or a bad [person]" (28b–d). As he left the court, Socrates asked the Athenians to treat his sons as he, Socrates, had treated his beloved city. That is, he asked them to be sure to teach them justice, for they and the citizens of Athens should be "ashamed to care for the acquisition of wealth and for reputation and honor, when you neither care nor take thought for wisdom and truth and the perfection of your soul" (*Apol.* 29d–e). He said to the jury, "But now the time has come to go away. I go to die, and you to live; but which of us goes to the better lot, is known to none but God." (*Apol.* 42a).

Firenze explains that Voldemort, killing unicorns and drinking their blood to save his own life, will pay "a terrible price.... [He] will have but a half-life, a cursed life" (*Stone* 258). Voldemort does not understand that he is damaging himself precisely because he thinks freedom means taking whatever he wants from whomever he likes under whatever conditions. The unicorns are pure and innocent; Voldemort damages himself precisely because he uses them to stay alive. Harry wonders, "But who'd be that desperate? ... If you're going to be cursed forever, death's better, isn't it?" (*Stone* 258).

Voldemort embodies the tyrannical ideal, and Dumbledore reminds us that he, Voldemort, is the most miserable, the most afraid, for "tyrants fear the people they oppress. All of them realize that, one day, amongst their many victims, there is sure to be one who rises against them and strikes back!" (*Prince* 510). The men in Plato's dialogue have grown accustomed to living with the fear that others might try to harm them, and only agree not to harm others in exchange for not being harmed. They agree to follow the rules in order to avoid retribution, but there is little in the way of examining or seeking what would meet human need most fully. Plato explains how democracy devolves into tyranny when ordinary people make this very mistake about freedom, not understanding that harming others to gain whatever catches one's fancy is not really freedom but a kind of bondage (Rep. 573a–b). Socrates reminds his friends that the tyrant is not really free and is never really happy, for "someone with a tyrannical nature lives his whole life without being friends with anyone ... and never getting a taste of either freedom or true friendship" (576a).

Adeimantus says almost wistfully, "if you had all spoken in this way from the beginning and from our youth up had sought to convince us, we should not now be guarding against one another's injustice, but each would be his [or her] own best guardian, for fear lest by working injustice he should dwell in communion with the greatest of evils" (367a). What a shift that would be—to fear doing injustice rather than to fear suffering another's injustice. This is precisely the shift that concerns Dumbledore when Draco, acting on Voldemort's orders, threatens to kill the headmaster on the top of the highest tower in *Harry Potter and the Half-Blood Prince*. Readers learn near the end of *Deathly Hallows* that both Dumbledore and Snape are aware of Draco's attempts to kill Dumbledore and that Dumbledore is already dying from the curse in the Horcrux that had been Marvolo Gaunt's ring.

As Harry later learns from Snape's thoughts in the Pensieve, Dumbledore did not intend to let Draco kill him. It is not his own death Dumbledore is trying to avoid; he knows death is "coming for [him] as surely as the Chudley Cannons will finish bottom of this year's league." His concern is, rather, trying to spare Draco the permanent damage he will inflict on his own soul (or character) if he commits murder. When he says to Snape that Draco's soul is "not yet so damaged," Snape wants to know about his own soul, since he has promised to kill the already dying headmaster. Dumbledore responds, "You alone know whether it will harm your soul to help an old man avoid pain and humiliation" (*Hallows* 683).

At the end of the *Politeia*, Plato writes a story from beyond the grave. Er, believed to have died in battle, returns to life from his funeral pyre, to tell the story of death and choices. Each soul who went to the underworld drew a lot and was then given the choice of its next life. Most made choices that reflected the common view that money and position are most important. Yet the soul of Homer's Odysseus made a different choice. His soul "got to make its choice last of all, and since memory of its former sufferings had relieved its love of honor, it went around for a long time, looking for the life of a private individual who did his own work, and with difficulty it found one lying off somewhere neglected by the others. He chose it gladly and said that he'd have made the same choice even if he'd been first" (620c–d). Odysseus' choice reminds readers of the healthy city Socrates describes early in the *Politeia* in which each person works toward the good of the whole and in which there was neither poverty nor greed.

In "The Tale of the Three Brothers" near the end of *Harry Potter and the Deathly Hallows*, Rowling writes a story about human souls confronting mortality and morality, about what life is worth living. In Rowling's tale, each of the Peverell brothers chooses a gift from death, gifts which both reveal something about their characters and shape their future lives. The youngest, Ignotus, chooses the Cloak, which allows him to live his life accepting of his human mortality. Only Ignotus recognizes that he can live a moral mortal life, eventually departing friends with death (*Hallows* 409). He and Odysseus are like the ordinary citizens of Plato's healthy *polis*, who, after a long life of living well, "drinking their wine and hymning the gods, hand on a like life to their children" (372c–d), as Ignotus Peverell and James Potter handed on the Cloak to theirs.

In the Epilogue of *Deathly Hallows*, Harry and Ginny stand on Platform 9¾ seeing their son, Albus Severus, onto the Hogwarts Express. It seems as though Slytherin has been reconnected with its Gryffindor, Hufflepuff, and Ravenclaw friends and that there is more harmony in the world than there had been when Harry made his first trip to school. After a long conceptual journey through the night in Plato's *Politeia*, Socrates and his friends depart for home, both home and each of the friends transformed. Socrates wishes for them all, "both here and in that journey of a thousand years ... *eu prattomen*": May we, all of us, fare well (621c–d). Despite his grief over his son's departure, Harry reaches to the lightening scar on his forehead and realizes it "had not pained [him] for nineteen years. All was well" (*Hallows* 759).

Works Cited

Deavel, Catherine Jack, and David Paul Deavel. "Choosing Love: The Redemption of Severus Snape." *The Ultimate Harry Potter and Philosophy: Hogwarts for Muggles*, edited by Gregory Bassham, Wiley, 2010, pp. 53–65. Blackwell Philosophy and Pop Culture.
James, Jamie. *The Music of the Spheres: Music, Science and the Natural Order of the Universe.* Copernicus (Springer-Verlag), 1993.
Joost-Gaugier, Christiane L. *Measuring Heaven: Pythagoras and His Influence on Thought and Art in Antiquity and the Middle Ages.* Cornell UP, 2006.
Kingston, Maxine Hong. *The Woman Warrior: Memoirs of a Childhood Among Ghosts.* 1975. Vintage, 1989.
Laërtius, Diogenes. *Lives of Eminent Philosophers.* Translated by Mitchell Parks, Knox College.
Matthews, Susan R. "*Ich Bin Ein Hufflepuff*: Strategies for Multiple Skill Management in J.K. Rowling's Novels." *Mapping the World of the Sorcerer's Apprentice*, edited by Mercedes Lackey. BenBella, 2005, pp. 133–44. Smart Pop Books.
Moran, Bruce T. *Distilling Knowledge: Alchemy, Chemistry, and the Scientific Revolution.* Harvard UP, 2005.
Näsström, Britt-Mari. "The Rites in the Mysteries of Dionysus: The Birth of Drama." *Ritualistics*, vol. 18, 1 Jan. 2003, pp. 139–48, Scripta Instituti Donneriani Aboensis, doi: doi.org/10.30674/scripta.67288. Accessed 30 Aug. 2018.
Patterson, Stephen W. "Is Ambition a Virtue? Why Slytherin Belongs at Hogwarts." *Harry Potter and Philosophy: If Aristotle Ran Hogwarts*, edited by David Baggett and Shawn E. Klein. Open Court, 2004, pp. 121–31. Popular Culture and Philosophy 9.
Plato. *Apology*. Translated by Harold North Fowler. *Perseus*. Tufts University, www.perseus.tufts.edu/hopper/text?doc=Perseus%3Atext%3A1999.01.0168%Abook%3. Accessed 1 June 2017.
_____. *Lysis*. Translated by W.R.M. Lamb. *Perseus*. Tufts University, www.perseus.tufts.edu/hopper/text?doc=Perseus%3Atext%3A1999.01.0168%Abook%3. Accessed 1 June 2017.
_____. *Republic*. Translated by Paul Shorey. *Perseus*. Tufts University, www.perseus.tufts.edu/hopper/text?doc=Perseus%3Atext%3A1999.01.0168%Abook%3. Accessed 1 June 2018.
_____. *Timaeus*. Translated by Donald J. Zeyl. *Plato: Complete Works*, edited by John M. Cooper and D.S. Hutchinson, Hackett, 1997, pp. 1224–91.

Preus, Anthony. Personal conversation. June 2015.
Rowling, J.K. *Harry Potter and the Chamber of Secrets*. Scholastic, 1998.
———. *Harry Potter and the Deathly Hallows*. Scholastic, 2007.
———. *Harry Potter and the Goblet of Fire*. Scholastic, 2000.
———. *Harry Potter and the Half-Blood Prince*. Scholastic, 2005.
———. *Harry Potter and the Order of the Phoenix*. Scholastic, 2002.
———. *Harry Potter and the Prisoner of Azkaban*. Scholastic, 1999.
———. *Harry Potter and the Sorcerer's Stone*. Scholastic, 1997.
Sallis, John. *Being and Logos: Reading the Platonic Dialogues*. Indiana UP, 1996 (1974).
"What Is Alchemy?" Royal Society of Chemistry. 2017. www.rsc.org/periodic-table/alchemy/what-is-alchemy. Accessed 15 Aug. 2017.
Siculus, Diodorus. *The Library of History*, vol. VI. Translated by C.H. Oldfather, Loeb, 1954. 12 vols.

Epilogue

Friendship Hallowed, Pure, and Ever-Present

Through the power of friendship, our prime trio—Ron, Hermione, and Harry—Transfigure each other into more golden versions of themselves. Ron, Harry, and Hermione put parts of their souls into each other simply by sharing each other's lives. By contrast, Voldemort puts parts of his soul into Nagini, Harry, and inanimate objects (not really recognizing the abilities and intentions of natural elements) and never understands either the power of the natural world or of its microcosms in human society. Harry finds part of his own soul in the Resurrection Stone. He finds his parents, Sirius, and Lupin in himself; he discovers the Stone in himself. As Dumbledore asks him, "You think the dead we loved ever truly leave us? You think that we don't recall them more clearly than ever in times of great trouble? Your father is alive in you, Harry, and shows himself plainly when you have need of him" (*Azkaban* 427–28). Harry is stronger because he has shared himself with others and allowed them to touch him deeply.

Voldemort attempts to use Horcruxes to become immortal, tearing apart his own soul when he murders other people in his attempt. The stone of Marvolo Gaunt's ring is both Resurrection Stone and Horcrux. Voldemort knows nothing of the Hallows, even while possessing the Stone and the Wand, and his seven Horcruxes make him weaker, less human. Unlike Harry, he allows no one else to touch him deeply. Although choosing objects to transform into Horcruxes for their mystique, such as their connection to Hogwarts' founders—including his ancestor, Slytherin, in the case of the stone in Gaunt's ring—Voldemort never treats those items as having purposes of their own. He makes them into inert objects in the service of his own entirely self-absorbed obsession. He imprisons Nagini, "confid[ing] a part of [his] soul to something that can think and move for" herself, and also makes Harry into a Horcrux accidentally (*Prince* 506).

He has utterly perverted the power, desire, and protection of the Hallows in his attempt to live forever through his Horcruxes. He does not understand at all the joining of the heavens and the earth, the solid and the liquid, life and death of Hermione's and the alchemists' prime substance, Mercury, which was also sometimes represented by a serpent (rsc.org). In Buddhist and Hindu iconography, the serpent, Nāga (Nagini is the feminine form), is associated both with caverns and bodies of water, a guardian of treasures ("Nāga"). When Voldemort turns Nagini into a Horcrux, he reveals that he sees no one as an independent being with hopes, fears, purposes, and desires. He reveals that he does not treasure anything but his own shrinking life. The magical objects he seeks to extend his own life might have done so, if he could have understood the true magic of an enchanted universe and the unique power he lacks entirely and which Harry embodies: Love. It also reveals his fears: he fears death; he fears the people he has tyrannized; he fears being human (*Prince* 150).

Voldemort's murders and his tyranny are not the only way to tear one's soul. He is not the only one operating from fear in the series. Aunt Petunia's curiosity about Lily's magical abilities turns to bitter disappointment at not being invited to Hogwarts and erupts from her when she hurls the word "freak" at her sister (*Hallows* 669). Petunia's disappointment turns to fear of the world that killed Harry's parents and could well threaten her own son's safety. Draco Malfoy persists in his assignment to kill Dumbledore, largely out of fear. He is sure Voldemort will kill not only him but his parents if he tries to back out. He stands there on the top of the tallest tower, a desperate, frightened boy offered help and protection by the man he was sent to kill. Rowling is brilliant at making empathy and a healthy curiosity about different worlds, cultures, people, and experiences "normal." She suggests that reducing fear and disappointment might go a long way in reducing oppression.

It makes no difference, really, if one lights torches with a Spell or lamps with "eckeltricity," as Arthur Weasley calls it (*Goblet* 46). Each takes a kind of magic; each is entirely ordinary to one group of people and strange to another. Yet, Rowling gives us Mr. Weasley's delight in all things Muggle both as an endearing eccentricity and as a model for openness. At the same time, we see Hermione's parents at the Leaky Cauldron and Lily Evans' parents standing on Platform 9¾ drinking in the sights and sounds with obvious delight. The world becomes lighter, less leaden. Bruce Moran notes something of Galileo's delight in wine, which he described as "'light held together by moisture.' He might not have known it, but he had actually expressed a very old alchemical opinion, one that acknowledged the existence in wine, indeed in all of nature, of something celestial, pure, and life-enhancing; and something that might be got at by means of distillation" (11). Similarly, in *Quintessence*, Rupescissa "referred to the quintessence, essentially alcohol produced by distilling wine, as 'human heaven (caelum),' which, as DeVun has noted, had the dual meaning of the sky and heaven in a theological sense" (Nummedal 316).

On his first encounter with the Pensieve, the Magical basin in which thoughts can be stored for future examination, Harry describes the silvery contents looking "like light made liquid—or like wind made solid" (*Goblet* 583). This process of distilling what matters most in one's thoughts and practices is akin to the alchemical process of distilling the Quintessence from the elements for healing body and soul—of both the individual and the community as reflections of the heavens, the cosmos. The Mirror of Erised can lead to pitiable narcissism, like Narcissa Malfoy's, if it is not Transfigured into a kind of Pensieve, in which one can take stock of one's life and situation and try for some self-understanding in the larger context of friends, of the heavens, and of the earth.* Kingsley Shacklebolt reminds us of something like this on Potterwatch, under his code-name, Royal. He refuses to separate magic from Muggle, reminding those who say that in dangerous times it should be Wizards first that "[e]very human life is worth the same, and worth saving" (*Hallows* 440).

Understanding nothing of house-elves or children's tales, nothing of love or loyalty, Voldemort neither understands the alchemical power of the Philosopher's Stone, the transformative power of the Hallows, nor the possibility of distilling something healing from the Pensieve. In trying to deny death, he makes himself less human, denies the "star stuff" in himself, and makes only the faintest and corrupt shadow of the Alchemical journey. When Ron, Harry, and Hermione retrieve the Horcrux-locket from Dolores Umbridge, they retrieve a piece of Voldemort's soul, entrapped, cold, and alone, encased in metal that never takes heat from human hands. In the moments before Ron stabs the Horcrux with the venom-impregnated Sword of Gryffindor, Voldemort's soul taunts him, saying "*I have seen your heart, and it is mine*" (*Hallows* 375). That is, Voldemort tries to disempower Ron as he plays on Ron's insecurities; he attempts to hold Ron's heart hostage. By contrast, when Harry gives the house-elf, Kreacher, Regulus Black's imitation locket, he gives Kreacher part of Regulus' heart. The metal is a warm reminder of love and affection. Putting part of himself into Kreacher in the shape of the locket, Regulus (through Harry) makes Kreacher more of himself, freeing him (*Hallows* 199). The gift of Regulus' locket is like Fleur Delacour's gift to her guests on her wedding day, when it "beautified everybody it fell upon" (*Hallows* 144).

When Voldemort creates Horcruxes after murdering, he makes himself less—less human, less vibrant, less hallowed. He tears his soul seven

---

*Thanks to Sobhi Kazmouz, Monmouth College, '19, for this insight.

times, making seven not at all a magical number. As much as he has tried to deny the possibility of his own death, or rather because he has tried to deny it, Voldemort embodies the "grinding scream of death," "the hemorrhage none can staunch, the grief, the curse no man can bear" in Rowling's epigraph from Aeschylus at the start of *Deathly Hallows* (xi).*

While Harry and Voldemort are bound together, those bonds are not nearly as powerful as the bonds of love and support in the woods when Harry tries to die for his community. When Voldemort possesses Harry in *Order of the Phoenix*, Harry's thoughts of his godfather save him (816), because *Voldemort* cannot bear to entwine his soul with another person who feels love so strongly, just as Quirrell and Voldemort could not bear to touch Harry's mother's love "in [his] very skin" in *Sorcerer's Stone* (299). Through their trust in the power of friendship, through their desire to create a better world, our trio embodies the epigraph from William Penn's *More Fruits of Solitude* at the start of *Deathly Hallows*. Ron, Hermione, and Harry have put their souls into each other; the three "live in one another" (xvii).

The *tria prima* (Mercury, Sulfur, and Salt) and the four elements make the Philosopher's Stone. Harry, Ron, and Hermione, our literary *tria prima*, and the four elements—the dead Harry loves, who are always with him (his parents, Sirius, and Lupin)—make the Philosopher's Stone, the Stone of Wisdom. From these seven—"seven the most powerfully magical number"—comes the whole world (*Prince* 466). In their Alchemical Quest, Ron, Harry, and Hermione understand, finally, how to unite the Hallows. They are the "cure in the house," these children who triumph, transforming power, desire, and self/community into Love—hallowed, pure, and ever-present (*Hallows* xi).

---

*See John Granger's "Aeschylus Epigraph in *Deathly Hallows*" on Harry's connection with Orestes and an allegorical/alchemical reading of Rowling's epigraph.

Works Cited

Granger, John. "The Aeschylus Epigraph in 'Deathly Hallows.'" *Hogwarts Professor: Thoughts for Serious Readers*, 20 Oct. 2008, www.hogwartsprofessor.com. Accessed 2 July 2018.

Moran, Bruce T. *Distilling Knowledge: Alchemy, Chemistry, and the Scientific Revolution*. Harvard UP, 2005.

"Nāga." en.wikipedia.org/wiki/Nāga. Accessed 10 July 2018.

Nummedal, Tara. "Alchemy and Religion in Christian Europe." *Ambix*, vol. 60, no. 4, 27 Nov. 2013, pp. 311–22, Taylor & Francis, doi:10.1179/0002698013Z.00000000036. Accessed 31 July 2018.

Rowling, J.K. *Harry Potter and the Deathly Hallows*. Scholastic, 2007.

_____. *Harry Potter and the Goblet of Fire*. Scholastic, 2000.

_____. *Harry Potter and the Half-Blood Prince*. Scholastic, 2005.

_____. *Harry Potter and the Order of the Phoenix*. Scholastic, 2002.

_____. *Harry Potter and the Prisoner of Azkaban*. Scholastic, 1999.

_____. *Harry Potter and the Sorcerer's Stone*. Scholastic, 1997.

"What Is Alchemy?" *Periodic Table*. Royal Society of Chemistry. 2017. www.rsc.org/periodic-table/alchemy/what-is-alchemy. Accessed 15 Aug. 2017.

About the Contributors

Tamyra **Dixon-Rankin** taught science at West Central Middle School in Stronghurst, Illinois, from 1991 until her retirement in 2020. She teaches advanced chemistry and physics at West Central High School and earth, life, and physical science at Immaculate Conception Middle School in Monmouth, Illinois. She has an MA in science education from Western Illinois University. Tamyra's interests include growing healing and culinary herbs in her organic garden, traveling, playing the mandolin for NoReason, an alt-folk music band, doting on her dogs and cats, and, of course, all things Harry Potter.

Lawrence W. **Farris** is a retired Presbyterian minister living in Minneapolis, Minnesota. He is the author of *Dynamics of Small Town Ministry*, *Ten Commandments for Pastors New to a Congregation*, and *Ten Commandments for Pastors Leaving a Congregation*. A voracious reader, he also loves to garden, cook, travel, walk, cycle, and sing. He is a graduate of the University of Michigan and Princeton Theological Seminary.

Kate **Fulton** is an associate professor of psychology at San Juan College in Farmington, New Mexico, and a licensed clinical mental health counselor in Colorado and New Mexico. She taught a Harry Potter learning community for four years with Alicia L. Skipper, pairing English composition and psychology classes with a Harry Potter theme.

John **Granger**, tagged "The Dean of *Harry Potter* Scholars" by *Time* magazine's Lev Grossman, is the author or editor of eight books on Rowling's series and has been a keynote and featured speaker at more than twenty academic and fan conferences. He has a BA in classics from the University of Chicago, an MFA in creative writing, and is writing his Ph.D. thesis at Swansea University (Wales).

Ella Victoria **Greer** lives happily in the North Country of New York with her family of six not including two dogs, a cat, and a previously uncountable amount of goldfish. She loves to read, and her parents retell stories of fishing overdue books out of her backpack. She is an aspiring writer, and her favorite spell is *Aguamenti*, because it's an instant pool party minus the guests.

Sophia **Imafuji** is a fifth grader who enjoys reading. Her favorite books are the series of Harry Potter, Keeper of the Lost Cities, and Percy Jackson. She also enjoys Greek mythology. She writes Harry Potter fan fiction with four of her friends.

About the Contributors

Lorrie **Kim** is the author of *Snape: A Definitive Reading* (2016), an analysis of the Harry Potter series from Professor Snape's point of view. She lives in Philadelphia with her grumpy, magical husband and their geeky offspring, one born between *Order of the Phoenix* and *Half-Blood Prince* and one in gestation during the publication of *Deathly Hallows*.

Anne J. **Mamary** is a professor of philosophy at Monmouth College in Monmouth, Illinois. A chemistry major at Bryn Mawr College, which might actually be Hogwarts, her Ph.D. is from the Philosophy, Interpretation, and Culture program at SUNY Binghamton. She is editor, with Gertrude James Gonzalez, of *Cultural Activisms* (SUNY). She learned Morris dancing from Bryn Mawr chemistry professor George Zimmerman and dances with the B.F. Harridans.

Anne **Parker-Perkola** is a Ph.D. candidate in the Rice University Department of Religion doing interdisciplinary and comparative work in medieval and religious studies. She pays particular attention to mapping interrelationships of mind, art (whether visual, performative, or literary), spirit, and body. Her dissertation focuses on the roles of reading, writing, and books in contemplative practice in medieval European and pre-modern Tibetan monastic literary communities.

Sean **Paulsgrove**, a double major in communication studies and philosophy, graduated from Monmouth College in 2018. He lives with his family in his home town, Monmouth, Illinois. An avid fan of exploring philosophical principles through art, his favorite musicians give him many lenses through which to view the world. He is pursuing a master's degree in communication studies at Western Illinois University.

B.L. **Purdom** studied classics and anthropology at Temple University and has presented at *Harry Potter* symposia and science fiction/fantasy conventions across North America since 2003. She is the host of "Quantum Harry, the Podcast," based on her book, *Quantum Harry: A Unified Theory of the Potterverse*, and she has appeared on other podcasts, authored the *Psychic Serpent* series, and co-founded FictionAlley.org.

Mary **Pyle** has a degree in English literature, which she taught, and she later trained in psychoanalysis, which she has practiced and taught for many years. Partially retired, she is completing her doctorate in English literature at Trinity College, Dublin. Her thesis, "Harry Potter and the Unconscious Dimension," examines the phenomenal success of the series and the reasons for its appeal to readers of all ages.

Charles M. **Rupert** has an MA in philosophy is from West Chester University of Pennsylvania He teaches philosophy at several Philadelpha-area colleges, is an active member of the Philly Socialists and the Democratic Socialists of America, raises his two sons, and works hard to lead a moral existence. His essay "Locke, Marx, and Two Theories of Labor" won first prize in the Next System Project's international essay competition in 2017.

S.P. **Şipal** has analyzed the mysteries behind the Harry Potter series for over a dozen years and is the author of *A Writer's Guide to Harry Potter* and *Fantastic Secrets Behind Fantastic Beasts*. She has presented at fan, writing, and academic conferences, including LeakyCon, Sectus, Ascendio, and Nicholls State University Jubilee

Jambalaya. She is now dissecting Rowling's newest creation with other like-minded fans on her YouTube channel at BeastChaser.com.

Alicia L. **Skipper** has an MA in English from the University of North Carolina at Wilmington and a Ph.D. in English from Arizona State University. Before accepting a position at Bakersfield College, where she is professor of English, she taught at San Juan College in Farmington, New Mexico, for six years. Her research interests include the constructions of epistolary identity in the letters of early twentieth-century women; the Beats; and, of course, Harry Potter.

Julie Loveland **Swanstrom** is an assistant professor of philosophy and religion at Augustana University in Sioux Falls, South Dakota. She teaches a range of courses, including philosophy of religion, ancient and medieval philosophy, ethics, philosophy of science, philosophical theology, and historical theology. In her research, she explores Medieval theories of causation, specifically focusing on how the concept of divine creation fits within the structures of causation as understood by Aquinas and Avicenna.

Robert **Tindol** is an associate professor of English at the Guangdong University of Foreign Studies in Guangzhou, China. He has published peer-reviewed articles on a variety of topics in British and American literature and contributed an Anti-Oedipal reading of Jane Austen's *Mansfield Park* to the journal *Rhizomes*. His other research interests include late capitalism, the conceptual metaphor, and the interaction between modern science and literature.

Isaac **Willis** is an MFA candidate at the University of Illinois at Urbana-Champaign. He writes poetry, dictates work to his cat, who has yet to transfigure into a human and actually transcribe any of it, and lives with his wife, Andi. He majored in philosophy and English at Monmouth College and is the former coordinating editor of the college's *Midwest Journal of Undergraduate Research*. His poems have appeared in *The Cresset* and *Bluffs Literary Magazine*.

Index

Numbers in bold italics indicate pages with illustrations

Abraham, Lyndy: "Nabokov's Alchemical Pale Fire" 32, 34, 36, 37, 40, 44
Ackermann, Zeno: "Rocking the Culture Industry/Performing Breakdown: Pink Floyd's *The Wall* and the Termination of the Postwar Era" 186
Acts 200
Adam and Eve 47
Adeimantus *see* Plato
Adorno, Theodor W., and Max Horkheimer: *Dialectic of Enlightenment* 231, 242
Advanced Potion Making (Hogwarts textbook) 8, 33, 136; *see also* Potions (class)
Aelian, Claudius 126
"'Aeschylus Epigraph' in *Deathly Hallows*" *see* Granger, John
Aether *see* Plato
agape 146, 150, 151, 152, 153, 154, 263
"Albertus Magnus on Alchemy" *see* Kibre, Pearl
"The Alchemical Process of Transformation" *see* Hamilton, Nigel
alchemical stages 9, 90; Black (*nigredo*) 9, 10, 34, 36, 37, 38, 39, 40, 41, 42, 129; *Calcinatio* 10; Calcination 118, 123, 124; *Coagulatio* 10; Coagulation 118, 124; *Coniunctio* 10; Conjunction 34, 41, 43, 70, 118, 123, 246; Dissolution 34, 36, 38, 40, 54, 118, 123, 125, 127, 129, 131, 132, 137, 138; distillation 8, 10, 36, 118, 120, 124, 288; Fermentation 118, 124; Red (*rubedo*) 9, 34, 35, 36, 37, 38, 40, 41, 42, 43, 44, 129; Separation 113, 118, 123; *Solutio* 10; *Sublimatio* 10; Sublimation 46; White (*albedo*) 9, 34, 35, 36, 37, 38, 39, 40, 41, 43, 90, 129; Yellow (*citrinintas*) 35; *see also* Black, Sirius; Dumbledore, Albus; Hagrid, Rubeus; Hogwarts alchemical symbolism; Snape, Severus
Alchemical Studies see Jung, Carl G.
alchemical wedding 10, 34, 35, 41, 43, 80, 162; Red Queen and White King 34; *see also* mercury; sulfur; Weasley-Delacour wedding
Alchemy *see* Cotnoir, Brian

Alchemy, Ancient Art and Science see Pyrites, Argo
Alchemy and Finnegan's Wake see DiBernard, Barbara
"Alchemy and Religion in Christian Europe" *see* Nummedal, Tara
"Alchemy and the Hermetic Tradition: Mircea Eliade and Carl Jung" *see* Ceaser, Cerena
alchemy, literary *see* literary alchemy
alchemy of the soul 24, 244, 247
"'Alchemy of the Word': Alchemy, Allegory, and Individuation in Angela Carter's Passion of New Eve" *see* Cooke, Alana Bolton
Alchemy: Science of the Cosmos, Science of the Soul see Burckhardt, Titus
Alchemy: The Medieval Alchemists and Their Royal Art see Fabricius, Johannes
alembic 40, 120, 125, 127, 129, ***130***, 132, 133, 137, 138
Alexandria 129
Alexandrov, Vladimir E.: *Nabokov's Otherworld* 44
al-Kimia 11, 281
Allen, Paula Gunn: "The Woman I Love Is a Planet, the Planet I Love Is a Tree" 6, 25
Allen, R. Michael: *Reformed Theology* 191, 208
American College of Heraldry 199, 208
Amusing Ourselves to Death: Public Discourse in the Age of Show Business see Postman, Neil
Ancient Egypt, vol. 1 see Petrie, W.M. Flanders
Ancient Runes (class) 9
Anelli, Melissa, and Emerson Spartz: "The Leaky Cauldron and Mugglenet Interview Joanne Kathleen Rowling: Part Three" 34–35, 44
anima and animus *see* Jung, Carl G.
animagus 3, 197; *see also* McGonagall, Minerva; Padfoot; Prongs; Wormtail
ankh *see* Horus
"Another Brick In the Wall, Part 2" *see* Waters, Roger
Anti-Oedipus: Capitalism and

295

296   Index

Schizophrenia see Deleuze, Gilles and Felix Guattari
Apology see Plato
Apparition 143
aqua vitae 69
arcanum 143
Ariston *see* Plato
Aristotle 21, 25, 276, 284; sublunary 280, 281; *see also* celestial
Arithmancy (class) 9
The Art of Loving see Fromm, Erich
Arthurian images 42; *see also* Weasleys
asphodel 116
astronomy 9, 121, 212, 267, 279, 280, 281; *see also* Plato; Thoth
Astronomy (class) 9, 212, 267, 281
Atlanta Fugiens see Maier, Michael
Aunt Marge *see* Dursley, Marge
Aunt Muriel 42
Aunt Petunia *see* Dursley, Petunia
"The Aurelian" *see* Nabokov, Vladimir Vladimirovich
auror 20, 111, 156, 166
authoritarianism 231
Avada Kedavra 20, 45, 95, 105, 107, 110, 129, 134, 147, 156, 157, 158, 160, 161, 164, 165, 166, 199, 200, 205, 263; *see also* Voldemort
axis mundi 191, 195, 197
Azkaban 64, 112, 123, 125, 173, 269
Azoth of the Philosophers see Valentine, Basil

Babel 200
baboon 121, 126
Bacon, Roger 69
badger *see* Hogwarts House animals
Bagshot, Bathilda 104, 193; house 43, 193
Baptist, Ron the 42; *see also* Weasley, Ron (Ronald Bilius)
Baptists 191
Bar/Bat Mitzvah 200, 208
Barrett, David V.: *Secret Societies: From the Ancient and Arcane to the Modern and Clandestine* 210, 224
The Basic Writings of C.G. Jung see Jung, Carl G.
basilisk 39, 123, 125, 127, 128, 132, 133, 190, 200, 201, 202, 213, 221, 256, 257, 263; fang 126, 133, 138, 201, 202; glance 214; venom 19, 213; *see also* mandrake; petrification
Bassham, Gregory: "Love Potion No. 9¾" 18n, 25, 26, 77, 175, 186, 284
Battle of Hogwarts 19, 35, 43, 84, 126, 147, 148, 181, 205, 223
Battle of the Doomed Gods see Heine, Friedrich Wilhelm
Beater 191, 206; *see also* Hogwarts Quidditch teams
Beauxbatons 194
"Before a Screen Door" *see* Harrington, Janice N.

Being and Logos: Reading the Platonic Dialogues see Sallis, John
Bendis *see* Plato
Benson, Amy 159; *see also* orphanage
bereavement 65
Bertie Bott's Every-Flavor Beans 220
Bishop, Dennis 159; *see also* orphanage
Black, Regulus Arcturus 83, 166, 175, 181, 232, 250, 277, 289
Black, Sirius 33, 39, 66, 69, 106, 119, 123, 153, 181, 197, 214, 216, 217, 221, 222, 238, 239, 249, 269, 272, 277; *nigredo* 38, 42; Padfoot 216; *see also* alchemical stages; animagus; Hogwarts alchemical symbolism; Marauders
Blavatsky, H.P.: *Isis Unveiled* 123, 138; *see also Emerald Tablet*; Vablatsky, Cassandra
Bloody Baron *see* Hogwarts ghosts
Bludger 191
The Book of Beasts see White, T.H.
The Book of Gramarye see Stanton, Will
The Book of the Dead see Budge, E.A. Wallis
borage (plant) 8
Borage, Libatius 8
Borgin and Burkes 268
Bosky, Bernadette Lynn: "Liminal Places and Liminal States in John Crowley's *Little, Big*" 195, 208
The Boy Who Lived 23, 92, 93, 175, 192, 207, 241
Brazilian Boa Constrictor 47, 48, 49, 52, 59, 128
Brown, Sara: "From Abjection to Alchemy: Tolkien's Middle-earth Legendarium" 32, 44
Browne, Thomas: *Pseudodoxia Epidemica* 13, 245
Brunschwig, Hieronymus 69
Bryce, Frank 199, 256
Buchanan, Ian: *Deleuze and Guattari's "Anti-Oedipus"* 102, 106, 107, 108, 109, 110, 113
Buckbeak *see* Hippogriff
Budge, E.A. Wallis: *The Book of the Dead* 122, 138
Bulgaria 191
Burbage, Charity 43; *see also* Muggle
Burckhardt, Titus: *Alchemy: Science of the Cosmos, Science of the Soul* 245, 263
Burns, William E.: *Knowledge and Power: Science in World History* 245, 263
The Burrow 95, 194, 199
butterbeer 180

caduceus *see* Hermes
Calvin 191
Campbell, Joseph: *Hero with a Thousand Faces* 202, 208
Capital: A Critique of Political Economy see Marx, Karl
capitalism 7, 100, 231
Care of Magical Creatures (class) 9, 22, 198, 212, 213

Carey, Brycchan: "Hermione and the House-Elves" 179, 180, 186
Carroll, Lewis 117
Carter, Angela: *The Passion of New Eve* 30, 32, 44
Castro, Adam-Troy: "From Azkaban to Abu Ghraib: Fear and Fascism in Harry Potter and the Order of the Phoenix" 173, 179, 186
cauldron cake 220
Cavanaugh, William: "Religious Violence as Modern Myth" 7, 25
Ceaser, Cerena: "Alchemy and the Hermetic Tradition: Mircea Eliade and Carl Jung" 14*n*, 25; *see also* Eliade, Mircea; Jung, Carl G.
celestial 280, 288; *see also* Plato; Quintessence
centaur 24, 265, 267, 280; Firenze 161, 212, 256, 280, 281, 282; *see also* Mars (red planet)
Cerberus 201; *see also* Fluffy
Chamber of Secrets 19, 47, 81, 118, 119, 120, 121, 125, 126, 127, 128, 131, 132, 201, 213, 257, 258
Chan, Deborah M.: "Love Is the Strongest Family Tie" 252, 263; *see also* Prinzi, Travis, and Kathryn N. McDaniel
Chang, Cho 194; *see also* Hogwarts Quidditch Teams
Chappell, Drew: "Sneaking Out After Dark: Resistance, Agency, and the Postmodern Child in JK Rowling's Harry Potter Series" 101, 113
Charms 21, 152; class 8, 9,
Chaser 191, 206; *see also* Hogwarts Quidditch teams; Quidditch
Chaucer, Geoffrey 30, 32
chiasmus *see* ring composition
"The Chiastic Structure of Harry Potter" *see* Parker, Joe
Chocolate Frog 220; card 1, 11, 204, 220, 232; *see also* Dumbledore, Albus; Flamel, Nicolas; Flamel, Perenelle; Paracelsus
choices 12, 13, 16, 24, 55, 79, 93, 94, 95, 110, 132, 133, 145, 154, 170, 190, 237, 239, 242, 262, 266, 274, 275, 276, 277, 278, 281, 283
"Choosing Love: The Redemption of Severus Snape" *see* Deavel, Catherine Jack, and David Paul Deavel
Christian 151, 200, 209, 221, 244, 280; alchemists 1, 8, 246; Christ 32, 34, 35, 43, 241; sacrament 41; symbolism 30, 31, 41, 42, 200; *see also* Baptists; Quakers
Chronicles of Narnia see Lewis, C.S.
Chudley Cannons 283
Cloak of Invisibility *see* Deathly Hallows, Invisibility Cloak
Cloninger, Susan C.: *Theories of Personality: Understanding Persons* 80, 81, 85, 96
Coleridge, Samuel Taylor: "Rime of the Ancient Mariner" 70, 77
Collected Works of C.G. Jung, Psychological Types see Jung, Carl G.

Collected Works of C.G. Jung, Psychology and Religion; East and West see Jung, Carl G.
Collected Works of C.G. Jung, Structure and Dynamics of the Psyche see Jung, Carl G.
conscious and unconscious 17, 79, 80, 81, 85, 88, 98, 99, 102, 104, 108, 236, 238, 245; *see also* Deleuze, Giles, and Felix Guattari; Jung, Carl G.
Cooke, Alana Bolton: "'Alchemy of the Word': Alchemy, Allegory, and Individuation in Angela Carter's Passion of New Eve" 32, 44
Cooper, Susan: *The Dark Is Rising* 219
Corinthians 194
cosmos 2, 8, 10, 248, 257, 260, 261, 263, 267, 279, 280, 281, 289; divine 24, 247; enchanted 4, 9, 244; *see also* God's active work in the world
Cosmos and Psyche: Intimations of a New World Order see Tarnas, Richard
Cotnoir, Brian: *Alchemy* 244, 245, 246, 254, 255, 260, 263
Cowper, William 63
Crabbe, Vincent 201, 206, 230; *see also* Goyle, Gregory; Malfoy, Draco
"Cracking the Planetary Code: Harry Potter, Alchemy, and the Seven Book Series as a Whole" *see* Sweeney, Erin
Crime and Punishment see Dostoevsky, Fyodor
Crites, Stephen: "The Narrative Quality of Experience" 152, 153, 155
Crockatt, Philip: "Freud's 'On Narcissism: An Introduction'" 227, 242
Crouch, Barty 178, 179, 180
Crouch, Barty, Jr. 157, 238; *see also* Moody, Alastor (Mad-Eye)
Crowley, Aleister: *Liber Al vel Legis* 58, 61
Crowley, John *see* Bosky, Bernadette Lynn
"Crowning the King: Harry Potter and the Construction of Authority" *see* Mendlesohn, Farah
the cupboard under the stairs 37, 47, 48, 49, 52, 92, 195, 247

The Daily Prophet 82, 274; *see also* Skeeter, Rita
D.A. *see* Dumbledore's Army
Darius' gold *see* Plato
The Dark Is Rising see Cooper, Susan
"The Dark Lord's Descent: How Voldemort Falls from Soul to Body through Reverse Alchemy" *see* Deans, Rochelle
Dark Mark 258
Darke Hierogliphicks: Alchemy in English Literature from Chaucer to the Restoration see Linden, Stanton
Dastin, John 245
Deans, Rochelle: "The Dark Lord's Descent: How Voldemort Falls from Soul to Body through Reverse Alchemy" 261, 263

Death Eaters 140, 149, 160, 162, 164, 183, 194, 204, 206, 233, 234, 238, 259, 262, 277
The Death of Nature: Women, Ecology, and the Scientific Revolution see Merchant, Carolyn
Deathly Hallows *12*, 13, 23, 73, 108, 141, 154, 196, 242, 254, 263; Elder Wand 2, 3, 12, 14, 17, 18, 21, 108, 110, 127, 128, 142, 157, 166, 204, 205, 207, 234, 235, 254, 279; Invisibility Cloak 2, 12, 14, 20, 21, 50, 51, 101, 108, 110, 141, 207, 216, 230, 241, 250, 254, 266, 270, 272; Resurrection Stone 2, 12, 13, 14, 15, 16, 17, 58, 63, 73, 74, 90, 101, 108, 110, 142, 194, 199, 206, 254, 287; *see also* Dumbledore, Albus
The Deathly Hallows Lectures see Granger, John
Deavel, Catherine Jack, and David Paul Deavel: "Choosing Love: The Redemption of Severus Snape" 73, 77, 277–78, 284; *see also* redemption
Defense Against the Dark Arts (class) 9, 196, 257
De Jong, Helena Maria Elisabeth 46, 61
Delacour, Fleur 35, 198, 223, 289
Deleuze, Gilles, and Felix Guattari: *Anti-Oedipus: Capitalism and Schizophrenia* 17, 98–99, 100, 101, 102, 103, 106, 107, 108, 109, 110, 111, 113; *see also* conscious and unconscious; Oedipus complex; psyche
Deleuze and Guattari's "Anti-Oedipus" see Buchanan, Ian
Della Stufa, Gismondo 57; *see also* Ficino, Marsilio
Deluminator 15; *see also* Dumbledore, Albus; Weasley, Ron (Ronald Bilius)
dementor(s) 19, 63, 64, 71, 76, 196, 203, 247
Dementor's Kiss 151, 197
Department for the Regulation and Control of Magical Creatures 178
desiring-production 100, 101, 102, 108, 111
Devil's Snare 28, 220
Devine, Megan: "'Stay Strong,' and Other Useless Drivel We Tell the Grieving" 67, 77
Dialectic of Enlightenment see Adorno, Theodor W., and Max Horkheimer
diary (Tom Riddle) 81, 119, 127, 128, 133, 135, 137, 200, 201, 202, 223; *see also* Horcruxes
DiBernard, Barbara: *Alchemy and* Finnegan's Wake 195, 208
Dickens, Charles: *Tale of Two Cities* 34
Dictionary of Alchemical Imagery see Abraham, Lyndy
Diggory, Cedric 22, 41, 199, 238, 275, 276; *see also* Dumbledore, Albus; grave(yard)
Dionysius II see Plato
disarming see Expelliarmus
Distilling Knowledge: Alchemy, Chemistry, and the Scientific Revolution see Moran, Bruce T.
divination 208, 212, 256, 257, 267
Divination (class) 9, 33, 212, 215; *see also* Vablatsky, Cassandra
divine cosmos see Cosmos
Dobby 74, 145, 151, 153, 175, 179, 180, 181; grave 42, 43, 185, 253; *see also* grave(yard)
dog and dogfish 213
Doge, Elphias "Dogbreath" 42
dogma 20, 31, 169, 171, 172, 173, 174, 175, 176, 177, 178, 180, 181, 182, 183, 184, 185
Donegality 32; *see also* Lewis, C.S.
Dostoevsky, Fyodor: *Crime and Punishment* 77
Doty, William G.: *World Mythology* 121, 138
Douglas, Mary: *Thinking in Circles* 16, 30; *see also* ring composition
dragon 9, 40, 42, 45, ***196***, 198; egg 40; Hungarian horntail 39, 40; *see also* Principe, Lawrence
Dumbledore, Aberforth 42, 91, 176, 216, 217; *see also* Dumbledore, Albus; Dumbledore, Ariana; Grindelwald, Gellert
Dumbledore, Albus 3, 6, 17, 41–42, 68, 69, 73, 75, 77, 83, 85, 99, 119, 122, 124, 125, 143 –44, 153, 158–59, 176–77, 180, 181, 189, 193, 197, 213. 214, 216, 221, 222, 225, 234, 238, 252, 257, 262, 268, 269, 279, 282; and Aberforth 91, 216, 217, 251; *albedo* 33, 37, 38, 54*n*, 89; *albedo* stage 33, 37, 38, 54*n*, 89, 90; and Ariana 56, 72, 89, 91, 103, 105, 176, 216, 217; and Cedric Diggory 22, 275; Chocolate Frog card 1, 204, 220; choices 94, 145, 190, 237, 242; Deathly Hallows 12, 13, 18, 20, 74, 90, 105, 108, 194, 204, 205, 206, 237, 241, 254, 270; deluminator 15; and Draco Malfoy 88, 90, 166, 204, 204, 270, 283, 288; Dumbledore's Army 20, 82, 169, 172, 178, 202, 203, 205, 217, 250, 251; Fawkes the phoenix 131, 200, 213, 263; and Flamels 3, 13, 32, 142, 211, 240; and Grindelwald 56, 89, 90, 176, 178, 204, 205, 255; Harry as Dumbledore's man 39, 42, 43; "having and being" 23, 231, 232, 236, 239 –40; Headmaster 37, 38, 235–36; and Horcruxes 84, 161, 164–65, 200, 201, 202, 204, 237, 241, 251, 254; "house-elves and children's tales" 4–5, 14, 175, 289; King's Cross Station 13, 17, 36, 89, 106, 107, 163, 174, 207, 216–17, 222, 223, 224; *Life and Lies* 41, 42, 89; and Love's power 17, 74, 144, 147, 149, 154, 158, 162, 212, 237, 240, 241, 254, 262, 265, 287; Mirror of Erised 3, 50, 54–56, 57, 58–59, 68, 70, 103, 113, 197, 210, 23637; "old man's mistake" 18, 154, 238–39; Order of the Phoenix 86, 205, 217; persona and shadow 80, 81, 88–89, 90, 91–92, 94–95; power 90, 154, 177, 178, 222, 254–55, 259, 262; remorse 18, 176, 177, 183, 184, 217, 254; "secrets and lies" 216, 251, 259; and Snape 86, 87–88 , 90, 151–52, 205, 217, 224, 235, 277, 278 283; and Tom Riddle 1, 81, 92, 124, 133, 141, 159, 233, 258; tomb 18, 108, 270; Voldemort duel 35, 98; *see also*

alchemical stages; Chocolate Frog; Deathly Hallows; deluminator; Diggory, Cedric; Dumbledore, Aberforth; Dumbledore, Ariana; Dumbledore's Army; grave(yard); Grindelwald, Gellert; "having and being"; Hogwarts alchemical symbolism; Horcruxes; King's Cross Station; Malfoy, Draco; Order of the Phoenix; persona and shadow; remorse; Riddle, Tom Marvolo; Skeeter, Rita; Snape, Severus
Dumbledore, Ariana 14, 56, 72, 89, 90, 91, 103, 176, 177, 183, 216, 217, 240; see also Dumbledore, Aberforth; Dumbledore, Albus; Grindelwald, Gellert
Dumbledore's Academy 23, 188, 189
Dumbledore's Army 20, 82, 169, 172, 173, 178, 202, 203, 205, 218, 250; see also Dumbledore, Albus; Granger, Hermione Jean
Durmstrang 13, 198
Dursley, Aunt Marge 38, 247
Dursley, Dudley 2, 14, 47, 48, 203, 219, 231, 235, 247, 248, 262, 269, 270, 279, 289
Dursley, Petunia Evans 2, 47, 52, 73, 181, 219, 248, 269, 288; see also Potter, Lily Evans
Dursley, Vernon 2, 4, 47, 48, 181, 195, 247, 248, 269
Dursleys: 1, 2, 3, 4, 5, 14, 15, 37, 48, 49, 52, 92, 145, 146, 162, 194, 222, 231, 235, 247, 248, 266, 267, 269, 279; see also Dursley, Aunt Marge; Dursley, Dudley; Dursley, Petunia Evans; Dursley, Vernon; number four, Privet Drive

eagle see Hogwarts House animals
Écrits see Lacan, Jacques
Edgecomb, Marietta 252
Egypt 10, 120, 121, 123, 126, 138, 209
The Egyptian Hermes see Fowden, Garth
Egyptian Religion: The Beliefs of Ancient Egypt Explored and Explained see Gahlin, Lucia
Ehrenreich, Barbara, and Diedre English: *Witches, Midwives, and Nurses: A History of Women Healers* 7, 25
Elder Wand 2–3, 12, 14, 17–18, 21, 108, 110, 128, 142, 157, 158, 166, 204, 205, 207, 234, 235, 254, 264, 270, 287; Death Stick 18, 241; of Destiny 18; see also wand
Eliade, Mircea: *The Forge and the Crucible* 14, 25, 190, 208; see also Ceaser, Cerena
Elixir of Life 3, 11, 30, 69, 70, 97, 104, 105, 141, 190, 192, 199, 200, 209, 210, 262
elm and dragon heartstring wand see wand
embalming 121
The Emerald Tablet see Hauck, Dennis William; see also Blavatsky, H.P.; Everard, John; Thoth
"Emotional Abuse: Destruction of the Spirit and the Sense of Self" see Keith-Oaks, Judy
Empedocles 9

enchanted cosmos see cosmos
Er see Plato
eros see love
Escape from Freedom see Fromm, Erich
eternal life 3, 8, 22, 24, 56, 70, 105, 112, 121, 122, 127, 134, 136, 137, 211, 240, 246, 247, 253, 254, 255, 256, 260, 261, 262; see also immortality
eudaimonia 237
Europe 1, 4, 5, 6, 7, 8, 17, 25, 143, 209, 290
Everard (Hogwarts Headmaster) 123
Everard, John 123; see also *Emerald Tablet*
Expelliarmus 199, 203, 204, 205, 207
"Experimental Corpuscular Theory in Aristotelian Alchemy: From Geber to Sennert" see Newman, William R.
extendable ears 217; see also Weasley, Fred and George
Eye of Horus see Horus
Eye of Horus Fractions see Stella, Benoît
Ezrin, Bob see Waters, Roger

Fabricius, Johannes: *Alchemy: The Medieval Alchemists and Their Royal Art* 263
fairy tales 4, 65, 66, 72
Fantasia 64
Fat Friar see Hogwarts ghosts
Fat Lady 216
Faust see Goethe
Fawkes (phoenix) 35, 125, 129, 131, 132, 133, 137, 163, 200, 201, 202, 213, 249, 263; see also gold; peacock; phoenix song; phoenix tears
Feather of Maat 121
Feist, Jess: *Theories of Personality* 81, 88, 96
Fenrir **203**
Ficino, Marsilio: *The Letters of Marsilio Ficino* 57, 58, 61; see also Della Stufa, Gismondo
Fiendfyre 201, 206, 250
fifth essence see Quintessence
Filch, Argus 51, 72, 73, 214; see also Mrs. Norris
Filibuster firework 198
Finch-Fletchley, Justin 128
Finnegan, Seamus 82
Finnegan's Wake see Joyce, James
Firebolt 216
Firenze see centaur
First Matter 11, 281
Fisher, Philip: *The Vehement Passions* 66, 67, 71, 75
Flame-Freezing Charm 7
Flamel, Nicolas 32, 33, 50, 104, 142, 258, 259, 260; see also Chocolate Frog; Dumbledore, Albus; Flamel, Perenelle; Philosopher's Stone
Flamel, Perenelle 1, 3, 13, 15, 134, 156, 211, 221; see also Chocolate Frog; Dumbledore, Albus; Flamel, Nicolas; Philosopher's Stone
Flaubert, Gustave: *Madame Bovary* 77
Fluffy 201, 212; see also Cerberus
Flying Red Dragon see Principe, Lawrence

300 Index

Forbidden Forest 43, 212, 241
Forbidden Planet 102
Forest of Dean 42
The Forge and the Crucible see Eliade, Mircea
Fortune, Dion: *The Mystical Qabalah* 50, 61
four elements (Earth, Air, Fire, Water) 9, 244, 280; *see also* Aristotle; Hogwarts alchemical symbolism
Four Treatises of Theophrastus Von Hohenheim see Paracelsus
Fowden, Garth: *The Egyptian Hermes* 122, 138
fox *see* Principe, Lawrence
Frankenstein see Mary Shelley
Freud, Sigmund 99–100, 229, 231; "having and being" 228; *Interpretation of Dreams* 61; id, ego, superego 98, 227, 102; Oedipus complex 100, 228; *see also* id, ego, superego; Oedipus complex
"Freud's 'On Narcissism: An Introduction'" *see* Crockatt, Philip
friendship 147, 148, 149; *see also* love
"From Abjection to Alchemy: Tolkien's Middle-earth Legendarium" *see* Brown, Sara
"From Azkaban to Abu Ghraib: Fear and Fascism in Harry Potter and the Order of the Phoenix" *see* Castro, Adam-Troy
Fromm, Erich: *Escape* 238, 239; *Loving* 237, 242; *To Have* 226, 227–28, 237, 240–41; *see also* "having and being"
Fudge, Cornelius 82, 125, 238, 250

Gahlin, Lucia: Egyptian Religion: The Beliefs of Ancient Egypt Explored and Explained 138
Gale, Dorothy 101
Galen 210
Galileo 288; *see also* Moran, Bruce
Garden of Eden 47, 48, 84
Gaunt, Marvolo 230; ring 152, 283, 287; *see also* Horcrux
Gaunt, Merope (Riddle) 18, 174–75, 257
ghost 68, 69, 72, 73, 75, 160, 161, 192, 222, 265; specter 64, 68, 75; *see also* Hogwarts ghosts
Glauber, Johann Rudolf: "Quintessence" 10, 11, 12; *The Works of the Highly Experienced and Famous Chymist* 25
Glaucon *see* Plato
Gloria Mundi 218
gnome(s) 199
Gnosis and Hermeticism from Antiquity to Modern Times see van den Broek, Roelof, and Wouter J. Hanegraaff
Goblin *see* Griphook
Goddard, David: *The Tower of Alchemy: An Advanced Guide to the Great Work* 210, 222
Godric's Hollow 33, 42; Potters' house 33, 119; *see also* Wright, Bowman
God's active work in the world 244–45; *see also* enchanted cosmos
God's Philosophers: How the Medieval World Laid the Foundations of Modern Science see Hannam, James
Goethe, Johann Wolfgang von: *Faust* 210, 224
gold 1, 24, 30, 32, 33, 35, 43, 69, 71, 93, 119n, 122, 128, 195, 199; as connection 15, 20, 158, 163–64, 200, 248, 252, 253, 259, 277, 278; Fawkes' beak and tail feathers 129, 137, 249, 263; golden chain 19, 217–18, 253; golden flames 20, 21, 110, 129, 156, 157, 165, 166, 263; golden light 20, 37, 164, 199, 263; Golden Snitch 23, 127, 191 192, 193–94, 198, 205, 206; material wealth 2, 13, 70, 73, 97, 100, 103, 104, 105, 118, 200, 209, 210, 263, 273, 277, 281; mercury and sulfur 9, 10, 12; personal transformation 8, 17, 23, 24, 34, 70, 79, 80, 96, 97, 118–19, 142, 143, 157, 197, 210–11, 219, 223, 244, 245, 247, 263, 273, 287; Philosopher's Stone 30, 34, 100, 104, 127, 128–29, 190; solid light 34; Weasley-Delacour wedding 34, 41, 43, 163; wisdom; *see also* Fawkes (the phoenix); Philosopher's Stone; Plato: Glaucon and Gyges' ring; *prima materia*; Principe, Lawrence; Snitch, Golden; *tria prima* (mercury, sulfur, salt); Weasley-Delacour wedding
Golden Snitch *see* Snitch, Golden
Goldenberg, Michael ix
Golpalott's Third Law 135, 157
Gorski, William T.: *Yeats and Alchemy* 32n, 44
Goyle, Gregory 206, 236; *see also* Crabbe, Vincent; Malfoy, Draco
grace 197, 203, 206, 207
"Grandma's Story" *see* Trinh, T. Minh-ha
Granger, Hermione Jean 13, 15, 16, 19, 20, 21, 28, 38, 42, 43, 49, 82–83, 85–86, 87, 88, 89, 94, 97, 104, 111, 112, 126, 127, 133, 135, 145, 147, 149, 150, 157, 160, 165, 172, 175, 176, 184, 186, 193, 197, 200, 201, 202, 204, 205, 216, 251, 258; Dumbledore's Army 250; house-elf liberation 178–80, 181, 185; as mercury 10, 12, 35, 124, 252–53, 287–88, 289, 290; Muggle-born 177–78, 179, 181, 220, 268, 274n; petrified 214, 221; quarreling couple 35, 37, 124, 216, 221, 234, 238; troll 148, 220; *see also* Dumbledore's Army; Hermes; mercury; petrification; quarreling couple; Society for the Promotion of Elfish Welfare; time turner; Weasley, Ron (Ronald Bilius); Weasley, Rose
Granger, John: "Aeschylus Epigraph" 289n, 290; "Alchemy 101" 1, 10, 14n, 16, 25; Hallows Lectures 42, 44; "PotterMore: J.K. Rowling Discusses Alchemical Colors" 33, 44; *Unlocking Harry Potter* 30n, 69, 70, 77, 148, 155, 245, 246, 252, 254, 256, 261, 262, 263; *Spell* 31, 36, 44
grave(yard) 40, 41, 42, 116, 163, 199, 204, 222, 230; *see also* Diggory, Cedric; Dobby; Dumbledore, Albus; Plato
Great Flood 119

Great Work 16, 19, 35, 37, 41, 59, 118, 124, 129, 131, 134, 136, 143–44, 198, 210, 224; Magnum Opus 142, 143, 153–54; Royal Art 210–11, 263; *see also* Philosopher's Stone
Greece 1, 4, 8, 9, 25, 100, 119, 123, 145–46, 151, 201, 212, 237, 265, 266, 267, 280
Green Lion 1
Greig, Georgie: *Tatler Magazine* 224
Grey Lady *see* Hogwarts ghosts; Ravenclaw, Helena
Greyback, Fenrir 35, 87; *see also* werewolf
grief 1, 16, 17, 56, 57, 60, 61, 63, 65, 66, 67, 68, 69, 70, 71, 72, 73, 74, 75, 76, 77; stages of 23, 78, 90, 103, 151, 152, 159, 160, 162, 163, 175, 176, 177, 182, 199, 217, 222, 284, 290; *see also* Kübler-Ross, Elisabeth; Lewis, C.S.
A Grief Observed see Lewis, C.S.
Grimes, M. Katherine *see* Whited, Lana A.
Grindelwald, Gellert 204, 205; *see also* Dumbledore, Aberforth; Dumbledore, Albus; Dumbledore, Ariana
Gringotts *see* Lestrange vault
Griphook 175, 185, 263
Groves, Beatrice: *Literary Allusion in Harry Potter* 31, 36, 44
Gryffindor, Godric *see* Hogwarts founders
Gryffindor House *see* Hogwarts houses
Gryffindor, Sword of 23, 136, 192, 201, 202, 204, 207, 249, 289; *see also* Horcruxes; lightning scar
Guarino, Ben: "This Chemist Is Unlocking the Secrets of Alchemy" 9, 25; *see also* Principe, Lawrence
Guattari, Felix *see* Deleuze, Giles
Gyges' Ring *see* Plato

Hagrid, Rubeus 2, 3, 4, 15, 20, 21, 24, 40, 49, 52, 69, 72, 80, 81, 92, 93, 125, 126, 145, 149, 161, 177, 179, 180, 200, 215, 219, 220, 252, 256, 257, 267, 276, 281; Care of Magical Creatures 198, 212, 213; Fluffy 201, 212; gamekeeper 212; half-giant 43, 63, 214; Keeper of the Keys 200; *rubedo* 33, 43, 89, 280; *see also* alchemical stages; Hogwarts alchemical symbolism; St. Peter
Half-blood Prince *see* Snape, Severus
Hall, Manly P.: *The Secret Teachings of All Ages* 142–43, 145
Hallows *see* Deathly Hallows
Hamilton, Nigel: "The Alchemical Process of Transformation" 4, 9, 25
Hanegraaff, Wouter J. *see* van den Broek, Roelof
Hannam, James: *God's Philosophers: How the Medieval World Laid the Foundations of Modern Science* 246, 251, 263
Harpur, Patrick: *The Philosophers' Secret Fire: A History of the Imagination* 213, 217–18, 224; *see also* imagination
Harrington, Janice N.: "Before a Screen Door" 63, 77

Harry Potter: A History of Magic (British Library) *see* Pavord, Anna
Harry Potter & Imagination: The Way Between Two Worlds see Prinzi, Travis
"Harry Potter and the Acquisition of Knowledge" *see* Hopkins, Lisa
"Harry Potter and the Greatest Virtue" *see* St. Hilaire, Jenna
"Harry Potter and the Post-Traumatic Stress Disorder Counselor" *see* Lackey, Mercedes
"Harry Potter and the Young Man's Mistake: The Illusion of Innocence and the Temptation of Power" *see* Moloney, Daniel P.
Harry Potter for Nerds: Essays for Fans, Academics, and Lit Geeks see Prinzi, Travis
Harry Potter for Nerds II: Essays for Fans, Academics, and Lit Geeks see Prinzi, Travis, and Kathryn N. McDaniel
"Harry Potter, Radical Feminism, and the Power of Love" *see* Smith, Anne Collins
"Harry Potter's World as a Morality Tale of Technology and Media" *see* Sheltrown, Nicholas
Hauck, Dennis William: "AZoth Ritual" 125, 129, 138; *Emerald* Tablet 118, 119n, 138; *Sorcerer's* Stone 109n, 125, 127, 129, 138
"having and being" moral identity 227–28, 229, 232, 233, 234, 236–37, 239, 241–42; *see also* Dumbledore, Albus; Fromm, Erich
Hedwig 153, 222; *see also* St. Hedwig
Heine, Friedrich Wilhelm *203*, 208
Heir of Slytherin 125, 126, 258
Heisenberg Uncertainty Principle 99
Heliopolis 122
The Herald see Simpson, Anne
Heraldic colors *see* Hogwarts Houses heraldic colors
Herbology (class) 9, 33, 111, 199, 212, 214, 224
"Here Be Dragons (and Phoenixes)" *see* Whited, Lana A.
Hermaphrodite 34, 131, 195; *see also* Rebis
Hermes 35, 123, 124, 138; Pillars of 119; rod or caduceus 47, 127, 128, 132, 133; Trismegistus 123, 127, 211, 217; *see also* Granger, Hermione Jean; Snitch, Golden; Thoth
Hermes' rod *see* Hermes
Hermes Trismegistus (the Thrice Great) *see* Hermes
Hermeticism 16, 25, 30, 32, 35, 36, 39, 96, 123, 127, 208, 210
"Hermione and the House Elves" *see* Carey, Brycchan
Hermopolis (Temple of Thoth) 126
Hero with a Thousand Faces see Campbell, Joseph
"Heroic Hermione: Celebrating the Love of Learning" *see* Shade, Patrick
heron 123
"Hey You" *see* Waters, Roger

Highfield, Roger: *The Science of Harry Potter: How Magic Really Works* 245, 263
hippogriff 213, 214; Buckbeak 35, 214, 216, 221; *see also* Malfoy, Draco
"'His Majesty the Baby': Narcissism and Royal Authority" *see* Schwartz, Peter Hammond
History of Magic (class) 9
A History of Magic see Bagshot, Bathilda
hoarding 13, 228, 230, 213
Hod, the Sephirah 50
Hogsmeade 42, 216, 272
Hogwarts Alchemical symbolism Black (*nigredo*) Stage 37, 38, 39, 40, 41 42, 129, 133; Red (*rubedo*) Stage 35, 38, 39, 40, 41, 42, 43, 129; White (*albedo*) Stage 35, 37, 38, 39, 40, 41, 90, 129; Yellow (*citrinintas*) Stage 35; *see also* Black, Sirius; Dumbledore, Albus; four elements (Earth, Air, Fire, Water); Hagrid, Rubeus
Hogwarts Castle 43, 65, 125, 131, 215, 216, 249, 255, 257, 266
Hogwarts Express 1, 14, 76, 93, 111, 172, 195, 232, 273, 274
Hogwarts Founders: Godric Gryffindor 21, 35, 43, 193, 201, 230, 231, 278, 284; Helga Hufflepuff 21, 170, 278, 284; Rowena Ravenclaw 21, 170, 202, 205, 206, 278, 284; Salazar Slytherin 21, 35, 43, 94, 125, 126, 128, 131, 132, 230, 231, 232, 237, 256, 257, 258, 276, 278, 284, 287
Hogwarts Ghosts 65, 266; The Grey Lady (Helena Ravenclaw) 128, 256, 128, 256; Nearly Headless Nick 213; *see also* ghost
Hogwarts Great Hall 35, 36, 128, 134, 215, 267
Hogwarts House animals: Gryffindor lion 198; Hufflepuff badger 199; Ravenclaw eagle 198; Slytherin snake 201
Hogwarts Houses: Gryffindor 22, 28, 35, 37, 41, 43, 93, 94, 112, 136, 148, 150, 172, 192, 193, 194, 198, 205, 207, 231, 240, 275, 277, 278, 284; Hufflepuff 22, 34, 136, 199, 205, 275, 276, 277, 278, 284; Ravenclaw 22, 35, 93, 136, 198, 205, 275, 277, 284; Slytherin 22, 35, 37, 41, 43, 84, 86, 88, 92, 93, 94, 136, 193, 198, 199, 205, 206, 230, 231, 232, 237, 249, 250, 258, 269, 275, 276, 277, 278, 284, 287
Hogwarts Houses Heraldic colors and elements: Gryffindor red, gold, fire 10, 22, 35, 135, 198, 199, 250; Hufflepuff black, yellow, earth 22, 34, 135, 199, 250; Ravenclaw blue, air 22, 35, 135, 198, 250; Slytherin green, water 22, 35, 135, 198, 250
Hogwarts letter 2, 22, 49, 50, 55, 92, 192, 195
Hogwarts Library 97, 212; Restricted Section 50, 117
Hogwarts Quidditch teams: Gryffindor 85, 112, 150, 192, 193–94, 195, 198, 205; Hufflepuff 205; Ravenclaw 194, 205; Slytherin 86, 191, 205, 206, 269
Hokey 256
Holy Spirit 200, 202

homo faber 190
Hopkins, Lisa: "Harry Potter and the Acquisition of Knowledge" 235, 242
Horcruxes 135, 136, 137, 165, 166, 192, 201, 202, 204, 205, 206, 207, 258, 289; *see also* Dumbledore, Albus; Gaunt, Tom Marvolo; Horus cross; Voldemort
Horkheimer, Max W. *see* Adorno, Theodor
horse and seahorse 213
Horus 120, 121, 126; cross 121; Eye of 19, **134**, **135**, 136, **137**, 138, 139; Horcrux 120, 121; *see also* Seth
House of Black 38, 42, 181; family tree 163–64; *see also* number twelve, Grimmauld Place
Hufflepuff's cup *see* Horcruxes
Hughes, Jonathan: *The Rise of Alchemy in Fourteenth-Century England: Plantagenet Kings and the Search for the Philosopher's Stone* 244, 245, 246, 251
human genius *see* Matthews, Susan R.
Hungarian horntail *see* dragon

Iamblichus: *On the Mysteries see* Taylor, Thomas
Iberian Peninsula 1
"Ich Bin Ein Hufflepuff: Strategies for Multiple Skill Management in J.K. Rowling's Novels" *see* Matthews, Susan R.
id, ego, superego: ego 36, 79, 80, 92, 94, 149, 227, 237, 255, 261; id 98, 102; superego 98; *see also* Freud, Sigmund
imagination 4, 5, 10, 20, 78, 106, 141, 145, 168–69, 171, 172–74, 181, 184, 185, 188, 218, 226, 266, 280, 281; *see also* Harpur, Patrick; Prinzi, Travis, and Kathryn N. McDaniel; *Very Good Lives* (Rowling)
immortality 1, 19, 20, 30, 69, 70, 73, 74, 77, 82, 85, 97, 104, 118, 119, 127, 128, 129, 132, 140, 144, 153, 156, 160, 164, 190, 192, 194, 200, 203, 209, 211, 212, 221, 232, 233, 246, 260, 287; *see also* eternal life
Imperious curse 238
India 1
Inferi 175
Inklings *see* Lewis, C.S.
Internet Sacred Text Archives see Ophiolatreia
The Interpretation of Dreams see Freud, Sigmund
Introductory Readings in Ancient Greek and Roman Philosophy see Reeve, C.D.C., and Patrick Lee Miller
Invisibility Cloak *see* Deathly Hallows
Ireland 32, 191
"Is Ambition a Virtue? Why Slytherin Belongs at Hogwarts" *see* Patterson, Stephen W.
"Is Desire Beneficial or Harmful in the Harry Potter Series?" *see* Piippo, Taija
Isis 120–21, 123, 126, 136, 138
Isis Unveiled see Blavatsky, H.P.

Index 303

James, Jamie: *The Music of the Spheres: Music, Science and the Natural Order of the Universe* 284
James, William: "On a Certain Blindness in Human Beings" 20, 169–70, 171–72, 186
Jewel of Eternity *see* Philosopher's Stone
Jewish 6, 208
Jobs, Steve 100
"John Steinbeck: A Literary Biography" *see* Lisca, Peter
Joost-Gaugier, Christiane L.: *Measuring Heaven: Pythagoras and His Influence on Thought and Art in Antiquity and the Middle Ages* 279–80, 284
Jorkins, Bertha 234, 256
Jörmungandr **203**
Joyce, James: *Finnegan's Wake* 1, 32; *see also* DiBernard, Barbara
Juhasz, Suzanne: *Reading from the Heart: Women, Literature, and the Search for True Love* 60, 61
Jung, Carl G. 14, 17, 81, 82 *Alchemical Studies* 98, 113, 208; anima and animus 80, 198 *Basic Writings* 79, 80, 90, 95, 96; *Memories, Dreams, Reflections* 79; *Mysterium Coniunctionis* 97, 98, 112; *Psyche* 84, 96 *Psychological Types* 85, 86; *Psychology and Religion* 96; *see also* persona and shadow; psyche
Jung's Map of the Soul: An Introduction see Stein, Murray
Jupiter, King of gods 129, **130**, 131, 138; peacock 129, **130**, 131, 133; *see also* Fawkes
"Just Another Brick in the Wall" *see* Waters, Roger

Kampf der untergehenden Götter see Battle of the Doomed Gods
Karkaroff, Igor 238
Keeper of the Keys *see* Hagrid, Rubeus
Keith-Oaks, Judy: "Emotional Abuse: Destruction of the Spirit and the Sense of Self" 247, 263
Kets de Vries, Manfred: *The Leader on the Couch: A Clinical Approach to Changing People and Organizations* 51, 61
Khem 10, 11, 281
Kibre, Pearl: "Albertus Magnus on Alchemy" 244, 263; *see also* Magnus, Alberto
Killing Curse *see* Avada Kedavra
King's Cross Station 13, 17, 36, 56, 64, 89, 106, 121, 137, 163, 174, 207, 216, 217, 220, 222, 224; *see also* Dumbledore, Albus
Kingston, Maxine Hong: *The Woman Warrior: Memoir of a Girlhood Among Ghosts* 265–66, 284
Klein, Melanie 219, 227; *see also* Meltzer, Donald
Knight Bus 177; *see also* Shunpike, Stan
Knowledge and Power: Science in World History see Burns, William E.

Kohlberg, Lawrence 229–30, 243
Kreacher 175, 181, 289
Kripal, Jeffrey: *The Serpent's Gift: Gnostic Reflections on the Study of Religion* 49, 61
Krum, Viktor 198–99, 206
Kübler-Ross, Elisabeth: "Stages of Grief" 66; *see also* grief

labyrinth *see* Triwizard Tournament
Lacan, Jacques: *Écrits* 227, 242
Lackey, Mercedes "Counselor" 66, 78; *Mapping the World of the Sorcerer's Apprentice* 25, 186, 243, 284
Laërtius, Diogenes: *Lives of Eminent Philosophers* 265, 284
lead 9, 30, 32, 34, 70, 118–19, 142, 288; Harry Potter as 5, 10, 11, 17, 80, 263; lightning shape 9; white (Albus Dumbledore) 54, 166; *see also* Dumbledore Albus; lightning scar
The Leader on the Couch: A Clinical Approach to Changing People and Organizations see Kets de Vries, Manfred
The Leaky Cauldron 20, 50, 92, 168, 177, 288
"The Leaky Cauldron and Mugglenet Interview Joanne Kathleen Rowling: Part Three" *see* Anelli, Melissa, and Emerson Spartz
Lectures on Literature see Nabokov, Vladimir Vladimirovich
L'Engle, Madeleine: *A Wrinkle in Time* 75
Leo (constellation) 198
Lestrange, Bellatrix (née Black) 66, 87, 149, 259
Lestrange vault 263
The Letters of Marsilio Ficino see Ficino, Marsilio.
Lewis, C.S.: *A Grief Observed* 78; Inklings 147; *Narnia* 31, 32, 75, 221; *see also* Donegality; grief; Londonness
Libavius, Andreas 8, 244–45; *see also* Moran, Bruce
Liber Al vel Legis see Crowley, Aleister
The Library of History see Siculus, Diodorus
The Life and Lies of Albus Dumbledore see Skeeter, Rita
light 17, 32, 36, 37, 57, 71; golden 20; lunar 34, 36, 37, 41; from shadow 79, 82, 83, 86, 87, 88, 96; solar 9, 41; solar and lunar wedding 41, 127; solid light (gold) 34; *see also* Lovegood, Luna; Lunar Queen; Plato; Solar King; Weasley-Delacour wedding
lightning scar 9, 92, 202, 207, 219; *see also* Gryffindor, sword of; lead; Thor
"Liminal Places and Liminal States in John Crowley's *Little, Big*" *see* Bosky, Bernadette Lynn
liminality 13, 23, 191, 195, 197, 199, 201, 204, 206, 207, 208
Linden, Stanton: *Darke Hieroglyphicks: Alchemy in English Literature from Chaucer to the Restoration* 30n, 32, 44

lion *see* Hogwarts House animals
Lisca, Peter: "John Steinbeck: A Literary Biography" 77, 78; *see also* Steinbeck, John
literary alchemy 16, 30, 31, 36, 39, 44; *see also* ring composition
Literary Allusion in Harry Potter see Groves, Beatrice
Little, Big see Bosky, Bernadette Lynn
Lives of Eminent Philosophers see Laërtius, Diogenes
Lockhart, Gilderoy 126, 137, 251
Lolita see Nabokov, Vladimir
London Underground 75
Londonness 32; *see also* Lewis, C.S.
Longbottom, Neville 19, 42–43, 111, 125, 147, 158, 192–93, 198, 200, 201, 202, 204, 218, 223, 234, 252–53, 257, 258; *see also* prophecy orb; Remembrall
love 12, 15, 17, 19, 20, 42, 43, 51, 52, 54, 55, 56, 57, 58, 73, 74, 76, 77, 80, 84, 87, 136, 137, 140, 144, 154, 155, 158, 159, 160, 174, 175, 237, 240, 241, 246, 247, 248, 256, 266, 290 *Agape* 146, 151, 152, 153, 263; affection (*Storge*) 145–46; children's tales, loyalty, and innocence 5, 14, 15, 289; *Eros* 53, 146, 148, 149, 150; friendship (*Philia*) 146, 147, 148, 149, 212, 252; Lily's for Harry 3, 15, 60, 124, 141, 162, 163, 168, 192, 203, 229, 249, 254, 255, 256, 290; missing element 19, 118, 134, 136; most powerful magic 83, 128, 153, 176, 222, 242; potion 18, 174, 175, 250, 251, 257; of power 19, 140, 141, 176, 261, 283; Snape's for Lily 33, 60, 73, 87, 88, 90, 116, 150, 151, 152, 206, 224, 272, 277; *see also* friendship
"Love Is the Strongest Family Tie" *see* Chan, Deborah M.
love potion *see* love
"Love Potion No. 9¾" *see* Bassham, Gregory
Lovegood, Luna 148, 253; friends 19, 164, 218, 253; lunar (moon) 37, 41; Patronus 19, 147, 223–24; *see also* light; Lovegood, Xenophilius; moon (lunar); sun (solar); Weasley-Delacour wedding
Lovegood, Xenophilius 19, 41; *see also* Lovegood, Luna; *The Quibbler*; Weasley-Delacour wedding
Lubac, Henri: *Scripture in the Tradition* 200, 208
Luke 246
Lumos Foundation 153, 155
Lupin, Remus John 38, 43, 106, 196, 197, 203, 217, 221, 272, 277; Moony 216; shade of 21, 203, 223, 287, 290; *see also* Lupin, Teddy; Marauders; Tonks, Nymphadora; werewolf
Lupin, Teddy 248; *see also* Lupin, Remus John; philosophical orphan; Tonks, Nymphadora
Lysis see Plato

Maar, Michael: "Why Nabokov Would Have Liked Harry Potter" 31

Maat *see* feather of Maat
Madame Bovary see Flaubert, Gustave
Magic and Alchemy: Mysteries, Legends, and Unexplained Phenomena see Place, Robert M.
Magic Is Might 42
Magnum Opus 142, 153; *see also* Great Work; Philosopher's Stone
Magnus, Albertus 244; *see also* Kibre, Pearl
Maier, Michael: *Atlanta Fugiens* 46, 47, 54, 59, 61
Malfoy, Draco 28–29, 92, 93, 94, 111, 112, 177, 193, 197, 201, 206, 210, 214, 259, 271; Dumbledore's death 88, 91, 152, 204, 288; *see also* Buckbeak; Crabbe, Vincent; Dumbledore, Albus; Goyle, Gregory
Malfoy, Lucius 21, 29, 125, 149, 157–58, 165, 180, 201, 230, 253, 259, 268, 271, 276–77
Malfoy, Narcissa (née Black) 29, 147, 180, 230, 253, 268, 289; *see also* Narcissus; Naso, Quintus Ovidius
Malfoy Manor 19, 175, 185, 277
Malleus Maleficarum (The Hammer of Witches) 7
mandrake 214–15; *see also* basilisk; petrification; Sprout, Pomona
map 170, 244; London Underground 75; Marauder's 216, 230
Mapping the World of the Sorcerer's Apprentice: Science Fiction and Fantasy Writers Explore the Bestselling Fantasy Series of All Time see Lackey, Mercedes
Marauders (Moony, Wormtail, Padfoot, Prongs) 216; *see also* Black, Sirius; Lupin, Remus John; Pettigrew, Peter; Potter, James
Mars (red planet) 213, 280–81; *see also* centaur
Marvell, Andrew 63
Marvolo Gaunt's ring *see* Gaunt, Marvolo
Marx, Karl 109–10; *Capital: A Critique of Political Economy* 100*n*, 113; Marxists 108; *see also* MCM
The Master and His Emissary see McGilchrist, Iain
master of death 13, 20, 23, 74, 154, 205, 207, 254, 262
Matthew 232
Matthews, Susan R.: "Ich Bin Ein Hufflepuff: Strategies for Multiple Skill Management in J.K. Rowling's Novels" 21, 25, 277–78, 284
McDaniel, Kathryn N. *see* Prinzi, Travis
McGilchrist, Iain: *The Master and His Emissary* 210, 224
McGonagall, Minerva 3, 75, 148, 193, 195, 216, 220, 238; tabby cat animagus 4; *see also* animagus
McGonigal, Jane: *Reality Is Broken: Why Games Make Us Better and How They Can Change the World* 190, 208
MCM 108–09, 110; *see also* Marx, Karl
Measuring Heaven: Pythagoras and His

Influence on Thought and Art in Antiquity and the Middle Ages see Joost-Gaugier, Christiane L.
Medieval Science and Technology *see* Whitney, Elspeth
Meltzer, Donald: *Sexual States of Mind* 219, 224; *see also* Klein, Melanie
Memories, Dreams, Reflections see Jung, Carl G.
Mendlesohn, Farah: "Crowning the King: Harry Potter and the Construction of Authority" 236, 242
Mephistopheles *see* Goethe
Merchant, Carolyn: *The Death of Nature: Women, Ecology, and the Scientific Revolution* 6–7, 25
mercury (element) 9–10, 40, 127, 244–45, 273; Hermione Granger Hg 35, 252; *prima materia* 244, 288; quarreling couple (sulfur and mercury) 34, 35; *tria prima* (mercury, sulfur, salt) 11, 129, 290; *see also* alchemical wedding; gold; Mercury (god); *prima materia*; *tria prima* (mercury, sulfur, salt)
Mercury (god) 12; *see also* mercury (element); Snitch, Golden
mermaids *see* merpeople
mermen *see* merpeople
merpeople 198, 213
Merton, Thomas 140, 154
"A Meta Model for the Unifying of Psychological Theories" *see* Zerin, Edward, and Marjory Zerin
Metamorphoses see Naso, Quintus Ovidius
Meyer, Stephenie: *Twilight* 34
Mickey Mouse 64
Miller, Patrick Lee *see* Reeve, C.D.C.
Ministry of Magic 82, 169, 192, 194, 215, 252, 274*n*; Harry's trial 112
Mirror of Erised 2, 3, 16, 50–51, 52–53, 55–56, 59–60, 61 195, 19, 113, 145, 195, 236, 237–38, 289; Dumbledore and socks 14; Harry's family 14, 51–52, 54, 58, 68–69, 103; Philosopher's Stone 105; Ron glorified 14, 103; *see also* Quirrell, Professor
missing element *see* love
Moaning Myrtle 125, 126, 206, 256
Moloney, Daniel P.: "Harry Potter and the Young Man's Mistake: The Illusion of Innocence and the Temptation of Power" 18, 25, 242–43
monkey 126; *see also* Thoth
Montagues and Capulets *see* Shakespeare
Moody, Alastor (Mad-Eye) 120, 122, 157, 238; *see also* Crouch, Barty, Jr.
moon/lunar 36–37, 41, 214, 280–81; Bendis 265, 266; Lunar Queen 131; *see also* Lovegood, Luna; Plato; sun/solar; Weasley, Ginny (Ginevra); Weasley-Delacour wedding
Moony *see* Mauraders
Moran, Bruce T.: *Distilling Knowledge:*

Alchemy, Chemistry, and the Scientific Revolution 5, 6, 8, 11, 25, 69, 78, 98, 103–04, 113, 273, 279, 280, 284, 288, 290; *see also* Galileo; Libavius, Andreas
More Fruits of Solitude see Penn, William
Moses 217
"Mother" *see* Waters, Roger
Mrs. Cole 81, 159; *see also* orphanage
Mrs. Norris 51, 72, 214; *see also* Filch, Argus
"Mudblood" *see* Muggle
Muggle 2, 13, 33, 35, 48, 50, 56, 69, 73, 84, 97, 103, 131, 140, 146, 159, 162, 172, 174–75, 176, 177; "Mudblood" 73, 177, 181, 185, 187; Muggle Studies (class) 9, 20, 43, 178, 179, 194, 195, 197, 201, 215, 220, 231, 259, 288, 289; post 22, 49; protection legislation 89; *see also* Burbage, Charity
Muggle Studies (class) *see* Muggle
Murphy, G. Ronald: *The Owl, the Raven, and the Dove: The Religious Meaning of the Grimms' Magic Fairy Tales* 200, 208
The Music of the Spheres: Music, Science and the Natural Order of the Universe see James, Jamie
Muslims 6, 280
Mysterium Coniunctionis: An Inquiry Into the Separation and Synthesis of Psychic Opposites in Alchemy see Jung, Carl G.
The Mystical Qabalah see Fortune, Dion
myth of Er *see* Plato

Nabokov, Vladimir Vladimirovich 16, 30, 31, 32, 44, 45; "The Aurelian" 32; *Lectures on Literature* 30–31, 31*n*, 45; *Lolita* 31
"Nabokov's Alchemical Pale Fire" *see* Abraham, Lyndy
Nabokov's Otherworld see Alexandrov, Vladimir E.
Nāga 288, 290
Nagini 42, 43, 84, 94–95, 135, 137 193, 202, 206, 223, 252, 287–88; *see also* Horcruxes
Naneferkaptah, Prince 122
Narcissus (myth of) *see also* Malfoy, Narcissa (née Black); Naso, Quintus Ovidius
"The Narrative Quality of Experience" *see* Crites, Stephen
Naso, Quintus Ovidius: *Metamorphoses* 52–53, 55, 61; Narcissus 53–54; *see also* Malfoy, Narcissa; Narcissus (myth of)
Näsström, Britt-Mari: "The Rites in the Mysteries of Dionysus: The Birth of Drama" 267, 284
Nearly-Headless Nick (Sir Nicholas de Mimsey-Porpington) *see* Hogwarts ghosts
Newman, William R.: "Experimental Corpuscular Theory in Aristotelian Alchemy: From Geber to Sennert" 245, 264
Nollius, Heinrich: *Theoria Philosophiae Hermeticae* 208; *see also* Rebis

306   Index

number four, Privet Drive 1–2, 4, 14, 21, 37–38, 64, 94, 152, 194, 195, 217, 222, 235, 247, 266, 269; *see also* Dursley
number twelve, Grimmauld Place 181, 217; *see also* House of Black
Nummedal, Tara: "Alchemy and Religion in Christian Europe" 8, 25

Occlumency 83, 151; *see also* Snape, Severus
Odin **203**
Odysseus *see* Plato
Oedipus complex 98, 100; *see also* Deleuze, Giles, and Felix Guattari; Freud, Sigmund
Oedipus Tyrannus see Sophocles
Ollivander: prisoner 19, 158, 164; Wand Shop 18; *see also* Malfoy Manor
"On a Certain Blindness in Human Beings" *see* James, William
Ophiolatreia 127, 138
The Order of the Phoenix 82, 86, 217, 251; *see also* Dumbledore, Albus
Orphanage 81, 82, 83, 136, 159, 160, 256; *see also* Benson, Amy; Bishop, Dennis; Mrs. Cole
Orpheus 60, 217
Osiris 120–21, 126
Ovid *see* Naso, Quintus Ovidius
The Owl, the Raven, and the Dove: The Religious Meaning of the Grimms' Magic Fairy Tales see Murphy, G. Ronald

Padfoot *see* animagus; Black, Sirius; Marauders
Paracelsus: *Four Treatises of Theophrastus Von Hohenheim* 10, 11, 198, 199, 208, 210, 279; *see also* Chocolate Frog
Paris 142; May 1968 protests 106, 107*n*
Parker, Joe: "The Chiastic Structure of Harry Potter" 45
Parseltongue 47, 94, 125, 126, 128, 131, 201, 204, 237
The Passion of New Eve see Carter, Angela
The Passion of the Western Mind: Understanding the Ideas That Have Shaped Our World View see Tarnas, Richard
Patronus 19, 64, 147, 196–97, 201; Kingsley Shacklebolt's lynx 41; Prongs 221; silver doe 87, 151, 201; *see also* Potter, James; Potter, Lily Evans; Shacklebolt, Kingsley; Snape, Severus
Patterson, Steven W. 21, 25, 276, 278, 284
Pavord, Anna: *Harry Potter: A History of Magic* (British Library) 214, 224
peacock *see* Jupiter
pelican 133
Penn, William: *More Fruits of Solitude* 191, 290
Pentecost 200, 202
persona and shadow 17, 79–80, 84–85, 86, 88, 90–92, 94, 95–96; *see also* Dumbledore, Albus; Jung, Carl G.; Voldemort

Personality Types: Jung's Model of Typology see Sharp, Daryl
Petrie, W.M. Flanders: *Ancient Egypt, vol. 1* 121, 122, 138
petrification 126, 213, 214, 221; *see also* basilisk; Granger, Hermione Jean; mandrake
Pettigrew, Peter 38, 197, 203, 222, 277; Wormtail 162, 216, 259; *see also* animagus; Marauders
Peverell brothers 12, 283 Antioch (Wand) 12; Cadmus (Stone) 12, 13, 135, 137, 201; Ignotus (Cloak) 12, 24, 283–84; "Tale of the Three Brothers" 12, 24, 204, 281, 283; *see also* Plato: Myth of Er
The Philosophers' Secret Fire: A History of the Imagination see Harpur, Patrick
Philosopher's Stone 1, 2, 9, 12, 13, 17, 23, 30, 34, 39, 40, 46, 54, 69, 73, 79, 97, 98, 99, 100, 113, 118, 123, 124, 128–29, 138, 141, 142, 190, 192, 195, 201, 204, 209, 210, 211, 217, 218, 220, 245, 246, 255, 289, 290; Great Work 16, 198; Harry Potter as 35–36, 81, 197, 199, 200; Jewel of Eternity 211, 222; rosy pink 10; Snitch/Remembrall as 85, 193, 194; *see also* Dumbledore, Albus; Flamel, Nicolas; Flamel, Perenelle; gold; Great Work; *prima materia*; Quirrell, Professor; resurrection stone; secret fire; *tria prima* (mercury, sulfur, salt); Weasley, Rose
philosophical orphan 34, 39, 43; *see also* Lupin, Teddy
phoenix feather and holly wand *see* wand
phoenix feather and yew wand *see* wand
phoenix song 35, 41, 156, 157, 164–65; *see also* Fawkes
phoenix tears 19, 133, 202, 213; *see also* Fawkes
physis 5, 97
Piippo, Taija: "Is Desire Beneficial or Harmful in the Harry Potter Series?" 236, 243
Pillars of Hermes *see* Hermes
Pink Floyd 20, 168, 169, 173, 174, 176, 181, 182, 183, 184; *see also* Waters, Roger
Place, Robert M.: *Magic and Alchemy* 191, 205, 208; *The Tarot* 195, 208
Planet Narnia see Ward, Michael
Plato: Aether 9, 280; *Apology* 236, 243, 284; Ariston 265, 274; Bendis 265; Cave 17, 81, 82, 83, 86, 87, 278, 279; Darius' gold 277; Er 24, 230, 281, 283; Glaucon 81, 82, 265, 266–67, 268, 269, 270, 271, 272, 274, 278–79; Gyges' Ring 246, 270; *Lysis* 277, 284; Myth of Metals 273, 274, 274*n*, 275; *Republic* 24, 96, 265, 284; Socrates 81, 82, 83, 86, 236, 265, 266–67, 269–71, 272, 273, 274, 275, 277, 278, 279, 281, 282, 283, 284; *Symposium* 197; *Timaeus* 9, 274, 280, 289; *see also* astronomy; cave; celestial; gold; grave(yard); light; moon (lunar); Peverell brothers; wall

Index   307

Polkis, Piers 48
Polyjuice Potion 220, 253
Pomfrey, Poppy 214
Postman, Neil: *Amusing Ourselves to Death: Public Discourse in the Age of Show Business* 240, 243
Postmodernism 5n, 14n, 26, 98, 101, 103, 106, 107, 112–13
Post-Potter Depression (PPD) 67, 78
Potions (class) 9, 22, 33, 116, 117, 135, 157, 212; *see also* Advanced Potion Making
Potter, Albus Severus 43, 87, 248, 250, 278, 284
Potter, James 194, 197, 200, 221–22, 277; Invisibility Cloak 108, 284; Prongs 16, 197, 216; Snape, Severus 86–87, 88, 152, 201, 224; *see also* animagus; Black, Sirius; Deathly Hallows; grave(yard); Lupin, Remus John; Marauders; Patronus; Pettigrew, Peter; Potter, Lily Evans
Potter, Lily Evans 52, 60, 192, 194, 222, 277, 278, 288; and Petunia Evans Dursley 72–73, 288; self-sacrifice 43, 107, 134, 141, 163, 176, 185, 192, 194; and Severus Snape 33, 60, 73, 87–88, 116–17, 150, 151, 152, 185, 201, 224, 272, 277–78; *see also* Dursley, Petunia Evans; Mirror of Erised; Patronus; Pettigrew, Peter; Potter, James; Snape, Severus
Potters' house *see* Godric's Hollow
prima materia (prime matter) 10, 11, 34, 36, 118, 129, 195, 218, 244, 245, 246, 288; *see also* gold; *tria prima* (mercury, sulfur, salt)
prime substance *see prima materia*
Principe, Lawrence 9; *see also* gold; Guarino, Ben
Prinzi, Travis: *Harry Potter & Imagination: The Way Between Two Worlds* 5, 65, 78, 96; *Harry Potter for Nerds* 264; *Harry Potter for Nerds* II (with McDaniel, Kathryn N.) 263; *see also* Chan, Deborah M.; imagination; Sweeney, Erin
Prongs *see* animagus; Marauders; Potter, James
the prophecy 38, 108, 158–59, 175–76, 192, 251–53, 257; Ministry of Magic 192; *see also* Longbottom, Neville; prophecy orb
prophecy orb 192–93; *see also* Longbottom, Neville; the prophecy; Remembrall; Snitch; Golden
"Prophetic Thought in Postmodern Times" *see* West, Cornel
Pseudodoxia Epidemica see Browne, Thomas
psyche 67n, 79, 81, 84–85, 96, 98, 102; *see also* Deleuze, Gilles, and Felix Guattari; Jung, Carl G.
pumpkin pasties 220
Pyrites, Argo 33

Quakers 191, 204
quarreling couple 34, 35, 37; *see also* Granger, Hermione; mercury; sulfur; Weasley, Ron

The Quibbler 6; *see also* Lovegood, Xenophilius
Quidditch 38, 40, 65, 105, 127, 170, 172, 191, 192, 193, 194, 195, 196–97, 199, 201, 203–04, 205–06, 220–21, 250, 253; World Cup 178, 191, 199, 206, 215; *see also* Hogwarts Quidditch teams
Quiditich World Cup *see* Quidditch
Quintessence *see* Rupescissa, John of
Quintessence (Fifth essence) 8, 9, **11**, 13, 118, 136, 288; *see also* celestial
Quintessence: A Quest 8, 135
Quirrell, Professor 3, 58, 60, 123, 124, 141, 159, 162, 197, 231, 232, 234, 251, 268, 290; *see also* Mirror of Erised; Philosopher's Stone; Voldemort

Ragnarök 202
Ramses 122
Ravenclaw, Helena *see* Hogwarts ghosts
Ravenclaw, Rowena *see* Hogwarts founders
Ravenclaw's Diadem *see* Horcruxes
Reading from the Heart: Women, Literature, and the Search for True Love see Juhasz, Suzanne
Reality Is Broken: Why Games Make Us Better and How They Can Change the World see McGonigal, Jane
Rebis 34, 36, 43, 195, **196**, 199, 208; *see also* Hermaphrodite; Nollius, Heinrich
Red King 34; *see also* alchemical wedding
Red Lion 34
redemption 18, 60, 73, 87, 183, 204, 225, 241, 246, 270, 284; *see also* Deavel, Catherine Jack, and David Paul Deavel
Reeve, C.D.C., and Patrick Lee Miller: *Introductory Readings in Ancient Greek and Roman Philosophy* 4, 25
Reformed Theology see Allen, R. Michael
"Religious Violence as Modern Myth" *see* Cavanaugh, William T.
Remembrall 192–93, 197, 201; *see also* the prophecy; prophecy orb; Snitch, Golden
remorse 18, 42, 73, 95, 122, 138, 145, 160, 162, 166, 175, 176, 183, 184, 257, 262, 270, 272; *see also* Dumbledore, Albus; Snape, Severus; Voldemort
resurrection 17, 34, 35, 40, 52, 73, 74, 121, 124, 127, 128, 132, 134, 176, 199, 222, 223, 224; *see also* Deathly Hallows
Resurrection Stone *see* Deathly Hallows
retort (Alchemical instrument) 125, 143
The Rhind Mathematical Papyrus: An Ancient Egyptian Text see Robins, Gaye, and Charles Shute
Riddle, Tom Marvolo 124, 143, 153, 165, 174, 241; Chamber of Secrets 19, 81, 126, 128, 200; contrast with Gaunt, Merope 18n, 83, 175, 233–34, 257; contrast with Harry Potter 92, 93–94, 147, 149, 162, 176, 237, 247, 256; diary 81, 119, 127–28, 131–32, 133, 135, 137,

200, 201, 223, 258; duel with Harry Potter 137, 241; "having and being" 230–31, 233; orphanage 82–83, 92, 147, 159; persona of Voldemort 17, 80–81, 82, 83–84, 95; *see also* basilisk; Dumbledore, Albus; Gaunt, Merope; "having and being"; Horcruxes; persona and shadow; Riddle, Tom Sr.; Slughorn, Horace; Voldemort; Weasley, Ginny (Ginevra)

Riddle, Tom, Sr. 18*n*, 174, 175, 257; *see also* Gaunt, Merope; Riddle, Tom Marvolo; Voldemort

"Rime of the Ancient Mariner" *see* Coleridge, Samuel Taylor

"Ring Alchemy" *see* Sprague, William

ring composition 16, 30, 39, 44; chiasmus 16, 30, 45; uroboros loop 43; *see also* Douglas, Mary; Granger, John

The Rise of Alchemy in Fourteenth-Century England: Plantagenet Kings and the Search for the Philosopher's Stone see Hughes, Jonathan

"The Rites in the Mysteries of Dionysus: The Birth of Drama" *see* Näsström, Britt-Mari

Robins, Gaye, and Charles Shute: *The Rhind Mathematical Papyrus: An Ancient Egyptian Text* 135, 138

"Rocking the Culture Industry/Performing Breakdown: Pink Floyd's The Wall and the Termination of the Postwar Era" *see* Ackerman, Zeno

Romeo and Juliet see Shakespeare

rooster 125; *see also* Principe, Lawrence

Royal Art *see* Great Work

Royal Society of Chemistry 11, 26, 285, 290

Rupescissa, John of: *Quintessence* 8, 8*n*, 69, 288; *see also* quintessence

St. Hedwig 222; *see also* Hedwig

St. Hilaire, Jenna: "Harry Potter and the Greatest Virtue" 246, 254, 255, 261, 264

St. Peter 200; *see also* Hagrid, Rubeus

Sallis, John: *Being and Logos: Reading the Platonic Dialogues* 266, 285

Salt 9, 10, *11*, 12, 129, 290; *see also* tria prima (mercury, sulfur, salt)

Sayre, Kenneth: *Unearthed: The Economic Roots of Our Environmental Crisis* 6*n*, 26

Schwartz, Peter Hammond: "'His Majesty the Baby': Narcissism and Royal Authority" 227, 229

The Science of Harry Potter: How Magic Really Works see Highfield, Roger

Scrimgeour, Rufus 39, 41, 202, 215; *see also* Dumbledore, Albus

Scripture in the Tradition see Lubac, Henri

Secret Fire 217–18; *see also* Philosopher's Stone

Secret Societies: From the Ancient and Arcane to the Modern and Clandestine see Barrett, David V.

The Secret Teachings of All Ages see Hall, Manly P.

Sectumsempra 136

Seeker (Quidditch position) 23, 112, 127, 128, 170, 191, 192, 193, 194, 195, 199, 203, 204, 206, 207, 220, 269

Seekers (17th century dissenters) 23, 191, 204

Selkies 198

Semina 245

The Serpent's Gift: Gnostic Reflections on the Study of Religion see Kripal, Jeffrey

Seth 120–21, 134; *see also* Horus; Setna

Setna 122; *see also* Seth

seven: alchemical stages 118–19, 122, 123–24; the most powerfully magical number 11, 192, 289–90; seven Harrys 21, 165, 166, 253; seventh Horcrux 119, 136, 160, 192, 211, 287; *see also* Horcruxes

Sexual States of Mind see Meltzer, Donald

Shacklebolt, Kingsley 41, 289; *see also* Order of the Phoenix; Patronus

Shade, Patrick: "Heroic Hermione: Celebrating the Love of Learning" 117, 172, 174–75, 177, 185, 186

Shadow *see* Jung, Carl G.

Shakespeare, William 30, 32; Montagues and Capulets of Verona 34; Tybalt and Mercutio in *Romeo and Juliet* 34

shaman 191, 195

Sharp, Daryl: *Personality Types: Jung's Model of Typology* 92, 96

Shelley, Mary: *Frankenstein* 76, 78

Sheltrown, Nicholas: "Harry Potter's World as a Morality Tale of Technology and Media" 243

Shrieking Shack 18–19, 38, 197, 203, 221–22; *see also* Pettigrew, Peter

Shunpike, Stan 177, 179, 203; *see also* Knight Bus

Shute, Charles *see* Robins, Gaye

Siculus, Diodorus: *The Library of History* 169*n*, 284

silver doe 42, 87, 151; *see also* Patronus; Potter, Lily Evans; Snape, Severus

Simpson, Anne: *The Herald* 1, 26, 45, 209, 224

Skeeter, Rita 42, 89, 238, 274*n*; *see also* *Daily Prophet*; Dumbledore, Albus

Slughorn, Horace 135–36, 143, 157, 161, 162, 165, 230, 251, 253, 258; *see also* Horcruxes; Riddle, Tom Marvolo

Slytherin, Salazar *see* Hogwarts founders

Slytherin's Locket *see* Horcruxes

Smith, Anne Collins: "Harry Potter, Radical Feminism, and the Power of Love" 18*n*, 26

Smith, Hepzibah 128, 256

snake *see* Basilisk; Brazilian Boa Constrictor; Hogwarts House animals; Nāga; Nagini

snake and eel 213

Snape, Severus 28, 74, 85–86, 89–90, 119, 124, 158, 165, 192, 201, 230, 238, 262, 272; and

Albus Dumbledore 86, 87, 88, 91, 152, 217, 277–78, 283; betrayal of Potters 33–34, 152; Black (*nigredo*) stage 37, 38; Half-blood Prince 33–34, 136; and James Potter 87, 146; love for Lily Evans Potter 33, 60, 73, 87, 88, 116, 151, 152, 272, 277–78; Occlumency 83, 150; Pensieve 87, 94, 152, 217, 224, 250, 283; persona and shadow 17, 80, 85, 86, 88, 95; silver doe Patronus 87, 201; Slytherin 43; Voldemort's murder of 21, 205, 206, 235; *see also* Dumbledore, Albus; Occlumency; Patronus; persona and shadow; Potter, Lily Evans
"Sneaking Out After Dark: Resistance, Agency, and the Postmodern Child in JK Rowling's Harry Potter Series" *see* Chappell, Drew
Snitch, Golden 127, 191, 193, 194, 195, **196**, 197, 198, 199, 200, 202, 203, 204, 205, 206, 207; Harry as 23, 192, 193, 194, 196, 200, 206, 207; *see also* Hermes; Mercury (god); prophecy orb; Remembrall; Wright, Bowman
Society for the Promotion of Elfish Welfare (S.P.E.W.) 178; *see also* Granger, Hermione Jean
Socrates *see* Plato
solar orb 127
Sophocles 99
Sorting Hat 21, 93, 94, 193, 202, 230, 237, 249, 250, 273, 274n, 275, 276
Spain 209
Spartz, Emerson *see* Anelli, Melissa
specter *see* ghosts
"Specters of Thatcherism: Contemporary British Culture in J.K. Rowling's Harry Potter Series" *see* Westman, Karin E.
Splendor Solis 129, **130**, 13, 138, 139; *see also* Trismosin, Salomon
Sprague, William: "Ring Alchemy" 39, 45
Sprout, Pomona 28, 199, 214, 215; *see also* mandrake
squib 73
Stages of Grief *see* Kübler-Ross, Elisabeth; grief
Stanton, Will: *The Book of Gramarye* 219
stargazers 24, 265, 267, 278–80, 281
"'Stay Strong,' and Other Useless Drivel We Tell the Grieving" *see* Devine, Megan
Stein, Mary: "A Study of Common Beliefs and Misconceptions in Physical Science" 251, 264
Stein, Murray: *Jung's Map of the Soul: An Introduction* 80, 81, 83, 84, 94, 96
Steinbeck, John 77, 78; *see also* Lisca, Peter
Stella, Benoît: *Eye of Horus Fractions* 139
Stevens, Wallace: "Sunday Morning" 75, 78
"Stop" *see* Waters, Roger
"A Study of Common Beliefs and Misconceptions in Physical Science" *see* Stein, Mary
Sublunary *see* Aristotle

Sufi 4
sulfur 9–10; *prima materia* 244, 288; quarreling couple (sulfur and mercury) 34, 35; Ron Weasley as 10, 15; *tria prima* (mercury, sulfur, salt) 11, 129, 290; *see also* alchemical wedding; gold; *prima materia*; *tria prima* (mercury, sulfur, salt); Weasley-Delacour wedding
sun (solar) gold 9, 10, 11, 36, 41, 83, 137, 150, 207, 210, 279; Sun King (Harry Potter) 131; *see also* citrinitas stage; Lovegood, Luna; moon (lunar); Weasley, Ginny (Ginevra); Weasley-Delecour wedding
"Sunday Morning" *see* Stevens, Wallace
Sweeney, Erin: "Cracking the Planetary Code: Harry Potter, Alchemy, and the Seven Book Series as a Whole" 80, 96, 260, 264; *see also* Prinzi, Travis, and Kathryn N. McDaniel
Sword of Gryffindor *see* Gryffindor, Sword of
sylphs 198
Symposium see Plato

"The Tale of the Three Brothers" *see* Peverell brothers
Tale of Two Cities see Dickens, Charles
The Tales of Beedle the Bard 204–05, 207, 208, 224
Tarnas, Richard *Cosmos* 4, 5, 26 *Passion* 6n, 7n, 26
The Tarot: History, Symbolism and Divination see Place, Robert M.
Tatler Magazine see Greig, Geordie
Taylor, Thomas: *Iamblichus: On the Mysteries* 119n
Temple of Thoth (Hermopolis) 126
Thatcher, Margaret 38, 243; *see also* Westman, Karin E.
Theoria Philosophiae Hermeticae see Nollius, Heinrich
Theories of Personality see Feist, Jess
Theories of Personality: Understanding Persons see Cloninger, Susan C.
Thinking in Circles see Douglas, Mary
"This Chemist Is Unlocking the Secrets of Alchemy" *see* Guarino, Ben
Thomas, Dean 19, 185
Thor 202, **203**; *see also* lightning scar
Thoth 120, 123, 125, 126, 127, 128, 135; *Book of the Dead* 121: *Emerald Tablet* 122; *see also* astronomy; Hermes
time turner 16, 216; *see also* Granger, Hermione Jean
To Have or to Be? see Fromm, Erich
Tolkien, J.R.R. 30, 32, 32n, 44, 117
Tonks, Nymphadora 41, 43; *see also* Lupin Remus John; Lupin, Teddy
The Tower of Alchemy: An Advanced Guide to the Great Work see Goddard, David
transfigurations 3, 9, 16, 21, 23, 202; class 1, 8, 9, 102–03

"Transitional Objects" *see* Winnicott, D.W.
transmogrification 245
transmutation 19, 40, 46, 70, 140, 143, 211, 242, 244, 245, 246
Tree of Life 50*n*
Trelawney, Sybill 175, 192, 193, 249, 281
Trevor (Neville's toad) 125
Tria Prima (*Tria Principia*) 10, **11**, 12, 290; *see also* gold; *prima materia*
"The Trial" *see* Waters, Roger (and Bob Ezrin)
Trinh, T. Minh-ha: "Grandma's Story" 4, 26
Trismosin, Salomon: *Splendor Solis* 139
Triwizard Tournament 197, 198, 199, 200, 201; labyrinth 40, 41
Turkey 22, 135
Twain, Mark 43
Twilight see Meyer, Stephenie

Umbridge, Dolores Jane 20, 38, 82, 169, 173, 183, 185, 193, 205, 250, 274*n*
Uncle Vernon *see* Dursley, Vernon
Unearthed: The Economic Roots of Our Environmental Crisis see Sayre, Kenneth
Unfogging the Future see Vablatsky, Cassandra
unicorns 157, 212, 280; blood 161, 212, 213, 260, 282
Unlocking Harry Potter: Five Keys for the Serious Reader see Granger, John
Updike, John 31
Updike, Martha Ruggles (née Bernhard) 31
urboros loop *see* ring composition

Vablatsky, Cassandra: *Unfogging the Future* 123; *see also* Blavatsky, H.P.
Valentine, Basil 9, 118, 123; *Azoth of the Philosophers* 118
van den Broek, Roelof, and Wouter J. Hanegraaff: *Gnosis and Hermeticism from Antiquity to Modern Times* 90, 96
Vane, Romilda 250, 251
veelas 35, 198
The Vehement Passions see Fisher, Philip
Verona *see* Shakespeare
Very Good Lives (Rowling) 144, 149, 155
Voldemort 2, 4–5, 19, 20, 24, 28, 55, 59, 68, 70*n*, 89, 94, 101, 106, 109, 122, 140, 142, 145, 146, 149, 153, 169, 174, 175, 177, 178, 180–82, 210, 221, 223, 225, 230, 237, 249–50, 258, 274*n*; Avada Kedavra 36, 107, 129, 147, 154, 156, 157–58, 160, 164, 165, 166, 201, 205, 241; Battle of Hogwarts 35, 43, 98, 108, 111, 127, 134, 147, 202, 204, 241, 242, 256; Chamber of Secrets 213, 263; Dark Mark 258; Death Eaters 140–41, 160–61, 162, 164, 183, 194, 206, 234, 259; duel with Dumbledore 210; Dumbledore's tomb 108, 270; Elder Wand 3, 108, 128, 166, 204, 205, 207, 235, 270, 287; Forbidden Forest 60, 98, 107, 108, 223, 241, 254, 290; graveyard duel 41, 87, 199, 203, 222, 230, 251, 275; having and being 23, 232, 233, 239, 240; heir of Slytherin 92, 126, 258; Horcruxes 13, 14, 21, 23, 42, 73, 74, 82, 83, 84–85, 90, 107, 110, 119, 120, 126, 136, 137, 141, 143, 144, 165–66, 175, 192, 194, 197, 199, 201, 202–03, 205, 207, 222, 230, 241, 247, 252, 260, 261, 277, 287, 289–90; King's Cross Station 107, 137, 157, 176, 222, 224, 230, 236; Ministry of Magic and Dolores Umbridge 82, 169, 194, 218, 238, 250, 274*n*; murder of Lily and James Potter 33, 125, 152, 159, 163, 192, 229; Nagini 84, 94–95, 193, 206–07, 223, 287, 288; Pettigrew, Peter 162, 221–22, 277; the prophecy 38–39, 87, 158–59, 175–76, 192, 253, 257; Quirrell and Philosopher's Stone 3, 58, 60, 70, 105, 123–24, 141, 159, 196, 220, 231, 232, 289, 290; remorse 18, 73, 95, 160, 184, 225, 252, 262, 268, 270; shadow of Tom Marvolo Riddle 17, 80–81, 83, 84, 85–86, 87, 95, 128; Snape, Severus 150, 151, 152, 206, 217, 234–35, 272, 283; unicorns 17, 161, 212, 213, 260, 280, 282; yew and phoenix feather wand 157, 163, 199; *see also* Dumbledore's tomb; grave(yard); having and being; Horcruxes; persona and shadow; Pettigrew, Peter; Quirrell, Professor; Riddle, Tom Marvolo; Snape, Severus

"Waiting for the Worms" *see* Waters, Roger
wall of dogmatism 168, 169, 171, 172, 174, 176, 181, 185; Pink's 7, 168, 172, 182–83, 184; Platform 9¾ 172; Plato's cave 81–82, 112; portal to Diagon Alley 7, 20, 50, 168, 177; Privet Dr. 5; *see also* Plato's cave
The Wall see Waters, Roger
wand 65, 178, 204, 205, 234, 242; elm and dragon heartstring (Lucius Malfoy) 21, 157, 158, 165; hawthorn and unicorn hair (Draco) 166; Hermes 127; phoenix feather and holly (Harry) 14–15, 18, 21, 42, 50, 64, 141, 156, 157, 158, 163, 164–65, 192, 199, 204; phoenix feather and yew (Voldemort) 21, 141, 156, 157, 158, 163, 164, 199, 222; *see also* Elder wand
Ward, Michael: *Planet Narnia* 31, 32, 45
Waters, Roger "Hey You" 176, 181, 182–83, 186; "Just Another Brick in the Wall" 173, 182, 186; "Mother" 186; "Outside the Wall" 7, 185, 186; *Pink Floyd The Wall* (and Bob Ezrin) 2, 168, 174, 181, 186; "Stop" 183–84, 186; "The Trial" 184, 168, 186; "Waiting for the Worms" 183, 186; *see also* Pink Floyd
Weasley, Arthur 177, 180, 288; snake attack 95; *see also* Arthurian symbolism
Weasley, Bill 47, 53, 132, 175, 223, 235; *see also* Delacour, Fleur; Weasley-Delacour wedding
Weasley, Fred and George 173, 198, 200, 216; Weasleys' Wizard Wheezes 173; *see also* extendable ears; Weasleys' Wizard Wheezes
Weasley, Ginny (Ginevra) 191, 193–95, 201, 206, 249; and Tom Riddle's diary 35, 120, 128, 131, 221

Weasley, Molly 217
Weasley, Ron (Ronald Bilius) 35, 200, 201, 202, 204, 205; Deluminator 15; as sulfur 10, 15, 35; Rose 43, 248; *see also* Deluminator; Granger, Hermione Jean; moon (lunar); *tria prima* (sulfur, mercury, salt); Philosopher's Stone; quarreling couple
Weasley, Rose 43, 248; *see also* Granger, Hermione Jean; Philosopher's Stone; Weasley, Ron (Ronald Bilius)
Weasleys 15, 146, 177, 249; *see also* Weasley, Arthur; Weasley, Bill; Weasley, Fred and George; Weasley, Ginny (Ginevra); Weasley, Molly; Weasley, Ron (Ronald Bilius); Weasley-Delacour wedding
Weasley-Delacour wedding 35, 41, 42, 43, 163, 223, 289; *see also* alchemical wedding; gold; light; Lovegood; moon (lunar); sun (solar)
Weasley's Wizard Wheezes *see* Weasley, Fred and George
Weltanschauung 230
Wendolyn the Weird 7
Werewolf 35; *see also* Greyback, Fenrir; Lupin, Remus John
West, Cornel: "Prophetic Thought in Postmodern Times" 5n, 26
Westman, Karin E.: "Specters of Thatcherism: Contemporary British Culture in J.K. Rowling's Harry Potter Series" 235, 243
"What Would Harry Do? J.K. Rowling and Lawrence Kohlberg's Theories of Moral Development" *see* Whited, Lana A., and M. Katherine Grimes
White, E.B. 117
White, T.H.: *The Book of Beasts* 219, 224
White Queen 33, 34; *see also* alchemical wedding
White Stag 35
Whited, Lana A.: "Here Be Dragons (and Phoenixes)" 35, 45, 242
Whited, Lana A., and M. Katherine Grimes: "What Would Harry Do? J.K. Rowling and Lawrence Kohlberg's Theories of Moral Development" 230, 243
Whitney, Elspeth: *Medieval Science and Technology* 244, 264
"Why Nabokov Would Have Liked Harry Potter" *see* Maar, Michael
Winfrey, Oprah 65, 78
Winky 178, 179, 180
Winnicott, D.W.: "Transitional Objects" 51, 52, 60, 62
Witches, Midwives, and Nurses: A History of Women Healers see Ehrenreich, Barbara, and Deidre English
wizard chess 220
"The Woman I Love Is a Planet, the Planet I Love Is a Tree" *see* Allen, Paula Gunn
Woman, Native, Other: Writing Postcoloniality and Feminism *see* Trinh, T. Minh-ha
The Woman Warrior: Memoirs of a Childhood Among Ghosts *see* Kingston, Maxine Hong
Wood, Oliver 127, 192, 193; *see also* Hogwarts Quidditch teams
World Mythology *see* Doty, William G.
Wormtail *see* animagus; Marauders; Pettigrew, Peter
Wright, Bowman 193; *see also* Godric's Hollow; Snitch, Golden
A Wrinkle in Time *see* L'Engle, Madeleine

yin-yang 206
Yule ball 193, 198

X-Men and X-Women 49
Xavier's School for Gifted Youngsters 49

Yeats, William Butler 32, 44; *see also* Gorski, William T.
Yeats and Alchemy *see* Gorski, William T.

Zerin, Edward, and Marjorie: "A Meta Model for the Unifying of Psychological Theories" 227, 243

www.ingramcontent.com/pod-product-compliance
Ingram Content Group UK Ltd.
Pitfield, Milton Keynes, MK11 3LW, UK
UKHW041924140426
5217IPUK00014B/300